TRANSFORMING INDIA

TRANSFORMING INDIA
Social and Political Dynamics of Democracy

Edited by

FRANCINE R. FRANKEL

ZOYA HASAN

RAJEEV BHARGAVA

BALVEER ARORA

OXFORD
UNIVERSITY PRESS

OXFORD
UNIVERSITY PRESS

YMCA Library Building, Jai Singh Road, New Delhi 110 001

Oxford University Press is a department of the University of Oxford. It furthers the
University's objective of excellence in research, scholarship, and education
by publishing worldwide in

Oxford   New York

Auckland   Cape Town   Dar es Salaam   Hong Kong   Karachi   Kuala Lumpur
Madrid   Melbourne   Mexico City   Nairobi   New Delhi   Shanghai   Taipei   Toronto

With offices in

Argentina   Austria   Brazil   Chile   Czech Republic   France   Greece   Guatemala
Hungary   Italy   Japan   Poland   Portugal   Singapore   South Korea   Switzerland
Thailand   Turkey   Ukraine   Vietnam

Oxford is a registered trademark of Oxford University Press
in the UK and in certain other countries

Published in India by Oxford University Press, New Delhi

ISBN-13: 978-0-19-565832-3
ISBN-10: 0-19-565832-9

Printed by Rashtriya Printers, New Delhi 110 032
Published by Oxford University Press
YMCA Library Building, Jai Singh Road, New Delhi 110 001

Preface

This volume emerged from a conference at India International Centre on 'Democracy and Transformation: India Fifty Years After Independence' in November 1997. Our intention was to take stock of the democratic experience in India, conceptualized as a set of interactions—those between liberal ideas and institutions on the one hand, and hierarchical social structures and heterogeneous cultures on the other. In other words, we wanted to present a dynamic understanding of how democratic forms of governance are able to adapt to unequal and divided societies, and in doing so, also change the cultural expression of rights and obligations, and patterns of social and political power.

The academic organizing committee consisting of the four editors worked to identify the participants, including the scholars invited to give papers and act as discussants. We invited Dr E. Sridharan, Academic Director, University of Pennsylvania Institute for the Advanced Study of India (UPIASI) to join us for substantive discussions, and requested UPIASI to take on the responsibilities of coordinating the arrangements for the New Delhi conference. This task was greatly facilitated by the superb cooperation we enjoyed from N.N. Vohra (Director), N.H. Ramachandran (Secretary) and Lalit Joshi (Manager) of India International Centre, and the staff, in overseeing the smooth functioning of the conference, among the first to take place in the state of the art facility and beautiful natural surroundings of the new Annexe building.

We feel fortunate that so many outstanding scholars from across disciplines and professions, based in India, the United

States and Europe enthusiastically responded to the challenge of this enterprise. All of the scholars represented in this volume revised their original papers in response to the discussions at the conference, circulated in the form of proceedings. They also updated their papers, as appropriate, to take account of the outcome of the February–March 1998 elections; the last revised paper, by Balveer Arora, also addresses the implications for democratic governance of the loss of confidence of the BJP-led coalition in April 1999.

All of us owe a special debt of gratitude to Victoria Farmer, Assistant Director, Center for the Advanced Study of India until October 1998, and Professor Douglas Verney, Adjunct Professor, South Asia Regional Studies, University of Pennsylvania for the meticulous editing of each paper and queries to the authors for revision. Ritu Menon, a professional publisher, provided invaluable assistance in completing the final copy-editing, to tighten the writing and standardize the style for publication according to specifications of Oxford University Press. All of these efforts saved valuable time in bringing out the volume as quickly as possible.

Finally, I want to express my personal appreciation to David D. Arnold and Dr Terrence George, then Representative, and Program Officer, respectively of The Ford Foundation, New Delhi, for the confidence they displayed in this project by approving the grant which made the November 1997 conference possible.

Francine R. Frankel
Center for the Advanced Study of India
May 5, 1999   University of Pennsylvania

Contents

Contributors

BALVEER ARORA is Professor of Government and Politics at the Centre for Political Studies, Jawaharlal Nehru University, and Honorary Director, ICSSR, Northern Regional Centre, New Delhi. Earlier, he has been a visiting fellow at the National Political Science Foundation, Paris and the Center for the Advanced Study of India, University of Pennsylvania, USA. He has co-edited *Multiple Identities in a Single State: Indian Federalism in Comparative Perspective* (1995) and *Federalism in India: Origins and Development* (1992).

SANJAYA BARU is Editor, *The Financial Express* and formerly professor at the Indian Council for Research in International Economic Relations, New Delhi. He has been an associate professor in economics at the University of Hyderabad and also a visiting fellow at the University of East Anglia (UK). He is the author of *The Political Economy of Indian Sugar* (1990) and the *Mid-Year Review of the Indian Economy* (1998). He is also a newspaper columnist and a television commentator.

AMRITA BASU is Professor of Political Science and Women's and Gender Studies at Amherst College, Massachusetts, USA. She has been a visiting scholar at the South Asian Institute, Columbia University, USA. She is the author of *Two Faces of Protest: Contrasting Modes of Women's Activism in India* (1992) and has co-edited *Appropriating Gender: Women's Activism and Politicized Religion in South Asia* (1998).

RAJEEV BHARGAVA is Professor of Political Theory at the Delhi University. Earlier he has been a senior fellow in Ethics at Harvard

University, Cambridge. He is the author of *Individualism in Social Science* (1992) and a contributor in and editor of *Secularism and Its Critics* (1998). Recently he has co-edited and contributed in *Multiculturalism, Liberalism and Democracy* (1999). Besides being a contributor to the *Encyclopaedia of Philosophy* (1998), he has written numerous articles for various well-known journals and edited volumes.

PAUL R. BRASS is Professor Emeritus of Political Science and International Studies at the University of Washington, Seattle. His most recent books are *Theft of An Idol: Text and Context in the Representation of Collective Violence* (1997); *Riots and Pogroms* (1996); and *The Politics of India since Independence*, 2nd ed. (1994). His other books include *Ethnicity and Nationalism: Theory and Comparison* (1991); *Caste, Faction and Party in Indian Politics*, 2 vols (1983 and 1985); and *Language, Religion and Politics in North India* (1974). He is currently working on a book on Hindu–Muslim communalism and collective violence in India.

RAJEEV DHAVAN was educated at Allahabad, Cambridge and London Universities. A former academic, he taught at Queen's University (Belfast, Ireland) and at the University of West London, with visiting and other assignments at the Universities of London, Austin, Madison and Delhi. He is an honorary professor of the Indian Law Institute and Director of Public Interest Legal Support and Research Centre (PILSARC). Author of many books and articles on constitutional law, policy and public affairs and called to the Bar in India and England, he is now a Senior Counsel practising in the Supreme Court of India.

VICTORIA L. FARMER is formerly Assistant Director of the Center for the Advanced Study of India, University of Pennsylvania and South Asia Program Associate, The Asia Society. She has taught comparative politics, American foreign policy and international relations at the University of Pennsylvania and Drexel University. The author of numerous articles, she is currently completing her Ph.D. dissertation in political science at Penn, entitled "Televising the Nation: Television, Politics and Social Change in India."

FRANCINE R. FRANKEL is Professor of Political Science and Director, Center for the Advanced Study of India, University of Pennsylvania, and a founding member of the University of Pennsylvania Institute for the Advanced Study of India, New Delhi. She is the author of *India's Green Revolution: Economic Gains and Political Costs* (1971); and *India's Political Economy 1947–77: The Gradual Revolution* (1978). Among other writings, she is a contributor and co-editor of *Dominance and State Power: Decline of a Social Order*, 2 vols (1989 and 1990) and contributor and co-editor of *Bridging the Non-Proliferation Divide: The United States and India* (1995). She is currently at work on a comparative analysis of the making of foreign policy in the United States and India titled *Different Worlds*.

ZOYA HASAN is Professor of Political Science at the Centre for Political Studies, Jawaharlal Nehru University, New Delhi. She has been a visiting fellow at the Center for Advanced Study of India, University of Pennsylvania, USA. She is the author of *Quest for Power: Oppositional Movement and Post-Congress Politics in Uttar Pradesh* (1998). She has also edited *Forging Identities: Gender, Communities and the State* (1994), and has contributed numerous articles to reputed journals and edited volumes.

CHRISTOPHE JAFFRELOT is Director of the Centre d'Etudes et de Recherches Internationales, France. Chief editor of *Critique Internationale*, he is also the author of *The Hindu Nationalist Movement and Indian Politics, 1925 to 1990s* (1991) and has co-edited *The BJP and the Compulsions of Politics in India* (1998).

SUDIPTA KAVIRAJ teaches in the Department of Political Studies at the School of Oriental and African Studies, London. He has earlier taught at the University of Burdwan and Jawaharlal Nehru University. He is the author of *The Unhappy Consciousness: Bankimchandra Chattopadhyay and the Formation of Nationalist Discourse in India* (1995) and has edited *Politics in India* (1997) and co-edited *Perspectives on Capitalism* (1989). Besides these, he has contributed several articles on political theory, Indian politics, and Bengali literature in well-known journals.

PRABHAT PATNAIK is Professor of Economics at the Centre of Economic Studies and Planning, Jawaharlal Nehru University, New Delhi. He is the author of *Economics and Egalitarianism* (1991), *Accumulation and Stability under Capitalism* (1997), *Whatever Happened to Imperialism and Other Essays* (1995) and also has edited *Macroeconomics* (1995) and *Lenin and Imperialism* (1986).

R.K. RAGHVAN (IPS) is formerly Director, Central Bureau of Investigation (CBI), Government of India. He was also Vice-President of the Indian Society of Victimology and Asia Editor for *Police Practice and Research*, published by the International Police Executive Symposium, USA. His publications include *Policing a Democracy: A Comparative Study of India and the US* (1999) and *Indian Police: Problems, Planning and Perspectives* (1998), besides several articles for periodicals and journals.

DOUGLAS V. VERNEY is Professor Emeritus of Political Science at York University, Toronto and Adjunct Professor, South Asia Regional Studies at the University of Pennsylvania. He is the author of five books, among them *British Government and Politics: Life Without a Declaration of Independence* (1976) and *Three Civilizations, Two Cultures, One State: Canada's Political Traditions* (1986). He has co-edited *Multiple Identities in a Single State: Indian Federalism in Comparative Perspective* (1995). In recent years he has published numerous articles on comparative parliamentary and federal systems in American, British, Canadian and Indian journals and is currently working on a book titled *Choosing a Regime: Eight Major Models*.

YOGENDRA YADAV is Fellow at the Centre for the Study of Developing Societies, Delhi, and Director, Institute of Comparative Democracy (a research programme of the CSDS). Besides contributing several research papers to reputed academic journals, he is on the editorial board of *Samayik Varta* (a monthly political journal in Hindi). He is also well known as an election analyst, both on television and in print.

INTRODUCTION
Contextual Democracy: intersections of society, culture and politics in India

FRANCINE R. FRANKEL

The preservation of democratic governance in India has presented a standing challenge to theorists of historical and comparative development. The preconditions associated with the origins of democracy in the United States and Europe, ranging from the prior formation of a nation-state, a homogeneous population, an industrial economy, a strong middle class, and shared traditions of civic culture were notably absent in 1950 when India first became a democratic, secular republic. The issue of India's survival as a single entity was still at the forefront of concerns in the minds of its founders.

The representatives of free India confronted unprecedented obstacles to the creation of an overarching national political identity. It is doubtful that even the minuscule class of English-educated professionals felt a loyalty to 'India' higher than the sentiments they experienced towards their religious community, linguistic region, or clan or caste. Domestic big business, despite bases in the major cities of Calcutta, Madras, Bombay, Hyderabad and Kanpur could not be characterized as a national bourgeoisie: Marwari entrepreneurs tended to be predominant in all these areas. In western India, Gujaratis and Parsis were preeminent. Traders and businessmen in smaller towns and cities were not far removed from their origins in the agrarian economy. Indeed, the 'middle classes' as a whole were intimately connected to the most rigidly hierarchical and compartmentalized social structure inherited by any modern state, a social structure which kept opportunities for upward mobility exceedingly small. Under Indian conditions, the middle classes lacked virtually all the attributes identified by theorists like Putnam to

make democratic institutions work: a common social background, participatory attitudes of mind, networks of civic interaction, feelings of trust, and a tradition of mutual cooperation in the interest of common benefit.[1]

However improbable, not only India, but India's democracy
endured. This has not been without crisis, as during the period
of Emergency Rule imposed by Prime Minister Indira Gandhi
during June 1975 and January 1977. Fears persist that political
institutions weakened by personal rule and the corruption of
normal politics in the post-Emergency period will be over-
whelmed by the accelerated participation of historically marginal groups, and that democratic India will eventually become
ungovernable.

Such pessimism, however, is confounded by another anomaly
of India's democracy, one which also sets it apart from comparative trends in the United States and Western Europe. This
is the upward trajectory of voter turnout in the absence of laws
for compulsory voting.

Political scientists have long been concerned about low voter
turnout in the United States and other democracies, amid evidence
that voter participation and class inequality are negatively linked.
Democratic theorists have labelled unequal participation the unresolved dilemma of democracy, since it biases representation and
influence in the direction of the better educated, more wealthy
and advantaged citizens. Paradoxically, India seems to be fulfilling the unrealized expectations of political analysts writing
at the end of the nineteenth and beginning of the twentieth centuries when universal suffrage was first introduced in many
countries. Their prediction was that the better educated and
more advantaged citizens would be least likely to vote since
their preference would be submerged among the votes of the
'great crowd'.[2]

As Yogendra Yadav demonstrates in this volume, sociologically biased turnout in India actually tends to favour the more
unequal and historically disadvantaged groups. The puzzle of
India's largely illiterate electorate is that even in the first two
elections, aggregate voter turnout was as high as 46–8 per cent.
This level soon reached (and exceeded) the average level in the
United States, pushing above 60 per cent by 1967, and staying
within the range of 55 per cent to 64 per cent in the ten general

elections between 1962 and 1998. More striking, voter turnout for state assembly elections has remained close to these levels during the same period, surging to 67 per cent in elections held during 1993–6. By 1989, the percentage of voter turnout was higher in rural than in urban areas, and this increase was connected to the sharp reduction in the gap between average turnout rates and those registered by the most disadvantaged groups. Survey data show that Other Backward Classes (lower castes), dalits (erstwhile untouchables) and tribals are more likely to vote than upper caste Hindus, and this is also true of the very poor, relative to the upper classes.

Clearly, democracy has struck very deep roots in the inhospitable soil of India. It has done so disproportionately among historically marginal groups, especially the most depressed among them. Equally important, democratic values have become entrenched among intellectual élites and institutions vital to the consolidation of democracy. Investigative reporting in national newspapers has exposed corruption and forced political accountability; meticulous planning by the Election Commission has assured free and fair general elections; and as Rajeev Dhavan shows, the Supreme Court's activism led to the prosecution of the highest elected politicians when evidence surfaced of their wrongdoing in office, as well as to continuously expanding public interest litigation for protection of civil liberties.

The phenomenon of democracy in India—a multicultural state of steadily growing scientific and military capabilities, projected to become the world's most populous country in the early twenty-first century, the fourth largest economy, and the largest consumer market next only to China—is so important, that the tendency of comparative-historical scholarship to treat India as a 'deviant case', when it is considered at all, impoverishes our understanding of democratization. Now that India has passed the half-century mark of Independence, it is time to take stock of her experience with democratic forms of governance and bring this knowledge into the mainstream of historical and comparative scholarship on national development.

The approach taken by the contributors to this volume is sensitive to the historical, social and cultural context in which fundamental rights, consensual procedures of governance and the rule of law were introduced. Like the founders of the Indian

Constitution, the authors recognize that under Indian conditions certain exceptions to universal criteria of the liberal state, based on guarantees of individual freedoms and protection of minority rights had to be made, both to ensure national unity and provide equality under the law for all groups of citizens. At the same time, the foundational values of western democracies remained the frame of reference for democratic principles. India did not set out to abridge democratic freedoms, or to rationalize departures from liberal democracy by invoking political or cultural relativism. On the contrary, provisions for state intervention that could temporarily override individual rights to restore political order, or to protect permanent religious minorities and strengthen the competitiveness of socially disadvantaged groups, were intended to create the political and social conditions essential to effective participation in the democratic process of individuals of all socio-economic strata and ethnic–religious identities.

Contextual Democracy

The contributors to this volume analyse the development of democratic institutions and practices in India, and their performance over time, from the perspective of the specific historical–social context in which they were established. More profoundly, they seek to understand the transformations unleashed by the introduction of political democracy in India's hierarchical society and plural cultures. The contributions focus on ways in which the historical–social context of India shaped the democratic institutions that were introduced, and reciprocally, how social hierarchy and preferences for group rights were affected by the introduction of egalitarian and liberal principles of governance. This broad analytic approach is summarized in the concept of contextual democracy.

The process of democratization in India revolves around the impact of a revolutionary principle, that of individual equality, imposed on interlocking hierarchical social structures and cultural norms whose configurations differ across regions. This diversity leaves room for several patterns of intersecting political, social and cultural change within a similar framework of democratic institutions. A contextual approach is therefore also appropriate in understanding the internal dynamics of democracy, including the timing and style in which marginalized social groups are incorporated into an inclusive political process, the alternative political alliances and alignments that are available, and the transformation that these new patterns work on the parameters of stable governance.

The vantage point provided by the concept of contextual democracy sheds light on the manifestations of the democratic process in India that might otherwise remain shadowed by bewildering complexities. Among the transformations discussed in this volume are the electoral upsurge of historically disadvantaged groups, the political organization of lower castes and dalits in competition with each other and in opposition to upper castes, fragmentation of national political parties, violence between Hindus and Muslims including spatial separation between the communities within urban centres, and the emergence of Hindutva (Sanskritic-based cultural Indian-ness) as the most important ideological challenge to the constitutional vision of the liberal state. It is a matter of debate whether such unanticipated outcomes were all along inherent in the diversity and social compartmentalization of Indian society, once integrating hierarchical structures were breached; or if pre-existing divisions are being deliberately manipulated by politicians to widen social conflicts in order to advance their own power and economic gain from state office, in the name of the poor.

Contextual democracy, in its origins, had a liberal vision. The efforts made to adapt universal principles to ground realities of group identities and plural cultures were motivated by the aim of preserving national integration without sacrificing the substance of individual rights. This involved finding compromises, for example, between fundamental rights and group identities, a strong Union and linguistic states, and equality under the law and compensatory discrimination. The aim was to carry along the electorate through a strategy of political accommodation that would safeguard their core cultures and ensure equal opportunities, while strengthening popular allegiance to the inclusive liberal democratic state.

The 'Democratic Vision'

The most important issue before the framers of India's Constitution was how to maintain national unity and also assure representative government. Rajeev Bhargava identifies one leitmotif of this challenge by examining the implications, for liberal democracy, of the fact that democracy arrived in India in the form of nationalism. He argues that individual liberties and universal franchise had been accepted by leaders of the nationalist movement as the only legitimate means through which self-representation of the nation and all of its component parts could be effectively expressed.

Still, the gap between vision and reality at the time of Independence appeared almost unbridgeable. The prolonged polarization between the Indian National Congress and the Muslim League during the nationalist movement ended in the partition of the subcontinent, to create the Muslim nation of Pakistan. Frenzied communal violence and mass killings whose immense magnitude has been estimated at anywhere from 600,000 to one million dead, can never truly be measured. Nevertheless, the Hindu majority, and Muslims remaining in India in the aftermath of this trauma, were caught in the grip of what Bhargava calls a 'majority–minority syndrome'. The Muslim minority could reasonably fear that their rights would not be guaranteed by the introduction of universal franchise. Rather, democracy, in its majoritarian form, was more likely to reinforce their position as a permanent minority, thereby alienating their allegiance from the new nation.

The religion-based majority–minority syndrome, as well as other social inequalities (for example, the problem of providing equal opportunity for historically disadvantaged communities like untouchables and tribals), raised a new kind of historical dilemma for the development of democracy based on equal rights under the law for all individuals regardless of religion, ethnicity, caste, gender or other social identity. In particular, a solution had to be found to protect the group rights of permanent minorities within a secular constitution that enshrined the fundamental rights of all individuals. Bhargava describes the solution to this dilemma as one premised on 'principled distance' between government and religion. His argument is that under Indian conditions, state intervention was required in areas impinging on religion, depending on social context, to safeguard the equal group rights of permanent minorities against the tyranny of majoritarian democracy.

Thus, the first compromise required to assure *de facto* equality of all citizens under the law was adaptation of the *de jure* principle of individual equality to the need for 'contextual secularism'. State intervention in religion, for example, to allow Muslims to retain their family law, or to outlaw untouchability and reserve seats for erstwhile untouchables or Scheduled Castes and Scheduled Tribes in elected bodies proportionate to their population, became essential to achieve the substance of secular equality in the context of Indian society. Such devices transformed, or averted the majority–minority syndrome of permanent exclusion and alienation. They converted the constitutional arrangements into a 'majority–minority framework' that could provide the basis of real political equality among groups as well as individuals. The effective operation of democratic norms in India's society rested not only on the acceptance of individual rights and universal franchise, but also the accommodation of group rights to safeguard minority freedoms.

As Paul Brass points out, Hindu-Muslim communalism was not the only aspect of the situational context that persuaded the framers that they needed to establish a strong centralized state that could intervene in society under turbulent conditions to temporarily suspend individual freedoms. A generalized 'fear of disorder' held sway. This fear arose from political movements that, in addition to Partition, were associated with threats from militant Hindu nationalism, regional secessionism and revolutionary communism, accompanied by serious acts of violence. There was also concern that the sentimental basis for the Indian Union was not strong enough to presume that people of all state units would always act in the interests of unity of the country as a whole, or that India could do without a strong Centre as an instrument for combating forces of disintegration.

The preoccupation with ensuring India's permanent and indissoluble Union, responding to well-grounded fears at the time of Independence, led to the Emergency provisions of the Constitution. Article 356 allowed 'President's Rule' or direct rule of any state by the Union government, on receipt of a report from

the governor of the state that its legislature could not function
in accordance with the provisions of the Constitution, and also
allowed for suspending the operation of any part of the Constitution in the state, except provisions relating to High Courts.
More draconian, Article 352, eventually invoked by Mrs Gandhi,
provided for a 'Proclamation of Emergency' to be issued by the
President in the event of external aggression or internal disturbance, and gave to the Union executive power to make laws
and other regulations for the states, including the suspension
of Fundamental Rights.[3] Beyond this, the Constitution enabled
passage of several other acts for preventive detention against
citizens suspected of terrorist or other anti-national activities.

Reviewing the record of the use of Emergency powers, preventive detention and internal security laws, Brass argues that
in the first two decades of independence, dominated by the Indian National Congress and the leadership of Prime Minister
Jawaharlal Nehru, a constitutional style of governance, commitment to secular principles, economic programmes of centralized
planning and strategies for peaceful social revolution moderated
the fundamental tension between the strong state and representative democracy. Nevertheless, by the mid-1960s, as the
Congress party failed to deliver on promises of economic growth
and social redistribution, the 'Nehruvian consensus' came under attack. According to Brass, the political debate revealed an
underlying lack of agreement on the form of the strong state and,
among some groups, resistance to the very goal of creating a nation-state in the absence of a dominant culture. The tension between centralizing and decentralizing tendencies found heightened
expression by the late 1980s. As the Bharatiya Janata Party (BJP)
set out to rally popular support for a powerful nation-state unified around Hindu nationalism, they were opposed by a growing
number of state and local parties embedded in regional identities
and demanding greater autonomy within the framework of what
might be called 'state-nations'.[4] Ironically, as Brass asserts, it was
Nehru's reluctant acquiescence in the creation of linguistic states
in non-Hindi speaking areas—a concession he feared would
strengthen disintegrative tendencies—that currently stands in the
way of the BJP's effort to succeed the Congress as the dominant
national party, and create a powerful nation-state on the basis of
the polarizing Hindutva ideology.

Political Dynamics of Expanding Participation

The framers of the Constitution faced not only a religion-based 'majority–minority syndrome' and well-founded fears of disorder, they also confronted a social structure characterized by caste and class hierarchies. As Sudipta Kaviraj argues, the introduction of the formal principle of political equality could not overcome the actual unequal economic structure of Indian society, reinforced by the uneven distribution of gains under a predominantly capitalist economy. Although the Congress party continued to pay lip service to the goal of a socialistic pattern of society until the early 1990s, anti-poverty programmes were the product of populist electoral mobilization, first adopted by Mrs Gandhi to bypass state party bosses after the 1969 Congress party split. During the 1971 elections, Mrs Gandhi made a direct appeal to the disadvantaged lower castes and classes with the promise to "abolish poverty".

As Kaviraj argues, one unintended consequence of populist politics was to fundamentally alter the structural properties of caste in the electoral arena. As political parties became concerned more with the spatial concentration of castes than their status within the caste hierarchy, electoral politics resulted in a 'democracy' of caste groups in place of a hierarchy. The search for 'contextual majorities' reinforced the voters' group orientation, while at the same time reservations of seats and jobs for Scheduled Castes and Scheduled Tribes, and reservations for admission into educational institutions and the administrative services in several states for Other Backward Classes, gave rise to the doctrine of equal treatment of caste groups, rather than of individuals.

The introduction of democracy into India thus weakened, over time, the legitimacy of caste hierarchies and privileges associated with upper caste status of superior social esteem and educational and occupational opportunities. The 'democratic upsurge' inevitably reflected the mirror opposite of this hierarchical structure and form of social inequality. Leaders of lower castes, starting with the Backward Classes in the mid-1960s, began to organize their own parties in order to achieve equality with the upper or Forward Castes in terms of social dignity and political power. Their immediate demands, for social and political equality rather than equality of economic condition, arose from the reality that deprivation of educational and economic opportunities had been a consequence of the caste system. The political logic of this assumption led to the demand for reservations in educational institutions and the prestigious government services, as the essential first step in overturning the Brahmanical hierarchy, to gain access to state patronage which eventually could be translated into economic gains.

The dominant Indian National Congress suffered most from the political dynamics of social mobilization in this context. Defecting leaders from the lower castes seized opportunities created by expanded participation to form their own parties and mobilize support from their own ranks. The 'second democratic upsurge' in the 1990s, tracked by Yogendra Yadav, shows a higher trend in increased voter turnout by marginalized groups in the most backward areas of the country, that were also most divided along caste and communal lines. In the north Indian heartland, voter turnout increased at the state level relative to the national level, in rural areas relative to the cities, and among dalits and Scheduled Tribes.

Uttar Pradesh, asserts Zoya Hasan, is the pivotal site of potentially the most radical challenge to the dominance of the upper castes, and the arena in which the contest among and between lower caste parties, and the Bharatiya Janata Party, will influence the content of democratization and the course of democratic politics at the national level. Two strategies of political inclusion, allied to opposing forms of political mobilization, are locked in contention in the state. One is based on the BJP's efforts to construct a majoritarian religious identity, aimed at reintegrating the lower castes into the traditional Hindu hierarchy. This strategy reached its apogee in the movement to demolish the Babri masjid at Ayodhya, believed to have been built on the site of the birthplace of Lord Ram. After the violent demolition of the mosque in 1992 by militants affiliated with the BJP's parent organization, the Rashtriya Swayamsevak Sangh (RSS), and the Vishva Hindu Parishad, a religious organization included in the Sangh Parivar or family, committed workers have ignored court orders, building, pillar by pillar, the architecture to erect a Ram temple at that site.

The second strategy represents an effort to use the polarizing politics of caste-bloc identities to disrupt the traditional Hindu hierarchy. The aim of lower caste leaders is to change the power structure through the formation of regional and local parties representing the backward classes and the dalits, to gain direct control over the state. Hasan argues that the most important phenomenon for the transformation of politics in the state is the growth of backward caste politics, and the strategy of extending reservations for the Other Backward Classes, including Muslims, to state educational institutions and administrative services. This has produced an enduring confrontation between the upper castes clustered around the BJP and the backward castes currently supporting the Samajwadi Party.

Nevertheless, the conflict between the upper castes and backward classes does not exhaust group claims. Both contenders confront militant dalit leaders organized around the Bahujan Samaj Party (BSP) which primarily concentrates on consolidating the 20 per cent of Scheduled Castes into a dalit bloc that can hold the balance between the BJP and the Samajwadi Party and take state power in their own right.

Democratization in Uttar Pradesh, conditioned by rough parity in numbers between the most privileged upper castes, the bloc of backward castes and the dalits indicates both the promise and limits of political transformation in north India. Expanded participation has succeeded in rectifying discrimination among disadvantaged groups at the level of political party organization and elected government bodies because of the extraordinary stress placed on symbolic equality of representation. It has also increased representation of a privileged minority of the lower castes in government positions, educational institutions and the professions. Under a dalit chief minister, democratization has even produced a small measure of land security, employment, housing and scholarship money for dalits. Yet, the major gains so far have been from symbolic acts of social recognition rather than economic benefits for the majority.

The most crippling limitation of caste bloc politics for achieving the structural change required for greater economic equality, according to Hasan, is the narrow horizon and bitter competition between the backward castes and the dalits for access to scarce state resources, and the absence of a common agenda for structural change to achieve redistributive reform. This has prevented a stable alliance between the Samajwadi Party and the Bahujan Samaj Party which could defeat the upper castes and the BJP in Uttar Pradesh.

The ability of the BJP to win power in Uttar Pradesh by exploiting the divisions between the lower caste parties has profound implications outside north India. Uttar Pradesh is India's largest state of 140 million people, and one of the most socially and economically backward states in the northern heartland. Most crucial, the state sends eighty-five of 545 MPs to the Lok Sabha, making it politically the most influential state for the formation of the central government in New Delhi. The success of the BJP in splitting the alliance of the lower caste parties in U.P. became the backbone of its greatest achievement when it formed a national coalition government in 1998.

Fragmentation of Political Parties

Democracy and expanding participation in the Indian social and cultural context, resulting in a 'democracy of castes' and caste and communal competition and conflict, has placed the majority–minority framework at risk, and also exacerbated the fundamental tension between a strong government and decentralizing tendencies.

The increased participation in electoral politics of groups long considered peripheral, has ratcheted up pressure on the cohesion of national and even state political parties in the wake of voter fragmentation along regional, religious and caste lines.

The destabilizing results of these trends first became evident at the national level in 1989 when state-based parties joined together in a minority National Front government. At that juncture, the National Front relied for support from parties outside the government, the BJP and two communist parties, the Communist Party of India (CPI) and the Communist Party of India–Marxist (CPI-M), whose only point of agreement was the negative goal of excluding from power a common enemy, the Congress (I).[5]

The continuing decline of Congress (I) as a national party was obscured during 1991–6 when the party returned to power as a minority government, whose pre-poll allies and post-election supporters (alleged to have been won over with bribes) allowed it to govern as a majority until 1996. It was during this period that the Congress (I) government of Prime Minister Narasimha Rao introduced major economic reforms to deregulate the private sector and liberalize trade and foreign investment.

In 1996, the Congress (I)'s defeat was decisive. A 14-party United Front government was formed, this time including the left parties inside the government. They relied on the 'like-minded' secular Congress (I) to offer support from outside the government, again with a negative aim, that of preventing the BJP, then the largest party in Parliament, from coming to power. The minority coalitions, both those formed in 1989 and 1996, were toppled within eighteen months when their supporters outside the government, the BJP and the Congress (I) respectively, withdrew support.

The trend towards fragmentation was more pronounced in 1998. By then, this tendency was no longer confined to northern India, but had spread to all regions of the country. In the 1998 national elections, a record number of 41 'parties' won representation in the Lok Sabha: seven of these groupings have two or three members and fourteen have one member each. Six MPs were elected as Independents.

Many more 'parties', 176 in 1998, were registered by the Election Commission, of which only 30 were 'recognized' as state parties and seven as national parties. Yet, 11 per cent of the electorate voted for registered parties (compared to 3 per cent in 1996) and almost 20 per cent voted for state parties, (as opposed to 21 per cent in 1996), accounting altogether for more than 31 per cent of the electorate.[6] The steady decline in voter support for parties classified as national parties is obvious from the comparison with 1980 when the national parties altogether received 85 per cent of the vote.

As Arora's paper shows, the Congress (I), whose aggregate vote level in 1998 fell to 25 per cent, intersecting with the rising vote for the BJP of 25 per cent, still retains the most even spread among regions. The BJP, by contrast, enjoys disproportionate support in the north and northwest (from Uttar Pradesh to Rajasthan). It's ability to strike pre-poll alliances and post-poll bargains with single-state parties, localized parties within states, splinter groups and Independents allowed it to win a vote of confidence and form the government as leader of a disparate 13-'party' coalition, buttressed by 'post-electoral adhesions' of groups not represented among pre-poll partners. Yet, neither the BJP leadership, nor that of the Congress (I) professed willingness to give up the notion of attaining a single party majority in the Lok Sabha.

Economic Reforms

A new factor, from the 1990s, tending to exacerbate regional differences, and also strengthen single state parties, are the economic reforms introduced in 1991. Deregulation drastically cut back the number of industries reserved for the public sector, removed compulsory central licensing and regulation of almost all private sector enterprises, and lifted most restrictions on foreign investments. The cumulative effect was a marked shift of political power away from the Centre to the states. State-level politicians and bureaucrats, with power to expedite or delay the various sanctions required at local levels to purchase land, arrange power connections, instal telecommunications and many other essential services, have become the gatekeepers of private investment by national enterprises and multinational corporations. Other new central government policies to encourage development of badly needed infrastructure have augmented the authority of the states to enter into negotiations with independent power producers and electricity distribution companies, to seek project loans from the World Bank and to make deals with multinationals involving direct investment.

Uneven implementation of the economic reforms has contributed to disparities between states. The largest share of domestic and foreign investment has been directed to the relatively developed and more stable states of Maharashtra, Gujarat, Karnataka, Goa, Tamil Nadu and Andhra Pradesh.

Sanjaya Baru's analysis of the historical emergence of regional capitalists of agrarian origin and rural roots in states with agricultural surpluses suggests a symbiotic relationship between new business groups and the rise of prominent state parties. The regional capitalists, arising from prosperous peasant castes who invested in education, acquired urban property, and then moved into non-farm business, have been able to draw on funds provided by kinship and caste networks. They have made the greatest headway, relative to older, national big business houses, in Punjab, Haryana, Maharashtra, Rajasthan, Gujarat, Karnataka, Andhra Pradesh and Tamil Nadu, and over a wide range of industries, including sugar, textiles, cement, pharmaceuticals and electronics. Many of these states' financial institutions tended to favour 'local' capital. On their part, regional capitalists 'invested' in state

political parties to ensure their access to them. The most successful new entrepreneurs have been able to strike collaborations with foreign investors to gain increasing market share. The
importance of regional capitalists and their financiers to the electoral fortunes of state parties may be strong enough, Baru suggests, to convert a 'national' party like the BJP into a 'regional'
party government, as in Gujarat.

This proposition gains some circumstantial support from recent political trends. State-based parties have done well in states
with the highest growth rates. Among the seven states ranked
in 1996 as having had the highest rates of growth—Tamil Nadu,
Andhra Pradesh, Karnataka, Arunachal Pradesh, Maharashtra,
Punjab and Assam—only the small north-eastern state of
Arunachal Pradesh was still governed by the Congress (I), and
Karnataka was ruled by an officially designated national party,
the Janata Dal, which subsequently disintegrated.[7] As Baru's
analysis helps explain, the uneven impact of economic reforms,
accompanied by political alliances in high growth states between
regional capital and state-based political parties, exacerbates
problems of reconstituting a strong national party that can provide a stable democratic government.

Prabhat Patnaik goes further. He warns that IMF stabiliza-
tion and structural adjustment programmes forced on much of
the developing world to deal with balance of payments crises,
such as the one preceding economic reforms in India, can help
to abridge political democracy itself.

Patnaik asserts that emphasis by international financial institutions on trade liberalization, and removal of restrictions
on capital flows, represents the converging interests of multinationals, sections of the domestic bourgeoisie seeking to expand
into the international market, larger agriculturists lured by the
promise of export agriculture, and third world élites eager for
opportunities and products accessible from globalization. Above
all, however, Patnaik argues that financial liberalization benefits international finance capital that no longer has any national character. According to him, the fear that this 'hot money'
will flow out of the domestic economy if fiscal deficits are allowed to increase, results in reduction of government expenditure and the adoption of neo-liberal policies, such as increasing
administered foodgrain prices, and cutting back on government

expenditure in rural areas and on infrastructure. After deregulation and the initial burst of production gains created by
bottled-up domestic investment, poor infrastructure and weak
purchasing power present new obstacles to further expansion.
This is reflected in declining growth rates, depressed exports,
widening trade deficits, increased inflation, and an arrested
decline of poverty. Although India, through prudent financial
management and sheer size of its domestic economy, has so far
escaped the worst manifestations of this contraction, Patnaik
nevertheless believes that the coexistence of widening disparities with democracy can become more problematic in the future. The hope of betterment among sections of the poor so far
sustained by slow social mobility and embedded in the politics
of populism and reservations for backward classes, could be
curtailed by economic stagnation associated with neo-liberal
economic policy. Indeed, Patnaik advances the general proposition that structural adjustment policies are antithetical to democracy in multicultural societies. The very process of 'globalization' helps to fracture national consciousness, thereby widening the political space for assertion of divisive communal,
fundamentalist and secessionist movements.

Nationalizing Institutions

It may appear that against the force of the centrifugal tendencies described above, India's political cohesion, no less than its
democracy is undergoing severe strain. Yet, few concerns are
expressed by even those most pessimistic about the performance
of India's democratic institutions with respect to the enduring
nature of India's Union.

One contextual factor which has not received much attention is the historical colonial legacy of centralization in national
media, the police and the judiciary that served state interests in
maintaining political control of a potentially rebellious population. As Victoria Farmer points out, until the early 1990s, and
the advent of transnational satellite television, the government
successfully used the legal structure first set down by the British
in 1885 for control of telegraphs, to establish a monopoly over
All India Radio (AIR), and then to create state ownership and
control of new television technology through the government

broadcasting corporation, Doordarshan. The stated purpose of the national television network, to support developmental programming, subsequently shifted emphasis to the creation of a national identity. Nevertheless, as Farmer argues, the depiction of national identity in such a diverse society, was bound to be contested, and indeed such programmes as the serialization of the *Ramayana* helped the BJP to advance its Hindutva agenda. The media's credibility was also questioned at times when it was misused by the ruling party, especially in the 1989 general elections to publicize Congress (I) party leaders at the expense of their opponents. Despite all of this, efforts to create an autonomous corporation to administer Doordarshan, since 1989, have yet to be fully implemented. As a result, Doordarshan still remains by far the largest source of television programming in both urban and rural India.

Similarly, as R.K. Raghavan demonstrates, the Indian police remains governed, by and large, by statutes going back to 1861 which reflect the colonial government's preoccupation with using police forces to preserve law and order. This function, and the types of police forces created to implement it after independence, has grown indiscriminately. The centrally recruited officers of the Indian Police Service (IPS), assigned to state cadres, have provided an indispensable institutional basis for cooperation between the central government and the states to handle public order problems, while the strength of the police forces has grown steadily. Equally important, centrally controlled police forces have been created, such as the Border Security Police and the Central Industrial Security Force, which have been deployed to nearly all states, at their request, to restore public order in 'disturbed areas'.

The determination to ensure a strong central government after independence, with capabilities to combat any threat to national unity, as noted by Brass, opened the way to the political involvement of the police in maintaining public order across a diverse range of threats, with little parallel in other democracies. As enumerated by Raghavan, centrally controlled police forces have been deployed against secessionist movements, linguistic agitations, agrarian revolutionaries, terrorism, caste clashes and communal violence. The most positive achievement of the police, according to Raghavan, was their professionalism

during the long years of terrorism in Punjab, which finally ended
with the restoration of democratic elections in 1992.

At the same time, such extensive use of the police to tackle
civil conflicts has had serious negative consequences for the
insulation of the forces from political interference, corruption
and communal biases. The police are generally viewed with
suspicion by the public, and distrusted by the courts for excessive use of force and human rights violations. Raghavan, who
served as Director-General of Police in the state of Tamil Nadu,
and was subsequently appointed to the highest police post of
Director of the Central Bureau of Investigation, expresses support for the activist role of the Supreme Court in landmark cases
that have increased public scrutiny of police investigations and
also provided some protection from political interference.

Indeed, as Rajeev Dhavan's sweeping overview of the evolving role of the judiciary in India's democracy makes clear, the
decades since the Emergency have witnessed the political manipulation and corruption of virtually all institutions of governance.
As a result, the higher judiciary has come to play a pivotal role
in asserting an independent status 'forcing other institutions of
governance to take steps to do what they are supposed to be
doing. . .'. According to Dhavan, the judiciary, which was an
institution of state during the colonial period, interpreting the
meaning of laws, first changed its character during the Nehru
years. During this period, the high courts and Supreme Court
functioned in institutional polarity to the government, scruti-
nizing legislation and striking down some acts for violating the
fundamental rights guaranteed by the Constitution.

The greatest transformation, however, occurred during the
1980s, in the immediate post-Emergency phase, when the judiciary began the transition to an independent institution of governance. Dhavan argues that in vastly expanding its powers to
encompass public interest litigation, the Supreme Court provided social activists, lawyers and journalists with recourse to
the protection of the law against abuses of it by other institutions of governance, and thereby took on the responsibility of
upholding the essential goal of social justice under the Constitution. The higher judiciary, in his interpretation, attempted to
fill a political vacuum created by the failure of governance on
almost all fronts. During the 1980s and 1990s, governance was

permeated with corruption, the relationship between some political parties and criminals with money and muscle power to influence the outcome of some local elections started to come into the open, and the police perpetrated human rights violations against secessionist groups and agrarian revolutionaries in 'disturbed areas'.

Among the most significant additional powers asserted by the judiciary, as Raghavan also points out, are the 1996 Supreme Court orders declaring its right to examine evidence collected by the revenue authorities or the Central Bureau of Investigation, when official reports cite the absence of any material reason to proceed further against an accused person; and the 1997 ruling which frees the CBI from having to seek prior permission of the government in initiating investigations of corruption against senior civil servants. Yet, as Dhavan observes, the judiciary's success in establishing an agenda independent of the government has made 'it the most controversial institution of Indian governance'.

Hindutva and the Redefinition of the National Political Community: Search for a New Regime?

Democratic institutions and practices, adapted to the Indian historical and social context, have had a powerful transforming effect. They have undermined the legitimacy of the hierarchical social structure, and destroyed the historical capability of the upper castes to enforce unequal status and power relations as the basis of stability in society. Rather, democratization has unleashed an upsurge of participation from among the poor and the illiterate of the lower social strata, and a 'democracy of caste groups', which has dramatically increased their representation in elected institutions of governance. Similarly, reservations in educational institutions and the civil services for dalits and the Other Backward Classes, have provided more opportunities for social mobility among the top layers of the disadvantaged.

Democracy has not, however, accomplished an overall increase of equality in social and economic life. Rather, after five decades of competitive politics, caste and communal conflict have intensified in a struggle to control the scarce resources of the state. Most of all, the second democratic upsurge, concentrated in the traditional northern heartland of the ancient Sanskritic culture, threatens to finally end the domination of the upper castes and upper classes in the bureaucracy, as well as in parliamentary institutions of government, once their impregnable strongholds.

Meanwhile, the rapidly growing urban middles classes, as the major beneficiaries of economic reforms, seek protection from the corruption and political disorder that threaten opportunities for further gains. Democratization has fragmented political parties along state, sub-regional, caste and religious lines, creating unstable coalition governments, paralyzed from within, without the capacity to carry out unfinished reforms. Apprehension that political stability will indefinitely remain elusive because of shifting tactical calculations by rival groups in local arenas has raised the question of whether the parliamentary system has run its course in India.

Both Christophe Jaffrelot and Amrita Basu, in their chapters on Hindu nationalism, concentrate on the implications for democracy of the BJP's rise to national power, and the controversial interpretations by their leaders of secularism, minority rights and a strong centre, organized as a presidential system of government. The BJP, founded in 1980 as the successor party to the Jan Sangh, the proponent of Bharatiya ideology stretching back to 1951, began its climb to national power in the late 1980s, supporting the Vishva Hindu Parishad's campaign to tear down the Babri mosque at Ayodhya and build a temple to Lord Ram on the site. This campaign to reintegrate the Hindu community around common religious beliefs was inescapably linked with the BJP's opposition to the minority United Front government's decision in 1990 to implement the recommendations of the 1980 Mandal Commission. Overnight, 27 per cent of all posts in the élite Indian Administrative Service and Indian Police Service, the virtual prerogative of the upper castes, stood reserved for candidates from the Other Backward Classes, including Muslims. The 'Mandir–Mandal' debate came to symbolize the contest, especially in north India, between the upper castes and the lower castes and dalits, over how the national political community should be defined, and the way in which the political system should be organized.

The Hindutva ideology favoured by the BJP as a unifying basis of national cultural identity, was criticized by virtually all other parties for reviving the majority–minority syndrome. It has the potential, in addition, of turning back the second democratic upsurge by splitting alliances between lower caste groups, Dalits and Muslims. Allied to a political agenda for advancing presidential government, it can also be seen as strengthening the authoritarian tendencies in the Constitution. The debate, in the 1990s, reopened the question, answered in the affirmative by the 1950 Constitution, whether the universal values of Western democracies embodied in the Westminster system of parliamentary democracy are relevant to India.

Jaffrelot's answer to the question of whether Hindu nationalists fully adhere to democracy raises serious doubts about their democratic credentials. He refers to arguments by leaders of the RSS, as well as to the 1996 statement by Atal Behari Vajpayee, who became prime minister in 1998, that the Westminster model adopted in the 1950 Constitution represents British-style institutions that are different from India's indigenous democratic traditions. Such ideas, propagated in the BJP by mainstream theoreticians, emphasize participation by the group rather than the individual as the relevant unit, and recommend, as an ideal, the vertical organization of society in an organic dharmic system based on geographic and functional or occupational representation that has no place for class. Jaffrelot also argues that Hindu nationalists cannot accommodate the notion of a plural democracy that protects minority rights. Their leaders are advocates of democracy in principle, endorsing 'one man, one vote'. Yet, this formulation merges democracy and majoritarianism, placing Hindus in a permanent majority to avoid the 'dangers of minorityism'.

The debate on changing from a parliamentary to a presidential system has been taken up among politicians across the spectrum seeking a solution for short-lived coalitions, but according to Jaffrelot, the version favoured by the BJP has authoritarian implications. Ideas sketched out so far rest on allowing the president to rule at the Centre with the help of his own advisers if political parties are unable to form a government. Finally, Jaffrelot's painstaking data for major parties in the Hindi belt through the 1998 elections, by occupation, caste and community, indicates that for all the BJP's success in expanding its social base among Other Backward Classes, the party remains disproportionately representative of upper castes as well as traders and businessmen, with no ability to contribute to the social democratization of Indian politics.

Amrita Basu's answer to a similar question posed in terms of the implications for Indian democracy of Hindu nationalism, is not much more reassuring. Indeed, she considers the rise of the BJP one of the major challenges to Indian democracy over the last 50 years. Like Jaffrelot, Basu addresses the puzzle of whether the BJP's adherence to formal democratic principles coexists with an intent to undermine democracy. She argues that the grounds on which the BJP supports secularism undermines the western concept of separation between religion and state. It is based on the criticism of the state for unequal treatment of Hindus and Muslims which discriminates against Hindus and appeases Muslims. Hindu festivals and religious practices are considered by nature, secular in assimilating all sects as part of the fabric of Indian cultural life. By contrast, Muslim religious observance is characterized as intolerant and a major obstacle to secularism, especially when protected by the state. Basu agrees with Jaffrelot that the BJP has redefined democracy as majority rule and opposes state protection for minority rights.

Nevertheless, she seriously considers the arguments of other scholars that all parties which seek power in India are subject to centripetal forces which drives them to the Centre; and that the BJP which suffered electoral losses in north India after the destruction of the Babri mosque also embarked on a strategy of relative moderation to win over coalition partners in the states. She concludes, nevertheless, that these changes in strategy are more likely to be cyclical than permanent, noting that the BJP engages in 'doublespeak', simultaneously using communal appeals and precipitating violence to influence election outcomes, while employing the language of legality and consensus to appease electoral allies. Moreover, even if moderate leaders of the BJP were inclined to follow a centrist position, they would be constrained from doing so by membership of the party in the broad network of Hindu organizations, especially the militant RSS which provides the large majority of BJP officials, as well as a mass base. Not least, according to Basu, is the actual experience of the Jan Sangh/BJP, that a double-edged approach alternating militancy and moderation or combining militant and populist appeals pays greater electoral dividends. Finally, Basu notes the different implications for democracy of identity politics based on ethnic as opposed to religious movements. Accommodation by the state of the first type of movement tends to strengthen democratic politics by satisfying demands for recognition of cultural pluralism that simultaneously enhance the need for political alliances which uphold national identities. By contrast, when the BJP assumes power at the state level, its ambition to rule at the Centre results in an assertion of the overriding importance of Hindu identity as the basis of a majority constituency, encouraging a political climate antithetical to minority Muslim, and more recently, Christian rights.

If Hindu nationalism challenges fundamental principles of cultural pluralism and minority rights, the renewed debate on whether the parliamentary regime should be replaced by presidential government, creates alarm about the future of India's democracy. Verney's analysis of what a presidential regime would involve in India's multicultural society, suggests that this alarm is well founded.

According to Verney, there is good reason for skepticism about a presidential system in India, especially the form adopted in France of a presidential/quasi-parliamentary government. Unlike France, with its homogeneous society, India's heterogeneity would place an impossible burden on the president who would find it hard to stay above the fray and represent all important regions and minorities. The French president, moreover, is not responsible to the National Assembly. A comparable arrangement in India would increase the danger of an authoritarian form of government under conditions of a fragmented and polarized party system. Neither is the French Constitution federal. Any adaptation to Indian conditions would require complicated modifications from a presidential/quasi-parliamentary regime, to a 'presidential/quasi-parliamentary federation' to ensure representation of the states. Such a regime, whose complex components Verney sketches out in some detail, has not been successfully implemented in any country.

Verney's argument that a presidential system cannot be an 'add-on' to India's democracy is a sobering one. He considers any approach that is analogous to facilitating 'President's Rule' at the Centre, a high-risk gamble. It could allow the president to pursue his own policies without any elected body that can adequately integrate the states into the formulation of national decisions. Over time, the Centre's influence relative to the states could well be weakened. Short of a grave unforeseen crisis, Verney argues, it would be preferable to make modifications in the direction of a more decentralized administration rather than choose a new presidential regime. This would avoid concentration of power in the office of an authoritarian president, and alienation from an arbitrary government with its danger of accelerating the fragmentation, and even disintegration, of the Indian polity.

The magnitude of ideological and group conflicts so far contained within democratically elected institutions is perhaps the best argument for the contextual democracy encompassed by constitutional arrangements that have held since 1950. Traditional questions of how well democratic institutions have performed, or how conflicting societal demands have affected the ability of government to implement policy choices, miss the deeper meaning of the dynamics of democracy under Indian conditions.

Democracy in India has neither 'succeeded' nor 'failed'. It has done something more remarkable. In little more than fifty years since colonial rule, the introduction of individual freedoms, minority rights and universal suffrage have significantly transformed historically rigid hierarchical structures, social relations and cultural attitudes. Democratic institutions in contemporary India are giving voice to what was the largest oppressed population in any ancient civilization or modern state. No future ruling party or coalition—or new regime—can hope to achieve stability, preserve the Union, and attain national greatness, without proceeding from this new reality.

Notes

[1] Robert D. Putnam, *Making Democracy Work: Civil Traditions in Modern Italy* (Englewood: Princeton University Press), 1993, Chapter 6.

[2] Arend Lijphart, 'Unequal Participation: Democracy's Unresolved Dilemma', *American Political Science Review*, vol. 91, nos. 11–14 (March 1977).

[3] The Constitution (Forty-fourth Amendment) Act, 1978, substituted

'armed rebellion' for 'internal disturbance' as the only situation apart from a grave threat to the security of India or any part of its territory, justifying a Proclamation of Emergency by the president.

4 See the discussion on democracy and multinational states by Juan J. Linz and Alfred Stepan, 'Toward Consolidated Democracies', in Takashi Inoguchi, Edward Newman and John Keane (eds), *The Changing Nature of Democracy* (United Nations University Press), 1998, pp. 61–3.

5 After a second split in the Congress party forced by Indira Gandhi, (the first occurring in 1967), the party was renamed Congress (I), for Indira, indicating the personalization of party power.

6 The Election Commission classifies political parties in three categories: 'national parties' with a presence across states; 'state parties' based in a single state; and 'Registered (Unrecognized) parties which are registered with the Election Commission and allowed to contest elections, but have not been given official recognition. For an analysis of the decline of support for national parties, and increase of vote share for state and registered parties, see Douglas V. Verney, 'Improving Coalition Government in India', *Denouement*, vol. 9 (January–February 1999), pp. 17–22.

7 Francine R. Frankel, 'The Problem', 'Unity or Incoherence', *Seminar*, 459 (November 1997), p. 14.

Democratic Vision of a New Republic: India, 1950

RAJEEV BHARGAVA

We live in a world of radical plurality: differences abound, contestation is rampant, every perspective appears to have a unique taker, and a deep-rooted scepticism exists about unified narratives. In this context it is almost blasphemous to speak of *the* democratic vision of a new republic, but I venture to speak of a single vision on the assumption that, despite the absence of a unified collective subject, a loose, disjointed, somewhat incoherent vision of India, with the potential of an overlapping consensus among its most active members, did emerge briefly in 1950.

Here, I try to rearticulate that vision. I argue that (*a*) democracy came to India *as* nationalism and, therefore, that arguments for nationalism were coterminous with arguments for democracy; that (*b*) the character of this democracy, in one significant sense, just *had* to be liberal not only because of its commitment to civil liberties but also because of its vision of equality and social justice; that (*c*) the predominantly cultural character of nationalism in India and its traditional proclivity for recognizing the importance of collectivities forced the makers of the Constitution to move beyond individualist liberalism, in order to wrestle with the tension between constitutive attachments and personal liberty, between group disadvantage and personal merit, and that all these factors shaped the character of the emergent secular–democratic state of India.

In presenting this view, I believe I challenge the accepted wisdom of much current history and social science.[1] In particular, I question the view that has considerable currency in intellectual circles today, i.e., that the crisis of liberalism stems directly from the opposition it faced at its birth.[2] This view claims that liberalism came to India along with the British ruling élite, rubbed off on to the skin of Indian imitators who came into contact with it, but was shed soon after because it remained only skin deep. This version of the story of liberalism in India is stunningly simplistic. The Constitution did not emerge miraculously out of calm deliberations around a table, but from the political struggles of an élite eager to give India a new social order. My objection, then, is that this view fails to see the link between the Constitution and the continuous intellectual and political labour in the country for over a century. An argument sustaining this objection constitutes the first section of the paper. In the second section, I more fully delineate the vision of a democratic India that animated the framers of the Constitution. This was a vision marked by a commitment to universal franchise, to rights of linguistic and religious minorities, and to a variant of secularism shaped by sensitivity to such group-specific rights.

Was the Vision Liberal-Democratic?

There is an undeniable crisis of liberal democracy in India today. It appears that the institutions associated with liberal democracy are worn out and frayed at the edges. Given the Western origins of liberal democracy and its unmistakable distance from traditional Indian culture, and because liberal democratic institutions appear so totally to lack legitimacy in contemporary India, it is tempting to believe that whatever else it might be, Indian democracy never was and never can be liberal. However, this view is not convincing. On the contrary, the current crisis of liberal democracy is due in large part to its own success. The introduction of civil liberties gave voice to the mute, and the stage for action was set by the democratic process for those hitherto debarred from the public domain. They entered it with new modes of speech and action to which the initiators of liberal democracy were unaccustomed, and in numbers that greatly exceeded the tiny upper crust that led the national movement. It is no doubt true that those empowered by institutions of liberal democracy do not come from a cultural background with an obviously liberal or democratic character. However, it would be mistaken to conclude from this that this newly empowered class is wholly maladjusted to these institutions. Considerable evidence exists of its successful adaptation to these western institutions (and of these institutions to these groups!). More importantly, tempting as it is, one should not succumb to the implausible idea that liberal democracy was forced out very quickly from the minds of the major political actors in the movement for Indian independence.

Yet something approaching this view has been advocated by Sunil Khilnani in his book, *The Idea of India*. For him, Indian liberalism was crippled from its beginnings: stamped by utilitarianism, squeezed into a culture that had little room for the individual.[3] Khilnani claims that, 'The idea of natural right, essential to modern liberalisms, was only faintly articulated and failed to find a niche in nationalist thought.'[4] In India, 'Liberty was understood not as an individual right but as a nation's collective right to self-determination.'[5] The discourse of rights was disengaged from its individual moorings and attached quite naturally to groups, particularly to religious communities in a society fashioned for centuries by a collectivist mentality. With its emphasis on separate individuals moved by internal requirements of personal autonomy and tied to others by choice rather than circumstance, liberalism was bound to fail in this culture and it did. The final nail in the coffin was hammered in by the very political agent that liberalism had nurtured in its initial encounter with India, the Indian National Congress. Gandhi's strategy of turning the Congress into a mass movement made a commitment to liberal and democratic institutions look shallow and irrelevant. 'By the 1930s and 40s, Congress nationalism was divided between opinions that had little interest in liberal democracy.'[6] Not surprisingly, political representation was granted only to ascriptively defined groups, i.e., those with immutable interests.

Khilnani's is an attractive portrayal of the intellectual and political history of modern India, not least because it brings order to criss-crossing, often mutually incompatible, ideas of diverse origin and value. It does this by an explanation of charming simplicity and economy, by nicely reinforcing the view that the current crisis of liberal institutions can be traced all the way back to their origins. But is this not the cultural-inadaptability thesis all over again? Does it not bolster the view that western ideas cannot really take root in a cultural environment seemingly hostile to them? Khilnani reconfirms the idea of India as a country whose individuality was throttled at the top by a small group of upwardly mobile men, lacking in self-confidence from years of powerlessness and swept off their feet by the first great tide of modernity. Without the effort required to change the course of history but with a great deal of good fortune, they used the power which they found in their hands to impose on an unwilling populace a set of ideas from which the souls of the poor people naturally turned away.

This argument appeases our hunger for coherent narratives and fulfils the need for collective individuality instilled in us by romanticism. It also falls in line with a cultivated sympathy for the marginalized. Yet, it presents a very skewed picture. It is nourished by a lopsided view of liberalism, a biased view of the history of liberal democracy in India. Above all, it is guilty of reverse anachronism. It extrapolates features of contemporary India into the past, sees continuity in the wrong places, and projects our own concerns on to remote relatives whose world was markedly different from ours. Views that appear constrictive to us were liberating for our forefathers; they were not exactly the same views, anyway. Besides, this perspective fails to properly account for much that is crying out for explanation. Why did India adopt the Constitution that it did? Why were fundamental rights accorded a central place within the Constitution? Why adopt a constitution in the first place? Why the scramble to protect the rights of individuals and only a grudging acceptance for group rights? And, in a deeply hierarchical society, why such scant opposition to universal franchise, to the ban on untouchability, and to formal gender equality?

Proponents of the argument that liberal democracy is alien to cultural and social norms in India can respond by claiming that they do possess a meaningful account of the birth of constitutional democracy in India. The Constitution, which was 'squarely in the best western tradition', this view believes, was given to the people of India by the political choice of an intellectual élite within a remarkably unrepresentative body.[7] Moreover, it was established in 'a fit of absentmindedness'; the élite had no idea of the political implications of their actions or of the consequences that lay in store once they had extended the franchise to the poor and the uneducated.[8]

I find this an extraordinary perspective on the making of the

Indian Constitution: chosen, but unwittingly, by a body that claimed to represent the real interests of everyone but was in fact wholly unrepresentative, in the best traditions of the West because it turned its back sharply on the homegrown traditions of the national movement. By what magic was this miracle performed? How could the *very* people who allegedly rejected the liberal-democratic vision, at the same time adopt a Constitution in the finest traditions of western liberal democracy? How could some of the most outstanding figures of the century choose a basic structure for their society without a clue about its impact on that society or on its inherited traditions? This is not an easy question to answer and certainly not one to be dealt with in a few pages. But it is worthwhile to ask whether a response that appears attractive at first sight retains plausibility on closer examination. I do not think it does.

The Liberal Strand in Indian Politics

It is more plausible to argue that at least since Rammohun Roy, and well before the radical politicization of the Indian National Congress, a distinct liberal stream existed which merged with and inherited a diffused but persistent strain of something akin to a liberal view within local Indian traditions; that western modernity made considerable inroads into an aspiring middle strata of Indian society because it genuinely articulated and responded to their needs; and that there is more to utilitarianism than its strong collectivist trappings. Therefore, even if liberalism came to India through utilitarianism, it washed up ideas that were neutral, to say the least, between the individual and the collective; British imperialism, by installing the machinery of a modern state simultaneously opened up opportunities for resistance to it. Therefore, a classical political libertarianism with its emphasis on individual rights came to India as a structural feature of modern political life. Above all, democracy grew in India, as it did in many other places, under the guise of nationalism, and its commitment to political equality fitted in neatly with the egalitarian strands of liberalism as well as of utilitarianism. In the last instance, this meant that even outside the polity, liberal demands for equality of opportunity and for treating individuals as equals were considerably strengthened. If all this is true then it is a gross exaggeration to assert that constitutional democracy in India was established in a fit of absentminded-ness, that the discourse of rights was detached entirely from its classical individualist and political moorings, and that Indian nationalism had little interest in liberal democracy. These points need elaboration.

I begin with the claim that the transformation of nationalist demands into a mass movement ended the short phase of lib-eral politics in India. I do not wish to contest that the politics of mass movement is deeply at odds with the politics of insti-tutionalized opposition. Undeniably, a great distance exists between a politics of resistance to the state, one that tries—with popular mandate if not direct pressure from below—to force rulers out of power, and a politics conducted within parameters of institutionalized opposition permitted by the state. Rather, my point is that the first kind of politics is as much a part of the liberal tradition as the second. Any plausible form of liberalism incorporates within it a right to actively resist illegitimate state power, a right that can hardly be exercised within normal po-litical process. The form taken by this politics of resistance var-ies in different contexts. People guided by a strong liberal vision, keen to set up a liberal state, may have to adopt even violent methods to do so. How else does one explain the American War of Independence or even, perhaps, the French Revolution? The fact that in periods of transition the Americans and the French adopted 'revolutionary', non-institutional politics does not mean they rejected liberalism. Similarly, Gandhi's adoption of mass politics, a politics of 'coercion and seduction' does not indicate that a liberal agenda had been abandoned, just as the revolu-tionary phase in France or America does not prove that liberal-ism had been jettisoned. The plain fact is that liberalism, while admitting the right to resistance to an illegitimate state, is not clear on the methods to be adopted for such resistance. These can vary from violent overthrow to passive resistance, and quite easily accommodate Gandhi's eclectic politics of satyagraha. At any rate, a distinction needs to be made between Gandhian methods of revolt against an oppressive regime and the sub-stantive vision that impelled these methods. Gandhi's programme for the abolition of untouchability; of equality for women; of the extension of franchise to every person; and his deeply individualistic vision of spirituality have much in common with any reasonable interpretation of a number of liberalisms.

My second point about the commitment to civil liberties flows directly from acceptable norms of dissent and the availability of political liberty within the confines of a liberal state. As early as the beginning of the nineteenth century, Rammohun Roy protested against a regulation curtailing the freedom of the press. He argued that a state that is responsive to the needs of individuals and ready for intervention on their behalf, makes available to them the means by which such needs are communicated, and, therefore, must permit unrestricted liberty of publication. The demand for a free press and opposition to its gagging persisted throughout British rule, particularly when the press was the principal instrument for the propagation and consolidation of India's nationalist ideology. Consider the fierce opposition to the infamous Rowlatt Act which gave the colonial state enormous emergency powers, similar to wartime controls. It is true that opposition to this act was not expressed in ways that were obviously liberal, but in its substantive content it was fundamentally liberal. An opposition to arbitrary detention is as classically liberal as you can get, and yet there is simply no one, particular, liberal method of opposing it, anytime, anywhere in the world.

Similarly, the claim that liberalism arrived in India already gravely compromised because it was introduced by utilitarianism in its rampantly collectivist and paternalist mood is severely overstated. For a start, liberalism did not come to India only as a well-articulated philosophy through standard processes of ideological transmission, such as education and the press. On the contrary, many of its core values originated simply as a consequence of practices and institutions set up by the rulers to directly serve British interests, rather than by deliberate design. Consider, for example, the introduction of the postal system or the railways and their dramatic impact on social mobility; or the system of education introduced for the convenience of the rulers, but of immense advantage to the ruled. Many local upper caste men may indeed have been transformed into efficient servants of the empire, but education also unwittingly created Indian nationalists who eventually challenged both the empire as well as some oppressive tendencies within their own social order. Similarly, by introducing the Indian penal code, the imperial legal system established the doctrine of equality of all before the law. By a curious dialectic, every practice that began as a functional requirement of the Raj contributed at least partly to its own undoing over time. Liberalism did not come to India only through the spoken or printed word; it was directly embedded in practices as a structural feature of institutions and technologies. Unsurprisingly, British rulers were unaware, or at least appear to have miscalculated the potential implications of their actions. Whether or not they had *created* the empire in a fit of absentmindedness, it appears that they had certainly *consolidated* it in that mood!

Let me come to the real point. It is no particular flaw of the Indian élite that constitutional democracy was established in a fit of absentmindedness. Human agents anywhere in the world are unlikely to be clairvoyant about *all* the potential implications of their actions. It was to counter the myth of this Cartesian translucency, the presumption that agents always have a clear idea of what they are doing, that philosophers such as Hegel introduced the concept of 'the cunning of reason'. Much safer, I believe, is to presume that agents never grasp the *full* implications of their actions or fully know what they are doing. The Indian élite was unaware to the same degree as any set of reasonable agents would be; indeed, they knew what they were doing to the extent possible even though they could not have been fully aware of all the potential implications of their actions.

My next point pertains to the characterization of utilitarianism and liberalism. An emphasis on the collectivist ingredient within utilitarianism should not ignore other components compatible with a rights-based version of liberalism. Likewise, the centrality of rights or autonomy within liberalism should not be interpreted in such a way that other key values within liberalism are overlooked. To be sure, the point about the strong collectivism of utilitarianism is not entirely mistaken; one of its glaring flaws is its failure to appreciate the true significance of the separateness of persons. Utilitarian calculation allows some individuals to subsidize, even at their own expense, the projects of other individuals; from the point of view of an impartial, benevolent observer, some individuals may count for nothing. This is deeply disturbing from an alternative standpoint of moral equality and fairness. Insofar as utilitarianism possesses this collectivist ingredient, it can only have strengthened the unjust, anti-individualist biases of Indian tradition.

However, utilitarianism also contains strands neutral towards the individual and the collective, and may strengthen individualist tendencies against traditional, inegalitarian collectivism. Here, I wish to draw attention to three such features: first, its stress on happiness and well-being, and its repugnance for suffering. Second, its idea that in the utilitarian calculus every unit of happiness carries *equal* weight, and therefore a desire cannot be ignored merely on account of the current social rank of its holder or some obscure metaphysics. Finally, the right answer to a moral question is determined by measuring human happiness rather than by relying on ramshackle tradition or a dubious spiritual leader.[9] Utilitarianism may have generated its own brand of authoritarian collectivism but it was also destined to upset the inegalitarian collectivism of several Indian customs. Indeed, by its emphasis on desire and happiness, on the avoidance of suffering and by its implicit attack on social hierarchy, it was more than likely to nourish individualist ideas. To cut a long story short, if it is important to point out the link between utilitarianism and collectivism, it is equally necessary to register the precise form of collectivism encouraged by it. The 'happiness of the greatest number' is galaxies apart from 'the happiness of the smallest number', which was the hallmark of traditional collectivism. Indeed, the individualist implications of utilitarianism could hardly have failed to contribute to the development of ideas that eventually coalesced into a set of fundamental rights in the Indian Constitution.

The Tension between Individual and Community Rights

Against the view that a rights-based liberalism was crippled in India from its very beginnings, I have argued that for the Indian political élite, civil liberties mattered a great deal, and that these had to be construed individualistically, i.e., essentially as features of individuals rather than of groups. True, little interest in the philosophical justification of these rights was evident, but in their practical engagement with an alien, oppressive state, political actors in India fully realized their importance. A practical knowledge that these rights belong to them qua individuals could not have escaped them, even though they did not articulate this knowledge in terms of an indigenous, grand theory. Perhaps the language and culture of individual rights was not pervasive and did not go very deep; but it went as far and as deep as it possibly could at that time, and for the 50 years or so before the adoption of the Constitution, every single resolution, scheme, bill, national demand or report mentioned it, not just in passing, but as a *non-negotiable value*. The section on fundamental rights in the Indian Constitution, with a core of civil liberties, did not fall from the sky fully formed. It grew out of struggles with an oppressive, humiliating political regime. Despite attacks and instrumentalist attitudes towards it, the idea of fundamental rights remains potent even today. After all, the discourse of civil rights has not exactly disappeared from India! The fact that it has not gone deeper requires explanation, but recognition of this is a far cry from accepting the idea that it was knocked out in India before it even took its first faltering steps.

More importantly, liberalism must not be viewed only as a doctrine of individual rights; nor was it believed to be so by more articulate members of the Constituent Assembly. For example, take the views of Sardar K.M. Panikkar who, in the Sarojini Naidu Memorial Lecture (1961) argued that Indian liberalism was made up of two streams each with 'a fairly long history'.[10] For Panikkar, the founder of the first stream was Rammohun Roy who, 'by emphasizing the right of women to freedom and the establishment of casteless society put the Hindu people on the road to liberal transformation and contributed to the growth of liberal thought in India'.[11] The second stream comprised figures like K.C. Sen and M.G. Ranade, but more importantly Swami Vivekananda, who 'introduced into orthodox Hinduism the spirit of social justice'. By disassociating institutions such as caste and prohibitions like widow remarriage from the Hindu religion, and by espousing the view that the reform of such practices is a matter essentially of social justice, Vivekananda spurred a movement of reordering Hindu society infused with liberal principles. Panikkar also argues that Gandhiji's ascendancy within the Congress initiated a programme of political action based on the same ideas for which liberalism stood. The Congress not only advocated political liberalism but emphasized the 'rights of the individuals and the value of essential freedoms, the rule of law, secularism in politics and faith in social justice'. Two features stand out in this account as constitutive of liberalism: equality and social justice. Panikkar's vision of liberalism in general and of Indian liberalism in particular is far more in consonance with the core values of liberalism than the identification of it exclusively with individualistically construed rights.

A concern for liberal justice is nowhere more evident than in constitutional provisions for affirmative action programmes.[12] To tackle the basic inequalities already existing in the Indian social structure, and to make the formal political empowerment of severely disadvantaged groups more effective, the introduction of constitutionally protected preferential treatment of these groups was thought necessary. A mere right to vote and to equality of opportunity, it was widely recognized, is insufficient to ensure meaningful, effective social and political equality. Thus, apart from several general provisions to the right of equality, special constitutional measures were taken to protect and advance the interests of the Scheduled Castes and Scheduled Tribes. For example, Article 334 provides for reservations for seats in legislatures for these groups; similarly, under Article 335 the claims of Scheduled Castes and Tribes are taken into consideration while making appointments to public services. Here, the makers of the Constitution appealed not only to backward-looking principles justifying compensation to victims of past harm, but also to a forward-looking liberal principle that aims at future equality of opportunity. Indeed, it was precisely because past injustice continued to be a source of current injustice that programmes of affirmative action were believed to be necessary.

The claim that in India 'liberty was understood not as an individual right but as a nation's collective right to self-determination' is deeply problematic.[13] To begin with, the two are not mutually exclusive. Some rights are irreducibly collective, such as the right to self-determination and the right to preserve a culture against potential threat from other cultural communities. Other rights are irreducibly individual: the right not to be subject to bodily harm, not to be detained arbitrarily, not to be prosecuted for expressing dissent against the state or the more positive right to, say, gainful employment are all individual possessions. Both kinds of rights can be granted, and though they may occasionally conflict, they coexist as well. Proponents of the view that individual rights had no place within Indian discourses may accept this but still argue that the ineffective presence of individual rights is explained by the fact that in Indian culture 'the only place for the individual is in the form of a renouncer'.[14] But I doubt if this account is plausible even for traditional Indian society and it is certainly less so for urban, middle-class India in the post-Rammohun Roy world, in which Indians tried somehow to combine or reconcile traditional collectivist and modern individualist strands. To assert that the issue was settled from the beginning in favour of one is to fail to understand the complex world of these persons.

Indeed, the world-view of intellectuals in the late nineteenth century was markedly different from the intellectual landscape of left-liberals after the Second World War. Attempts to reconcile individual and collective identities were not uncommon within liberal writing at the turn of the century and for roughly three decades thereafter. T.H. Green, L.T. Hobhouse and John Dewey, to name three prominent liberals, recognized the importance of belonging to a cultural community with its memories, traditions, customs, and a shared way of thinking and feeling, a common language.[15] Without devaluing individual liberty, such liberals recognized community rights with great philosophical ease. The intellectual environment that informed Indian thinking is imbued with liberalism of this hue, rather than the classical libertarianism of the eighteenth century, or the deontological liberalism of the second half of the twentieth century.

The question of group rights needs further scrutiny. The prospect of the breakdown of hierarchical communities, i.e., emotional solidarities that are shot through with asymmetrical relations, provoked many responses. One such viewpoint, known in India as 'communalism' legitimizes a full-blooded conflictual relationship between communities that may view each other as equals, but are obsessively self-focused and intent upon maximizing their own interests at the expense of the other. Distinct from hierarchical communitarianism and an egalitarian communalism, is *individualist egalitarianism*, a view committed to equality among individuals and marked by a drive towards abstract universalism; and *communitarian egalitarianism* that forges a relationship of equal *respect* among communities. Two features distinguish the aforementioned views: one has to do with their attitude to difference, and the other, with their understanding of the source of this difference. In individualist egalitarianism, differences are due to individual choice or to a culturally neutral, socially generated circumstance that must be ignored or eliminated in order to achieve an egalitarian order. In communitarian egalitarianism, differences are a result of irreducibly diverse cultural backgrounds, and need to be properly recognized and affirmed rather than be jettisoned from the egalitarian framework.

The strategy of the individualist response is at best to treat difference as a disadvantage suffered by a group; the removal of disadvantages by working through and eventually dissolving groups into individuals is therefore a natural objective of state policy. From the perspective of the collectivist viewpoint, this strategy fails to understand how groups sustain culture and why every cultural difference is not a disadvantage that must be shed; the eradication of difference is undesirable and impossible. Instead, a parity between irreducibly different cultural communities is required. This does not mean that particular cultural communities never disappear or assimilate into other communities; however, it does mean that a culture-neutral, homogeneous society consisting only of radically self-directing individuals is an impossibility. Though both the individualist and the collectivist responses were in the making in the early twentieth century, post-War liberalism articulated and theorized the former at the expense of the latter.

It is important not to read the mind of the political élite in India with the interpretive grid of post-War liberalism which, to ward off hierarchical communitarianism and communalism, relies exclusively upon the resources of individualist egalitarianism. The Indian political élite may not have made a distinction between hierarchical and egalitarian communities—they frequently failed to keep the idea of communalism distinct from egalitarian communitarianism. But it is difficult to deny that the discourse of mutual respect between cultural communities was always within their reach.[16] To counter the challenge of hierarchical communitarianism and communalism, they relied on and frequently wavered between individualist and non-individualist egalitarianism. The Constituent Assembly debates reflect this tension. The political élite in India, working with the resources of a ragbag liberalism, was sensitive to both individual and group rights, and wrestled with the tension between them within the context of a forever threatening anti-liberal conception embedded in the then existing political practice. The Constitution too, reflects, perhaps was even born out of, this turmoil, and uneasily tries to reconcile individual with group rights.

The Majority–Minority Framework

Articles 29 and 30 of the Constitution granted special rights to groups in order to protect their interests and, in particular, to enable them to establish and administer their own educational institutions. These group-specific rights were frequently viewed as the rights of minorities. By the time the Constitution came to be written, that is, after Partition, the language of majority–minority had taken a firm hold on the dominant political discourse. A special sub-committee on minorities was constituted and most of its members accepted the idea that permanent minorities needed special safeguards. So, by incorporating group rights, the framers of the Indian Constitution accepted what might be called the *majority–minority framework*. Was this move on their part defensible? In this section I argue that it was.[17]

There are two alternative ways of understanding the notions of majority and minority. One is from within the problematic of communitarianism and nationalism, and the other from the vantage point of a certain conception of democracy. The most familiar democratic notion of majority–minority rests on the rule of preference aggregation. No matter what its content or who its holder, every preference must be taken into account and placed on the same scale. Social status and economic position attached to preferences, the intensity of their expression, judgments about their worth, their impact and on whom, are irrelevant. A majority and a minority emerges when such preferences are aggregated and counted. Notions of majority and minority within this framework are predicated on preference.[18] I shall call them *preference-based* majority and minority. The idea of preference appears to but does *not* depend on the notion of a self-defined independently of fundamental commitments, constitutive attachments and communities. All it requires is that the self be treated as if, upon entering a common public space, it can leave behind commitments and attachments. This implies that the only feature relevant in public contexts is the capacity of the self to choose among desires it happens to have. Because the preferences of people are never taken as immutable within this conception, the idea of a permanent majority or minority makes little sense.

It is in the nature of preference-based democratic institutions that the minority of today becomes the majority tomorrow. Popular elections constantly reconfigure majorities and minorities, yet constitutional safeguards may still be required because the basic interests of an individual must not be impaired, even temporarily. At any rate, even in this preference-based model, majorities and minorities may become practically permanent if the outcome of democratic procedures repeatedly favours one kind of preference expressed by a set of individuals. Constitutional safeguards are necessitated by the need to check the injustice of such outcomes, to prevent pitfalls of an intolerable and congealed stability. Therefore, certain preferences are excluded from the arena of aggregation and decision-making so that, were they to congeal, they would not affect the position or value of other preferences. (For example, if majority preferences persistently express that meat-eating be banned, and a minority equally persistently expresses preference in favour of eating meat, then any preference one way or another is excluded from decision-making.) On the whole, all constitutions are attempts to prevent democracy from sliding into despotism by controlling the tyrannical elements of political majoritarianism.

The move from an aggregative to a constitutional model of democracy involves granting some guarantees to individuals. This diminishes insecurity among individuals who reason thus: suppose that it turns out that a set of given preferences held persistently by a small number of people is always opposed to or incompatible with those held by larger numbers. Given further, that in a democratic system governed entirely by preferences, policy making is unlikely to be shaped by minority preferences, it is reasonable and in the interest of all to inhibit this untrammeled majoritarianism by assuring all relevant individuals that policies exclusively meant for them be formulated by their own internal preferences and not by external ones.[19] Hence, the necessity of individual rights.

There is, however, a second conception of majority–minority which arises when individuals define themselves and others not in terms of preference, i.e., the desires people choose to have, but rather by the more or less permanent attributes that they happen to possess. These attributes are widely believed to constitute the very identity of individuals.[20] Such individuals also see themselves as constituting a group around this feature. Assume two such groups with differing numerical strengths—a minority and majority exists then on the basis of such identity—constituting features. Let me call these *identity-dependent* majority and minority. In a large society where people do not share the same identity-constituting features, majorities and minorities exist more or less on a permanent basis. (For example, Tamils in Sri Lanka, the Quebecois in Canada, the many linguistic groups within India, Muslims in Britain.) Here we can even speak of permanent majorities or minorities.

When such permanent identity-dependent majorities and minorities enter the democratic arena, they bring along desires possessed simply by virtue of the kind of people they are. I am not of course claiming that these desires are natural or immutable, only that because they are culturally inherited and collectively reinforced they are relatively stable. In such contexts, the outcome of democratic procedures is likely to repeatedly favour not only the preferences of a set of individuals but the more or less permanent desires of a group. Moreover, these desires of the majority may be about the basic structure and organization of society, so that minorities within that society may live as permanent aliens, in perpetual insecurity. When this occurs in reality, a society may be wracked by what I call the *majority–minority syndrome*.[21] It follows that constitutional guarantees are needed for permanent (religious or linguistic) minorities and therefore more imperatively, a majority–minority *framework* is necessary to prevent a society from swirling into the vortex of a majority–minority syndrome.[22]

I started off with a minority–majority framework and later referred to the minority–majority syndrome. The two terms are not interchangeable—syndrome suggests something stronger and pejorative. When a deep malaise sets into the framework causing, for one or other intrinsic reason, a spiralling estrangement between the minority and the majority, we are saddled

with a minority–majority syndrome. On the other hand, a minority–majority framework rests on different self-identifications
and a modicum of distance between the two groups but implies
no galloping alienation or the chronic malaise typical of syn-
dromes. It is important here to note that the majority–minority
framework operates with strictly egalitarian premises. A demand
for minority rights is occasionally made under conditions where
the group claiming such rights has the resources as well as the
inclination to dominate and oppress other groups in society.
(The system of apartheid in South Africa is an obvious example.)
However, the entire point of introducing minority rights, on the
view outlined here, is to eliminate hidden inequalities and possible injustice. The idea is to give minorities some power to
shape the social and political structure so that they too are able
to do or get what the majority group routinely procures by virtue of the structural conditions in that society. A society that
needs to deploy a majority–minority framework is not the best
of all possible worlds, but in my use of the term it is not at all
obvious that it connotes a terrible, avoidable state of affairs.[23]

Can the syndrome be sidestepped in some way other than by
the use of the majority–minority framework? Given the distance
it creates between groups is this framework necessary? Why have
notions like majority or minority at all? Why not rid ourselves of
the syndrome by jettisoning the framework itself? There are two
issues here. One is the question of feasibility: are other alternative ways of dissolving the syndrome available? Which of these
is really feasible? Second, of those that are feasible which, in
the given context, is ethically sustainable?

Several alternatives are indeed available. By delving deep into
the resources of our distinctive traditions, particularly of religion, we may rediscover ways of living together woven into the
fabric of lived experience and embedded in traditional practices. This alternative is developed on the more or less correct
assumption that the majority–minority framework is linked to
modern democratic politics and to the formation of modern
nation-states. Modernity is the bête noire here; it begets the
minority–majority framework and carries all its ills. In this view,
then, the only way to get rid of the syndrome (and the framework) is to eject the framework, which in turn is done by a
rejection of modernity itself. There is a second alternative. This

involves the homogenization of individuals or their treatment, as if differences amongst them do not matter. This is believed possible by transforming ascriptive, identity-constituting features into preferences. This involves a conceptual and practical move from a communitarian identity-constituting to an individualist, preference-based understanding of the categories of majority and minority. Usually, this entails a refusal to bestow special rights or a withdrawal of privileges from minority groups and replacement with a uniform charter of rights.

A third alternative is the homogenization of individuals, not by the process mentioned in the preceding paragraph, but by assimilating the minorities within an overweening majority, by a stipulation that only the identity-constituting features of the majority count in society. Special rights are wrested away from the minority; for example, a watchdog minorities commission may be disbanded. It is not uncommon to find that when enforced uniformity is resisted, it results in the withdrawal of general rights as well. Finally, a fourth way in which this syndrome/ framework can be done away with is by the politics of 'overlapping good'. This would entail that different groups and individuals, from their respective standpoints, gather to deliberate over the good life, each contributing distinctively from its original perspective but converging ultimately on a conception shared to some extent by all.

Which of the above are desirable and can be met? The first alternative, delving into tradition to discover ways of living together, is partially desirable. Why only partially? Modernity is a contradictory phenomenon; it contains two blended ribbons of the good and the bad. By exploring resources of tradition it provides an alternative to the evils of modernity, but by exaggerating its importance it remains wholly blind to its inescapability or its good, and fails to harvest its enormous benefits. Really, it is too caught up in the simple-minded binary opposition of a pristine tradition contrasted with the unrelieved evil of modernity. Therefore, it is not a wholly desirable option, and in any case, it is not even a real possibility. The second alternative, treating individuals as if group-based differences do not matter, requires a certain pattern of modernization that is sociologically naive in its underestimation of the importance and desirability of constitutive social attachments in the life of

people. I rule it out because of its insensitivity to cultural identities. People in India are hardly likely to shed their religious
identity; indeed, religion continues to be rather more like the
colour of the skin than a consumable item to be chosen from an
array on offer in the marketplace. The third alternative, the assimilation of minorities, is undesirable because it can be realized, if at all, only by outright manipulation or force. However,
modern politics is not a zero-sum game and has at best only
temporary winners and losers. Besides, equalization, an integral and irreversible feature of modern societies, has meant that
strategies of enforced assimilation have lost even the minimal
legitimacy they once possessed. Any asymmetry between groups
is resisted sooner rather than later. As a result, it is extremely
difficult to forcibly assimilate or coerce any group into the mainstream. The final alternative, the politics of 'overlapping good'
is wonderful, if realizable. However, conditions for its realiza-
tion do not always exist and even when they do, the need for a
fall-back strategy remains.

Though a political condition of 'overlapping good' is a valuable regulative ideal, the makers of the Constitution retained
the minority–majority framework as the only realistic option
by which to realize a society free of the majority–minority syndrome. They sought its abandonment by specific constitutional
safeguards, i.e., by transforming a simple majoritarian democracy to one with a constitution, by granting groups a degree of
control over their affairs by different rights of self-government,
including the right to express cultural particularity. They believed this strategy would contain discrimination and rectify
perceptions of disadvantage among minorities.

It might be argued that their position severely underestimates
problems generated by the minority–majority framework. Why
must we put up with a permanent state of radically distinct
groups, which see themselves in numerical terms and remain
potentially divided, distanced, somewhat alienated from one
another? Why not aspire to a political society that recognizes
the equal standing of all viable groups and simply jettison talk
of minorities and majorities?[24] Indeed, why at all take refuge in
a divisive discourse of rights? My straightforward response to
this objection on behalf of the framers of the Constitution is
that the best available option is not *always* realizable. Condi-

tions that enable its exercise may be present in a society but once the opportunity thrown up by the historical process is missed, it may altogether lose even the chance of securing other morally defensible but second-best options.

Let me explain this point. A pervasive myth within modernist self-understanding is that modern conditions destroy every collective formation and unleash different forms of individualism. In this view, collective identities and commitments cannot survive the modernist onslaught. Even a cursory glance at the processes of modernity however, reveals that while they undermine some *kinds* of groups, they simultaneously generate and bolster others. The most obvious example of a group made possible and supported by modern processes is the nation (and other sub-national groups).[25] Now, the same processes that generate national identity also produce a sense of equality and intense competitiveness, ingredients that contribute substantially to the formation of what I called the majority–minority syndrome. It is of course true that a syndrome is not inevitable. A mechanism ensuring equality and mutual respect may well be introduced before competitiveness among groups goes too far. If a society succeeds in doing so, then it secures dignified and peaceful coexistence of groups without even resorting to a framework of rights. However, in most instances, the very formation of groups is dependent upon and accompanied by a sense of equality and radical competitiveness. Indeed, groups are formed within a process of rivalry that threatens to spiral out of control. One possible solution to contain it, to foster institutionalized tolerance is to have a system of group rights. Collective self-government rights, special rights for representation within legislatures, or rights to express distinctive cultural particularities enable viable groups in society to live with dignity. At this stage, a society possesses a system of group rights without talk of minority and majority, without what I have called the majority–minority framework. However, if such rights are not granted at the appropriate time, complex feelings of disadvantage and marginalization grow and a majority–minority syndrome sets in, and once entrenched—precisely this is my argument—the only way to eliminate it is to introduce a majority–minority framework.

This point can be formulated differently. Group rights need not always be perceived as minority rights. They are viewed as rights of minorities if introduced after an irreversible condition of radical alienation between groups has come into existence. A minority–majority framework is then needed to get rid of the syndrome; no need for the former to exist, if the latter did not exist in the first place. In short, the framework *follows* the syndrome. To insist upon the futility or irrelevance of the framework when in fact the syndrome is already entrenched is to belie, at best, a shallow utopianism and, at worst, to shamelessly disguise inequalities between groups. The point I am hammering home is that societies that grant equal recognition to groups at an opportune moment avoid the majority–minority syndrome, and therefore have no need for a majority–minority framework. However, once they miss this opportunity and a syndrome bedevils them, the only ethically defensible option then is to live with a minority–majority framework. Other ways of ridding the syndrome are, quite simply, morally unsustainable. On a constructive interpretation of the intentions of the framers of the Constitution, this was the logic behind their acceptance of the majority–minority framework.

A Modern, Indian Secularism

The acceptance of group rights and the majority–minority framework had a profound impact on the conception of secularism implicit in the Constitution. A variant of secularism was developed which is at once Indian and modern.[26]

There is a tendency in the literature on secularism in India to first posit a highly idealized version of secularism derived partly from, say, the American or the French experience, and then judge the practice of the secular state in India by standards evolved from these models. (Secularists have often done this and then lamented the failure of Indian secularism. Likewise, opponents of secularism have used the ploy to first highlight the inconsistencies of Indian secularism and then conclude that the collapse of secularism in India is imminent.) To illustrate this point let me take the example of Donald Smith's *India as a Secular State*, still the locus classicus on the subject.[27] Smith's conception of the secular state involves three distinct but interrelated relations concerning the state, religion and the individual. The first relation concerns individuals and their religion, from which the state is excluded. Individuals are thereby free to decide the merits of the respective claims of different religions without any coercive interference by the state. They are free to revise or reject the religion they were born into or have chosen. (This is the liberal ingredient within secularism.) The second concerns the relation between individuals and the state, from which religion is excluded. Here, the state views individuals without taking into account their religious affiliation. The rights and duties of citizens are not affected by the religious beliefs held by individuals; for example, no discrimination exists in the holding of public office or taxation. (This is the egalitarian component within secularism.) Finally, for Smith, the integrity of both these relations is dependent on the third relation, between the state and different religions. Here he argues that secularism entails separation of powers, i.e., the mutual exclusion of state and religion in order that they may operate effectively and equally in their own respective domains. Just as it is not the function of the state to promote, regulate, direct or interfere in religion, just so is political power outside the scope of religion's legitimate objectives. So, for Smith, secularism means the strict separation of religion and the state for the sake of the religious liberty and equal citizenship of individuals.

Clearly, on this account of secularism, any intervention in Hinduism—for example the legal ban on the prohibition of Dalit entry into temples—is illegitimate interference in religious affairs and therefore compromises secularism. Similarly, the protection of socio-religious groups (minorities) is inconsistent with an individualistically grounded secularism. For example, the right to personal laws entails a departure from secularism simply on the ground that it depends on a communally suspect classification. Together, these policies violate the ideal of neutrality or equidistance that plays a pivotal role in Smith's view of secularism. Smith believed that despite these flaws the Indian state, at least in the early 1960s, was secular. However, he also believed that these constituted serious deviations from the model of secularism and unless quickly brought in line, the secular state in India would plunge into crisis. Was he correct?

I do not think so. Smith remained in the grip of a particular model of western secularism and therefore, was unable to get a handle on the basic features of Indian secularism. The distinctiveness of the Indian variant of secularism can be understood only when the cultural background and social context in India is properly grasped. At least four such features of this socio-cultural context call for attention. First, there exists the mind-boggling diversity of religious communities in India. Such diversity may coexist harmoniously but it invariably generates conflicts, the most intractable of which, I believe, are deep conflicts over values. Second, within Hinduism in particular and in South Asian religions more generally, a greater emphasis is placed on practice rather than belief. A person's religious identity and affiliation are defined more by what she or he does with and in relation to others, than by the content of beliefs individually held by them. Since practices are intrinsically social, any significance placed on them brings about a concomitant valorization of communities. Third, many religiously sanctioned social practices are oppressive by virtue of their illiberal and inegalitarian character and deny a life of dignity and self-respect. Therefore, from a liberal and egalitarian standpoint, they desperately need to be reformed. Such practices frequently have a life of their own, independent of consciously held beliefs, and possess a causal efficacy that remains unaffected by the presence of conscious beliefs. Furthermore, a tendency to fortify and insulate themselves from reflective critique makes them resistant to easy change and reform. It follows that an institution vested with enormous social power is needed to transform their character. Fourth, in Hinduism, the absence of an organized institution such as the Church has meant that the impetus for effective reform cannot come exclusively from within. Reform within Hinduism can hardly be initiated without help from powerful external institutions such as the state.

In such a context, India needed a coherent set of intellectual resources to tackle inter-religious conflict and to struggle against oppressive communities, not by disaggregating them into a collection of individuals or by de-recognizing them, but by somehow making them more liberal and egalitarian. A political movement for a united, liberal, democratic India had to struggle against hierarchical and communal conceptions of community, but without abandoning a reasonable communitarianism. Besides, the state had an important contribution to make in the transformation of these communities; for this reason, a perennial dilemma was imposed on it. The state in India walked a tight rope be-

tween the requirement of religious liberty that frequently entails non-interference in the affairs of religious communities,
and the demand for equality and justice, which necessitates intervention in religiously sanctioned social customs. Secularism
in India simply had to be different from the classical liberal
model that does not recognize groups, and dictates strict separation between religious and political institutions.

If we abandon the view such as Donald Smith's, that political
secularism entails a unique set of state policies valid under all
conditions, that provide the yardstick by which the secularity
of any state is to be judged, then we can better understand why
despite 'deviation' from the ideal, the state in India continues
to embody a model of *secularism*.[28] This can be shown even if
we stick to Smith's working definition of secularism as consisting of three relations. Smith's first relation embodies the principle of religious liberty construed individualistically, i.e., as
pertaining to the religious beliefs of individuals. However, it is
possible to make a non-individualistic construal of religious liberty by speaking not of beliefs of the individuals, but rather of
the practices of groups. Here religious liberty would mean distancing the state from the practices of religious groups. The first
principle of secularism can then be seen to grant the right to a
religious community to its own practices. Smith's second relation embodies the value of equal citizenship for all individuals.
But this entails—and I cannot substantiate my claim—that we
tolerate the attempt of radically differing groups to determine
the nature and direction of society as they best see it.[29] In this
view, then, the public presence of the religious practices of
groups is guaranteed and entailed by the recognition of group-
differentiated citizenship rights. Smith's version of secularism
entails a charter of uniform rights for all individuals. But it is
clear that the commitment of secularism to equal citizenship
can dictate group-specific rights, and therefore differentiated
citizenship. Smith's third principle pertains to non-establishment,
and therefore to a strict separation of religion from state, under
which religion and the state both have the freedom to develop
without interfering with each other. Separation, however, need
not mean strict non-interference, mutual exclusion or
equidistance, as in Smith's view. Instead, it could be a policy of
principled distance, which entails a flexible approach on the

question of intervention or abstention, combining both, dependent on the context, nature or current state of relevant religions.

It is important to understand that principled distance is not mere equidistance. In the strategy of principled distance, whether or not the state intervenes or refrains from action depends on what really strengthens religious liberty and equality of citizenship for all. If this is so, the state may not relate to every religion in exactly the same way, intervene to the same degree or in the same manner. All it must ensure is that the relation between religious and political institutions be guided by non-sectarian principles that remain consistent with a set of values constitutive of a life of equal dignity for all.

It was largely this group-sensitive conception of secularism of the principled distance variety that legitimized the practices of the state wherein religion was alternately excluded and included as an object of state policy. By its refusal to allow (i) separate electorates, (ii) reserved constituencies for religious communities, (iii) reservations for jobs on the basis of religious classification, and (iv) the organization of states on religious basis, the Indian state excluded religion from its purview on the ground that its inclusion would inflame religious and communal conflict and produce another Partition-like scenario. However, the very motive that excluded religion from state institutions also influenced its inclusion in policy matters of cultural import. For example, a uniform charter of rights was not considered absolutely essential for national integration. Separate rights were granted to minority religious communities to enable them to live with dignity. Integration was not seen as identical to complete assimilation. Similar liberal and egalitarian motives compelled the state to undertake reforms within Hinduism. By making polygamy illegal, introducing the right to divorce, abolishing child marriage, legally recognizing inter-caste marriages, regulating the activities of criminals masquerading as holy men, introducing temple-entry rights for dalits and reforming temple administration, the state intervened in religious matters to protect the ordinary but dignified life of its citizens.

To sum up: (a) modern secularism is fully compatible with, indeed even dictates, a defence of differentiated citizenship and of rights of religious groups; and (b) the secularity of the state does not necessitate strict intervention, non-interference or equidistance but, rather, any or all of these, as the case may be. If this is so, the criticism that the Constitution envisages a state that cannot be secular because it explicitly abandons equidistance is mistaken. A secular state need not be equidistant from all religious communities and may interfere in one religion more than another. A critique of constitutional secularism on the ground that it acknowledges group rights or that it gives up on neutrality, simply does not wash.

Why Universal Franchise? Or Democracy as Nationalism

Franchise in India was restricted before the adoption of the Constitution. Citizenship was based on what Dahl calls 'the contingent principle of inclusion' i.e., restricted to only those qualified to rule and who could claim citizenship. [30] Citizenship in the Constitution was based instead on the categorical principle of inclusion: to be an adult member in the society is sufficient qualification for full citizenship of the state. Rights of citizenship, including the right to vote, were justified by exclusive reference to this principle. In a society ravaged by persistent social inequalities and marked by a subordinate role for women within the patriarchal system, how could this come about? I offer three possible reasons: first, the influence of liberal individualist ideas in which the self is constituted not by a place within the group arena, but in abstraction from it. Such ideas are unlikely to have influenced those who played a key role in public deliberations. [31] A second reason may well have to do with the less explicit, unselfconscious motivations of political actors. In a country dominated by poor peasants belonging either to backward castes or falling altogether outside the caste structure, a restricted franchise would certainly have meant their exclusion from the political process. In a numbers-dominated democratic system, this could significantly weaken the bargaining power of Hindus. I remain unpersuaded by this strongly communitarian, almost communal argument. A third reason might have to do with the growth of the idea of the nation. It is more or less integral to the concept of the nation that members who comprise it are equal. If so, and if the idea of democracy has been accepted, then no member of the said nation can be excluded from the exercise of franchise. This response needs further examination.

In 1916, nineteen members of the Imperial Legislative Council that included Madan Mohan Malaviya, Tej Bahadur Sapru and Mohammad Ali Jinnah sent a signed memorandum to the viceroy, outlining a scheme of self-government for India which claimed that without self-government, Indians in India feel that 'though theoretically they are equal subjects of the king, they hold a very inferior position in the British empire'.[32] 'Humiliating as this position of inferiority is to the Indian mind', the memorandum continues, 'it is almost unbearable to the youth of India whose outlook is broadened by education and travel in foreign parts where they come in contact with other free races. In the face of these grievances and disabilities, what has sustained the people is the hope and the faith inspired by promises and assurances of fair and equal treatment by the sovereign.'[33] The signatories argued that to regain self-respect the Indian people needed not merely good government or efficient administration but a government 'that is acceptable to the people because it is responsible to them'.

The memorandum to the viceroy reflects how western modernity was lived from the inside by the élites of a conquered culture. A traditionalist refusal of Western modernity would have entailed a turning away from popular rule, but Indian élites embraced the idea and complained in the name of that very idea, that to be denied self-rule is to be demeaned, to be diminished in one's own eyes. Moreover, this loss of self-esteem was a shared experience—the experience of humiliation was irreducibly collective. The emotional power of nationalism is derived from this register of collective pride and humiliation.[34] Therefore, self-respect could only be restored and felt collectively. Self-government had to be a collective matter too.

But how large must this collectivity be? Should it be restricted to the aspiring élite, denied full access, but already on the margins of power? It is of course true that a link exists between nationalism and self-governance and the nationalist demand is indistinguishable from the demand for self-governance; but why should the nation include the entire people? Why could it not have been restricted to a small élite? Why should everyone govern or why should some govern in the name of everyone? Why have universal franchise? Why must nationalism be almost identical to democracy?

One possible answer to these questions may be that the particular form of community known as a nation is a functional requirement of a distinctively modern society where social ranks, no longer fixed and immutable, are up for grabs, and the smooth operation of which requires flexible, context-free agents who not only move freely across physical and social space, but communicate easily with each other. This freedom from social rank and content brings with it the ideas of symmetrical (equal) relations as well as a degree of individualization. It follows that ideas of equality and individualism go hand in hand with the idea of a nation. The making of a nation, therefore, is the process of binding together a particular kind of people, those who have begun more or less to see themselves as individuals and relate to each other as equals. The functional tie envisaged by this account assures that no particular temporal sequence need be followed; a nation-state may precede or succeed a modern society of individualized and equalized human beings.

If what is said above is true, then we have at least some explanation for why no one within the social order can really be left out of the nation. If social hierarchy and strongly particularized identities cease to matter, then no reason exists to exclude anyone. (Or so it appears, because nationalism brings with it its own forms of strong exclusions.) Liah Greenfeld has helpfully drawn our attention to a change in the semantics of the term 'nation'.[35] In the late thirteenth century the term 'nation' meant a community of opinion where the constituents of the said community were representatives of cultural and political authority. In short, a nation was a group of social élites. In the sixteenth century however, the reference term 'nation' changed; it began to be applied to the entire population of a country and became synonymous with the word 'people'. This change in meaning signalled the symbolic elevation of the rabble into an élite, its movement from the wings onto centre stage, from irrelevance to relevance. Henceforth, every member of the population could partake of this superior, élite quality. The transformation of a rabble into a people and of the people into an élite, presupposes a profound change in the way societies are imagined, i.e., from hierarchical communities to networks consisting of free and equal individuals.

This effected yet another change; in their self-understanding, the nation exists prior to and independent of the political organi-

zation of society which has the power to give itself a constitution.
I have already touched upon the background which makes this
possible and which includes, among other things, complex constituents such as a particular frame of time and of common action. The important point I want registered is that the idea of
the basic rules of society as stemming from the common action
of a people, of a nation, is identical with the democratic idea
for which sovereignty is located within a people fundamentally
equal to one another. As Greenfeld puts it 'nationalism was the
form in which democracy appeared in the world, contained in
the idea of the nation as a butterfly in a cocoon'.[36]

This is precisely what appears to have happened in India.
Once the idea of a nation took root among the élite, a conception of a political order growing out of the will of every single
member of society, and eventually the idea of democratic self-
government could not but have followed. The idea of universal
franchise lay securely within the heart of nationalism.[37] In the
Constitution of India Bill (1895), the first non-official attempt
at drafting a constitution for India, the author, probably Tilak,
did not contest that the 'sovereign power of India is vested in
the sovereign of Great Britain and Ireland, the supreme head of
the Indian nation' or challenge the authority of the viceroy as
representative of the sovereign. He did, though, declare at the
same time that every citizen, i.e., anyone born in India, had a
right to take part in the affairs of his or her country and be
admitted to public office, and therefore hoped that 'under the
benign government of the British', Indian citizens would 'in future enjoy and use the rights proposed to the greatest advantage of their country and the British government'.[38] The Motilal
Nehru Report (1928) reaffirms this conception of citizenship.
Section 9 of the report reiterates that every person of either sex
who has attained the age of twenty-one is entitled to vote for the
House of Representatives or Parliament. It defines the word citizen as any person who is born or whose father is either born or
naturalized within the territorial limits of the commonwealth and
has not been nationalized as a citizen of any other country.[39] The
Motilal Nehru Report is unequivocal about the powers of government as derived from the people. In his presidential address
to the National Convention of Congress Legislators (1937),
Jawaharlal Nehru opposed the Government of India Act (1935)

for not representing the will of the nation. He declared that the convention stands for a genuine democratic state in India where political power has been transferred to the people as a whole. Such a state, he said, can only be created by the Indian people themselves, through the medium of the Constituent Assembly elected on the basis of adult suffrage, and having the power to determine finally the constitution of the country.[40] Not much more evidence is required to substantiate my claim that democracy came to India in the guise of nationalism, with universal franchise as the most important and legitimate instrument by which the will of the nation was to be properly expressed.

Notes

[1] By not taking into account or drawing upon the world of subalterns, I plead guilty, of course, to the charge of élitism.

[2] Though I explicitly have in mind Sunil Khilnani's *The Idea of India* (London: Hamish Hamilton), 1997, this is also the predominant impression I have gained from several scholars, most notably from Sudipta Kaviraj.

[3] Khilnani, op. cit., 26.

[4] Ibid., p. 24.

[5] Ibid., p. 26.

[6] Ibid., p. 27.

[7] Ibid., p. 34.

[8] Ibid.

[9] For utilitarianism's attractive qualities, see Will Kymlicka, *Contemporary Political Philosophy: An Introduction* (Oxford: Clarendon Press), 1990, pp. 10–12.

[10] K.M. Panikkar, *In Defence of Liberalism* (Bombay: Asia Publishing House), 1962.

[11] Ibid.

[12] In all fairness, this is recognized by Khilnani. He acknowledges that 'reservations had been intended to be a temporary expedient to a less just society' (Khilnani, op. cit. p. 37), but my point is that he fails to see it as reflecting liberal principles.

[13] Ibid., p. 26.

[14] Ibid., p. 26.

[15] On this see, for example, Will Kymlicka, *Liberalism, Community and Culture* (Oxford: Clarendon Press), 1989, Chapter 10.

[16] On this, see for example, the *Constituent Assembly Debates*, vol. VIII, 16 May–16 June 1949, p. 326.

17 For my reading of the Constitution as embodying a majority–minority framework and for a substantiation of my view that it is justified and that this justification can be found in the debates of the Constituent Assembly, see B. Shiva Rao (ed.), *The Framing of India's Constitution* (New Delhi: IIPA), 1967, vol. II, part III, pp. 309–86. See particularly the reply to a questionnaire prepared by K.M. Munshi on the nature and scope of the safeguards for minorities, by M. Ruthnaswamy, who explicitly makes a distinction between political and national/religious minorities, and a good case (at least as a temporary measure) for minority rights; and by Jagjivan Ram who argued that while political safeguards for minorities may be eliminated after they are convinced that their rights shall be protected even after they remain unrepresented in the legislature or the administration, some of the other safeguards, such as those guaranteeing religious and cultural freedom, shall have to remain for all time in the Constitution. (See pp. 312–18 and 330–6. Also see B. Shiva Rao, *The Framing of India's Constitution*, op. cit., pp. 741–80.

18 By preference I mean a desire that we have because we have chosen it. Preferences may be short term or long term. For the purposes of this paper, a long-term preference is an aggregation of short-term preferences. A long-term preference for something is a chain of short-term preferences for the same thing.

19 External preferences are preferences held by people on what others may desire to do. This is roughly the same as the distinction between personal and external preference drawn by Ronald Dworkin. See his *Taking Rights Seriously* (London: Duckwort), 1977, p. 234.

20 It may be noted that majority and minority cannot be defined independently of each other; this presupposes, in turn, a common framework and some commitment, however tenuous, of living together.

21 Since when have majorities and minorities existed? At least since the formation of states. For example, numerically small religious groups existed in Empire states, such as the Jews in the Holy Roman Empire. However, enumeration, though necessary, is not sufficient for the constitution of minority and majority. Three other features enter into its current understanding. First, groups must view themselves as a minority or a majority. Self-identification or the persistent identification by others in these terms, simultaneously or subsequently recognized by the group in question, is central to majority–minority formations. Second, the group must believe that its own identity-constituting features have the power to shape the structure of some social and political order, usually the one they happen to live in. In large democracies this is likely to happen through representative institutions. It is only when this belief is accompanied or followed by the inability to exer-

cise power that the resulting sense of impotence breeds a perception of disadvantage. Indeed, a majority–minority syndrome has set in when this sense of disadvantage slides into an enduring feeling of insecurity.

[22] The syndrome need not always be well justified. A group may wish to shape the structure exclusively but not be allowed, or it may try participating with others in determining it but not be permitted to do so. In the first example, there is no effective discrimination against the group, but a minority–majority syndrome is well grounded when the majority really discriminates against minorities. In such instances, minorities do not merely see themselves in terms of constitutive features that differentiate them from a larger group, but are seen so, and this difference forms the basis of persistent disfavour.

[23] The majority–minority syndrome can also be set off when a minority resists the attempt by the majority to exclusively shape the social and political institutions in accordance with its own cultural predilections. Equally, a well-grounded syndrome may be caused by discrimination of the majority, as the case of blacks in South Africa testifies.

[24] J. Raz, *Ethics in the Public Domain* (Oxford: Clarendon Press), 1994, p. 159.

[25] It would likewise be mistaken to believe that pre-modern social processes undermine every version of individualism and uphold all forms of collectivism. These processes also support some individualist tendencies while disrupting others.

[26] For a detailed defence of this view and for further elaboration of the idea of principled distance, see my article 'What is Secularism For?' in Rajeev Bhargava (ed.), *Secularism and Its Critics* (New Delhi: Oxford University Press), 1998, pp. 486–542.

[27] D.E. Smith, *India as a Secular State*, (Englewood: Princeton University Press), 1963.

[28] For an interesting critique of Smith's interpretation of Indian secularism as derived from the American model with an 'extra dose of separation', see Marc Galanter, 'Secularism, East and West', in Rajeev Bhargava (ed.), *Secularism and Its Critics*, op. cit., pp. 234–67.

[29] T.M. Scanlon, 'The Difficulty of Tolerence', in Rajeev Bhargava (ed.), *Secularism and Its Critics* (New Delhi: Oxford Univeristy Press), 1998, pp. 54–70.

[30] Robert Dahl, *Democracy and Its Critics* (New Haven and London: Yale University Press), 1989, Chapter 9.

[31] It is not implausible to claim, however, that for the leaders of the national movement a part of the self could be abstracted from the substantive commitment flowing from one's tradition and custom, from family and community. In short, a domain existed where a person could

be legitimately viewed simply as an individual rather than as a member of this or that particular community. Significantly, in this domain a person's unequal status within a particular community also had no relevance. The process of individualization went hand in hand with the process of equalization. Once this idea of political equality—equality in the public domain—grew in importance, universal adult franchise was only a small step away.

³² B. Shiva Rao, *The Framing of the Constitution: Select Documents*, vol. I, op. cit., p. 21.

³³ Ibid.

³⁴ On this aspect of nationalism, see Charles Taylor, *Nationalism and Modernity*, unpublished.

³⁵ Liah Greenfeld, *Nationalism: Five Roads to Modernity* (Cambridge: Harvard University Press), 1992, 'Introduction'.

³⁶ Ibid., p. 10.

³⁷ I might have given the impression that nationalism can be extremely exclusionary, which of course, is not true. Nationalism can be extremely exclusionary as attested by the case of Germany or Russia. However, the point I am making is that both the need to include everyone and the temptation to exclude certain categories of people come from the same source, namely from a sovereign body of free and equal citizens who are bonded together in a common enterprise of self-rule. Modern conceptions of democracy and popular sovereignty rule out the possibility of a notion of citizenship that is differentiated and unequal. This means either that every member of the population, regardless of religion or ethnicity, is viewed as constituting 'the sovereign people' or that only some or just one religious or ethnic group is believed to constitute it—other groups are excluded from the 'people'. Since there is no place for unequal groups within a democracy, we have either the option of including everyone or simply excluding certain ethnic or religious groups. It follows that democratic self-rule is consistent with an exclusionary nationalism. As Charles Taylor, from whom I borrow this argument, says, 'Just because a successful democracy requires strong common allegiance, there can be an all but irresistible pull to build the common identity around the things that strongly unite people, and these are frequently ethnic or religious identities. The very functional requirement of a democratic "people" that seems to make (say), secularism indispensable, can be turned around and used to reject it.' See Charles Taylor, 'Modes of Secularism', in Rajeev Bhargava (ed.), *Secularism and Its Critics*, op. cit., pp. 31–53. If the above is true, then my claim that in India ideas of nation and democratic self-rule came more or less together is compatible with both inclusionary and exclusionary nationalisms. The Congress party clearly articulated an

inclusionary nationalism, while the Hindu Mahasabha and the Muslim League represented the exclusionary variant.

[38] B. Shiva Rao, *The Framing of the Indian Constitution*, vol. I, op. cit., pp. 5–14.

[39] Ibid., p. 59.

[40] Ibid., pp. 86–92.

The Strong State and the Fear of Disorder

PAUL R. BRASS

India's Constitution was born more in fear and trepidation than in hope and inspiration. Its proceedings began on December 9, 1946 in the midst of the final negotiations for the transfer of power, which culminated with Independence on August 15, 1947, and the communal bloodshed associated with the partition of the subcontinent. Negotiations were also taking place under the leadership of Sardar Patel and his principal advisor, V. K. Menon, for the integration of the Indian states (that is, the Princely States) into the Union of India. These negotiations were fraught with tension that culminated in the use of armed force in three situations, namely, in Junagadh, Hyderabad and, most seriously, of course, in Jammu & Kashmir.

The Constituent Assembly concluded its deliberations with the passage of the Constitution of India on January 24, 1950. In the intervening years, the mass migrations of perhaps 12 million Hindus and Muslims across the partition lines had been concluded with a loss of several hundred thousand lives. So had the integration of the Indian states, including Hyderabad, after the entry of the Indian army into that state on September 13, 1948. In Kashmir, whose ruler acceded to India on October 26, 1947, the cease-fire mandated by the United Nations came into force on January 1, 1949, dividing the state into two areas of control, with India holding the Kashmir Valley, Ladakh and a large part of Jammu, while Pakistan held the western portions.

Two other ominous violent forces had also appeared forcefully on the Indian political scene: militant Hinduism and revolutionary communism. A militant Hindu had assassinated Mahatma Gandhi on January 30, 1948, an act which was then followed by a ban on the activities of the leading organization of Hindu nationalism, the Rashtriya Swayamsevak Sangh (RSS), with which Gandhi's assassin had been previously associated. In the Telengana region of Hyderabad state, the issue of its integration into the Indian Union was complicated by the communist-led insurrection there, ultimately suppressed by the Indian army after its takeover of the state.

There was, finally, the food crisis that faced India at Independence. An estimated three million people had perished in Bengal during the famine in 1943, precipitated by food shortages and the failure of the British during the War to take adequate measures to cope with them.[1] The framers of the Constitution no doubt felt that stringent measures might have to be taken to deal with continuing shortages of food and potential price rises, as well as possible urban disorder. The national leaders feared that the "provincial governments might not be able to bear the strains" under these and other threatening circumstances of the times.[2]

Thus, India's Constitution-makers thought they had good reason to be fearful of disorder, even chaos, in the subcontinent as a consequence of a multiplicity of dangerous forces arising out of political movements associated with Muslim separatism, militant Hindu nationalism, Hindu-Muslim communalism, secessionism and revolutionary communism. Moreover, these forces were associated with significant acts of violence, extending from assassination of the country's founding father, to revolutionary insurrection and extensive communal killings and war. The response of India's Constitution-makers to these threats and dangers was to frame a Constitution with numerous provisions designed to deal effectively with the threat of disorder through the creation of a strong, centralized state. While the threats and dangers were real, the Constitution-makers had other motivations as well for the creation of such a state, which will be explored further below.

The Fear of Disorder in the Constituent Assembly Debates

The fear of disorder did not arise only from the objective circumstances just mentioned. Several members of the Assembly considered disorder an endemic condition of the people of India, of which the many forms of real turmoil that the country was passing through were manifestations. Among such members was Naziruddin Ahmad, who spoke at length in favour of granting the president the authority to proclaim an emergency in the country whenever it might be threatened by war or external aggression or "internal disturbance". In this speaker's mind, as in the minds of many other participants pro and con, the primary question was whether or not the president should have such powers to deal with "internal disturbance", nowhere defined in precise terms.

The issue of defining an "internal disturbance" came up in the Constituent Assembly in connection with what ultimately became Article 355 of the Constitution—part of the emergency provisions—which assigned to the Union the duty "to protect States against external aggression and internal disturbance". Shri H. V. Kamath, who was the most consistent critic of these emergency powers and of the aggrandizement of the powers of the Indian Union at the expense of the states and the fundamental rights of the people, argued that the term was too broad; he argued that it would "whittle down provincial autonomy", giving the Union government the right "to intervene in the internal affairs of the State on the slightest pretext of any internal disturbance".[3]

Naziruddin Ahmed, on the contrary, saw no need to define the term "internal disturbance" precisely, nor to limit, in any way, the powers of the president to declare an emergency to deal with them, whatever their cause. He began his speech by comparing the people of India unfavourably with those "in many other countries" where "democratic institutions" were well established. In such countries, he reasoned, the people "are highly law-abiding and there is very little danger of internal disorder as there is likelihood in India". By contrast, in India, "forces of disintegration and disorder" were "already visible everywhere". However, Naziruddin Ahmed did not refer in his opening remarks to the specific forms of disorder, violence, separatism and insurrection noted above, but to a whole host of other characteristics he attributed to Indian society, including "corruption, nepotism, favoritism and inefficiency"! All these, he thought, "may lead to small disorders and gradually to misgovernment and grave general disorder", against the last of which it was "necessary to guard ourselves". He saw "forces of disorder . . . everywhere in the land"

and cited everyday criminal events as "pointers" to situations that "may develop into a general breakdown, and then a Proclamation of Emergency may be necessary".[4] In short, for this member, the prospect of disorder lurked everywhere and arose out of the nature of the Indian people and their daily practices. It was, in effect, against the Indian people and all their wayward characteristics that the powers to proclaim an emergency were required.

Shri Mahavir Tyagi, a prominent Congressman from Uttar Pradesh who became a minister in the central government, also spoke in favour of the provisions for a proclamation of emergency, including assigning to the president the duty to declare one even "before the actual occurrence of war or aggression or disturbance". Shri Tyagi's support was based primarily upon his belief in the preeminent necessity to maintain the unity and peace of India at all costs. He went so far as to say that this clause in particular was "the only thing that binds the units [of the Indian Union] together and prevents the people of one unit acting in a manner prejudicial to the interests of the country as a whole". He noted in support of his contention that there was "no contractual agreement between the units and the Union", and nowhere mentioned in his speech the existence of any sentimental basis for the Union. It was, therefore, the duty of the Centre to maintain "India as one unit", which could be achieved only if "there is absolute peace in all India, and to take prompt action when that peace is threatened". Shri Tyagi was clearly concerned about the threat of secession, rather than the generally wayward characteristics of the Indian people. Yet, his speech too reflects an anti-people bias, for he urged not only the necessity to prevent "the people of one unit" acting against the interests of the unity of the country, but "even the tendency to act in such a manner". If one follows Shri Tyagi's argument to its logical conclusion, it amounts to this: there is no contractual or sentimental basis for the Indian Union, which can be maintained only through the suspension of the Constitutional balance between the Union and the states and the civil liberties of the people, along with the implied use of force or the threat of force to maintain "absolute peace".[5]

Brajeshwar Prasad, a Congressman from Bihar, feared that the emergency provisions in the draft Constitution were not sufficient. Among other possibilities for strengthening those provisions further, he opposed the constitutional prohibition against the extension of a period of emergency within any state beyond three years. He thought there was no way of knowing beforehand that an emergency would not last "beyond three years". He was concerned especially that there be no such time restriction because he thought that "the forces of disorder and lawlessness are increasing and spreading fast in this country".[6]

Yet another prominent Congressman, Pandit Thakur Das Bhargava of Punjab, spoke on the provisions of what became the famous Article 356 in the final version of the Constitution, allowing for the takeover of the administration of any state in the Union by the central government, in case the governor of the state reported that "the government of the State cannot be carried on in accordance with the provisions of this Constitution". Although several members thought this provision for president's rule was so sweeping and the conditions for declaring it so vague, that it threatened to undermine the autonomy of the states in their own sphere, Pandit Bhargava had no such fears. On the contrary, he "wanted to see that the Centre was given powers even when there was no breakdown of the Constitution" to ensure that "conditions" in any state did "not deteriorate into chaos".[7]

Fifty years later, after numerous uses and abuses of the emergency powers provided for in the Constitution of India, opinion among political scientists is divided concerning the continuing threat of disorder, its sources and the abilities of the Indian state to manage it. Atul Kohli writes of "India's growing crisis of governability", associated with "growing civil disorder" in the country. Its sources are not so much in the Indian people as such but in the decline of the effectiveness of authoritative institutions in accommodating and resolving the inevitable conflicts that arise in a competitive polity such as India's.[8]

James Manor, in contrast, holds a more sanguine view of the abilities of India's leaders and its institutions to accommodate and manage conflict and prevent institutional decay. He sees no "downward spiral leading to collapse" because India's democratic institutions have demonstrated repeatedly a "capacity for. . . regeneration". Furthermore, in all the post-Independence years in which numerous violent conflicts and disorder have broken out in different parts of India, none have turned into "nationwide convulsions".

Finally, throughout all these years of conflict and disorder, the Indian authorities and its political leaders have developed a discernible and effective mode and sequencing of action to contain and resolve them. The sequence begins with "coercive force to quell disorder", but is then "swiftly followed by accommodationist management".[9] In other words, while disorder and violent conflict have been endemic in India throughout much of the post-Independence period, they have all been localized, never a threat to the Indian polity as a whole. Although many of India's institutions have declined in effectiveness, there is every reason to believe they will recover. Finally, during the past 50 years, a consistent and effective pattern of conflict management has been in operation and has almost always worked effectively.

The Fear of Disorder, 1947–97: A Critical Assessment

I believe that all these views, whatever the differences among them, are of a piece in their focus on disorder, whether managed effectively or not, and despite disagreements among members of the Constituent Assembly and contemporary political scientists on the sources of disorder. There are at least two—and probably many more—problems with this focus. The first has been well put by Gurharpal Singh in considering the case of Punjab, which has evidently followed the accommodationist sequence that Manor has so clearly described. But, Gurharpal, in the aftermath of the death and destruction that engulfed the people of Punjab in 10 years of bloody conflict, asks us to change the "problematic", to shift our attention away from how "disorder" has been managed to "how 'order' has been maintained, justified, and sometimes legitimized".[10] What is this "order" that has been maintained in India—and other parts of South Asia—at the increasing cost of human lives? What great and noble purposes have been served by this quest for order that continues in Kashmir, that has been mirrored in Sri Lanka and Pakistan and Bangladesh, as well, from time to time? The second problem with the focus on disorder is its neglect of the structures of dominance and subordination, the power relations that are maintained in societies so strongly oriented to the quelling of disorder and the maintenance of order. Marxists welcomed disorder, often provoked it in the hope that a new and more

just social order would be brought into being. Indian Constitution-makers and contemporary political scientists have rejected
this Marxist dream as a chimera, but we have also rejected the
construction of any serious critique of the social order that is
maintained by the Indian state, its ethnographic practices, and
its policies and non-policies.

We have neglected to see that this focus on combating disorder and maintaining order has been part of a whole range of
ideologies, policies, non-policies and practices that have been
sustaining not just "order" in the abstract, but a particular social and economic order, particular patterns of dominance and
subordination, and particular relations of power. For, this fear
of disorder has preoccupied the minds of India's dominant upper caste and upper class political, social, and economic élites
for the past 50 years. It is a fear not just of disunity, disintegration, decay and violence, but a fear of the people, of the dangers to their own status and well-being if the poor and the low
castes should at last begin to assert themselves, to organize, and
to challenge their dominance as many are now, at last, doing.
Fear of the poor has lain behind many post-Independence policies and non-policies: from food rationing and food price controls to prevent uprisings of the urban poor, to anti-inflationary
policies rigorously pursued for the same reason, to the non-
policy of eliminating child labour and providing compulsory,
universal primary education for the poor children of India.[11]

After Independence the fear of disorder and the desire for a
strong central government, termed a "strong Centre" in Indian
parlance, went together. On this subject there was virtual, if
not total, uniformity of opinion in the Constituent Assembly,
even including critics of the draft Constitution who opposed
some clauses that seemed to undermine state autonomy and
the fundamental rights of the people. One can almost sense a
sigh of relief, alongside the genuine pain felt by members of the
Assembly over the partition of the subcontinent, that the original (British) Cabinet plan envisaging a united India could now
be discarded. Under that plan, the Centre was to be weak, its
powers restricted to only three subjects—defence, foreign affairs,
and communications—and the residuary powers of the Union
would lie with the provinces. In an early speech in the Assembly,
before the acceptance of the Partition Plan, Dr S. Radhakrishnan,

a future president of India, remarked with resignation that, though "a strong Centre is essential to mould all the peoples [of India] into one united whole" and "events. . . in Bihar and Bengal" had demonstrated "an urgent need for a strong Centre", members of the Assembly would have to accept instead the development of "a multi-national State".[12]

Once the Cabinet plan was removed from consideration with the acceptance of the division of India, the strength of senti-ment in the Assembly for a "strong Centre" became evident. One member put the matter succinctly by saying that "we have always been fighting for a strong Centre".[13] Mahavir Tyagi, in the speech cited earlier, made it clear that he thought "that the Cen-tre should be strong" because, if it lacked the "right to interfere" in the governance of the states, "there will be a tendency to-wards disintegration", revolt by parties "wedded to violence", and secession on the part of state governments "in conjunction with a neighbouring province or a foreign country".[14]

In utter contrast to the deliberations leading to the creation of the United States, there was not even a murmur from the provincial governments themselves against the idea of a strong Centre. There was hardly any conflict between advocates of a centralized state and upholders of provincial autonomy.[15] Austin notes that "in twenty memoranda" submitted by the "provin-cial governments to the Assembly" concerning the allocation and distribution of revenue sources, no claims were made on grounds of the need to preserve provincial autonomy or "states rights", despite the evident fact that the revenue sources allo-cated to the states were insufficient for "their budgetary needs".[16]

For virtually all Assembly members, as well as, of course, for the framers of the Constitution, a strong Centre and a strong Indian state were underlying assumptions. This ideal of a strong Centre was itself so strong that members who criticized any of the emergency provisions of the Constitution felt obliged to preface their remarks with the defensive statement that they, too, shared the common goal. Over and over again members of the Assembly justified the desire for a strong Centre in terms of the imperative need to combat threats to the unity of the country that took many forms. Fear of disintegration was in the fore-front of their minds and they proclaimed that, under no circumstances, would any further secessionist moves by any groups or units of the Union or any of its peoples be tolerated. The Union of India was to be permanent and indissoluble.

It is also evident from the constitutional provisions concerning the fundamental rights of citizens, as well as the Assembly debates that took place concerning them, that the security of the Indian state took precedence over fundamental rights. The two values were presented as separate, requiring a choice between them. Shri Brajeshwar Prasad put it in his usual uncompromising manner when he said:

> I feel that if there is a conflict between the security of the State and the personal liberty of the individual, I will choose the former and lay stress on the security of the State. For the first time in the chequered history of India we have got an independent State of our own; are we going to barter it away in the name of some newfangled notions which have been discredited in their own homelands?[17]

In this member's mind, fundamental rights were not something sacred to be sacrificed only because of dire necessity or a grave threat to state security. On the contrary, it was the state that was sacred, and fundamental rights nothing but "newfangled notions" from abroad.

Although Brajeshwar Prasad's statements were generally more extreme than those of the Constitution's drafters, the latter clearly shared many of his sentiments and ignored the protests of H. V. Kamath, one of the tiny group of two or three members in the entire Assembly who consistently expressed their concerns over various aspects of the emergency provisions, including the complete abrogation of fundamental rights during the pendency of an emergency. Shri Kamath pointed out that the fundamental rights themselves were already "laden with five provisos"[18] that, taken together, in effect denied the fundamental character of the very rights granted in what ultimately became Article 19 of the Constitution.

Even Mahavir Tyagi who, as we saw above, generally defended the emergency clauses, opposed one that denied the people the right during an emergency even to approach the courts, including the Supreme Court, to seek enforcement of their fundamental rights. In remarks rather inconsistent with his earlier arguments, he bemoaned the implication of such a provision that, in effect, "the people were to be told that the State is supreme in India".[19]

These protests notwithstanding, the cumulative effect of the provisos in Article 19 and the emergency provisions of the Constitution was to provide a range of grounds, some of them extremely broadly stated, to nullify all the fundamental rights of the people. The constitutional authority, M. V. Pylee, counted not "five provisos" noted by H. V. Kamath but, with regard to "freedom of speech and expression", "seven restrictions", as follows: "the security of the State; friendly relations with foreign States; public order; decency or morality; contempt of court; defamation; and incitement to violence".[20] All these restrictions were imposed swiftly with the passage of the Preventive Detention Act under the authority of the Constitution. Others were added later and the state's powers against the individual strengthened still further under the Defence of India Act, the Maintenance of Internal Security Act, and the Terrorist and Disruptive Activities Act, among other acts less notable for the severity of their restrictions and the unlimited powers granted to the state against its citizens. Professor Pylee, a great admirer of the Constitution as a whole, was nevertheless alarmed in the first edition of his book (published in 1965) by the sweep of the first two of those acts. He feared that "under the cloak of emergency these powers could be abused by an unscrupulous and power-seeking party in office to destroy forever the cherished ideals of the Constitution",[21] a fear that seemed to many to have come true during the Emergency of 1975–7.

But were there no other underlying reasons behind the desire for a strong Centre, no other more positive goals? Indeed there were. Chief among them and, according to Austin, preeminent among all the goals declared in the Constitution and expressed in the Constituent Assembly debates, were the goals of economic development and even "social revolution".[22] "The immediate goals of the social revolution—improving the standard of living and increasing industrial and agricultural productivity—provided yet another reason for a strong central authority".[23] Moreover, the goals of economic development through centralized planning under the lead of the state, were shared by liberals, radicals and conservatives alike,[24] though not necessarily the goals of "social revolution".[25] Thus, it was...

both for the preservation of the newly-won independence and the planned development of the country" that "central direction" was considered "essential", and the decision was made "that what India needed was a strong Union and comparatively weak States".[26]

In effect, therefore, these very goals of economic development and social revolution provided a further justification not only for the strong state, but for restrictions on civil liberties and provincial autonomy, and for establishing the preeminence of the state itself in relation to all other corporate groups in society. Thus, freedom of religious practice was constrained by the right of the state to make laws for "social welfare and reform".[27] Similarly, the judicial review powers of the Supreme Court with regard to both property rights and "personal liberty" were restricted "in the name of the social revolution".[28] On the other side of the divide between labour and capital, the Indian state was also able to contain trade union and labour demands partly because it had "won wide acceptance for its claim that it has a special responsibility for nation building and economic development".[29] It could also be argued, as Weiner noted in the aftermath of the First General Elections in which "no national opposition party had emerged", "that as long as there was a pressing need for rapid economic development planned by the state, such a program could best be carried out if a single party, with a minimum of opposition, led the country".[30] Further, with regard to provincial autonomy, Dandekar noted that, although the Constitution provides a long list of subjects reserved to the states, most of them, like the protections for fundamental rights, contain "provisos and exceptions" that enabled the Indian state "to expand and extend its authority as and when it felt necessary".[31]

The Record

In his analysis of the Constitution of India, including its actual working during the first two decades of Indian independence, Granville Austin noted that, during this period of Congress hegemony, "cabinet government" had "provided India with stable and strong government" and "that Congress ministries" had "not aggrandized their authority at the expense of constitutional government either in the states or in New Delhi".[32] Thirty years later, no one could make the same statement concerning the record established since then. In the intervening years, the Indian people have been subjected to an Emergency, authoritarian regime, the undermining of fundamental rights through the excessive use of a multiplicity of preventive detention and internal security laws, gross abuses of human rights in Kashmir, Punjab, the northeast and Gujarat, and routine abuses of their powers by the police forces in many states of the Union. There has also been a considerable increase in numbers and a proliferation of types of armed forces directly under the control of the central government, but used primarily to maintain security within the states. These include the Central Reserve Police Force, the Border Security Force, the Central Industrial Security Force and the Home Guards.[33] The use of the military forces to suppress and control riots and other forms of internal disturbance and disorder has also vastly increased over the years.[34] As for the federal system, Dua concluded in 1985, in connection with his survey of the extensive use and misuse of the imposition of Presidents' Rule upon the states and union territories under Article 356 of the Constitution, that "the Indian system" amounted to "a case of the pathology of federalism".[35]

It needs to be stressed that there is no longer anything exceptional about the abuse of fundamental rights and human dignities by state agencies in India. David Bayley commented upon police misbehaviour in the early 1980s, and in 1987 Barnett Rubin placed their behaviour and that of other agencies within the broader context of the human rights situation.[36] Amnesty International, Human Rights Watch, and PIOOM (Interdisciplinary Programme of Research on Root Causes of Human Rights Violations) in the Netherlands have, year after year, since then published reports documenting in considerable detail the extent of those abuses, placing India in the category of the more extreme undemocratic states of the world on this measure.[37] Rubin also placed such violations of civil rights in India within the context of the original ideological justification for them that I have noted above, remarking that, above the abusive police and the "chaotic and corrupt" state and local governments, stands the "central 'state', promoting national 'security' and pursuing dreams of glory far removed from the goals of marginalized sectors of the population".[38] I have noted elsewhere that individual safety is not one of the implied guarantees of life in the Indian state, but is merely one value among others that is obtained through politics, through gaining the protection of the dominant political leaders and groups who control the police.[39]

In the years since Bayley and Rubin wrote their articles, the Government of India has added further to its enormous armory of powers and diminished the rights of its citizens in the struggle against imagined separatism in Punjab and a genuine secessionist movement in Kashmir. The former "totalitarian" Soviet state allowed the secession of numerous of its former Republics, for the most part without the use of its armed forces, while the federal government of Canada watched, without a drop of blood being shed, the resurgence of a secessionist movement and its near-success in Quebec. At the same time the Government of India was deploying, at a low estimate, above a quarter of a million armed men in several distinct forces to bring about a termination of the chaotic conditions in Punjab, using the very sequence of coercion–accommodation tactics described by Manor, first to destroy the terrorists and then to hold legislative assembly elections with the aid of these several forces.[40]

What has changed in these intervening years in such a way as to make some of the worst fears of that tiny band of critics of the draft Constitution, come true? There are several obvious changes that have taken place, each one of which—and more so, all in combination—provide some understanding. They include the shift in leadership quality and style from Nehru to Indira Gandhi to Rajiv Gandhi, which have been noted by many observers, including this writer, though it must be acknowledged as well that there is a strong opposite point of view. The latter argues that it was not primarily a difference between the ruthlessness, demagoguery, and interventionist tactics of Indira Gandhi compared to her father's more tolerant, principled and mediating tactics that explains the deterioration in Indian political life, including the erosion of provincial autonomy, the abuses of fundamental rights, and the rise of violence. Rather, it is the changing context of increased competitiveness; rising assertiveness and the mobilization of ever more segments of the population, particularly from the lower half; and the easy availability of advanced, destructive small weaponry that are responsible, not the actions of individual leaders. Others have pointed to the decline in effectiveness of India's leading institutions as a consequence of some of the latter factors, as well as because of rampant, pervasive, large-scale corruption.

One can go on in this manner, multiplying the causes of the present crises in contemporary Indian politics. But, there remains something broader that frames them all, that has shaped the fundamental, underlying set of tensions built into the Indian Constitution and Indian political practices and modes of thinking from the beginning. Those tensions have already been partly illustrated above, especially between centralizing and decentralizing tendencies, protection for fundamental rights versus the security of the state, authoritarian proclivities in the ready acceptance of all kinds of emergency provisions versus protections for the maintenance of liberal-democratic practices. They arise out of the very goal of creating a "nation-state", modelled on the monolingual states of Europe in which there is also a dominant culture and often a dominant religion, in which all who do not subscribe to the values of the dominant group are classed as minorities, to be tolerated in some cases, expelled in others, or exterminated.

In other words, with all the talk and agreement about the need for a strong state in India, there has never been a consensus on its form. The consequence has been that, while a continuing struggle has taken place—or rather has ebbed and flowed over the decades—over its proper form, the state itself has come to exist for its own sake. It is forbidden in India—informally, of course—to refer to India as a multi-national state. The secular principles promoted so vigorously by Nehru during his years of dominance provided a basis not for defining the shape of the Indian state, but for transcending and avoiding a debate over it. The focus was not on the place of all the distinctive religions, languages and cultures of the Indian peoples, but on economic development and some form of so-called socialist transformation of Indian society.

European economic ideologies and categories were transplanted to India, but the divisive potential of the ideologies of the European nation-state form were kept out of the discussion. Instead, Nehru and the socialist opposition took the position that all the religions and cultures and languages of the peoples of India were to be respected and protected, provided they did not make political demands for recognition as corporate political groups in the Indian state and society. In practice, during Nehru's time, many political rights were nevertheless conceded to corporate groups, for example, through the creation of linguistic states or the continued recognition of the partial legal autonomy of religious communities in India. In effect, as I argued in *Language, Religion, and Politics in North India,* India was developing under Nehru's leadership many of the features of a developing multi-national state rather than a homogenous nation-state.[41] This was done even as a consensus was maintained that the fundamental goals of the Indian state had nothing to do with these matters; rather, those goals were economic development and social transformation. Secularism was the ideology or, rather, a set of practices that prevented or halted in its tracks or compromised or suppressed the intrusion of religious, linguistic, tribal, and other cultural demands into the centre of Indian politics. These matters were nuisances for, and obstructions to, the main business of the Indian state.

Jaffrelot has articulated this opposition cogently in his book on *The Hindu Nationalist Movement* in which he shows how the drive to consolidate Hindu society and unify the Indian state with an ideology of Hindu nationalism was blocked throughout the Nehru period, largely by the focus of the Indian state and the then-dominant political parties in both government and opposition on "secularism and economic development". He notes also, however, that what he calls "Hindu traditionalist" tendencies in the Congress itself, especially in north India, undermined efforts by the Jan Sangh to capitalize on such demands as the promotion of the Hindi language and the displacement of Urdu.[42] After the death of Nehru, the failure of centralized economic development planning to transform India into either the socialist, industrial society of Nehru's and the Left's dreams, or into a dynamic capitalist society became increasingly clear. India failed even to provide for the basic, minimum needs of most of its people. The increased assertiveness of a multiplicity of new caste groups in Indian state politics led Mrs Gandhi, her son Rajiv, and the Bharatiya Janata Party (BJP) in different directions from those followed by the Congress under Nehru's leadership. Secularist practices and the focus on economic development planning were gradually discarded while the Congress sought to maintain its national strength by identifying with backward caste movements in several states and with Hindu sentiments in the northern states. A corrupted and divided Congress, however, under Rajiv Gandhi and P. V. Narasimha Rao, proved incapable of dealing with the forces it helped to unleash. In north India, the new assertiveness of the Scheduled and backward castes was fostered and channeled by the Janata parties and the Bahujan Samaj Party (BSP), while the BJP and the Vishva Hindu Parishad (VHP) captured overwhelmingly the resurgent and increasingly more explicit sentiments of Hindu nationalism and anti-Muslim feelings through the Ayodhya movement. The consequences of the prolonged movements leading to the destruction of the Babri mosque on December 6, 1992, were several waves of destructive riots across northern and western India that left thousands dead in their wake. It also left in tatters the idea that the dying Congress party could any longer provide even a semblance of protection for the Muslims of the country, or even knew any longer how to act upon the secular principles that kept militant Hindu nationalism and its organizations at bay during the first two decades of Indian independence.

Hindu Nationalism, Regionalism and the Future of Federalism

The leaders of the BJP are presently operating in their integrationist mode, as Jaffrelot would put it, rather than emphasizing the "ethno-religious" themes that have brought them to their present (1998) position of power in the Indian Union. Many observers believed that once they attained power at the Centre, they would become more moderate either because they really are moderate and democratic at heart, or because of the compulsions of operating within a culturally and politically heterogeneous society. The latter factor, the heterogeneity of Indian society, did indeed compel them to compromise with regional political forces to gain power at the Centre while attempting to hold at bay the RSS cadres whose lives have been built upon the dream of consolidating Hindu society and creating a Hindu nation-state that will become strong enough to gain the respect of the West. Caught between these two sets of forces, the BJP leadership found a way to temporarily transcend them and move towards the latter goal with the nuclear explosions of May 1998. At the same time, the BJP government, including one of its non-BJP members, George Fernandes, indulged in militant and antagonistic jingoistic rhetoric directed against India's neighbours, particularly Pakistan for its alleged continued support of the insurrection in Kashmir. He also made strident statements regarding the government's determination to suppress that insurrection by whatever means necessary, and responded defiantly to the protests of most of the great powers and the sanctions applied by them, especially the United States, in response to the government's nuclear policy. In effect, therefore, while being forced to compromise with regional forces to gain and retain power at the Centre, the BJP at the same time presented itself as the most forceful defender of the great Indian nation against all divisive internal foes and external rivals.

However, the BJP has by no means been able by this method, to avoid the obstacles posed by regional political forces to its free exercise of power at the Centre. I argued fifteen years ago that, despite the centralizing tendencies that were so prominent during Mrs Gandhi's rise and her consolidation of power, the long-term trend in Indian society and politics was towards pluralism, regionalism and decentralization.[43] I continue to believe that the tension between homogenizing and pluralist, national and regional, centralizing and decentralizing tendencies are at the heart of the struggle for power in Indian politics, and that the long-term prognosis remains in favour of the latter set of forces. Those forces are represented today by the Marxists in Bengal and Kerala, the secular parties representing the lower and backward castes acting as a brake upon Hindu consolidation, and the regional nationalist parties in the south, the northeast, and the Punjab.

Although the long-term interests of all these forces lie in resistance to excessive consolidation of power at the Centre by a single dominant party, it is also to be expected that compromises will be made on both sides, many of them in the form of rank opportunism so characteristic of Indian politics. The BJP assiduously sought electoral alliances and seat adjustments with regional parties in most of the Indian states in preparation for the 1998 Lok Sabha elections. It was equally assiduous in making deals with regional parties to either join or support its coalition government at the Centre or to at least abstain from voting against it. Its efforts led to the incorporation of both the Akali Dal and the AIADMK into the government, and an agreement with the Telugu Desam to either abstain from voting against it or to support it on crucial matters affecting its fate in Parliament. The BJP's alliance with the AIADMK has been particularly opportunistic on both sides, and has placed the two parties in somewhat paradoxical positions on the issue of Centre-state relations. The AIADMK leader, Jayalalitha, desperate both to squelch corruption charges against her and to regain power in Tamil Nadu, pressed the BJP to dismiss the DMK government and impose President's Rule. The BJP, however, not wishing to be seen as misusing the notorious Article 356 of the Constitution of India for this purpose and, thereby, alarming all other regional forces in the country about its future intentions, refused Jayalalitha's demands.

It is evident, therefore, that the fundamental tension in the Indian political order between centralizing and regionalizing forces remains its defining feature, and that it is likely to go on indefinitely without a decisive outcome. At the same time, it must be recognized that the organizations building militant Hindu nationalism represent a long-term tendency in Indian history that has by no means worked itself out. Moreover, it is not just power in Indian politics that they seek, but greatness in the world, a world of states dominated by western powers, in which India has been seen primarily as a country on the dole, a nuisance in international relations, with a vainglorious and pretentious leadership making demands for recognition that its achievements do not justify. They believe that their aspirations for greatness cannot be achieved until Hindus consolidate and India becomes a nation-state.

This striving for Hindu consolidation is something utterly different from previous efforts by the dominant Congress to maintain its power in the face of the pulls of a multiplicity of regional and local forces. Nehru, whose personal position went largely unchallenged after the death of Sardar Patel, maintained the support of the Indian people in two ways. One was through his forthright condemnation of all forms of "provincialism, casteism and communalism"; the other was his moulding of a

consensus on national economic development goals that embraced the Congress and the principal parties of the Left, and
that also shaped the dialogue with the parties of the Right. In
these ways, he also kept the communists and the Hindu nationalists constantly on the defensive. His success also depended
partly on the use of preventive detention laws—particularly
against the communists from time to time—and in banning, and
threatening to ban the RSS.[44] Extensive vote banks among dominant castes in the states and localities were developed by state
party bosses who were allowed free rein as long as they produced the majorities required for the Congress to maintain its
dominance in nearly every state of the Indian Union.

Mrs Gandhi, who began her first period of rule from a weak
position, and who considered the state bosses obstacles in the
way of her personal consolidation of power, had to seek alternative support bases. In the process of attempting to free her-
self from dependence on regional and local centres of power,
she adopted several methods, most of which worked against
the militant nationalist dreams of Hindu consolidation. She appealed directly to categories of voters who had a national spread,
particularly the Muslims, the Scheduled Castes, and the poor in
general. Secondly, she intervened in state politics on the side of
the newly assertive backward castes, particularly in states such
as Gujarat and Karnataka. Further, she intervened directly in
the politics of all the states of the Union, seeking to divide and
undermine the existing bases of support of all serious rivals to
the Congress. When, towards the end, she still felt that her support bases were insecure, and that she had lost some or most of
her following among Muslims, Sikhs and Scheduled Castes, she
too began to appeal to Hindu nationalist sentiment.

The strategies pursued by Nehru and Mrs Gandhi to maintain their leadership, the dominance of the Congress, and the
unity and strength of the central government were, therefore,
for the most part different from each other as well as different
from that of the BJP. Nehru himself believed in the idea of a
composite nationalism integrating all the cultural strands of the
Indian peoples, but he was not really interested in promoting it
as such. For the national leadership in Nehru's time (as for most
political science commentators on the issues and problems faced
by the new states generally in the early post-colonial years) of

equal, if not greater, importance than cultural diversity as a possible obstacle to national integration was the so-called "gap" between the Centre and the localities. Insofar as India was concerned, Weiner put it as follows: "From the point of view of the national leadership, it was 'politics'—in the sense of narrow ambitions for power and the parochial loyalties of small men— which threatened national unity, economic development and political order".[45]

Secularism was not an ideology for Nehru. On the contrary, he considered it nothing but civilized behaviour practised by all but a few contemporary states in the modern world.[46] His strategy could be characterized as one that sought to transcend cultural differences, accommodate conflicts arising out of them, combat parochial and militant Hindu nationalist forces, and get on with the business of the state as he saw it.

Mrs Gandhi, though she fought the RSS and the Jan Sangh and threatened them from time to time with legal restrictions, did not follow as consistent an anti-communal policy as her father. Furthermore, in her struggles with opponents, she built horizontal support bases that drew attention to divisions in Indian society between Hindus and Muslims, Hindus and Sikhs, and among Hindus as well. At the same time, she was a strident nationalist in world affairs, who apparently believed that the United States, in collusion with Pakistan and indigenous opposition forces, was out to undermine the unity and strength of India.

Mrs Gandhi and her son, Rajiv, also played upon the fear of disorder, disunity and instability in ways that Nehru never did. Nehru combatted forthrightly the enemies he identified. He named them, addressed them, used the powers of preventive detention against them when he thought it necessary or convenient, but he rarely, if ever, used alleged threats to the unity of the country as a basis for justifying his rule or that of the Congress, or the imposition of a countrywide emergency. He made it clear to the Nagas in the northeast, to Master Tara Singh in Punjab, and to others elsewhere in the country that secessionism would not be tolerated under any circumstances, but he did not use their demands and their movements to suggest that the country's survival was at stake. Mrs Gandhi, however, used such alleged threats to the country's unity, which she often never identified clearly, to justify her own indispensability in the shameless spreading of the slogan that "Indira is India". Rajiv did the same, as Hardgrave noted in connection with the 1984 election campaign, and as everyone, including this author who was there at the time, also noticed in full page advertisements in the daily newspapers, in his speeches and those of Congress-men throughout the country. The "message" conveyed "was that the nation's unity and integrity were threatened and that only Congress could provide strength at the Centre vital to the sur-vival of India". [47]

The BJP–RSS strategy, as everyone knows, is in sharp con-trast to those pursued by Nehru and Mrs Gandhi. They stand, on the one hand, for emphasizing the distinctness and great-ness of Hindu civilization as opposed to that of the Muslims and the West. On the other hand, they call for playing down the horizontal divisions among Hindus and the integration of all castes and sects, including the Sikhs, into one homogenous whole. These two aspects of the strategy of militant Hindu nationalism combine to form the one overarching goal of establishing India as a homogeneous, Hindu nation-state on its way towards the ultimate goal of achieving the status of a great power, the equal of the great powers of the West.

The BJP strategy is also different from that of Rajiv Gandhi. While it does not shrink from attacking those whom it consid-ers threats to the consolidation of Indian nationhood, its mes-sage is aggressive rather than defensive. Its leaders do not say that only the BJP can save India, but that only the BJP can trans-form India to enable it to achieve greatness.

What still stands in their way? The existence of linguistic states and the regional parties within them are the principal obstacles to the BJP's goals. The Congress under Nehru's leader-ship was reluctant to concede linguistic states, for many of the Congress leaders feared that these reorganized units would form the basis for new nations that might some day secede from the Indian Union, causing its further disintegration. That fear has so far proved largely unwarranted, but the linguistic states have, nevertheless contributed to a consolidation, in whole or in part, of regional identities, expressed politically by parties such as the DMK and AIADMK in Tamil Nadu, the Telugu Desam in Andhra Pradesh, the Asom Gana Parishad in Assam, the Akali

Dal in Punjab, and the Shiv Sena in Maharashtra. Some regional parties have already made alliances with the BJP, such as the Shiv Sena and the Akali Dal, but those parties that are more securely ensconced in their regional strongholds have not done so. The decision of such parties as the AIADMK and the Telugu Desam to ally with the BJP in 1998 or support it from outside, depended on concrete political dynamics within their regions rather than upon principled belief in "states' rights". In the case of the AIADMK, the party's interest was to use an alliance with the leading centre party against its rival in the state. For the Telugu Desam, neither an alliance with the BJP coalition nor with the United Front provided the necessary support it required to maintain its power in Andhra Pradesh against its principal rival, the Congress; on the contrary, more than the BJP it feared a central government coalition led by the Congress. Initially, therefore, it opted for a neutral stance in Parliament, but one leaning towards the BJP.

Pylee argued in 1965 that, with all the unitary features of the Constitution, "federalism has been a powerful decentralising force", in which "the formation of linguistic States was the most important single factor" contributing to that development.[48] His judgement was premature, for neither he nor most other observers at the time anticipated the centralizing drives that would follow, leading to the erosion of federalism during Mrs Gandhi's long years in and out of power. Today, however, the non-Hindi-speaking linguistic states remain the principal bastions of federalism and decentralization in Indian politics. From these states have come demands for increased regional autonomy and the elimination or clearer subordination of the IAS officers serving in the states, among others. But most of all, these states, no matter what opportunistic alliances they may make in the short term, represent centres of autonomous politics, into most of which the BJP has not been able to penetrate effectively.

In fact, the primary consequence of the decline of the Congress in all the states of India has been the continued regionalization of their party systems. In the summer of 1998, the Congress was in power in only two states, Madhya Pradesh and Orissa; the BJP alone was in power only in Rajasthan and Gujarat, in coalition with other parties in U.P., Himachal Pradesh, Punjab, Haryana and Maharashtra; various units or splinter groups of the Janata Dal ruled in Karnataka and Bihar; CPM-led Left Fronts were in power in Kerala and West Bengal; in Kashmir, Andhra, Tamil Nadu and Assam, distinctive regional parties controlled their respective state governments.

Although the BJP after the 1998 Lok Sabha elections had the broadest spread of any party except the Congress, it remained then—as it has always been—primarily a regional party in the states of Delhi, Gujarat, Madhya Pradesh, Rajasthan, Himachal Pradesh and Uttar Pradesh, all (except Gujarat) in the Hindi-speaking zone. It had significant electoral strength in Karnataka and Bihar, and gained a foothold in Andhra Pradesh as well, but lost ground in Maharashtra. In Punjab, Tamil Nadu, Haryana, Assam, West Bengal and Kerala, it is either insignificant or a minor party.

It is in the north, the historic centre of imperial India as well as the strongest post-Independence source of centralizing leadership, that the BJP has retained its strongest base. Here the principal obstacles to the further rise of the BJP have been the large Muslim populations and the continuing caste divisions among Hindus. In large parts of this vast region, Muslims have sufficiently large population concentrations in many Vidhan Sabha and Lok Sabha constituencies to hold the balance in electoral contests.

Insofar as the divisions among Hindus are concerned, the BJP's predecessor, the Jan Sangh, was stopped in its apparent gradual ascent to power in Uttar Pradesh—increasing its strength in each successive legislative assembly election in that state from 1952 to 1967—after 1967, when Chaudhuri Charan Singh left the Congress, formed a new agrarian party based primarily on the cultivating middle peasant, so-called "backward castes", and displaced the Jan Sangh as the primary opposition to the Congress. His party, the Lok Dal, became the central component in the Janata Party, from which all the contemporary left-oriented Janata parties are now descended. The BJP too arose from the remnants of the original Janata Party, the Jan Sangh having merged into it with the Lok Dal of Charan Singh and the other principal non-Congress parties in north India.

However, support for the BJP remained well behind the several Janata formations in north Indian politics until V. P. Singh made his (mis) calculated error in August 1990 of adopting the long-dormant Mandal Commission recommendations for reservations in central sector jobs for backward castes. This deliberate effort on the part of V. P. Singh to strengthen the hold of his Janata Dal on the backward castes, thereby intensifying divisions among Hindus while simultaneously appealing for the votes of Muslims, precipitated the BJP–VHP decision to intensify its mobilization of Hindus to remove the Babri masjid from Ayodhya and replace it with a temple to Ram. In the election campaign of 1991, the BJP followed the double strategy of seeking to consolidate all Hindus around the Ayodhya issue, including the deliberate targetting of constituencies with heavy Muslim population concentrations for special attention, on the one hand, while appealing to the resentments and fears of upper caste Hindus and middle castes left out of the Mandal list of backward castes. These double appeals were so successful as to completely transform the social base of the BJP in north India. It now became a new political formation quite distinct from its previous incarnations in terms of electoral support,[49] and became the strongest party in north Indian politics as well the principal contender for power at the Centre.

Nevertheless, the BJP continued to be blocked by three things. First was the solid opposition of Muslim voters; second, the division of the backward castes into supporters of the BJP and the left Janata parties; and third, the near-total hold of the relatively new Bahujan Samaj Party (BSP) upon the most numerous castes among the Scheduled Caste voters. Although the BJP has twice entered alliances in U.P. with the BSP, and has attempted to build its own base among the dalits, the bulk of the Scheduled Caste vote has remained closed in the hands of Kanshi Ram and Mayawati. The BJP has had to be content with some support from a few of the less numerous Scheduled Castes, such as the Balmikis and Sonkars.

Although, therefore, the mobilizing capacity of the BJP has reached a peak in the north, the forces arrayed against it are also divided. When the Muslims, half the backward castes, and the Scheduled Castes are united behind the Janata parties and the BSP, the BJP cannot win elections in the north. It can come to power in the north and at the Centre only by isolating the Muslim voters, capitalizing upon the divisions between the BSP and Janata parties, and extending its base among the backward castes. It has been working assiduously to do so in all three respects. Since the most recent legislative assembly elections in this state in 1996 which resulted in a hung assembly, the state has experienced president's rule and several changes in government. The latter included a period of alliance with the BSP that ultimately fell apart, and was then followed by a successful move on the part of the BJP to split the BSP and form a government with the support of a large segment of the divided party. This last event was accompanied by bloody violence inside the assembly among the contending political parties, scenes from which were filmed and broadcast round the world.

In 1998, the BJP was in power again in U.P. under the chief ministership of Kalyan Singh. Under his chief ministership and with his complicity in December 1992, the mosque at Ayodhya was destroyed. Under his leadership work was continuing in an area near the site of the former mosque, including the carving out of "stone pillars for the proposed temple".[50] Such activity is meant to satisfy the militant Hindu cadres of the party, but it also effectively maintains the Hindu-Muslim divide that the BJP and the VHP have worked to intensify over the past decade. At the same time, the BJP government has continued its efforts to woo the backward castes by providing reservations for those whose support it seeks, and supporting the "declassification" of those whose support has gone mainly to other parties. It also planned to "launch a drive to fill 70,000 vacancies in various [government] departments"[51] that would provide it with ample patronage to distribute among backward castes and other castes whose support it seeks.

What then remains of the desire for a strong state and the fear of disorder that has apparently accompanied it since Independence? In fact, all the principal parties in north India have been deliberately fomenting divisions and disorder for many years including violent disorders such as Hindu-Muslim riots, to assist them in gaining power locally, regionally and nationally. The sheer unscrupulousness of these efforts is at times awe-inspiring, but they also have a long history dating from before and after Independence. Yet the deliberate creation of division and disorder, while using them as a justification for the creation or restoration of a strong state, are hardly new features in the twentieth century. They were the trademark of all the fascist movements that rose to power in Europe during the first half of the twentieth century, and the strategy reappeared, as if in a time-warp, in the hands of Milosevic of ex-Yugoslavia with consequences the world has witnessed during the past few years.

India has often been commended for its adherence to democratic practices and other achievements. At the same time, we ought not to forget that there are two kinds of disorder: the disorder of Indian politics that is necessary for any kind of so-called "social revolution", economic transformation, or achievement of human dignity for its poorest classes; and the disorders that are manufactured to hide India's failures and to justify the maintenance of a strong state in search of glory. Those manufactured disorders, with all their violent consequences, are likely to continue without end at different times and places on the subcontinent, in India and in the other states of the region as well, as long as the tension between the desire for strength through homogeneity, on the one hand, and local autonomy and individual dignity on the other, is not resolved.

Notes

1 On the contrary, as Amartya Sen has noted, British policies exacerbated the problem by diverting food from the rural areas to Calcutta, among other disastrous actions and non-actions; see his *Poverty and Famines: An Essay on Entitlement and Deprivation* (Oxford: Clarendon Press), 1981, Chapter VI.

2 Granville Austin, *The Indian Constitution: Cornerstone of a Nation* (Oxford: Clarendon Press), 1966, p. 191.

3 H. V. Kamath, in India, *Constituent Assembly Debates: Official Report* [hereafter referred to as *CAD*], vol. IX (30 July 1949–18 September 1949) (New Delhi: Government of India Press), 1967, p. 138.

4 Naziruddin Ahmad, in *CAD* IX, pp. 116–17.

5 Mahavir Tyagi, in *CAD* IX, p. 121.

6 Brajeshwar Prasad, in *CAD* IX, p. 171.

7 Pandit Thakur Das Bhargava, in *CAD* IX, p. 168.

8 Atul Kohli, *Democracy and Discontent: India's Growing Crisis of Governability* (Cambridge: Cambridge University Press), 1990, pp. 17–18.

9 James Manor, 'Ethnicity and Politics in India', *International Affairs*, vol. LXXII, no. 3 (1996), p. 472.

10 Gurharpal Singh, 'Punjab Since 1984: Disorder, Order, and Legitimacy', *Asian Survey*, vol. XXXVI, no. 4 (April 1996), p. 421.

[11] Myron Weiner, *The Child and the State in India: Child Labor and Education Policy in Comparative Perspective* (Princeton, N.J.: Princeton University Press), 1991, p. 5.

[12] Sir S. Radhakrishnan, in *CAD* II (20 to 25 January 1947) (New Delhi: Government of India Press), 1966, pp. 272–3.

[13] Shibban Lal Saksena, in *CAD* IX, p. 109.

[14] Mahavir Tyagi, in *CAD* IX, pp.119–20.

[15] Austin, op. cit., pp. 186–9.

[16] Ibid., pp. 217–18.

[17] Brajeshwar Prasad, in *CAD* IX, pp. 170–1.

[18] H. V. Kamath in *CAD* IX, p. 183.

[19] Mahavir Tyagi in *CAD* IX, p. 194.

[20] M. V. Pylee, *Constitutional Government in India* (New York: Asia Publishing House), 1965, p. 226.

[21] Ibid., pp. 321–322.

[22] Austin, op. cit., pp. xi, 45.

[23] Ibid., p. 191.

[24] *Cf.* Baldev Raj Nayar, *The Modernisation Imperative and Indian Planning* (Delhi: Vikas), 1972.

[25] Austin, op. cit., p. 45.

[26] Pylee, op. cit., p. 512.

[27] Austin, op. cit., p. 64.

[28] Ibid., pp. 173–4.

[29] Lloyd I. Rudolph and Susanne H. Rudolph, *In Pursuit of Lakshmi: The Political Economy of the Indian State* (Chicago: University of Chicago Press), 1987, p. 273.

[30] Myron Weiner, *Party Politics in India: The Development of a Multi-Party System* (Princeton, N.J.: Princeton University Press), 1957, pp. 20-1.

[31] V. M. Dandekar, 'Unitary Elements in a Federal Constitution', *Economic and Political Weekly* [hereafter referred to as *EPW*], vol. XXII, no. 44 (31 October 1987), p. 1865.

[32] Austin, op. cit., p. 139.

[33] Myron Weiner, 'India's New Political Institutions,' *Asian Survey*, vol. XVI, no. 9 (September 1976), pp. 898-9 and David H. Bayley, 'The Police and Political Order in India, *Asian Survey*, vol. XXIII, no. 4 (April 1983), pp. 492–3.

[34] Stephen P. Cohen, 'The Military and Indian Democracy', in Atul Kohli (ed.), *India's Democracy: An Analysis of Changing State–Society Relations* (Princeton, N.J.: Princeton University Press), 1987, pp. 99–143.

[35] B. D. Dua, *Presidential Rule in India, 1950–1984: A Study in Crisis Politics*, rev. edn. (New Delhi: S. Chand), 1985, p. 5.

[36] David H. Bayley and Barnett R. Rubin, 'The Civil Liberties Movement in India: New Approaches to the State and Social Change', *Asian Survey*, vol. XXVII, no. 3 (March 1987).

37 See, for example, the PIOOM survey of reports from Amnesty International and the U.S. State Department between 1977 and 1988, scoring 93 countries on a scale relating to 'observance of integrity of the person'. On a scale of 1 to 5 in which 5 was the lowest ranking, India received a score of 4 on the basis of reports from one or both of those agencies in six of those years; *PIOOM Newsletter*, II, no. 2 (Autumn, 1990), pp. 19–20.

38 Rubin, op. cit., p. 388.

39 Paul R. Brass, 'National Power and Local Politics in India: A Twenty-Year Perspective,' *Modern Asian Studies*, vol. XVII, no. 1 (February 1984), pp. 89–118.

40 Singh, op. cit., pp. 413–14, among many other sources.

41 Paul R. Brass, *Language, Religion, and Politics in North India* (Cambridge: Cambridge University Press), 1974.

42 Christophe Jaffrelot, *The Hindu Nationalist Movement and Indian Politics, 1925 to the 1990s: Strategies of Identity-Building, Implantation and Mobilisation* (London: Christopher Hurst) 1996, citation from p. 9. See also Brass, *Language, Religion, and Politics in North India*, op. cit., pp. 203–11, where the discriminatory policies of the Congress governments towards Urdu in the post-Independence period are described in detail. For the role of 'Hindu traditionalists' in the Congress in Uttar Pradesh, see also Paul R. Brass, *Factional Politics in an Indian State: The Congress Party in Uttar Pradesh* (Berkeley: University of California Press), 1965, pp. 35–7.

43 Paul R. Brass, 'Pluralism, Regionalism, and Decentralizing Tendencies in Indian Politics', in A. Jeyaratnam Wilson and Dennis Dalton (eds), *The States of South Asia: Problems of National Integration* (London: Christopher Hurst) 1982, pp. 223–64; revised and republished in my *Ethnicity and Nationalism: Theory and Comparison* (Delhi: Sage), 1991, pp. 114–66.

44 On the latter, see especially, Jaffrelot, op. cit.

45 Myron Weiner, *The Politics of Scarcity: Public Pressure and Political Response in India* (Bombay: Asia Publishing House), 1962, p. 3.

46 How else to interpret the following remarks of Nehru in the Constituent Assembly debates? "Another word is thrown up a good deal, this secular state business. May I beg with all humility those gentlemen, who use this word often, to consult some dictionary before they use it? It is brought in at every conceivable step and at every conceivable stage. I just do not understand it. It has a great deal of importance, no doubt. But, it is brought in all contexts, as if by saying that we are a secular state we have done something amazingly generous, given something out of our pocket to the rest of the world, something which we ought not to have done, so on and so forth. We have only done something which every country does except a very few misguided and back-

ward countries in the world. Let us not refer to that word in the sense that we have done something very mighty." (From *CAD* IX, p. 401.)

[47] Robert L. Hardgrave, Jr., 'India in 1984: Confrontation, Assassination, and Succession', *Asian Survey*, vol. XXV, no. 2 (February 1985), p. 142.

[48] Pylee, op. cit., p. 601.

[49] Paul R. Brass, 'General Elections, 1996 in Uttar Pradesh: Divisive Struggles Influence Outcome', *EPW*, vol. XXXII, no. 38 (20 September 1997), p. 2418.

[50] *The Hindustan Times*, 16 June 1998.

[51] Ibid.

Democracy and Social Inequality

SUDIPTA KAVIRAJ

It appears to me beyond doubt that, sooner or later, we shall arrive, like the Americans, at an almost complete equality of condition.[1]

Alex de Tocqueville

I

This paper seeks to analyse the question of democracy and its relation to social equality in India from the point of view of historical sociology. Purely formalistic discussions of democracy which compare the formal–legal aspects of political institutions are at best, unincisive, at worst, can be seriously misleading. The reason for this is that in formalistic accounts of democracy, at least in the world of Indian social science, there is an equation between the idea of democratic institutions in the abstract and the specific constitutional arrangements of Britain and the USA, the forms that we learn about in our formative textbooks. This 'textbook' picture is likely to be dated: democracy in Britain and America might have dropped some of these individual forms and survived happily. Secondly, focusing on Britain and America gives us a parochial picture of what democracy historically has been. As some recent formal studies like Lijphart's[2] show, democratic regimes can take utterly different forms, depending on what they consider it their business to deal with. Democracy can be majoritarian or consociational, but this taxonomy itself can be read in two different ways. The first way would be to now look for consociational as well as majority forms, and rejoice at this addition to our earlier, somewhat narrower, conceptual repertoire. A second way, which I prefer, is to read this as evidence that institutional forms are mobile and plastic, and societies constantly improvise with their institutional tools to tackle the historical problems they face. In democracy therefore, as with many other modern processes, there is a process of differentiation rather than a singularity of forms. Forms of democracy change and its political and institutional repertoire increases with time. Formalistic views tend to lead to unnecessarily pessimistic implications. Since we equate democracy with either a single or a cluster of institutional rules, any deviation from these models leads to fears of its imminent collapse. If some rules of parliamentary privilege, produced by peculiar accidents of the history of British aristocracy, are eventually abandoned in Indian legislative practice, formalists might see this as a deplorable decline of democratic norms. Given a more sceptical or sympathetic historical sociology, we might see that as an incipient innovation. Take a striking example: when politicians we love to hate, BJP or Mayawati, decide to alternate as leaders of a coalition administration, we usually regard this as incongruous and laughable; but when European states decide to take turns in the EU presidency instead of following the militarist and muscular rules adopted by the United Nations, we applaud that as innovation in democratic procedure.

Why do we assume a connection between democracy and social equality? Democracy and a tendency towards social equality are usually seen as collusive or collateral *modern* processes. To understand this question, we must think of the relation between democracy and the larger developments of historical modernity. Modernity, in my view, is not the name of a single process, but a time in history in which several processes of social change tend to occur in combination. These processes are the familiar ones: the increasing centrality of the modern state and its forms of governmentality and discipline, social individuation, capitalist industrialization, the rise of nationalism and democracy. Yet these processes are not necessarily functionally related to each other. They differ from one society to another in two ways: in their internal sequences (like the sequence between consumer and capital goods industries within the process of industrialization); and the sequences *between* processes (e.g., whether universal suffrage comes *before* widespread literacy or not; whether secularization of the state occurs *before* democracy is established or *after*). The modernity of every society, what forms modernity would crystallize into and what its social consequences would be, depends to a large extent on these sequential connections and influences. Additionally, since modern processes transform traditional structures which differ from one society to another, it is normal to expect that modernity would take differentiated forms. A consequence of this line of thinking would be to treat democracy not as a set of rules strictly tied to any particular Western system, English, American or consociational, but as some general principles which we would *expect* to change through practical improvisation. Thus the judgement about Mayawati's suggestion would hinge not on whether similar procedures exist in any known western constitutions, but whether it is consistent with general principles of democratic government. Ironically, politicians who are less 'educated' have an advantage in their practical thinking: Kanshi Ram, unlike Nehru or Ambedkar, is unlikely to consult books on western constitutional law before deciding on a course of action; as a consequence, their decisions might be more unconstrained by historical precedents and they might be able to improvise more freely.

An analysis of the relation between democracy and inequality, however, requires a clearer perception of what is meant by the two terms. Although we might eventually conclude that it is in the nature of the two terms to be in some ways necessarily complex/polyvalent, it is essential to disambiguate them in order to understand clearly what might make the structure of this relation complex or unpredictable.

II

A Tocqueville's Argument

The connection between democracy and equality has been theoretically interpreted in several ways, but it might be useful to take one of the most extreme theses about this historic connection. Tocqueville argued that democracy is above all an egalitarian principle. I find his theory of democracy wonderfully suggestive, but that does not imply an acceptance of all of the propositions of which it is constructed. Democracy, he contends, bears a particularly strong affiliation not only with liberty but to the principle of equality. He also believes, as a separate thesis, that 'a complete equality of condition' would eventually come to all societies, and that the aristocracy in European societies must surrender to this historical tendency and come to terms with it, rather than try to resist its course. The choice before Europe was to be swept before this tide by trying to resist it, or to 'guide' it to serve other, more worthwhile, and less destructive, purposes. Tocqueville uses a traditional, in some senses, ancient conceptual tradition while talking about democracy. He uses the term in a manner that was current in discussions about the extreme tendencies of the French revolution, which radical observers celebrated and conservatives feared, equating democracy with the power of the poor majority. Yet, historically, it is quite clear that the structural logic of modern society is not so simple or univocal, or so completely determined by the political laws of a society. In Europe, the principle of political equality which Tocqueville found so important was read very differently by different propertied classes. Precisely because aristocracy was based on *formal* privilege, the principle of the political equality of citizens was fundamentally revolutionary for its adherents; yet a bourgeois conception of democracy would regard as compatible, the extreme equality of political citizenship and an equally extreme inequality generated by commercial society.

Another difficulty with Tocqueville's thesis was that the state of distributive relations he designated as 'equality of condition' was ambiguous. He appears by the use of that phrase to refer to two rather dissimilar states of affairs in distributive terms. The first is the condition of the early settlers in America, or·the condition he found in the outlying western townships during his visit, where there were no individuals or families pre-eminent in wealth, which is a condition of relatively low inequality. Yet at times he clearly means a very different situation—where great inequality of wealth does exist, but wealth is itself inherently uncertain and unstable, and in his language, is being daily acquired and lost. This second case is typical of a capitalist class structure as opposed to a feudal aristocratic one. Sometimes he implies a third and different reading of the same phrase: because great wealth is impermanent, unlike aristocratic society,

this does not create durable social prestige for the high bourgeoisie. They may be more wealthy than former aristocrats, but
they do not enjoy any social pre-eminence due to their wealth;
on the contrary, he could have added, in a general climate of
political egalitarianism, the very insecurity of their wealth in-
vites resentful hostility from lower classes. Capitalist classes,
in this argument, would find it particularly hard to establish
patriarchal relations with subaltern groups.

There are some cautionary points to be made in any use of
Tocqueville's ideas. First, the idea I am taking out of his work is
certainly one of the most powerful and vividly expressed, but
not by any means the only significant one; it is also not wholly
expressive of Tocqueville's 'theory'. Second, in some ways his
theory is so obsessed with democratic transformation that it
then does not pay attention to other strands of modern life or,
illegitimately and misleadingly, reduces them to mere effects of
the democratic principle. Thus it is the primacy thesis underpinning Tocqueville's theory that makes it brilliant and misleading at the same time. It illuminates precisely because it distorts,
it can see the logic of democracy so clearly precisely because it
has subtly introduced a prior bracketing which puts everything
else into abeyance. Within the European condition, there were
several things Tocqueville abstracted from his picture which we
would have to re-integrate: absolutism of the state, aristocratic
society, the strong growth of capitalist economies, etc. It is within
this context that the force of democracy is operating, and that
some structures that democracy is modifying and restructuring,
lie. If we are to learn from his theory, we must look similarly for
the conditions in which the logic of democracy has been introduced in India.

There is a second point which is probably more important for
the present discussion, and that is that there is an exaggeration
at the heart of Tocqueville's thinking, not merely about what democracy causes, but about what democracy is. Clearly, for
Tocqueville, democracy stands for, or symbolizes *all* forms of egalitarian tendencies: not only the formal *political* equality of treatment before the law, but also the *social* and cultural fact of the
loss of prestige of the aristocracy, and the *economic* fact of equality or equal insecurity of condition. These latter two are different
and are constantly invoked by Tocqueville, but somewhat con-

fusingly, either as a single process, or as entirely unavoidable consequences of the introduction of political equality. This way of
thinking leads him to the surely incorrect belief that through
the rise of democracy, economic inequality was beginning to be
modified towards a mean, being reduced at both ends. This picture of a constant reduction in economic inequality is ambiguous between two versions. If it is meant as a reduction of feudal
inequality, the picture is perhaps more persuasive; if it is to be
true against economic inequalities caused by capitalist production, it is surely implausible. Moreover, it is linked to a second,
and in this case correct, observation that although individuals
accumulated great wealth it was volatile and impermanent, because it was not based on landed property and not secured by
legal restrictions; nor did it produce the right conditions for
the creation of durable social prestige. The 'aristocracy' of manufacture could never be like the real aristocracy of landed property. In other words, if the democratic principle is construed as
narrowly political, its consequences would appear different than
if it were given this rather extreme and expansive form. In that
sense, the defect of Tocqueville's theory is the exact reverse of
Marx's. He underrated the disequalizing powers of the capitalist economy and its capacity to modify and often override the
egalitarian principles of formal democracy; Marx underrated the
power of the democratic political institutions and their capacity to impose more egalitarian distributive regimes on societies
against reluctant capitalist classes.

Equality and the Nature of Indian Society

Political principles, including theoretical ones, are invented
through pressures of practice, not deductions from abstract principles. Thus the principles of European and American democracy were aimed at destroying and fundamentally re-ordering
the basic principles of an aristocratic society. I would like to
argue that traditional Indian caste society was not aristocratic
in the strict sense. An aristocratic society, I suggest, is one in
which the various bases of social inequality—ritual-cultural status, control over political power, and over economic means—
tend to be symmetrical and unified. In caste society, there is a
tendency towards differentiation, if not systematic asymmetry,

between these aspects. It is the arrival of colonial power and the opportunities it opened up for the modern colonial élite, which brings into existence something similar to a real aristocracy in the Indian context. Even this process was subject to great regional variation, but the primary implication of this view is that democratic rules and provisions would have to undergo considerable adaptation if they are to attack the types of inequality specific to the Indian social form.

In discussions on the egalitarian principles of democratic politics or the socially egalitarian effects of the democratic principle the idea of democracy, which is a specific enough governmental form, is seen in relation to something quite unspecific and abstract—'social inequality'. The fault with this way of looking at the problem is that it treats inequality as structure-neutral. It speaks about inequality, but in an unhelpfully abstract fashion. Social inequality is always *formed* into a structure of some kind, and caused by the reproduction of specific types of social relations. Inequality can be structured very differently, according to different principles and with different social consequences. The question could in fact be more complicated, if we allow variation on the other end of the relation, to admit variations in democratic governmental forms as well. Purely formal differences, like parliamentary or presidential government, might not have a serious bearing on questions like this (though some would argue that they do: for instance, the attempt by some so-called 'radical' advisors to Indira Gandhi to popularize the idea of a presidential form of government, was based on the expectation that this formal change would facilitate more radical social reform, by making parliament and the courts even more pliant than they were to her orders). Clearly, however, formal distinctions of the kind discussed by Lijphart can have a serious effect on the pace of change, since consensualism would impart greater stability to the political order, but reduce the speed of radical reform by requiring the interlocking consent of a chain of groups. But even if we suspend these institutional differentiations on that side of the equation for the moment, it is important to see the structured nature of social inequality. A purely philosophical discussion would simply reflect on the relation between democratic doctrines and inequality as a principle, although in that kind of discussion, too, the question quickly turns to: an inequality of what? In sociological analysis, that question translates into the problem of the precise configuration of inequality given in a social form. In the Indian context, it would take us into a discussion of how democracy affects inequality structured in two different forms, as *caste* and as *class*.

For historical precedents, which might show us what the long-term social effects of the democratic principle can be, we must turn to the history of Europe. But the body of evidence from European history can be read in significantly divergent ways. To take only the most well-known traditions, there can be a 'necessary extension' thesis, which would assert that the underlying principle of democracy was not merely egalitarian in the political sphere, but that its introduction would *necessarily* extend from the political to the social and economic realms, though there might be a time lag. Following Marx, we can think of a possible, but not necessary, extension from political to social democracy, dependent on revolutionary mass action by the proletariat, to be inevitably obstructed by the bourgeois classes, and the bias built into the institutional structures of capitalist society. Using these distinctions between the application of the principle of egalitarianism to the various spheres (which does not appear entirely unproblematic to me for reasons that cannot be discussed here in detail), [3] we can then also think of a third sceptical line of argument which maintains that democracy is only political equality, and any possible extension of its egalitarianism would distort its logic, turning equality of opportunity towards equality of condition. We could call this a non-extension thesis. The introduction of democracy to any society could yield three distinct possibilities: equality might be established only in the economic sphere, or it might spread from the political to the social, leaving the economic a field of unrestricted inequality; or, the most radical and, in practical terms, the least likely, it might extend from the political to all spheres.

In fact, the problem of eradicating social inequality might raise further and more complex problems. Underlying our Constitution and much of our party politics, is an unstated consensus about how inequality has to be intellectually analysed and practically reduced. Often one significant aspect of this implicit understanding is not taken up for serious discussion. I shall call that a flattening of inequality instead of a structurally specific view of how it functions, and it is surprising to find that even Marxists and others given to a normally historical view of social problems, in essence agree with this approach. Inequalities are flattened if we take them simply taxonomically, and point out that in contemporary Indian society there are the following list of grounds which make people unequal. But each type of inequality might come from a different structural source. Caste inequality is grounded in practices of the caste order; these practices are quite specific, based on observance of restrictions on commensality, marriage, etc., denying access to lower caste groups to education or certain types of social functions, or forcing them to carry on the occupations of their ancestors. Inequality of income in modern sectors is produced by quite a different kind of structural logic: by the rise of industries generated and managed according to capitalist principles. If we take a structural view, we shall be forced to admit that these inequalities emerged at different points of time and, historically, one kind of structure might replace another. But if we believe in a minimally functional view of social systems, it would imply that trying to eradicate all types of social inequality at the same time might not be very promising. Thus the radical Jacobinism underlying our constitutional dispensation and reformist political practice of the Nehruvian era might be mistaken. A more traditional view, on the lines of Russian official Marxism, could argue that reduction of caste inequality might be achieved more efficiently precisely through unrestricted development of a capitalist economy and the labour market, rather than by a process in which the agency of the state tries to work against the structural logic of both capitalist and caste inequality. As evidence, it might be shown that where state-driven reform has been the only instrument of social change, the reduction of inequality has made little headway; whereas in the economic zones which experienced relatively unrestricted capitalist growth, either during the colonial period or after independence, capitalist economic processes have more successfully reduced the effectiveness of caste. It might then be a safer strategy to play one inequality against another rather than try to flatten them in a structure-neutral fashion, and attempt to eradicate them by the

single implement of state action.[4] I do not agree with this thesis, but I wish to suggest that we should not use the conventional structure-neutral treatment of social inequality, but adopt
a more structural and historical understanding instead.

Constitutional Democracy and Inequality

There was a sense in which the constitutional settlement in independent India was based on a form of Jacobinism,[5] a phase
in European history which most political groups admired,
though often for contradictory reasons. What was common to
nearly all branches of opinion in Indian nationalism was the
gesture of accepting and assuming a radical plasticity of the
social; an attitude of radical constructivism about the relations
that constituted society; a belief that all relations active in Indian society could be erased, as it were, and entirely new ones
written down through a heroic, comprehensive, legislative act.
In a sense this act of producing a 'clean slate' originary position, on which acceptable or rationally preferable social principles could then be written, was a precondition required by all
acts of constitutional construction. This idea had two parts: the
first was about the plasticity of the social world and the sovereign powers of the state in bringing patterns of action into being by legislative construction; the second part was constituted
by the pattern of society that was preferred, and sought to be
established in the space thus cleared by the sovereign acts of
the state. On the second point, there were obviously grave differences among political groups; but their very different
programmes presupposed the common idea of unconstrained
constructivism.[6] Communists admired not merely the radicalism of this constructivist attitude, they also wanted to imbue
radical content in the laws which would govern social life. Others, like Nehru or Ambedkar, whose tastes in social engineering were decidedly more moderate, also believed in the
constructivist premise. But there was something peculiar about
this acceptance of the Jacobin attitude in the Indian Constituent Assembly. In Europe the Jacobin gesture usually came from
politicians of the lower classes, the Parisian *sansculottes*, for example. In India, this Jacobinism drew upon traditions which
had been well established during British rule, of invoking the

power of the colonial state to introduce, and at times coercively apply, radical social reform. In cases like the banning of sati or encouraging widow remarriage in early colonial Bengal, social reformers established a tradition of seeking support from the alien state power to drive through reforms in Hindu society. [7] One particular strand of thinking in the Constitution-making process came directly from this social reform tradition, and Ambedkar, oddly situated between the élite and the downtrodden, instinctively resented its implicit elitism. This strand of social reform was also generous in giving away other peoples' privileges. Though these reform proposals were driven by groups, and individuals who usually originated from upper caste groups their fortunes were securely grounded in the professional occupations of the modern sector, and they had little to lose through such acts of apparent self-sacrifice. In fact, one can argue that Jacobinism in this sense produces, by its very extremism, the contrary effect.[8] Precisely by wishing away suspicion and mistrust and the weight of interest and opinion in favour of unjust practices, it mobilizes the opposition and gives a sharp and desperate edge to their hostility, forces them to reorganize, and therefore eventually retards, rather than accelerates, the reforms that it supports intellectually.

Consensualism and Social Reform

The attempt to reform social inequality was made at two different levels. At one level there was the constitutional effort to outline a structure of social relations which would constitute a basic map of everyday social conduct. In this map certain traditional practices were dramatically ruled out. Despite a long and deeply entrenched history of caste practices, practising caste in some forms was made illegal from the morning of 26 January 1950. Similarly, in a society which was still deeply religious, the use of religious considerations in state activities was banned from that day. One interesting question is: how could this kind of revolutionary gesture be made without trouble? The answer must be complex. Because of illiteracy and lack of information, this radical activity of construction was in effect the interior tumult of a small élite club, its historical significance quite different in scale and significance from the celebrated incidents of

European history that it sought to imitate. Thus, upper caste Hindus could happily go on practising untouchability for several decades, if they were in areas distant from the state's control or the media's scrutiny. Everyday discrimination or insult to low caste groups formed a very substantial part of social and political experience till very recently. Some part of the explanation must be in the reason Partha Chatterjee gives in his discussion on secularism. Laws which declared extraordinary changes in Hindu religious practice were in fact passed after the event. These legislative acts did not initiate changes, as in European revolutions, rather they ratified changes which had already been accepted by large parts of Hindu society through internal reform. The evidence of this lies in the dissimilar treatment given to Muslim rules of conduct; since Islamic society in India was strongly opposed to reforms on those lines, the state immediately resiled and gave way.[9] In a way, this illustrated the consensualism underlying Indian democratic politics under the Congress regime. During the national movement, it is easy to show, Congress functioned on the basis of a broadly consensual principle, rather than strict majorities overruling other opinions.[10] After independence, during the Nehru years, this implicit rule of consensus continued. Rajni Kothari's work illuminates how consensualism worked inside the Congress in spite of the formal divide between the government majority and opposition minorities.[11] I think we must supplement Kothari's discussion on the manner of party functioning with an argument about the coalitional nature of class power in Indian political life. It is the specific character of the structure of class power in Indian society which eventually imposes a coalitional logic on the party-political scene.

Experience of electoral politics after the collapse of Congress dominance since the late Eighties does not falsify this argument: it merely shows that the rule of consensualism is always at work, but it can take two forms. If government is controlled by a single party, like the Congress or the Janata after the Emergency, consensual forms operate *inside* the party, not explicitly in the government; if no single party exists which can achieve that result, government itself becomes explicitly a coalitional government, as in the recent cases of the BJP coalition and its predecessor. In fact, the extraordinary example of the BJP failing to form a government even as the largest single party in parliament after the national elections in 1996, indicates how strongly the political culture disapproves of an explicitly homogenizing, anti-coalitional politics based on unqualified majoritarianism.

Significantly, the Constitution abolished some forms of social inequality, and not others. Although a result of contentious debate and often uneasy compromise,[12] it eventually accepted a structural, not a flat, view of inequality. Untouchability was explicitly outlawed; practice of caste in other ways merely discouraged. Continuance of marriage within caste could not be similarly outlawed by the Constitution because it fell within the circle of private decisions implicitly conceded by constitutional provisions. This highlighted an interesting paradox: in some instances, a decision actually based on caste considerations could be passed off as a result of personal preference. By contrast, the right to property, the legal recognition of capitalist class inequality, was not seriously curbed.[13] Communists were therefore right in denouncing Nehru for taking a 'capitalist' path, despite the misleading official rhetoric of a 'socialist pattern of society'. The consigning of demands for economic equality directed against the capitalist principle into the Directive Principles of State Policy, might also indicate a deeply evolutionary belief on the part of the Nehruvian élite about how societies progress. They could well have believed that with the expansion and entrenchment of a capitalist economy, demands for economic equality would gain strength and lead to an historic shift in legal structures. However, at the time of Independence, legal institution of more egalitarian rules would have been premature. The general phrasing of the provisions in the Constitution reveals an interesting, but for its time, typical, treatment of problems of gender inequality: most of the provisions dealing with equality denounce differential treatment on the basis of race, caste, sex and language, but the reference to gender is basically part of a general rhetoric. The Constitution is almost entirely blind to the fact that gender inequality might require treatment exactly parallel to caste.[14] It does ensure equal treatment before the law, but undertakes no serious exertion to reduce or eradicate forms of unequal treatment known to exist in society.[15] Thus the nature of the constitutional settlement, what it seeks to achieve and what it deliberately leaves alone, can be understood at least in significant part, by paying attention to the implicit consensualism of decision-making inside the Congress party, and in the Constituent Assembly. It did not function by the rule of the majority as commonly understood, but by implicitly consociational principles, as did the Congress party afterwards. In legal terms, the Constitution consistently abolishes discrimination on the basis of 'race, caste, sex and religion', occasionally adding to this list, language and descent, which in structural terms are all directed against social, but not economic inequality.

Clearly, however, this is only part of the relation between democracy and social inequality, since by 'democracy' in ordinary language is meant at least two different things. It means first a fundamental constitutional order based on political equality which is meant to be inflexible and constant. But it also refers to a fluid everyday electoral process and its long-term tendencies. The question of the relation between democracy and social inequality must therefore be broken up into two: how the constitutional arrangement settles it, and how it is addressed by the electoral process. It is particularly important to see the question this way, to bring in the second, more sociological aspect, precisely because the relation between legality and social life in India is vastly different from that of the West. The second question, then, is twofold: can electoral democracy be said to have a long-term *historical* tendency? If it does, is this, as was widely believed, towards greater social equality?

Nehruvian ideology, which drove the high echelons of the Congress, clearly thought of democracy and electoral politics as part of a general functionalist logic of modernity. The processes of industrialization, on this view, tended inevitably to break down traditional solidarities like caste. The experience of electoral democracy was supposed, independently, to go in the same direction. All these discrete processes of modernity were expected to corrode traditional social structures and reinforce each other and the most fundamental process of a modern society, which was presupposed by all: individuation. Nehru was evidently entirely clear about the process of individuation being the basis of all other processes like industrialization and electoral politics. But what has actually happened has really confounded the Nehruvian ideology of social progress. From that perspective some features of present-day political reality in India would appear strangely contradictory, some trends shockingly retrograde, others astonishingly 'progressive'. It is impossible to make sense of what has really happened in Indian political life through the dichotomous models of modernity and tradition that lay at the centre of the Nehruvian world view.

Adaptability of Traditions

The progressivist ideology that dominated political thinking and practice in the Fifties seriously underrated the capacity of traditions to deal with historical change. There was in this sense a strong parallel between Nehruvian ideology and most academic modernization theories. They commonly misunderstood the nature of tradition, construing it to be primarily stagnant and unable to change. Successful traditions in fact demonstrate just the opposite: traditional structures maintain themselves for long periods precisely because of their flexibility in the face of historical change.[16] If we adopt a different view of tradition, mistrust its rhetoric of immutability and acknowledge its enormous capacity for structural adaptation, the actual historical process need not appear utterly inexplicable. In retrospect, it is not surprising that authors sceptical of the progressivist dichotomies of modernization theory were the first to discern the perplexing trends in electoral politics.[17] Caste groups, instead of crumbling with historical embarrassment,[18] in fact, adapted themselves surprisingly well to the demands of parliamentary politics. Congress itself had to submit to the pressure of instant electoral mobilization a year after the Constitution came into force, and faced three possibilities regarding the manner in which the electorate could be mobilized. First, and most improbable, was that they would be mobilized, like intellectuals, by the power of theoretical ideas. Second, they could mobilize themselves in terms of modern interest groups—as classes, in other words—which they did, wherever the historical conditions existed. But such pockets were very few quite and small. Thus, electoral mobilization, once the great unifying, ideological language of anti-colonialism became redundant, could take place only on the basis of the principles of the electorate's everyday self-recognition embedded in rural social practice, based on the logic of caste. So the use of caste in electoral mobilization was not, in retrospect, that surprising. But such mobilization immediately brought a new element into caste practice: in a curious sense, all caste groups acquired immediate political significance. Electoral politics thus altered the structural properties of caste in one fundamental respect: it created a 'democracy' of castes in place of a 'hierarchy'. For political parties, what was significant was their numbers and their spatial concentration, rather than their social status in the traditional ranking order. This was a wholly untraditional and modern use of the power of caste; instead of restricting groups to their traditional occupations and their relative status level in a hierarchy, this allowed them to deploy their numerical strength in electoral support for parties and candidates. To the extent castes were able to respond to this electoral need, they created for themselves a meaningful place in the modern political world. Thus, the way Nehru posed the alternatives was proved false.[19]

The institutional order within which Indian democracy had to function had some internal difficulties, although it seems incorrect to see them as inconsistencies or legal design faults. Rather these were compromises and concessions imposed by the peculiar circumstances of an independence marred by Partition. In the discourse of politics which developed through the nationalist movement, there was no serious defence or elaboration of liberal principles.[20] After the moderate constitutionalists, whose influence was swept aside by the extremists and later by Gandhi, no serious liberal and individualist political position was argued out consistently or acquired much influence. Rather, the two lines of argument which became widely influential were the idiosyncratic positions of Gandhi and various forms of leftism, which were both generally critical of individualism. Significantly, those in the national movement who were critical of Gandhi and the Left themselves showed little sympathy for liberal or individualist political thinking, favouring instead the idea that religious communities should be considered the fundamental political actors. Given this context of political discourse, the legal structure of the Constitution was a surprising one, since a large part of its fundamental principles and technical legal apparatus presuppose a liberal–individualist understanding of democratic politics.[21] The Constitution introduced some types of rights and legal provisions which recognized communities as bearers of rights. The fact that many of these provisions were meant to continue for strictly specified periods is evidence of the Constitution-makers' belief that these were situational adjustments; equally, the fact of the indefinite continuation of these provisions in actual practice shows that the society for which they legislated failed to think as they did.

Electoral Democracy and Inequality

Usually, when we refer to democratic forms, we mean two different aspects of institutions: the constitutional structure setting down permanent rules; and the electoral process and flux of everyday politics. Although the constitutional and electoral levels of democratic politics are distinct, there has to be a reciprocity between them, established through common understanding generated and upheld by quotidian political practice. The constitutional provisions securing minority rights and special advantages were formulated in a language which implied they were impermanent; but electoral practice often belied this. The exact character of the electoral appeal of the Congress to minority religious groups altered over time. Nehru was quite explicit and undefensive about the special protection needed by the Muslim minority in India after Partition; and the support of the Muslim vote for the Congress under Nehru could be defended by those strictly conjunctural arguments. Subsequently, however, Congress appeal to the minority vote cut loose from specific historical arguments and often degenerated into a distinctly less highminded search for permanent group loyalty in elections. This could not work efficiently if Muslims did not feel a certain vague but endemic insecurity. However, it is important to keep in mind that during the Nehru period, the question of social equality was quite central to ideological debates between main political parties. Communists, who rather surprisingly became the largest opposition group in parliament after the first general elections, construed that to mean inequalities of class and income. The response of the Congress to this criticism by fashioning the Avadhi resolution calling for a 'socialistic pattern of society' also clearly implied the same reading of the problem. Historically, however, political democracy appeared an unsuitable, or at least an ineffective, instrument in the cause of reducing class inequality. It became quite obvious fairly early in the history of the republic that the Congress under Nehru was unlikely to take serious initiatives in this direction. The communists, in retrospect, showed limited political imagination, confining themselves to voluble opposition to Nehru's policies instead of making seriously costed egalitarian policy suggestions. From the late Seventies, when communist governments enjoyed relatively long incumbencies in state governments, and a nearly permanent one in West Bengal, their policies showed very limited imagination about the strategies by which economic inequality could be reduced. Interestingly, by the Seventies, through increasing assertion of caste politics, the question of 'social inequality' came to stand almost exclusively for disadvantage based on caste rather than class.

A more striking example of the effect of democracy on social inequality could be found in the politics of caste. Often, the use of caste appeal in constituencies with a distinct caste majority was self-defeating in terms of strict electoral arithmetic, because all parties would normally nominate candidates from the same caste, cancelling out advantage for any one of them. Conversely, any party trying out a heroically idealist strategy of nominating a candidate from a different, locally undominant caste was bound to suffer. Under conditions of endemic caste rivalries, most parties played safe. Ironically, though this may have failed to secure any immediate advantage to any single party in a specific election, it legitimized the practice of caste-politics as a general democratic principle. Such electoral practices in everyday democratic politics made it impossible for the long-term trend to move unambiguously in the direction desired by Nehru, Ambedkar and other Constitution-makers. The nationalist movement was, apart from other things, a gigantic pedagogic process, in which ideas about how to look at and handle the political world were being constantly generated and disseminated through mass politics: meetings, demonstrations, discussions, calls upon people to act. The mobilizational politics of nationalism urged people to act in ways strikingly different from the segmentation and community-orientation in their daily life. With the arrival of independence, this immense pedagogic process falls silent, and because of the startling neglect of ordinary education in the Nehruvian development project, it is not replaced by any other expedient. Undoubtedly, a 'public spere' of the circulation and disputation of opinions on the fundamental constitution of society developed through the Nehru years, mainly through English-language national newspapers and journals. By the Seventies, this upper class public sphere was being slowly overtaken by a much wider circle of active interest expressed in politics by ordinary people who were outside this highly restrictive 'public opinion'. The sociological constitution of these groups is quite different, and their life-conditions sometimes considerably unstable. As this new 'public sphere' of social groups with much more heterogenous educational, social and cognitive compositions comes into being, its internal processes of operation are also bound to be utterly different. It was immediately apparent how different this political universe was in its political discourse—its rhetoric, its stock of information, its historical memory, its vernacular language. One of the most striking features of this discourse, which makes it utterly different from the discourse of high nationalism, is that it does not have a ready 'memory' of western history. Above all, the fragmentation of this political public sphere made it impossible for the traditional political élite to address all its segments and to perform its earlier functions of pedagogic instruction or public opinion formation. Even if the nationalist élites had the will to lecture their fellow citizens about the rules of modern behaviour, they had lost the means. It is interesting to note how segments of Nehruvian political opinion which still remain are confined to a mediating function between various regionally entrenched groups. They have lost the capacity to impose their model of politics on others; but they are still crucial in playing an essential role in mediating between groups with more regional, or often purely local, political horizons. Under these conditions, they simply do not have the capacity to set the terms of political discourse any more.

Quotidian democratic politics, however much we try to confute its majoritarian reading, brings into play a relentless search for contextual majorities, and thus creates a general potential for the mobilization of all possible social groups, not just the 'modern' ones. Actual electoral politics of the parties, particularly at the intermediate level of states and districts, had recourse to common peoples' everyday self-understanding in terms of caste for gathering voter support. The intensity of electoral democracy, therefore, contrary to the framers' historical beliefs, constantly reconfirmed ordinary people's community-orientations instead of undermining them. Gradually, the language of expressing grievances in terms of 'peoples' rights' became increasingly common, but the normal bearers of these rights were seen to be *primary* groups rather than individuals.[22] Since society outside the cities did not experience substantial sociological individuation, even grievances in everyday life about which political agencies were called upon to act—to demand preference, or redressal of ill-treatment—were expressed commonly in terms of group rights and discriminations.

Other institutional mechanisms also served to reinforce these identities. As the state was a main provider of employment, both high and low, reservation of jobs provided by the Constitution became a major channel for upward social mobility. The character of economic development in India, with its huge reliance on the state, made this tendency particularly strong. The protection and possible expansion of these employment avenues for the relevant groups began to occupy a central place in party political conflict. Political parties directly based on caste identities are sometimes blamed for this trend, unfairly, in my opinion. Indistinct caste-based policies were often pursued by Congress politicians in the years when their electoral dominance had not been threatened. The internal politics of Congress state organizations were already riven by caste-based political rivalries between chief ministerial candidates in many areas. The establishment of political parties directly interested in reservation politics merely brought this trend into the open. For several distinct reasons, and in several ways, the functioning of state institutions in India slowly worked towards a persistent reinforcement of caste identities instead of their erasure, as the framers of the Constitution had planned.

The intensification of caste politics has led to several interesting and unforeseen consequences. Conventional wisdom expected electoral politics, parallel to industrial economic practices, to break down and erase patterns of caste action, and increasingly produce an equality between individuals, irrespective of caste origins. The conventional view was right in anticipating that an aspiration towards equality was to be articulated through political democracy, but it was wrong in expecting that the operation of political institutions would lead to strong individuation. In fact, while caste practice declined in its traditional arenas of social behaviour, like commensality and marriage, it was given a powerful new life by electoral politics, where people started to claim equality *on the basis of* caste, without giving up their caste identity. The equality or dignity that caste politicians like Kanshi Ram or Laloo Prasad Yadav demand is not as individuals, irrespective of their caste, but emphatically as members of their caste. It is unprofitable to speculate about how intellectuals like Nehru would have responded to contemporary caste-based politics: they might have deplored its strident casteism and aggressive assertion of the difference between various groups, instead of a liberal, individualistic stripped-down equality; at the same time, they ought to be happy about the democratic, that is, egalitarian character of this politics. Caste politics in one sense has merely transposed to its own level the rules of equal treatment and equality of opportunity. Democratic equality has been mainly translated as equality between caste groups, not among caste-less individuals. Makers of the Constitution dreamt of a future of equality without caste; we might eventually have an unexpected historical stage of the equality of castes.

The reason for this apparently strange development is not difficult to understand. Electoral politics turns basically on numbers: political parties and groups naturally try to mobilize existing group loyalties or try to create new ones through political campaigns. Groups can vary according to their numbers, stability of membership and internal cohesion. Olson's work pointed out an inverse relation between numbers and cohesiveness.[23] In India, we have to inflect and modify this insight to include the peculiar nature of membership of individuals into caste groups. First, caste membership is not merely one of identity in the ordinary sense; because of the strong connection between caste affiliation and productive roles, it contains a powerful element of interest. Although appeals to caste and religion are both correctly regarded as examples of identity politics, it must be seen that caste has a much stronger and plausible relation with economic interest. Second, because of its stability (permanence) it imparts a strong cohesion to the group's perception of self-interest, unless industrialization dissolves these ties. Loyalties or affiliation to groups can be of two different types (to use classical sociology) according to whether these are primary or secondary groups, *communities* or *associations*. In classical western theory, the problem did not arise so prominently because of the specific historical sequence of western modernity. Capitalist industrialization transformed societies into vast fields of associational interest-based activity, the realm of the 'civil society'—at least that was what classical historical sociology wanted us to believe. In any case, it is not surprising that it is in Pareto, writing in relatively backward Italy, that we find the idea that the arrival of democracy brings into play both types of social groups, based on different forms of solidarity. In his writings on 'demagogic plutocracy' Pareto observed the different character of these two types of groups and their consequences for democracy, calling them 'aggregates' and 'combinations'.[24] Combinations, or class-based groups, suffer the obvious disadvantage of impermanence in two senses: the individuals constituting groups keep changing, and the groups themselves in their structure, solidarity and power, tend to depend on the volatile forces of a modern economy. In a society like modern India, the social and economic conditions in which 'classes' can form are particularly complex. It is in relatively small parts of the country that class-based combinations can be used by parties involved in democratic politics.[25] By comparison, Pareto's 'aggregates'—or caste-identifications in our case—are permanent, and since these are explicit and not latent, it requires little extra effort to bring them to self-consciousness. To play on a Marxian locution, there is no objective caste which is not a subjective caste. If such affiliations can be mobilized, their force in democratic politics is obvious.

This however brings us back to the conflict between participation and procedure: caste majorities are by nature permanent, and obviously any permanent majority would make democracy unbearable for other groups. This is precisely the paradox of the Mandal Commission politics: although it begins with arguments of social justice, it succumbs too easily and quickly to the strong temptation of a relentless majoritarianism.[26] Ironically, this shift to the majoritarian argument immediately incites responding to majoritarian ideas, particularly the vicious attempt to trump it with the alleged aspirations of the Hindu majority, to which the BJP has mysterious and privileged access. No doubt the primary purpose of this politics is to attack and render impossible the practice of social inequality in a particularly odious form; yet the manner in which it seeks to do so goes against one of the major principles of democracy. It is also quite clear that in some cases, like the administrations of Laloo Prasad or Mulayam Singh Yadav (as in the earlier precedent of Indira Gandhi) there is a tendency to use the logic of social reform against democratic *form*, in a way Tocqueville anticipated, leading to situations that come close to elective despotism, justified in the name of impatience for reform.

Several problems arising out of this democratic conflict for equality have become increasingly apparent in India. At times, it appears that the object of these political forces after capturing state power, is not to secure equality in the strict sense by opening the gates of opportunity to formerly disadvantaged groups, but to close them to other groups who have traditionally enjoyed dominance. It can be argued that often, because of the entrenchment of vested interests, this is the only way of securing greater access for backward groups, and eventually achieving equality. Nehru's thinking behind the introduction of reservations was clearly to enable backward groups to catch up with others: 'therefore, not only must equal opportunities be given to all, but special opportunities for educational, economic and cultural growth must be given to backward groups to enable them to catch up to those who are ahead of them'.[27] Interestingly, however, one aspect of such democratic power has been to deny access to others, rather than make it universal. Given the decline of the culture of consensualism and the fragmentation of a public sphere of debate in which such social principles are debated and generally accepted, dominant social groups take recourse to policies calculated to defend their advantage. This might intensify the upper class–caste groups' support for two types of policies in the economic and political spheres. They are likely to support policies of economic liberalization, wrenching large sectors of industrial employment out of the state's control and handing them over to the unrestricted market, which is bound to distribute opportunities disproportionately in their favour. This can be supplemented by support, in party politics, to the BJP which is the most powerful force opposing caste-based reservations. Although in the short term, the BJP is hostile to policies of liberalization, in the longer term, the logic of social support might reconcile them to these. Already there is some evidence in electoral statistics for a trend towards this kind of convergence in voting profiles.

There is another peculiarity of Indian democracy which takes it in an illiberal direction. Since the state is regarded by both Nehruvian reformists and populist politicians as the primary agency for creating equality, the pressure of democracy has para-doxically led to a constant increase in the powers of the state. The state is seen as an agency supporting equality for two reasons: first, in purely juridical terms, it is the legislature which has the power to enact reform legislations, and the executive to implement them; second, since the state is the major provider of employment, enlargement of the economic orbit under its control helps translate such legislation into reality. The discourse of this democratic force does not propose an encirclement of the state by an active, oppositional, constantly vigilant 'civil society'; on the contrary, it justifies expansion of the powers of the state, and sometimes shows scant respect for juridical re-straint in the name of the urgency of the reforms it undertakes. Analyses of Indian politics should pay more careful attention to the precarious balance between the *elective* and other aspects of democratic politics and procedure. Elections are surely an im-mensely significant element in the procedural structure of de-mocracy but there are other, equally significant procedural and deliberative aspects. An overvaluation of the elective side can lead to a collapse of confidence in the entire structure if politi-cians persist in the idea that elections are essential, because the party that gets the electoral mandate has the right to disregard legal rules.[28] It is particularly important to note a strong recent trend to argue, in cases of important appointments, that people belonging to a particular caste can only trust politicians or offi-cials from the same community. This might seem a plausible, even defensible, measure coming from disadvantaged groups; but it must be recognized that extension of such an argument would completely undermine impersonal rules of the operation of political power. It will make trust wholly segmentary, and make it impossible to run a modern democratic polity. To associate trustworthiness with individuals and their social identity implies a corresponding lack of confidence in trust working through impersonal institutions. This creates a sociologically unprecedented situation: instead of the segmentation of society in small, local groups it ushers in a period of segmentation into immense cross-regional entities. Persistent clashes between these groups might create a situation where the implicit assumption of western democratic forms adopted in the Constitution—that the majorities and minorities would be shuffling, impermanent and fluid rather than fixed—would become defunct.

Limits to Caste Mobilization

Already, however, some limits of this kind to caste politics can be seen fairly clearly. The election of Laloo Prasad Yadav or Mayawati has of course been of immense symbolic value for Indian society. It marks a decisive step ahead from the cultural presuppositions of the Seventies, when a politician of the stature of Jagjivan Ram could not be given a position of highest eminence for no other discernible reason than an implicit upper caste consensus against him. Yet, in some ways, the politics of reform that Jagjivan Ram represented, now replaced by the politics of challenge exemplified by Kanshi Ram or Laloo Prasad Yadav, had greater historical importance. An enormous amount of the energy of the new politics of the disadvantaged is spent in symbolic acts of retaliation which have increasingly tended to replace substantive measures directed against inequalities. State-funded statues of Ambedkar in every Indian village might give Dalit politics greater prestige, but does nothing to alter the structural bases of privilege in education, health and other opportunities, which serve to reproduce the inequalities against which the politics of the lower castes is directed. Ambedkar or Jagjivan Ram, presumably, would not have been satisfied with the symbolic humiliation of upper caste officials, or display of regal and courtly grandeur coupled with a quasi-absolutist contempt for procedures. If we divide the process of distribution into two and call some of these, access goods, the argument might become clearer. There is a level of distribution in income, honour, capital, power and so on, to individuals and groups constituting current society. But in the longer term, this is implicitly determined by other goods, by means of which access to these goods can be achieved—for example, education, health, literacy, etc. —and on which they ultimately depend. Politics of lower caste assertion has, in a sense, retreated from a more mundane reformism to a spectacular exchange of symbolic acts. Symbolic exchanges do not have the power to affect the level of primary distribution of access goods, concentrating on a spectacular redistribution of prestige on a very small scale. Thus this politics can create enormous spectator interest through the parliament and media, but the satisfaction drawn by lower caste groups is primarily symbolic and episodic. It does not touch the institutional sources which reproduce inequality in society. During the Nehru years the powers of the state were constantly increasing, along with its resources, though there is clear evidence that the state did very little to remove inequalities of either type, leading to the breakdown of trust in impersonal institutions. But symbolic politics of this kind is likely to prove equally ineffective, precisely because resources and legal authority to act upon these sectors are being wrenched from the state's grip. The more education and health are prised away from the control of the state in the process of liberalization, the more unequal their distribution is likely to become. The political equality of democracy would then lose its capacity to exert pressure towards social equality.

Capitalism and Democracy

To return to some of the themes mentioned in the first part of the paper: although the strategy for reduction of inequality appeared structure-neutral and, therefore, directed at both social and economic inequality, in fact the institutions of free India treated them differentially. Constitutional provisions contributed to the amelioration of caste practices in two different ways. They directly prohibited particularly egregious practices like untouchability, and instituted greater access to access goods through reservations in education. But the indirect effects of constitutional provisions were probably more far-reaching: by designating them as Scheduled Castes, instituting a new political category, these provisions encouraged a politics of electoral consolidation. Through electoral politics and by an increasing assertion of low caste groups, traditional caste discrimination has been reduced even further. Without any doubt, this has been one of the great successes of Indian democracy, but it appears to me to have been accomplished at a certain cost. Economic inequality generated by the expansion of capitalist production has faded from the centre of equality debates. Two different forces, emanating from different directions and using very different arguments, are creating a discursive climate suited to the rapid development of capitalist inequality. Although the recent politics of the BJP do not appear to explicitly support capitalist ideology, its hostility to affirmative action assists classes which are better placed in the distribution of access goods. Alongside, increasing pressure towards liberalization will tend to force the state to abandon the provision of these opportunities to poorer social groups. Privatization of these sectors would enlarge and intensify the inequalities in health and education that already exist. If we consider the distinction between these two types of social inequality relevant, then the historical lessons of Indian democracy are very interesting. Social inequality of the traditional type—the Indian equivalent of Tocqueville's aristocratic privilege—has been seriously undermined by the power of democratic politics; but the logic of democracy has not seriously opposed the logic of capitalist development and inequalities associated with that process.

Notes

[1] Alexis de Tocqueville, *Democracy in America*, Vol. I, p. 14.

[2] Arend Lijphart, *Democracies*, (New Haven: Yale University Press), 1984.

[3] The reason for that primarily is that concepts like the *economy*—or indeed *society* in the narrower and specific sense in which they begin to be used in Europe from the seventeenth century onwards—are historically specific. There is no reason to believe that these are wired into human minds transcendentally; and everywhere human beings would spontaneously think of segments of human life as these spheres. Conceiving a special sphere of reality called the 'economy' facilitates or makes possible some types of practices which are now considered to be autonomous, with their own laws, interference with which is thought to cause unspecified but horrendous damage to the life of society. While this line of reasoning is quite consistent and widespread

in the modern West, there is no reason to believe that social actors in all societies would use these precise distinctions.

[4] It should be noted that the tendency to translate inequality exclusively into deprivation is not always analytically, or even practically, helpful. For instance, caste inequality is hard to grasp by this conceptual grid unless it is expressed in terms of material disadvantage. It is true that Scheduled Caste groups would normally also be economically and educationally backward compared to others. But one can imagine a situation where two castes, scheduled and non-scheduled, may have very similar economic or deprivation levels; yet to treat them as equal victims of inequality would be grossly wrong, since the first would be victims of untouchability taboos, the second not.

[5] I am not using the term here to stress what is central to Gramsci's use, or the entire Marxist tradition, which emphasizes the social radicalism of this strand of thought and practice, their willingness to go to the most extreme steps to attain the revolutionary ends they wished to achieve. I wish to emphasize a different aspect of their political imagination: the idea that social relations through and inside which people lived could be radically altered by a deliberate willed action, reflected in the etymology of constitutionalism.

[6] For instance, the phrasing of Ambedkar's valedictory address to the Indian Constituent Assembly, and similarly, Jinnah's statement in his inaugural address to the Pakistan CA, declaring that from now on people are 'no longer Hindus or Muslims'. This is particularly astonishing coming from someone who played on the power of religious sentiments so crucially, yet considered these forces to be surprisingly resistible. When he wanted these forces to go back home, he clearly thought as did Nehru that they would obey his command.

[7] I do not wish to be misunderstood on this point. I am not at all suggesting that these reforms were imposed by a colonial power against universal opposition from Bengali society. On the contrary, colonial authorities were often hesitant, persuaded eventually by enthusiastic Hindu reformers. Nor did those who wish to introduce reform rely exclusively on the support of the colonial state. Each of these reforms was intensely disputed in the emerging vernacular public sphere. Eventual legal reform was first preceded by considerable open controversy, and usually had the support of a sizable part of the native élite society.

[8] There is an argument that is quite similar in Francine Frankel, 'Compulsion and Social Change in India'. It raises a whole host of other, difficult questions which ought to be discussed. My own feeling is that its predominantly economic view of inequality makes it susceptible to some of the criticism I have made earlier, though I did not get time to think about these things carefully. Broadly, I feel a sociological

appreciation of these problems, followed by a comparison with Frankel's more economic view could be highly instructive. Cf. Frankel, in Kohli (ed.), *The State and Development in the Third World* (Princeton: Princeton University Press, 1986.) Her criticisms of Myrdal's apparently 'radical' attitude of impatience should be analysed more seriously. I also believe that her line of argument comes very close to the differences Nehru expressed with more radical groups like the communists. But at the heart of Myrdal's thesis lies a confusion about the question of legality. A democratic state need not be a soft state; at least the 'softness' of the state does not derive from its democracy as Myrdal rather casually suggested, but from other sources, probably the *consensualism* of democracy, rather than democracy itself.

[9] Partha Chatterjee, 'Secularism and Toleration', *Economic and Political Weekly*, 9 July 1994.

[10] It is important to remember the famous exceptions, like Gandhi's obstinate refusal to be reconciled to Subhas Chandra Bose's majority; but despite these aberrations, it remains true that Congress decision-making followed broadly consensual principles.

[11] Rajni Kothari, *Politics in India* (Delhi: Orient Longman), 1970, Chapter 5.

[12] The debates in the Constituent Assembly on the legal arrangements about the justiciability of rights are highly instructive in this regard, because they show the divergent ideological positions being argued in their relatively pure forms, as well as the eventual shape these principles assume as a result of political compromise.

[13] The abolition of Article 31 and the relevant interconnected clause from Article 19 of the Constitution by subsequent amendments created a peculiar disjuncture between reality and legality. I feel it is dangerous to use the Constitution like an election manifesto—to include into its clauses formally legal principles which are at serious variance with actual social practice. I can understand the argument that such declarations announce a weak value consensus in the political system, but fear that it is in fact too weak to be read that way. It is more likely to give rise to the idea, particularly dangerous in a democracy, that rules included in the Constitution need not always be taken as literally enforceable. I acknowledge that this particular case about the right to property might not be specially vicious because it is a negative enactment—repealing a right, rather than installing one. But the brutish good health of Indian capitalism is difficult to reconcile with the fact that the Constitution does not guarantee a right to property.

[14] This is an evidently anachronistic criticism directed at the document, which simply reflected the context of political arguments of its time. But as a Constitution, precisely because of its importance, it contains

expedients making its alteration extraordinarily difficult; this becomes a particularly troublesome anomaly.

[15] However, the Nehru administration did introduce serious changes in the legal status of women in some important respects, like inheritance of property, by changes in the Hindu laws.

[16] It must be noted that Nehru uses both views of a tradition in his own writing. In the *Discovery of India* (Bombay: Asia Publishing House), 1972, at various points, the suppleness of the caste system is observed. However, when it comes to the large ideological reflexes, he falls back into the thesis that traditions are entirely static.

[17] Kothari, *Politics in India*, op. cit, Lloyd I. Rudolph and Susanne H. Rudolph, *The Modernity of Tradition* (Chicago: University of Chicago Press), 1968.

[18] Note Nehru's awkward but significant phrase: they are 'incompatible' (presumably with the zeitgeist, the spirit of the times,) he talks about in the same paragraph in *Discovery*, p. 521.

[19] 'In the context of society today, the caste system and much that goes with it are wholly incompatible(?), reactionary, restrictive, and barriers to progress. There can be no equality in status and opportunity within its framework, nor can there be political democracy and, much less, economic democracy. *Between these two conceptions conflict is inherent and only one of them can survive.*' (Nehru, *Discovery of India*, p. 257, emphasis mine.) But at other places in the same work, Nehru had a somewhat different view of caste as 'flexible and expanding', and capable of historical adaptation (p. 251). 'Somehow the new, though very different, appears in terms of pre-existing patterns, and thus creates a feeling of a continuous development from the past, a link in the long chain in the history of the race. Indian history is a striking record of changes introduced in this way, *a continuous adaptation of old ideas to a changing environment*, old patterns to the new.' (p. 517, emphasis mine).

[20] This does not mean that Indians were unfamiliar with principles of liberalism. The interesting historical fact is that liberal ideas spread into the Indian intelligentsia in the early phase of modern Indian culture. The Bengali intelligentsia of the mid-19th century read the works of Mill and Spencer with keen interest. The arguments for reform of Hindu society advanced by the progressive intelligentsia drew on rationalist critiques of Hindu religious orthodoxy. Liberal ideas exerted the greatest influence on the political ideas and activities of the 'moderate' constitutional nationalists. After the turn of the century, liberal–individualist ideas were subjected to serious criticism from two directions—Gandhi, and various strands of socialism. It is clear however that Nehru, unlike the communists, always regarded socialism as an extension of the political principles of liberalism.

[21] This was largely due to Nehru's understanding of socialism which was viewed as an extension, rather than an overcoming, of liberal practices.

[22] We are simply going with the general belief that secondary groups do not have harmful effects for democratic principles.

[23] Mancur Olson, *The Logic of Collective Action* (Cambridge: Harvard University Press), 1965.

[24] Vilfredo Pareto, *Selected Writings* (ed. S. E. Finer) (Oxford: Blackwell), 1966, p. 316.

[25] Though I think the success of the CPI(M) in rural West Bengal after 1977 has shown that class politics of a certain kind need not be confined only to urban and industrialized areas, I can immediately see that a counter-argument can claim that the influence of communists does not necessarily indicate class politics, and that the secret of the CPI(M)'s success in West Bengal is its ability to keep its class inclinations in check.

[26] Strictly speaking this might not be correct about the Commission's actual report, which begins by making a social justice case, but loses nerve and often seeks to firm it up by crudely majoritarian arguments. Unfortunately, however, the translation of the more careful Mandal Commission line has been into popular politics by politicians who use the second type of reasoning much more than the first.

[27] *Discovery of India,* p. 521.

[28] Once more it must be remembered that such trends were first shown by Indira Gandhi's Congress party and not by the present state governments of U.P. and Bihar. In our political commentary, there is a decided preference for English-speaking authoritarianism over more vernacular forms, reflected in recent times in the much greater hostility to the elevation of Rabri Devi to the post of chief minister, compared to the idea of bringing in Sonia Gandhi to the leadership of the Congress.

Understanding the Second Democratic Upsurge: trends of bahujan participation in electoral politics in the 1990s

YOGENDRA YADAV

This paper has a very limited ambition. It examines the available evidence to understand the changing nature of political participation in India in the 1990s. In particular, it disaggregates the turnout and other participation related figures in terms of regions and different social groups. Analysts of political participation have usually drawn their inferences either from the aggregate data on electoral turnout or from survey data on political behaviour. This paper brings both types of data, along with survey evidence on participation-related attitudes, together.

This decade—known and remembered both in popular and academic literature for its governmental instability, rise of coalition politics, decline of the Congress and rise of the BJP, and the subterranean politics of economic liberalization—has witnessed a fundamental though quiet transformation, best characterized as the 'second democratic upsurge'. Although overall turnout figures have not increased dramatically, the social composition of those who vote and take part in political activities has undergone a major change. There is a participatory upsurge among the socially underprivileged, whether seen in terms of caste hierarchy, economic class, gender distinction or the rural–urban divide. They do not lag behind the socially privileged as they did in the past; indeed in some respects they are more active today than the former. If this is true, this profile differs not only from India's own past but also from that of most existing democracies for which we have information. It also does not square with the dominant ways of making sense of Indian politics. As such, the limited point this paper makes may have deeper implications for our understanding of contemporary

Indian democracy; it concludes by reflecting on what those implications might be.

In characterizing this change as the 'second democratic upsurge', the point of reference is the decade of the 1960s which, by all accounts, marked the first democratic upsurge following the establishment of Indian democracy. Its basic thrust was towards an expansion of the participatory base of Indian democracy. Voter turnout went up at all levels as political competition became serious and alternatives to the one-party dominance of the Congress began emerging. There were some signs of the deepening of political participation as well, as 'lower' castes began to enter the world of politics. The second upsurge intensifies this downward thrust and involves in it nearly all the groups that suffer from one form of social deprivation and backwardness or another. Bahujan, a word drawn from the political vocabulary of the contemporary dalit movement, offers a better description of these diverse social groups than any concept drawn from modern social science. In its current usage it includes dalit, adivasi, Other Backward Castes (OBC) and all the minorities, but not women or the poor; the political scope of the concept allows, and in fact requires, us to expand its usage to include all other victim communities of social deprivation.[1]

National and Regional Turnout Patterns

If we focus our attention only on the aggregate turnout in parliamentary elections (Table 1), we are unlikely to find clear evidence for a democratic upsurge. Since much analytical attention is paid at this level, the upsurge at the lower levels and beneath the deceptive aggregates has been ignored by most analysts. After a steady rise in the first two decades of competitive politics, turnout in the Lok Sabha elections reached a plateau around the 1967 elections. There is no clear growth, or even clear pattern, discernible after that, except that the 'normal' elections after the Lok Sabha completed its full term (1977, 1984, 1989, and 1996) tended to attract a higher turnout than the mid-term elections (1971, 1980, 1991). However, the 1998 mid-term poll has upset this trend as well by recording an even higher turnout than the 'normal' election of 1996. It may be premature to read the rise in aggregate national turnout in 1998 as the

Table 1: Turnout in Lok Sabha and major assembly elections, 1952–1998

Lok Sabha elections		Major state assembly elections		
Year	Turnout (%)	Year	No. of states	Turnout (%)
1952	45.7	1952	22	46
1957	47.7	1957	13	48
1962	55.4	1960–62	15	58
1967	61.3	1967	20	61
1971	55.3	1971–72	21	60
1977	60.4	1977–78	24	59
1980	57.2	1979–80	16	54
1985	64.1	1984–85	18	58
1989	61.9	1989–90	18	60
1991	55.9	1991	—	—
1996	57.9	1993–96	25	67
1998	62.1	1998	4	63

Source: CSDS Data Unit.
Note: A 'major' round of assembly elections is defined here as one which involved, within a year or two, elections to at least 2000 assembly constituencies. The figures for the last column do not conform to this definition. Calculations include provisional figures for state assembly elections held in 1995, the report for which has still not been released by the Election Commission.

beginning of a more enduring trend, and there is no reason to be confident that another mid-term poll will not see a reversal of the 1998 picture. On the whole, then, average national turnout in the last four parliamentary elections is about the same as in the previous four elections during the 1970s and 1950, following the first democratic upsurge.

Turnout figures for the assembly elections aggregated at the national level (Table 1) do show an upward trend, though somewhat tentatively. In the first two decades of democratic politics turnout at the state level rose with each parliamentary election; but in the following two decades of plebiscitary politics at the national level, when assembly elections became a matter of endorsing the national verdict, enthusiasm for elections at the state level shows a clear decline, to a level lower than that of parliamentary elections. As politics became decentred in the 1990s, the democratic urge found primary expression at the state level. The aggregate national turnout of assembly elections held since 1989 shows an upward trend, specially in the elections held between 1993 and 1996 (which covered all the states except Jammu & Kashmir and Punjab). We can also note a weak trend in the same direction for the previous decade. As in the case of Lok Sabha elections, it is too early to say whether the rise seen in that round will carry forward, but it seems clear that electoral participation in state level politics is more intense than in national politics.

Does the same trend continue when we go further down to the third tier in democratic governance? Unfortunately, there is no reliable compilation of aggregate data on the turnout in panchayat elections across various states, but limited data and episodic newspaper reports indicate that the turnout at that level is much higher than both state and national levels.[2] Non-empirical fieldwork also confirms that since the 73rd Amendment, panchayat elections are fought with much greater intensity and invite more enthusiastic participation than assembly or parliamentary elections. If this reading is correct, we already have the first characteristics of the second democratic upsurge: its intensity varies by the proximity or otherwise of the tier of democracy to the citizen; the closer the democratic tier, the higher the participatory urge. It should be noted that this trend is unusual in the comparative democratic context: democracies in advanced industrial societies have often reported a lower turnout in local elections.

National level aggregates conceal regional trends and patterns that are far from uniform. The 1989 and 1998 Lok Sabha elections provide an interesting point of comparison for changes in the state-wise (Table 2) and zone-wise (Table 3) patterns of turnout during this decade. Though the overall turnout in both elections was about the same, the figures underwent an interesting change at the lower aggregates. Comparatively speaking, the turnout in the traditionally high-turnout states of the south declined by six percentage points. The east and the west also recorded a decline, though the quantum is less significant here. It is only in the north Indian Hindi heartland that the turnout has risen in the last decade: North India recorded a marginal gain (mainly in Rajasthan and Haryana); the real change came about in the Hindi-speaking region, namely Uttar Pradesh, Bihar and Madhya Pradesh, which registered a gain of nearly five percentage points during this period.

One must not rush to a quick generalization from these trends. First of all, at least in some of these states (e.g., Maharashtra,

Table 2: State-wise turnout in Lok Sabha elections, 1977–98

State	1977	1980	1984	1989	1991	1996	1998
Andhra Pradesh	62.5	56.9	69.0	70.4	61.4	63.0	66.0
Arunachal Pradesh	56.3	68.6	75.5	59.2	51.3	55.0	59.2
Assam	54.9	53.4	79.7	****	75.3	78.5	61.1
Bihar	60.8	51.9	58.8	60.2	60.4	59.5	65.2
Goa	62.8	69.5	71.8	58.2	42.4	56.3	61.2
Gujarat	59.2	55.4	57.9	54.6	44.0	35.9	59.3
Haryana	73.3	64.8	66.8	64.4	65.8	70.5	69.0
Himachal Pradesh	59.6	58.7	61.5	63.9	57.4	57.6	71.1
Jammu & Kashmir	57.9	47.7	66.4	25.7	****	49.0	41.2
Karnataka	63.2	57.7	65.7	67.5	54.8	60.2	64.9
Kerala	79.2	66.6	77.1	79.3	73.3	71.1	70.1
Madhya Pradesh	54.9	53.4	57.5	55.2	44.4	54.1	61.7
Maharashtra	60.3	56.8	61.8	59.9	48.8	52.5	57.1
Manipur	60.1	81.7	85.8	71.8	69.7	75.0	56.8
Meghalaya	49.9	51.2	54.5	51.9	53.6	61.6	74.4
Mizoram	49.9	56.1	****	58.3	58.6	73.4	69.6
Nagaland	52.8	63.9	66.5	74.7	77.1	88.3	45.4
Orissa	44.3	46.3	56.3	59.3	53.8	59.2	58.0
Punjab	66.8	62.7	67.6	62.7	24.0	62.3	60.1
Rajasthan	55.9	54.7	57.0	56.5	47.3	43.4	60.3
Sikkim	****	44.7	57.6	72.0	58.8	77.4	67.1
Tamil Nadu	67.1	66.8	73.0	66.9	63.9	66.9	58.0
Tripura	70.1	80.0	77.3	83.9	67.3	79.1	80.9
Uttar Pradesh	56.1	50.0	55.8	51.3	49.2	46.5	55.5
West Bengal	60.6	70.7	78.6	79.7	76.7	82.7	79.2
A & N Islands	71.0	84.5	78.8	71.7	64.4	62.0	63.7
Chandigarh	67.4	63.9	68.9	65.7	57.8	58.4	53.7
Dadra & Nagar Haveli	68.5	72.8	74.6	72.9	66.5	77.0	77.4
Daman & Diu	****	****	****	66.0	67.0	70.7	72.8
Delhi	71.3	64.9	64.5	54.3	48.5	50.6	51.3
Lakshwadeep	84.6	88.8	87.0	85.0	80.4	89.0	85.1
Pondicherry	73.6	80.4	72.3	66.7	67.7	75.4	62.8
All India	60.4	57.2	64.1	61.9	55.9	57.9	62.1

Source: CSDS Data Unit.

Notes: **** denotes no election / state did not exist.

M.P. and U.P.), there is also a considerable difference in the turn-out among the different regions within the state. Second, no single factor satisfactorily explains either the direction or the quantum of the change in turnout in different states. Usual explanations like the mobilization strategy of the political parties, greater keenness of the contest, context of regime alteration, or the Election Commission's efficiency, do not seem to

Table 3: Turnout by zone, Lok Sabha elections, 1977–98

Zone	1977	1980	1984	1989	1991	1996	1998
South	66.5	61.0	70.7	70.0	62.5	64.8	64.0
East	54.9	63.3	72.7	72.8	69.9	75.4	70.0
West	60.0	56.5	60.6	58.1	47.1	47.0	57.9
North	63.8	58.6	62.4	57.2	45.8	53.3	59.9
Heartland	57.5	51.0	57.1	54.9	51.5	51.9	59.6

Source: CSDS Data Unit.

Notes: States are grouped according to their geographical location. South = Andhra Pradesh, Karnataka, Kerala, Tamil Nadu, A & N Islands, Lakshwadeep, Pondicherry. East = Arunachal Pradesh, Assam, Manipur, Meghalaya, Mizoram, Nagaland, Orissa, Sikkim, Tripura, West Bengal. West = Goa, Gujarat, Maharashtra, Dadra & Nagar Haveli, Daman & Diu. North = Haryana, Himachal Pradesh, Jammu & Kashmir, Punjab, Rajasthan, Chandigarh, Delhi. Heartland = Bihar, Madhya Pradesh, Uttar Pradesh.

work here. Regime alteration or keen contests could well be the outcome rather than the cause of the increase in turnout.

In some ways this trend represents a convergence towards the national average due to a belated 'catching up' by the Hindi heartland. But even if this is the case it still remains for us to ask why it should occur at this juncture. While it would take more in-depth research to offer a satisfactory answer to this question, it may not be out of place to note the fact that the region and the period that have witnessed a rise in turnout have also been centres of the Mandalization of politics. In other words, what appears to be a regional difference may turn out to be a reflection of a deeper social difference.

Turnout Patterns by Social Groups and Sectors

If the argument about the democratic upsurge is valid, one would expect to find a clearer pattern when participation data are dis-aggregated by social categories rather than regions. Two of the distinctions relevant to our argument—the rural–urban and the gender divide—can be examined with a fair degree of precision by using the official election results released by the Election Commission itself.

The data on rural–urban turnout (Table 4) show a secular trend over the last two decades: the turnout in the rural areas has gradually overtaken the urban areas. Earlier evidence suggested that before the 1970s the urban turnout was significantly

Table 4: Locality-wise turnout, Lok Sabha elections, 1977–98

	Constituencies	1977	1980	1984	1989	1991	1996	1998
Rural	421	60.2	56.7	64.1	62.2	56.6	58.6	62.8
Semi Urban	59	60.4	57.8	64.8	62.7	56.8	59.0	62.9
Urban	63	62.1	57.9	62.9	60.0	50.4	53.4	56.7

Source: CSDS Data Unit.

Note: All the Lok Sabha constituencies were grouped according to the estimated percentage of urban electorate there: less than 25 per cent is 'Rural', between 25 and 50 per cent is 'predominantly Rural' and more than 50 per cent is 'Urban'. The estimates are based on a comparison of the 1991 Census figures for urban population with the size of the electorate in the 1991 elections.

higher than the rural; in the following two decades the gap narrowed steadily. The 1984 election was the dividing line, when the rural turnout overtook urban turnout for the first time. Since then the gap has increased and now stands at six percentage points.

To be sure, these conclusions are based on aggregate data for Lok Sabha constituencies grouped by degree of urbanity. The unit is still so large that one cannot rule out the possibility of ecological fallacy. It needs to be checked, ideally, by polling booth or at least assembly segment level turnout records, for the distinction between an urban and a rural unit is fairly neat (absolutely, in the case of polling booth) at that level, but the pattern shown in the table here is so clear and systematic that there cannot be much doubt about the direction of change. If anything, the booth-level data might show a sharper change in the same direction. Besides, this pattern does not vary across states or regions. The national trend of rural turnout being higher than urban turnout is replicated in virtually every major state. It can be safely concluded, therefore, that the participatory upsurge draws more underprivileged participants in the rural–urban divide.

Aggregate data give a clear picture of the trends in women's turnout, for the figures for this category are officially released, thus avoiding the need for sample survey or statistical inferences. Yet the conclusions on this are not obvious, for most analysts have adopted somewhat crude measures. Table 5 unfolds various possible readings. The first column looks at the percentage of women who turned out, but it does not enable us to

Table 5: Women's turnout and women as proportion of total voters, Lok Sabha elections, 1957–98

Year	Women % (turnout)	Men % (turnout)	Women % (of total voters)	Turnout index	Odds ratio
1957	38.8	55.7	38.3	0.81	0.50
1962	46.6	62.1	39.8	0.84	0.53
1967	49.0	61.0	42.0	0.88	0.62
1971	49.2	61.2	42.4	0.89	0.61
1977	54.9	65.4	43.6	0.91	0.65
1980	51.2	62.2	43.1	0.90	0.64
1984	59.3	68.4	44.5	0.93	0.67
1989	57.5	66.4	44.1	0.93	0.68
1991	50.5	60.7	42.9	0.88	0.66
1996	53.4	62.1	44.0	0.92	0.70
1998	61.0	65.9	46.9	0.98	0.81

Source: CSDS Data Unit.

Notes: (1) Column 4 shows the percentage of women as a proportion of the total turnout. (2) The turnout index controls for the uneven size of the male and female electorate by expressing the proportion of women in turnout relative to the proportion of women in the electorate. For example, in 1998, women accounted for 46.9% of the total voters and 47.7% of the total electorate. We can therefore express the proportion in turnout as a fraction of the proportion of the electorate. Thus, 46.9 / 47.7 = 0.98. If women had accounted for 47.7% of the total voters, then their proportion in turnout would have been equivalent to their proportion amongst the electorate and the turnout index would have equalled 1. (3) The odds ratio measure the ratio between the odds of women voting and men voting.

see this trend in relation to the turnout among men presented in the next column. Since both figures tend to vary in the same direction, this first measure can be seen as a not very useful guide to understanding women's participation relative to men's.

Once we control for the general changes and look at the *proportion of women among voters,* we get a clearer picture in the third column. We can see that despite an occasional increase in their turnout, there was very little discernible change in the proportion of women among voters in the two decades up to the 1996 elections. The ratio has jumped by nearly three percentage point in the 1998 elections and now stands at an unprecedented 46.9 per cent. In retrospect we can discern an upward trend since the 1991 elections. This needs to be fine-tuned further to control for the proportion of women among the electors. This picture, presented in the fourth column as 'Turnout Index' confirms our earlier reading that, compared to men, there has indeed been a significant rise in the turnout among women.

Table 6: Women voters as proportion of total voters by states, Lok Sabha elections, 1977–1998

State	1977	1980	1984	1989	1991	1996	1998
Andhra Pradesh	47.0	46.0	47.7	47.5	46.1	47.3	59.2
Arunachal Pradesh	41.6	44.8	47.5	44.4	43.1	44.8	46.2
Assam	39.9	39.0	46.4	****	44.3	45.8	46.4
Bihar	39.7	39.9	39.7	38.8	38.2	39.8	48.0
Goa	49.8	49.5	49.7	47.2	45.4	46.3	47.8
Gujarat	45.5	44.4	45.0	43.7	40.9	40.1	45.2
Haryana	45.3	43.1	43.5	42.4	43.6	45.0	43.4
Himachal Pradesh	44.9	34.9	47.1	47.7	46.1	48.4	49.9
Jammu & Kashmir	39.2	38.8	42.8	62.8	****	37.2	38.4
Karnataka	44.8	43.9	45.5	46.4	43.8	45.4	46.3
Kerala	50.8	49.4	51.1	50.9	50.5	50.9	51.4
Madhya Pradesh	41.0	39.8	41.8	41.1	38.6	42.0·	52.5
Maharashtra	45.8	44.7	46.2	45.1	42.1	43.7	44.9
Manipur	54.9	51.1	51.9	49.1	50.3	49.5	49.6
Meghalaya	45.6	46.7	46.0	46.9	46.1	49.2	50.0
Mizoram	44.7	50.7	****	47.5	48.1	50.4	49.9
Nagaland	42.4	46.7	44.6	44.9	45.5	46.1	44.9
Orissa	39.7	40.3	41.6	42.0	40.4	43.8	43.7
Punjab	45.5	44.1	44.6	43.0	40.2	46.5	45.5
Rajasthan	42.7	42.0	41.6	41.6	39.1	40.0	43.4
Sikkim	****	45.0	40.7	44.8	39.1	45.5	44.6
Tamil Nadu	48.3	47.3	48.8	47.9	47.6	48.1	47.0
Tripura	45.9	47.3	46.8	47.6	44.7	47.8	48.0
Uttar Pradesh	39.9	39.5	41.3	40.7	40.6	39.9	40.7
West Bengal	41.6	43.0	44.5	44.7	44.9	46.3	46.2
A & N Islands	36.5	37.7	40.7	41.2	41.7	42.3	43.3
Chandigarh	41.7	31.9	43.4	43.5	42.7	43.5	42.1
Dadra & Nagar Haveli	48.2	48.3	50.4	49.3	48.1	48.8	48.8
Daman & Diu	****	****	****	53.0	50.8	51.3	49.7
Delhi	42.9	42.9	44.9	42.7	40.5	41.8	40.3
Lakshwadeep	47.0	50.6	50.8	49.8	50.3	49.4	49.7
Pondicherry	48.9	49.4	49.0	48.1	48.6	49.9	49.6
Total	**43.6**	**43.0**	**44.5**	**44.1**	**42.9**	**44.0**	**46.9**

Source: CSDS Data Unit.

The odds ratio (see methodological note at the end about this measure used often in this paper) highlights the conclusion starkly: although the odds that a woman will vote are still lower than a man, there has been a non-trivial gain in this respect in the last decade. After a long stagnation, then, there are clear signs of participatory upsurge among women.

A closer look at the state-wise pattern of this rise in women's turnout shows a good deal of regional variation. Earlier, the turn-out deficit generally followed the map of women's deprivation in different states, with Bihar, U.P., M.P. and Rajasthan showing the greatest deficit. The generally lower level of turnout also seems to be related to the additionally lower turnout among women as in the case of Gujarat. It is interesting that the maximum rise in the proportion of women among voters has been recorded in Bihar, M.P. and Rajasthan, besides an extraordinary and somewhat puzzling leap in Andhra Pradesh.

The most significant question about bahujan upsurge in the 1990 relates to social groups whose turnout cannot be estimated from aggregate data alone. For any reliable estimate of the turn-out trends among dalits, adivasis or Muslims, we can only use some broad inferences from aggregate data. In the case of OBCs, even this is not possible. Survey data are necessary here both as independent evidence and a double check on the conclusions drawn from aggregate data.

Aggregate data-based inferences are most useful in the case of the reserved (ST) constituencies, for these constituencies are almost invariably areas of high adivasi concentration. Here the trend of the last decade (Table 7) is very striking, though hardly noticed by any analyst or newsperson. After decades of lagging behind the average turnout by nearly 10 percentage points, the

Table 7: Turnout (%) by different types of constituencies: Lok Sabha elections, 1962–1998

Year	All India	General	SC	ST	Gap: Gen-SC	Gap: Gen-ST
1962	55	56.6	53.6	43.7	3.0	12.9
1967	61	62.4	61.0	49.0	1.4	13.4
1971	55	57.0	51.4	43.4	5.6	13.4
No. of seats	543	425	77	41		
1977	60.4	61.5	59.5	48.6	2.0	12.9
1980	57.3	58.2	55.6	48.2	2.6	10.0
1984	64.1	65.2	62.6	54.1	2.6	11.1
1989	62.1	62.7	61.8	53.2	0.9	9.5
1991	55.8	56.6	55.4	48.8	1.2	7.8
1996	57.9	58.3	57.1	55.6	1.2	2.7
1998	62.1	62.2	62.0	59.9	0.2	2.3

Source: CSDS Data Unit.

Note: The 'gap' is the difference in turnout (in percentage points) between general and scheduled caste/scheduled tribe constituencies.

Table 8: Changes in the turnout gap between general and reserved (ST) constituencies in major states: Lok Sabha elections, 1977–1998

Year	All India	Andhra Pradesh	Bihar	Gujarat	Madhya Pradesh	Maha-rashtra	Orissa	Raja-sthan	West Bengal
1977	12.9	15.9	22.6	5.9	9.8	6.0	14.2	1.3	0.4
1980	10.0	8.0	14.7	3.1	10.1	11.4	16.8	1.7	1.2
1984	11.1	9.9	16.5	7.3	8.2	7.8	16.1	5.2	-1.3
1989	9.5	3.1	14.6	8.3	8.7	8.7	17.2	4.2	0.5
1991	7.8	1.9	12.3	5.7	8.0	5.2	10.6	2.0	1.0
1996	2.7	0.3	4.9	-2.8	-3.4	11.5	1.2	5.1	3.8
1998	2.3	1.4	5.5	0.5	2.4	11.0	0.6	6.4	-4.0

Source: CSDS Data Unit.
Note: Table entries stand for **Tg -Tst**, where **Tg** stands for turnout in general constituencies and **Tst** for turnout in the reserved (ST) constituencies in the state concerned. The states chosen here for comparison are those with a significant number of both kinds of constituencies.

Table 9: Turnout (%) in constituencies grouped by proportion of Muslim electorate: Lok Sabha elections, 1977–1998

Year	All India	Low (upto 10%)	Medium (11–20%)	High (21% +)	Gap High-Low
No. of constituencies	543	309	167	67	
1977	60.4	60.3	60.0	61.6	1.3
1980	57.2	58.0	55.1	59.3	1.3
1984	64.1	63.7	62.7	69.2	5.5
1989	61.9	61.7	62.0	63.2	1.5
1991	55.9	53.6	56.1	67.0	13.4
1996	57.9	57.5	56.1	64.9	7.4
1998	62.1	61.4	61.6	66.0	3.6

Source: CSDS Data Unit
Notes: (1) Table entries in the last column stand for the percentage point difference in the turnout of the two extreme categories. (2) Proportion of Muslim electorate as per estimates given in H.D. Singh, 543 Faces of India (New Delhi: Newsmen), 1996. These rough estimates have been found to be erroneous in many instances.

reserved (ST) constituencies have rapidly caught up with the rest in this decade. The 1989 election was the turning point in this respect. The gap reduced significantly in 1989 and 1991 and then very sharply in 1996. A further reduction in 1998 proves that the trend of 1996 was not an outlier. This is true of all the major states with a significant tribal population, except

Table 10: Odds ratio for voting: 1971, 1996 and 1998

	1971	1996	1998
Hindu Upper	1.11	0.90	0.97
Hindu OBC	0.82	1.07	0.94
SC	1.04	1.22	1.21
ST	0.65	0.91	0.95
Muslim	1.59	0.92	1.12
Sikh	1.53	0.86	1.60
Christian	2.29	1.13	1.05
Very poor	0.89	1.24	0.92
Poor	0.98	1.13	1.05
Middle	1.14	0.94	1.18
Upper middle	1.06	0.89	0.96
Upper	1.38	0.75	0.75
Illiterate	0.82	1.03	0.91
Up to middle	1.49	1.01	1.33
College	1.29	1.05	0.91
Graduate	1.07	0.70	0.66

Sources: National Election Study (NES) 1971, NES 1996 and NES 1998.
Notes: The variable for constructing the economic status of the respondents was derived from their type of occupation and amount of land owned, and in 1971 and 1996, family's monthly income, and in 1998, the type of accommodation.

Maharashtra and, to a lesser extent, Rajasthan (Table 8). The pattern of aggregate data thus clearly suggests that there is a definite though silent jump in tribal electoral participation. The survey data confirm that this conclusion was not an ecological fallacy. The odds that an adivasi will vote have improved substantially between 1971 and 1996 and have recorded an increase thereafter, the same trend as seen in the aggregate data. The odds that an adivasi will vote are now nearly as high as an upper caste or an OBC Hindu (Table 10).

In the case of dalits, a simple disaggregation of the turnout data by general and reserved (SC) constituencies is not helpful beyond a point. Reserved (SC) constituencies bear a very weak relationship to the size of the dalit electorate, given the latter's even demographic spread throughout the country and within most states. If we look at the turnout data with this limitation in mind, we find a steadily narrowing gap between the general and the reserved (SC) constituencies (Table 7). Between 1977 and 1984 the gap was in the range of two percentage points; it fell to around one percentage point after that. In the 1998 election it has become negligible. As mentioned above, it may be erroneous to draw any definite conclusions about dalit turnout from this difference; the gap is better interpreted as the difference between various degrees of competitiveness, for reserved constituencies hitherto witnessed less keen contests.

Survey data provide more reliable evidence regarding trends in dalit turnout (Table 10). It seems that dalit voters were already well mobilized by the first democratic upsurge. Their odds of turning up to vote were almost as high as the upper castes in 1971; since then their odds have registered a noticeable increase, although the pattern is still highly uneven across various states. Dalit turnout in Bihar, Madhya Pradesh and Rajasthan is still lower than that of upper caste Hindus. The gap is made up, above all, by Uttar Pradesh where the odds of dalit turnout are substantially higher than for the upper castes.

There are no signs of a dramatic change in the turnout of OBCs between 1971 and 1998 (Table 10). It has remained fairly close to the average, gradually moving from the lower edge to the upper in this period. Survey evidence does not offer anything more by way of a distinctive pattern for the OBCs. Perhaps OBC is too large and heterogenous a category to offer meaningful patterns. The data categorization does not yet allow us to separate the lower OBCs from the dominant peasant–proprietor OBCs. It is possible that this period has seen a significant internal movement within various strata of the OBC itself that we are unable to capture here, but it may be safe to infer that the first stage of OBC mobilization was completed before 1971. If OBC politics has gained during this period, it has done so not by increasing the volume of votes but by making them more effective with the help of better aggregation in social and political terms.

Conclusive evidence for long-term trends in Muslim turnout is no less difficult to obtain. Disaggregation of constituency-wise turnout data by proportion of Muslim electorate (Table 9) shows a general tendency for constituencies with high Muslim electorate to have a higher than average turnout. The turnout gap between the constituencies with high and low Muslim electors widened dramatically to 13 percentage points in the communally charged election of 1991, but has steadily declined thereafter to reach 'normal' levels. Whatever the gap, there is little to support the popular myth of extraordinarily high turnout among the Muslims. A higher turnout in constituencies with a high Muslim electorate does not mean a higher than average turnout of Muslims. In all likelihood, it is a function of the higher communal tension or keener political competition in such constituencies which leads to more intense mobilization of both communities. The period that saw an increase in turnout among higher Muslim electorate constituencies may have actually experienced a lower turnout among the Muslims. The figure for 1971 conforms to the usual impression that the odds of a Muslim were higher than that of an average Hindu when it came to voting. By 1996, the odds ratio had become slightly unfavourable to the Muslims; by 1998, however, there was a reversal as the odds ratio picked up again. This confirms a popular impression that the decline in Muslim turnout was only a temporary phenomenon in the post-Babri masjid demolition phase. It needs to be emphasized that the evidence for the decline in 1996 is not highly significant and cannot be relied upon in the absence of corroborative evidence. What we do know is that unlike the other deprived groups, there does not seem to be any simple linear trend among Muslims from a low to a high turnout. It is possible that here again treating the entire community as one group may have concealed internal but politically significant patterns among, say, lower caste Muslims.

With the partial exception of Muslims, then, we can say that the second democratic upsurge has a bahujan character. India is perhaps the only large democracy in the world today where the turnout of the lower orders of society is well above that of the most privileged groups. A comparison of upper caste Hindus, seen here as representing inherited social privileges, with all other caste groups or communities except the OBCs, shows the former in an unfavourable light. What is more important, the odds of an OBC, dalit or adivasi voting are much higher today than in 1971. In the case of upper castes however, the odds ratio is more unfavourable than it was in 1971. The trend is not exclusive to bahujans as defined in terms of caste or community. The same applies to educationally and economically privileged groups. The odds ratio for different economic strata in 1971 was quite like the rest of the world. The richer you were, the greater the likelihood that you would vote. By 1996 there was a neat reversal of this pattern. The data for 1998 show highest turnout for middle income groups, but the richest continue to be the lowest in turnout. The pattern of odds ratio for categories of education is more complicated, with the school educated most likely to vote. Yet it confirms the basic trend reported here: the group that has seen the sharpest decline in odds of voting is that of the highest educated. While the last two decades have witnessed a decline in the proportion of illiterates, they have also seen an increase in the propensity of illiterates to vote.

Beyond the Vote: Behavioural and Attitudinal Aspects

Is this trend confined to the act of voting? Can we read into it anything more than a habit, a reflex action? Does voting mean very much in terms of how ordinary citizens relate to democracy? These are valid questions and need to be responded to at this stage. Clearly, voting is not the only act of political participation. If the argument of a democratic upsurge has merit, one should expect other behavioural attributes of participation to register a similar change. Besides, the translation of voting as behaviour into the act of political participation depends on the meaning structures in which this act is embedded. A survey is not the ideal instrument for ascertaining the nuances of this meaning system, but in the absence of sensitive anthropological research we have to make do with the rough picture of attitudes and opinions offered by survey responses in a standardized setting. At the very least, it enables us to distinguish between voting as a mechanical response from voting as meaningful political action.[3]

Let us begin with a very simple behavioural indicator of participation in electoral politics other than voting, namely attendance at election meetings. Between 1971 and 1998 this attendance has more than doubled (Table 11). It is significant because the benchmark here is an election that is remembered for its fiery 'Garibi Hatao' campaign, and is being compared to two rather lacklustre campaigns of 1996 and 1998. More importantly the composition of those who attended at least one election meeting has changed along expected lines. The odds ratio of women, dalits, adivasis and the poor attending an election meeting underwent a striking improvement in this period; more

Table 11: Respondents (%) who attended at least one election meeting: 1971, 1996 and 1998

Category	1971	1996	1998	1971 Odds ratio	1996 Odds ratio	1998 Odds ratio
All	**12.0**	**16.3**	**25.8**	-	-	-
Women	2.5	7.7	13.4	0.19	0.43	0.44
Men	19.7	24.7	37.8	1.80	1.68	1.75
Hindu Upper	15.2	15.8	26.2	1.49	0.96	1.02
Hindu OBC	10.5	17.4	24.8	0.86	1.08	0.95
SC	9.5	17.8	27.3	0.77	1.11	1.08
ST	5.6	10.1	22.9	0.44	0.58	0.85
Muslims	15.0	16.9	28.9	1.47	1.04	1.17
Illiterates	4.7	9.4	18.7	0.36	0.53	0.66
Up to middle	17.8	19.1	29.4	1.59	1.21	1.20
High school	33.9	24.7	33.6	3.77	1.68	1.45
Graduate	39.7	20.5	30.4	4.84	1.32	1.26
Very poor	5.6	14.2	21.0	0.44	0.86	0.74
Poor	8.9	14.5	24.2	0.72	0.88	0.92
Middle	17.5	18.2	27.8	1.56	1.14	1.11
Upper middle	21.0	18.9	26.7	1.95	1.20	1.05
Upper	19.7	17.4	26.3	1.80	1.08	1.03

Sources: NES 1971, NES 1996, NES 1998.

remarkably, what is noted is the reduced effect of higher educational levels on political participation. In other words, greater participation need not be linked to better or more education.

A much higher level of activity on this continuum of political participation would be taking up membership of a political party. Notwithstanding widespread claims of depoliticization, the number of those who said they were members of a political party went up almost two times between 1971 and 1996 (Table 12B). While every section of society has registered an increase, the odds of a woman, and adivasi or illiterate citizen are still way below others in this more demanding form of political participation. Even for these groups, the change is substantial, as can be seen in the column percentages of the same figures (Table 12A). The proportion of men, upper castes and graduates among those who are party members has declined substantially since 1971. In other words, the direction and the extent of change in both these aspects of political behaviour is quite similar to what

Table12A: Changing social composition of party members, 1971 and 1996 column percentages

	1971	1996
Men	93.5	81.1
Women	6.5	18.9
Rural	64.5	71.1
Urban	35.5	28.9
Hindu upper	36.3	28.0
Hindu OBC	26.7	37.2
SC	12.6	18.8
ST	1.5	1.5
Muslims	16.3	10.0
Illiterate	16.9	16.6
Up to middle	47.1	37.9
High school	31.6	35.8
Graduate	4.4	9.7

Sources: NES 1971, NES 1996.
Note: Table entries here are different from the pattern followed above. These stand for the percentage of members who belong to the specified categories rather than the percentage of the respondents who are members in each category. Some of these groups do not add up to 100 per cent because some minor categories have been excluded here.

Table12B: Changing social composition of party members, 1971 and 1996 row percentages and odds ratios

	1971	1996	1971 Odds ratio	1996 Odds ratio
All	**3.6**	**6.3**	-	-
Men	6.1	10.0	1.76	1.66
Women	0.5	2.4	0.14	0.37
Rural	3.0	5.9	0.84	0.94
Urban	5.8	7.5	1.66	1.21
Hindu upper	4.5	6.8	1.27	1.09
Hindu OBC	3.1	7.2	0.86	1.16
SC	2.8	6.4	0.79	1.02
ST	0.8	2.2	0.22	0.34
Muslims	5.9	5.9	1.69	0.94
Illiterate	1.0	2.5	0.27	0.38
Up to middle	6.0	7.4	1.73	1.19
High school	11.3	11.1	3.44	1.86
Graduate	8.2	10.3	2.41	1.71

Sources: NES 1971, NES 1996.

Table 13: Interest in election campaigns among different sections, 1971 and 1996

	1971	1996	1971 Odds ratio	1996 Odds ratio
All	**27.9**	**35.3**	-	-
Men	37.1	45.0	1.52	1.50
Women	17.5	25.3	0.55	0.62
Rural	27.1	34.1	0.96	0.95
Urban	34.0	39.1	1.33	1.18
Hindu upper	34.0	38.3	1.33	1.14
Hindu OBC	23.3	35.9	0.78	1.03
SC	24.0	34.7	0.82	0.97
ST	22.2	22.5	0.74	0.53
Muslims	31.6	35.9	1.19	1.03
Illiterate	18.6	21.8	0.59	0.52
Up to middle	36.1	39.7	1.46	1.21
High school	54.3	51.4	3.07	1.94
Graduate	56.1	52.4	3.30	2.02

Sources: NES 1971, NES 1996.

we observed in the case of voting. It seems reasonable to think therefore that we are dealing not only with an upsurge in turn-out, but in political participation in general.

The increase in political participation has taken place not only in the realm of objective behaviour; it is also registered in the subjective assessment of participants. As compared to the high-pitched campaign of 1971, the proportion of those who felt that they took no interest in the election campaign declined, while those who took 'some' or 'a lot' of interest increased by nearly 50 per cent in the otherwise dull campaign of 1996 (Table 13). The increase in interest was more or less even across all sections. This means that the odds ratios have not changed as sharply here as in the earlier tables, though there has been a substantial reduction in the differences across various educational strata. If the class of those who took an interest is broken down into those who took 'some' interest and those who took a 'great deal' of interest, the real increase has been in the moderate category. The proportion of strong enthusiasts has not changed since 1971.

Table 14: Sense of efficacy among different sections, 1971 and
          1996

	1971	1996	1971 Odds ratio	1996 Odds ratio
All	**48.4**	**58.7**	-	-
Men	58.3	66.2	1.49	1.38
Women	35.9	50.9	0.60	0.73
Rural	44.2	56.9	0.85	0.93
Urban	64.4	64.1	1.93	1.26
Hindu Upper	56.2	61.0	1.38	1.10
Hindu OBC	45.7	57.6	0.90	0.96
SC	42.2	60.3	0.78	1.07
ST	30.5	47.5	0.47	0.64
Muslims	49.9	60.3	1.06	1.07
Illiterate	35.7	47.0	0.59	0.62
Up to middle	62.3	62.5	1.76	1.17
College no degree	76.8	70.9	3.53	1.71
Graduate and above	83.6	79.5	5.43	2.73
Very poor	37.9	50.7	0.65	0.72
Poor	43.4	54.9	0.82	0.86
Middle	54.8	61.5	1.29	1.12
Upper middle	68.9	67.7	2.36	1.48
Middle	68.0	66.1	2.27	1.37

Sources: NES 1971, NES 1996.
Note: Table entries are for the percentage of respondents who said 'has effect' to the question, "*Do you think your vote has effect on how things are run in this country or do you think your vote makes no difference?*"

Moving to the stronger attitudinal issue of efficacy, we find that in this period, the electorate's sense that their vote matters, that it affects the way things are run in the country, has become stronger (Table 14). The proportion of those who held no opinion on such a crucial question has declined sharply. In every group the number of those who responded positively to this question increased, although the socially privileged still feel more efficacious than the rest. Once again, the odds ratio has not changed dramatically, but the sharp effect of educational and economic privileges has been significantly reduced. The odds that a dalit believes that he makes a difference are about the same as that of an upper caste Hindu. It needs to be empha-

Table 15: Support for democracy among different sections, 1971 and 1996

	1971	1996	1971 Odds ratio	1996 Odds ratio
All	**43.4**	**68.8**	-	-
Men	52.4	73.4	1.44	1.25
Women	32.0	64.1	0.61	0.81
Rural	39.4	69.0	0.85	1.01
Urban	59.0	68.2	1.88	0.97
Hindu upper	50.9	73.7	1.35	1.27
Hindu OBC	38.8	65.5	0.83	0.86
SC	38.2	67.3	0.81	0.93
ST	41.2	66.4	0.91	0.90
Muslims	39.6	72.2	0.85	1.18
Illiterate	30.6	61.6	0.57	0.73
Up to middle	56.2	73.0	1.67	1.23
College no degree	75.8	75.9	4.08	1.43
Graduate and above	75.3	74.2	3.97	1.30
Very poor	32.3	63.5	0.62	0.79
Poor	37.2	67.8	0.77	0.95
Middle	54.1	72.3	1.54	1.18
Upper middle	59.2	72.2	1.89	1.18
Upper	55.7	69.6	1.64	1.04

Sources: NES 1971, NES 1996.

Note: Table entries are for the percentage of respondents who said 'no' to the following question: "Do you think that the government in this country can be run better if there were no parties or assemblies or elections?"

sized that unlike voting, the advantage of the deprived in this case is only relative. Those who belong to dominant social groups (men, well educated, upper caste, upper class) still have a much greater sense of power than those who don't.

Finally, does all this affect the way citizens react to the democratic system? If answers to standard stimuli in a survey setting are anything to go by, it does. Along with higher efficacy, people's trust in the legitimacy of the democratic system has also grown between 1971 and 1996 (Table 15). It needs to be remembered that the legitimacy of the political system need not translate into the legitimacy of the regime and that it certainly does not translate into trust in representatives and leaders. Interestingly, the highly educated are the only group among whom enthusiasm for democracy has declined during this period. Faith in democracy has registered highly significant gains among the most marginalized groups: dalits, tribals and Muslims. Unlike efficacy, the legitimacy of the regime is not necessarily higher in the eyes of the powerful. Like all other indicators we have discussed, the movement is unmistakeably in the direction of reduction of differences caused by social privileges.

Implications

What does all this add up to? At this stage it is easier to see the negative implications, to say what the evidence presented above does not support, rather than offer an alternative positive reading. The story of contemporary Indian politics is often recounted, in its popular and academic versions, in terms of an impending catastrophe: it is a story of the decline and collapse of the democratic edifice, of growing apathy and widespread indifference, and of a resultant loss of popular legitimacy for the political system. The evidence presented in this paper does pose serious difficulties for this popular reading. This reading appears to be based on assumptions that do not stand the test of empirical scrutiny. Even if democratic politics is headed for a catastrophe, it is not because there is any decline in the most obvious indicators of political participation. The impression that there is such a decline seems to be an unwarranted generalization of the behaviour and attitudes of the socially privileged. Trends and patterns of bahujan participation do not appear to have received the analytical attention they require.

At a general plane, this evidence also poses difficulties for some of the current middle level theories of democratization. The idea that political participation is a function of social privileges does not seem to apply in this case. That the recent Indian experience is almost exactly the reverse of the rules of established democracies calls for rethinking the received models of democracy and democratization. This evidence also does not sit comfortably with the suggestion that too much participation was after all not such a good thing for new democracies. First popularized by Samuel Huntington, this theory saw 'excessive' participation in the absence of early institutionalization as a recipe for revolution, of rising frustration and the eventual collapse of democracy. That too does not seem to have happened in India. Despite an ambiguous record on institutionalization, the democratic upsurge of the last decade has not resulted in the widespread erosion of legitimacy or sense of efficacy among the bahujan, those who should have experienced the highest degree of frustration. It seems that the trajectory of democracy in India is different from what the Huntingtonian model expected it to be.

One has to be more careful in spelling out the positive implications of this evidence. In particular, there is a need to avoid a hurried counter-reading, a simple-minded optimism about Indian democracy. If the dominant bleak picture of Indian democracy needs to be reviewed, we must not replace it with an all-is-well-with-our-democracy attitude. In this paper, we have looked at some indicators of participation and even fewer indicators of efficacy and legitimacy. At any rate, participation and political attitudes are only one aspect of democracy. There are various other aspects that cannot be read off from the logic of participation. In other words, what this paper calls for is not the celebration of the democratic upsurge but an attempt to understand its characteristics, achievements and pathologies in its specificity. In itself, the argument advanced in this paper does not provide us with or even indicate the contours of the big picture of Indian democracy. But I hope it contributes to that big picture, not only by providing some empirical evidence but also by indicating that our task is to theorize the trajectory of Indian democracy in its historical specificity.

I would like to thank the participants at the CASI seminar for bombarding me with questions and comments that helped me think through my argument. The main argument was also presented at a seminar organized by the Department of Political Science, Panjab University (Chandigarh) and has benefitted from the reactions of participants there. I am grateful to Professor Anthony Heath for reading the draft version and helping me with several technical issues regarding the Odds Ratio. I would also like to thank Alistair McMillan and Oliver Heath for research support and Himanshu Bhattacharya, and Hilal and Kanchan Malhotra of the CSDS data unit for data analysis.

Methodological Appendix

1. *Data Sources*

CSDS Data Unit: Centre for the Study of Developing Societies, 29 Rajpur Road, Delhi.
The aggregate data on elections are based on the official reports of the Election Commission.
Wherever official data have not been released, provisional data in the computers have been used.
National Election Study 1971 [NES1971] conducted by CSDS, data stored at CSDS data unit.
National representative sample: Size 3800 in 80 Lok Sabha constituencies. Cross-sectional.
National Election Study 1996 [NES1996] conducted by CSDS, data stored at CSDS data unit.
National representative sample: 9833 interviews in 108 Lok Sabha constituencies. Cross-sectional panel study, three waves.
National Election Study 1998 [NES1998] conducted by CSDS, data stored at CSDS data unit.
National representative sample: 8133 interviews in 108 Lok Sabha constituencies. Cross-sectional panel study, two waves.

2. *Odds Ratio*

Odds ratio can be understood as a ratio of two different ratios. This summary measure provides a standardized base for comparison, both over time and between groups. For example, the 1971 data revealed that 49.2 per cent of women voted in the Lok Sabha elections. This can be expressed as odds of 0.97:1, which in other words means that for every 100 women who did not vote, there were 97 women who did. The turnout for men was 61.2 per cent which reduces to odds of 1.58:1. For every 100 men that did not vote 158 did. Thus the ratio between these two odds can be calculated as (0.97:1) / (1.58:1) which equals 0.61. An odds ratio of 1.0 would have meant that the odds of women voting are exactly the same as the odds of men voting. In that case, we could have said that sex and turnout are independent of each other, which is to say that the former does not have an effect on the latter. The degree to which values deviate from this baseline represents the level of association. The same calculation for the year 1998 yields an odds ratio of 0.81. It means that over this period the association between sex and voting has declined. Thus an odds ratio of 0.61 has stronger association than an odds ratio of 0.81. On the other hand, an odds ratio of 1.8 indicates stronger association than 1.6.

3. *Reported Turnout and Actual Turnout*

The paper does not mention the raw percentage of reported turn-out (the number of respondents who responded positively to the query, 'Could you cast your vote in xxx election?' in a post-poll survey) for it can be highly misleading. The experience of survey research all over the world shows that the turnout reported in the survey tends to be higher than the actual turnout recorded officially. In the British context, Professor Anthony Heath has isolated three factors at work here. First, of course, there is misreporting, for the respondent wishes to conform to the perceived expectation of the surveyor and would rather say 'yes' than 'no' to a question involving civic virtue. Second, there is availability bias, for those who are available for survey interviews are also much more likely to have been available for voting. Third, inaccuracies in the official electoral roll mean that it contains several names of persons who could not have cast their vote for various reasons (death, permanent shift in residence, clerical errors, bogus names) and thus depress the official turn-out figure. Of these three factors, the first—misreporting—is actually a minor one. None of these factors, however, affects the utility of the reported voting figures for analysing the internal composition of the voters. Such an analysis operates on a safe assumption that these biases are not systematic, i.e., it does not lead to excess reporting for one group more than another.

For the record, the reported (actual in parenthesis) turnout figures for the three CSDS surveys are: 1971: 78.3 per cent (55.3 per cent); 1996: 87.2 per cent (57.9 per cent); 1998: 91.5 per cent (62.1 per cent). The increasing gap between the reported and the actual could be due to the progressive reduction in the time lag between the date of polling and that of survey. In 1998, the survey was carried out within a week (within 24 hours, for the third phase constituencies) of the polling when the availability bias operates at its strongest. There has been no study in India to empirically determine the respective strength of these three factors in causing over-reporting. Such a research is hampered by the fact that the information on who voted and who did not is not made available officially. NES 1996 included an exercise to gather background information about the sampled persons who could not be interviewed. Its findings confirm that the second factor operates very strongly. Of those who could not be interviewed, only 36.9 per cent were reported to have voted, as against 28.2 per cent who had not voted (as many as 34.9 per cent fell in the 'unsure' category). Even if we exclude the 'unsure', it is clear that those who were not interviewed were much more likely to be non-voters. The survey did not, however, find any significant deviation from the mean reporting bias for any social group except migrant labour. Thus we can conclude that the gap between the reported and the actual turnout does not affect the conclusions of this paper regarding the changing composition of those who turn out to vote.

Notes

[1] The other serious contender is the concept of *shudra* as used in the socialist tradition. For Ram Manohar Lohia it did not refer only to the shudra varna. It included all the non-twice-born among the Hindu social order, including dalits and adivasis. He also insisted that every woman, irrespective of her caste is a shudra. For Vivekananda too the concept was a general gesture towards all the deprived groups, but the non-existence of a significant political tradition of shudra politics has reduced the scope of this concept to its more narrow sociological usage.

[2]

State	Lok Sabha		Panchayat	
	Year	Turnout %	Year	Turnout %
West Bengal	1998	79.2	1998	80.0
Rajasthan	1996	43.4	1995	70.0
Madhya Pradesh	1996	54.1	1994	65.0

Sources: CSDS Data Unit & Data Centre on Panchayati Raj, Institute of Social Sciences, New Delhi. I would like to thank Dr George Mathew for his help in accessing these figures.

[3] It has often been asked if non-voting represents a questioning of the political system. This is a big question and some psychological aspects of it do not admit of an empirical answer. But survey evidence can help rule out some of the more obvious anxieties. All the CSDS surveys have probed reasons for non-voting in detail. None of the surveys found indifference or fear to be significant reasons. For example, the 21.8 per cent respondents in NES 1996 who reported that they had not voted gave the following reasons for not voting (per cent of valid responses in parentheses): "Out of station" (5.9); "Not well" (2.2); "Not interested" (1.7); "Fear of violence"/ "Was prevented" (0.3); "Someone else had already voted" (0.2); Other responses (2.4). Other surveys do not provide a different picture.

Representation and Redistribution: the new lower caste politics of north India

ZOYA HASAN

A complex scenario is unfolding in India: the state is in retreat, institutions are in decline, caste and communitarian assertions have grown and political instability has increased. The 1998 election was the twelfth since 1947, but its fourth since the last decade—a sign of the fragmented state of the polity. At the same time, there is evidence of the vitality of Indian democracy: throughout the 1990s, turnouts for elections to parliament and state assemblies have risen steadily and significantly. The data collected by the Centre for the Study of Developing Societies in Delhi make it clear that the steadiest increases in participation have come from those in the lower social order, from the poor and illiterate. This process has been aided by the regionalization of the polity, the emergence of a coalition of regional groups/parties, and the entry of hitherto marginalized groups into the political system.

Still there remains a central contradiction at the heart of Indian democracy: an inclusive polity has so far not made for a more just and equal society. What, then, is the meaning and significance of greater political participation? What is the relationship between democracy and social and economic equality? What are the consequences of appealing to the electorate in ethnic or group terms, or making group demands on the state? Do political parties merely mirror divisions, or do they help to deepen and extend them?

In 1949, B.R. Ambedkar noted an incongruity between political equality and social and economic inequalities that would effectively exclude sections of the population from the democratic process. He stated in the Constituent Assembly:

On the 26th of January, we are going to enter a life of contradictions. In politics we will have equality and in social and economic life we will have inequality. In politics we will be recognizing the principle of one man one vote value. In our social and economic life, we shall, by reason of our social and economic structure, continue to deny the principle of one man one value. How long shall we continue to live this life of contradictions? How long shall we continue to deny equality in our social and economic life? If we continue to deny it for long, we do so only by putting our political democracy in peril.[1]

Fifty years later, the contradiction persists. In fact, it has come to the fore in the last two decades of competitive politics. Seen from the vantage point of the 1998 elections, democratic politics is distinguished by a fundamental transformation: a dramatic upsurge in political participation in north India. That, of course, is not the whole story: the upsurge is most marked among the socially underprivileged in the caste and class hierarchy. Moreover, the downward thrust of participation is entwined with struggles of groups who have been mobilized under banners of ethnicity, caste and religion. In these processes, group identity has supplanted class interest as the chief vehicle of political mobilization; hence, the increasing dependence of all major political parties on ethnic appeals. Ethnic strategies of political mobilization have drawn new groups into the political arena; yet, these struggles occur in a world of great material inequality—staggering inequalities in income and property ownership, in access to employment, education and health care. In fact, material inequality is on the rise in India and the socially privileged remain economically powerful.

This chapter focuses on the relation between the two transformations: the upsurge in participation of hitherto marginal groups and the increasing dependence of political parties on ethnic appeals to facilitate participation. Opening up the institutional space to greater participation by marginal groups is vital; equally crucial however, is how this can be achieved and the terms on which it is taking place. In part, this means looking at the relationship between the 'struggle for recognition' of marginal groups, and social and economic equality. In addressing this problematic, I shall focus on axes of injustice that are simultaneously cultural and socio-economic, and paradigmatically, caste and class. In what follows, I consider only one aspect of the problem. Under what circumstances can the 'politics of recognition' foster participation and empowerment? Can such politics help promote redistribution? And when is it likely to undermine it?

These questions are addressed through an examination of the career of a lower caste political party, notably the Bahujan Samaj Party, and is based on secondary sources and interviews with political leaders in Uttar Pradesh, India's largest state. The BSP has made rapid progress on the electoral front. During the 1989 election it received 2.07 per cent of the votes and obtained three seats in the Lok Sabha. By 1996, its growth enabled the party to obtain the status of a national party winning 20 per cent of the vote and five seats. How and why has the BSP's mobilization strategy succeeded in attracting voters? And how successful has it been in achieving its goals from the standpoint of equality?

Why U.P.? For one thing, this mega-state of 140 million people, located in the northern Hindi heartland, is one of the most backward in India. It is also one of the most deprived economically, giving its citizens less than some of the worst performing economies in sub-Saharan Africa. However, it sends eighty-five members to the Lok Sabha, out of a total of 545. This makes it politically the most crucial region in terms of determining the formation of the central government in New Delhi. It is also the chief locale for the transition to a post-Congress polity, and is the pivotal site of contestation between non-Congress groups. Inter-caste conflict, assertive lower castes and Hindutva politics all manifest themselves in U.P. Potentially, the most radical challenge to upper caste hegemony, the outcome of which would affect the overall structure of social inequality, is taking place in U.P. The way in which conflicts between castes and communities are played out in U.P. will influence the course of democratic politics in north India and alter the ways of wresting and sustaining political power at the national level.

I

The impetus for political transformation originated in the rapid realignments that began to take place in the late 1980s. The state was controlled by the Congress party until 1989, with its social base drawn from the Brahmins, the Muslims and the

Scheduled Castes. Operating as a centrist party, Congress attracted the support of a wide range of groups. As elsewhere, the centrepiece of its hegemony was a strategy that vertically aggregated the interests of different sections of society. It was an aggregation based on an inclusive ideological package of nationalism, secularism and Nehruvian socialism. Congress succeeded in retaining its hold because it deftly persuaded the lower orders to believe that the existing political arrangements worked in their interest. It was quite a while before the Congress was challenged by the counter-hegemonies created by new social forces.

The main social conflict in U.P., apparent since 1977, has been between the upper castes, represented by the Congress, and backward castes, backed by socialists who had been a major political force in U.P. from the days of the anti-colonial struggle. Eventually, the backward castes were mobilized under the aegis of the Janata Dal formed in 1989 by V.P. Singh (who had left the Congress in 1988 to establish his own party), and included some of the older socialists. Dedicated to moral probity and social justice, he promised the backward castes reservations in education and government service. During the brief period from 1989 to 1990, the Janata Dal-led government in New Delhi carved out a distinctive ideology based on the dual demands of the rural majority. One was for greater opportunities through investment in agricultural infrastructure and employment, and the other for higher social status through quotas for lower castes and OBCs in recruitment to the élite all-India services. Ironically, the Janata Dal itself was the major victim of its political mobilization strategy. Subsequently, state and local leaders of the backward classes and dalits rejected the mediation of national parties such as the Janata Dal, even though it was essentially a party of OBCs. Instead, they attempted to enhance their access to public resources of the state through direct participation in the bargaining process that preceded the formation of governments at both the central and state levels.

The political pattern that emerged in the early 1990s demonstrated that the Hindu nationalists rather than the Janata Dal or its successor, the Samajwadi Party, had displaced the Congress as the dominant party. The growth of the BJP, which had not won even a quarter of votes or seats in the U.P. Assembly before 1991, was an extraordinary development. It changed the

dynamics of electoral competition and facilitated the emergence
of the BJP as a national contender to the Congress. The decisive
electoral battles of this period were fought in U.P., where Congress fortunes declined dramatically. The most significant factor responsible for its electoral defeat was the party's inability
to retain its traditional support base that had cut across caste,
class, and community lines. Furthermore, Congress' actions regarding Ayodhya, the disputed site of the Babri masjid, claimed
by Hindus as the birthplace of Lord Ram, alienated devout voters among both Hindus and Muslims, accelerating the party's
decline.

In 1986, a dispute about the status of the Babri masjid, built
centuries earlier by Babar on or near an ancient site sacred to
Hindus, took an unexpected political turn. The district judge,
presumably on instructions from Congress authorities at the
Centre, allowed the padlock to be removed to allow Hindus to
worship at the site. An unprecedented Ram Janmabhumi movement organized by the Vishva Hindu Parishad (VHP), an organization affiliated to the BJP and the Rashtriya Swayamsevak
Sangh (RSS) demanded the building of a new Ram mandir at
the site of the mosque. The Congress, in November of 1989,
allowed the foundation-laying ceremony of the Ram mandir to
take place on the disputed site. Although it later prohibited the
construction of the mandir, pending a court decision on the
rights of each community to the area, the foundation-laying
ceremony emboldened militant Hindus associated with the BJP.
This helped the VHP–RSS to start a popular movement which
significantly changed India's political agenda. Designed to reverse the dwindling appeal of the Congress by buttressing the
'Hindu' vote, the leadership's permissiveness in allowing the
foundation-laying ceremony, while holding the line against
building the temple, alarmed Muslims and disappointed Hindus, ironically contributing to the party's downfall.

At the national level, the political ground shifted in 1990
when the central government adopted the recommendations of
the Mandal Commission to establish reservations. The initiative, motivated by V.P. Singh's effort to strengthen the Janata
Dal's influence on the backward castes, intensified divisions
among Hindus. This confrontation spurred the BJP to support the
movement led by the VHP, and aimed at reintegrating lower castes

into the Hindu hierarchy through a religious appeal to all Hindus to demolish the Babri masjid and replace it with a Ram mandir.

In U.P., the BJP combine provoked stiff resistance from the Samajwadi Party led by Mulayam Singh Yadav, U.P. chief minister from 1989–91. Mulayam Singh was busy consolidating his own power base by extending reservations for the backward castes in state educational institutions and administrative services. Once the new reservation policy was set in motion, the upper castes reacted violently. The conflict between the Mulayam Singh government and the upper castes in 1990 spilled into communal conflagration that engulfed U.P. from October 1990 to March 1991. The disaffected upper castes, who had traditionally voted the Congress, transferred their support to the BJP. They resented the rise of backward-caste parties and leaders in the state, and the patronage extended by the central Congress leadership in New Delhi to Mulayam Singh. He maintained his hold on U.P., even after the minority Janata Dal-led National Front government collapsed at the Centre, once the BJP withdrew its support in the wake of the Mandal–Mandir controversy. The conflict between Mulayam Singh's government and the upper castes became the most enduring confrontation in U.P.'s contemporary political history.

Political leaders and party strategies played the determining role in instigating caste and communal crusades, and in supporting political mobilization around issues of caste discrimination, social recognition and religious identity. But the two mobilization strategies in question, caste and community, are quite different in the outcomes they produce, even though both speak to particularistic interests. By polarizing castes into blocs and demanding representation on a bloc basis, the politics of caste identity disrupts the traditional definitions of caste-based hierarchy in Hindu society. Using political rather than religious criteria, caste-based political mobilization converges on control of the state. Such strategies of caste polarization can destabilize the political system, but appear necessary to achieve justice for lower caste groups. In other words, what may be seen as destabilizing political process from one perspective, can be seen as deepening democracy by those groups who capture state power for the first time. By contrast, the politics of communalism practised by the BJP attempts to unify all Hindus within a traditional

and hierarchical social order. The BJP is not known for its commitment to justice or democracy. The very concept of pluralism
which is at the heart of India's democracy is challenged by its
project to privilege a singular, majoritarian identity.

II

Although the OBCs and Scheduled Castes constitute more than
half its population, and just over 20 per cent of U.P.'s population belongs to upper castes; it is this 20 per cent that has dominated U.P. society and politics. In recent decades, however, the
entry of OBCs into the political system has made a profound
difference. Even more important than the rise of Hindu nationalism for the transformation of politics in the state, is the growth
of backward and lower caste politics. Caste politics, admittedly,
are not new. For several decades, inter-caste conflicts have fur-
nished the principal cleavage in electoral mobilization and
played a key part in structuring inter-party competition. Caste
calculations have affected most aspects of social and political
relations in rural and urban U.P. They set the terms of political
competition for entitlement and status among groups who see
themselves as having equal claims to rights and power. The Hindi
satirist, Harishankar Parsai, captured this centrality in a liter-
ary piece. He claimed to have persuaded Lord Krishna to contest for a seat in the state assembly:

> We talked to some people active in politics. They said, 'Of course.
> Why shouldn't you? If you won't run in the election, who will?
> After all, you are a Yadav, aren't you?' Krishna said, 'I am God. I
> don't have a caste.' They said, 'Look, sir, being God won't do you
> any good around here. No one will vote for you. How do you ex-
> pect to win if you don't maintain your caste?'[2]

What is new is the heightened political awakening among the
lower castes and dalits, a process hastened by the fragmentation of the old Congress coalition into constituent groups of
upper castes; Muslims and dalits. What is also new is the formation of local and regional parties that represent marginal
groups hitherto under the Congress umbrella. The structure of
representation power-sharing conceived and practised by the
Congress was at odds with the way the new groupings wanted
to represent themselves. The drift has unmistakably been to-

wards seeking direct control over the state by hitherto excluded groups.

Among these disadvantaged groups, the Scheduled Castes constitute more than 20 per cent of the population of U.P. After Independence, policy measures for their uplift were designed to moderate the harshness of the caste system. Reservation for them in elected legislatures, and in recruitment to educational institutions and government services, as set out in the Constitution, were justified on grounds of the extreme social discrimination they had suffered for centuries, resulting in educational and economic backwardness. Most remained poor and illiterate, either casual or landless labour. Despite reservations, in 1991, only 22.92 per cent of Scheduled Castes were literate. Their level of urbanization was 11.80 per cent compared to 22 per cent for others. As many as 81.59 per cent were engaged in the agricultural sector, as against 69.42 per cent for others; and only 18.59 per cent were employed in non-agricultural occupations, while for others the proportion was 30.58 per cent. Although the disparity between groups in literacy had narrowed since 1971, as of the early 1990s only 14.43 per cent of Scheduled Castes population had received any kind of formal education.[3] Again, while blatant forms of caste discrimination have disappeared, more subtle forms remain widespread, especially in rural areas.[4] Compared to their upper caste peers, Scheduled Caste legislators seemed to have very little influence over the day to day implementation of public policies, underlining the real constraints on political empowerment. They could not bring about a substantial change in the distribution of agrarian assets, the most important determinant of the material condition of the rural population.[5]

In theory, zamindari abolition and land reforms should have empowered the dalit community in U.P. However, it is widely accepted that these reforms, which were only partially successful, merely undermined the power of the upper caste landlords. The wider benefits of reform reached out to the erstwhile tenants or the intermediate and backward castes, not to the untouchable communities or agricultural labourers and agrestic serfs.[6] In fact, the growing power of the backward castes in the wake of the Green Revolution obliged the states in north India, most notably U.P., to initiate the Mandal Commission reforms.

These translated the increasing political and economic influence of the backward castes into bureaucratic power.

Despite the limitations of land reforms, the logic of extending the franchise to all adults and allowing democratic politics, finally created a social milieu in the 1990s in which dalit voters at last confronted the dominance of the upper and backward castes. Aware of the logic of democratic politics in which a majority is won on the basis of the first-past-the-post-system, the numerical strength of lower caste groups gives them an advantage. It is important to note that dalit voters had already been mobilized by the democratic upsurge of the 1970s: the odds of the dalits turning out to vote became as high as those of the upper castes. Since then, the odds of dalit voter turnout is 70 per cent higher than that of the upper castes.[7] This encouraged dalit leaders to launch their own platforms. According to social anthropologist, R.S. Khare, the impact of the democratic culture is unmistakable when a dalit, 'who customarily has a non-competitive subjugated status', discovers through experience, especially of other groups, that competition is one of the major mechanisms of social recuperation.[8] To compete is to claim a political right.

In the forefront of dalit politics are the new professional and administrative élites, a group that is still very small but quite aware of its prestigious social placement. Politically conscious, better educated and assertive towards the hierarchy of caste and class, members of this group have contributed to strengthening the processes of socio-political change. The striking feature of this agenda is the belief that real improvement in their lives can only come through a discourse that focuses on political power and organization as the key to their social advancement. The logic of dalit politics, they argue, involves three major themes: a challenge to the very definition of Hinduism as the majority religion and the core of Indian tradition; an extension of this theme beyond dalits to include all sections of those oppressed and marginalized by the process of caste exploitation; and a synthesis of economic and political issues with the need for cultural recognition.[9] At the heart of the matter is whether it is more important to change state policy outcomes, or the processes that produce them. The strategy of dalit assertion clearly indicates it is more important to acquire power as a means of changing state outcomes, than to change the structures that produce them.

Given the dual inequalities of status and income/occupation built into the caste system, the dominant tendency among dalit leaders has favoured a change in the power structure, so that opportunities could be channeled to the deprived sections of society. The OBC-dominated Janata Dal, led by Laloo Prasad Yadav in neighboring Bihar, came to power on such a platform: 'smash the upper castes, destroy the Bhura-bal'. An example of his rhetoric is the following:

Just as peddlers visit your villages saying, choose what you like for four annas, the officers of my government will come to you with whatever you want. Free sarees, free dhotis. They will camp in your villages. They are your servants. Take what you want.

The centrality accorded to power was just as clear in the remarks of former Prime Minister, V.P. Singh, the chief architect of the social justice platform:

Through Mandal I knew we were going to bring in changes in the basic nature of power. I was putting my hand on the real structure of power. I knew I was not giving jobs, Mandal is not an employment scheme, but I was seeking to place people in the instrument of power through the use of governmental power.[10]

The most remarkable characteristic of lower caste politics is the pursuit of power. Like the OBC leaders, the dalit leaders are preoccupied with the question of who governs and how the new political order should be established and maintained. Both attach great importance to gaining government positions, and measure social and economic progress by their groups' share in public life: education, professions and public employment. Kanshi Ram, the pioneer of the movement to politically organize the bahujan samaj (which simply means the non-upper caste majority, Muslims included), puts the matter bluntly: 'We have a one point programme—take power.'[11] The BSP's principal slogans underscore this thrust: *mat hamara raj tumhara, nahi chalega nahi chalega or, vote se lenge PM/CM, arakshan se SP/DM.*[12] By contrast, in the 1970s, Kanshi Ram's activities were focused on welfare and reform. By the late 1970s his strategy had changed and he no longer believed in the primacy of social reform; rather, it is a share in political and administrative power which will bring about the desired social change.[13]

Opposed to this argument stand the unlovely structures of social dominance within north Indian society that traditionally compelled dalits to vote in accordance with the wishes of upper caste landlords. Ambedkarite in ideological inspiration, the new leadership wants to turn this structure upside down and construct, instead, a new political order based on the active participation of hitherto deprived groups in government and public administration. Through controlling power, they hope to ensure that members of lower castes secure jobs and places in educational institutions. Although reservations have secured some upward mobility, dalits have a major grievance that the reservation quota is seldom filled. In the early 1980s, only 5.8 per cent of Class I officials, and 6.23 per cent Class II officials were Scheduled Caste, although 18 per cent positions were reserved for them. Even when the quota was filled, the Scheduled Castes complained of social discrimination in promotions and postings. Hence the dalit upsurge was stirred principally by the upwardly mobile middle strata among the Scheduled Castes, who were powerless to secure important postings and proper recognition in government and society. The origins and support of the party among educated government employees is crucial for understanding both the institutional nature of its strategy and its success, a success that was limited to élite incorporation into state institutions.

III

A development of critical importance in U.P. has been the rise of the Bahujan Samaj Party which was able to form the government in 1995 and 1997. The BSP benefitted crucially from the collapse of the Congress in U.P. Its rise to prominence was partly due to the vacuum caused by the decline of the Congress, partly because of its own appeal, and also because the Congress discouraged highly assertive advocates of the oppressed castes and classes within its ranks. More importantly, the disintegration of Congress rule transformed the manner in which ethnic identities were catapulted onto the political arena. The waning of the Congress coincided with an escalation of direct caste-community appeals made by non-Congress parties, which led to an exodus of groups that were under the Congress umbrella towards the Samajwadi Party and the BSP. These two parties picked up additional support as they gathered momentum.

A crucial step in this direction was the formation in 1978 of an organization called the Backward and Minority Classes Employees Federation (BAMCEF) by Kanshi Ram. Established in Punjab, it was later extended to U.P. Its chief aim was to organize the élite of the bahujan samaj who had benefitted from quotas in government service. They became the chief ideologues and workers of the organization that eventually became the Bahujan Samaj Party. By the early 1990s, BAMCEF had almost 200,000 members.[14] It mobilized government officers on the assumption that their further individual progress was closely linked to the collective standing of their group.[15] It prepared the ground for the formation of the BSP in 1984; its goal was to create a coalition of minorities that actually constituted a majority: the Scheduled Castes, Scheduled Tribes, OBCs, Muslims, Christians and Sikhs, that is, all those not included in the Hindu upper castes. Unable to establish itself as a party of all the minorities, the predominant base of the BSP came from the politicized dalits who were receptive to its radical message of political empowerment. Today, its core support comes from those castes who have been the main beneficiaries of the state's reservation policies. The nucleus of its support comes from the Chamar caste, by far the largest and most politicized lower caste in U.P. Backed by the BSP, dalit assertiveness succeeded in undermining the domination of upper castes and, by the mid-1990s, they were beginning to supplant them in elected government bodies.[16]

The ascent of Mayawati to the powerful office of the chief minister of U.P. in less than a decade of Scheduled Caste mobilization, highlights the success of this strategy in U.P. Mayawati, a Jatav woman, became the chief minister in 1995. She is the first dalit woman to have reached the highest office in an Indian state, but gender was not the most important aspect of her accession. Its significance arises from the mobilization strategy of the BSP, centred on dalits themselves. The control of the government by a dalit had a stirring effect on dalits, who felt that they had unexpectedly pulled the ground from beneath the feet of upper castes, so that those at the bottom ruled over those at the top. This event established the dalits as a central political force in their own right and not as a vote bank to be exploited by upper castes.

Before the 1993 assembly elections, Kanshi Ram had entered into a winning alliance with Mulayam Singh. Against the back-

ground of the Mandal-Mandir controversies, this alliance assumed a new relevance for the Bahujan Samaj's access to power.
It helped the BSP and the Samajwadi Party to improve their support in the 1993 elections: the Samajwadi Party won 109 seats
out of 425 and 25. 83 per cent of the vote, and the BSP won 67
and 11.11 per cent of the vote, and formed the government
which lasted nearly two years. But the alliance was dogged by
differences over the distribution of benefits. This was by no
means a natural alliance, since the two communities were engaged in sometimes violent conflict over land and wages in the
villages. The BSP was worried by advances made by the Yadavs
under the chief minister Mulayam Singh Yadav's dispensation,
while backward castes used every opportunity to tease and tor-
ment dalits and also check the latter's efforts towards social mobility. The alliance fell through amidst considerable bickering and bitterness over atrocities against dalits in May 1995,
and the BSP quickly moved on to form a new alliance with the
BJP which helped Mayawati to become the chief minister in June
1995. But this alliance was just as expedient as the previous
one, its chief purpose being to control Mulayam Singh Yadav,
whose increasing political influence both partners wished to
curb. But, more importantly, it helped the BSP to be in government. Given the overwhelming importance of acquiring power
in the BSP scheme, its leadership was willing to enter into an
alliance with the BJP or any other party to form a government.

The BSP's approach is fundamentally different from other
parties. For it, political society is constituted by groups, and
not individuals. It treats group identity as the defining one and
does not consider class, gender or occupation as relevant. Hence,
its political strategy hinges on activating this identity. Implicit
in it is a belief that universalist ideas associated with the post-
colonial politics of the state were unjust, because they favoured
the dominant groups without making adequate allowance for
the inequities from which lower castes suffer. Seen invariably
in collective terms, disadvantage and inequity are regarded as
the unfair treatment of whole caste groups, by the state or others. The new lower caste politics draws upon a growing preference for the recognition of group claims on grounds of social
discrimination. This has been used to increase group-based representation in existing political institutions.[17]

In accordance with this strategy, the BSP advocates a one-point programme: proportional representation for all groups in government, bureaucracy and educational institutions. This system appealed to dalits precisely because it addressed their political aspiration, an aspiration neglected by the Congress. It effectively superceded the welfarist approach of the Congress that stressed material benefits such as jobs, houses and sanitation for dalits, minorities, and women, but did not offer them a share in power. It treated dalits primarily as an underprivileged group requiring a programme of action to ameliorate poverty. Quite deliberately breaking from this policy, the BSP defined dalits as a 'community of humiliated' who could be liberated only by gaining political power of their 'own', and not just material gains.[18] Under Congress rule, despite the importance of the dalit vote, they achieved very little representation in the government and party organization, and the few positions that they did get were due to the benefaction of the upper castes. In a word, the significance of the dalit vote did not translate into perceptible influence for individual members in the organization or government. By contrast, Mayawati's rise to the office of chief minister was the result of the autonomous mobilization of dalits, itself the product of democratic politics, and the politics of reservation, which has made available to them new forms of political self-definition. Dalits, as much as the OBCs, are a category of political action. Political action has been an important means of affirming their political equality vis-à-vis upper castes and a way of regaining self-esteem and self-respect.

Although Mayawati's first stint in power did not entail any structural changes in the economy or polity to benefit the vast numbers of the subaltern classes, the BSP nevertheless commanded pivotal support among the dalits throughout its period in office and even thereafter. By the 1996 election it had emerged as an important political force: it notched up an impressive 20 per cent of the vote and managed to get 59 seats in the Vidhan Sabha. This was an improvement of eight per cent on the 1993 election, a significant development. Significant because it derived not from militant mass mobilization, but from capturing state power via anti-high caste propaganda. An additional reason was Mayawati's distinctive style and culture of administration and her determination to promote Scheduled Caste officers. For example, all the upper castes holding important positions, such as chief secretary and chief minister's private secretary were replaced by Scheduled Caste officers. This change provoked resentment and, correlatively, the dalit assertion polarized the upper and lower castes.

During her two terms in office, and especially her second term, Mayawati succeeded in building a new political presence for dalits. She tried to make good the promise of political empowerment by filling the reserved quota for Scheduled Castes and appointing them to important positions in the government. This was accomplished through large-scale transfers of bureaucrats; 1350 civil and police officials were transferred during her six month tenure in 1997. As many as 467 members of the Indian Administrative Service, 380 officers of the Indian Police Service, 300 members of the Provincial Civil Service and 250 Provincial Police were transferred. Dubbed as a 'transfer industry' by the Allahabad high court, the large-scale transfers placed dalits in key positions in the state and local administration. At the end of Mayawati's second term in office, a quarter of the district magistrates and superintendents of police and more than a quarter of the principal secretaries in 1997 belonged to the Scheduled Castes.

In terms of new policies or programmes there was little to show from her two terms of government. But it could be argued that the BSP had not been in power long enough to initiate major development programmes. Mayawati, however, claimed that her government had done some indispensable work for dalits during two short stints in power. These achievements were: (*i*) sharpening the emancipatory campaigns among the dalits; (*ii*) confronting the existing upper caste bias of the state apparatus in order to make way for lower castes; (*iii*) accelerating the passage of resources and funds via government programmes for the Scheduled Castes; and (*iv*) securing dalits' access to some government land. Serious land reform was not on the BSP agenda. It limited itself to efforts that enabled dalits to take possession of land they had already been allotted. Nonetheless, land reforms have given a measure of land and security to the dalits: 158,000 dalits were given possession over 1.20 lakh acres of land. In addition, unauthorized possession by dalits of Gaon Sabha land prior to June 1995 was regularized, benefitting 1500 Scheduled Caste families.[19]

The most significant programme of her second term was the Ambedkar Village Development Scheme, which provided development funds and infrastructure to 15,000 Ambedkar villages, with a 30 per cent dalit population. Basically, model villages were built by transferring funds and resources from other programmes spread over large areas, and concentrating them in smaller pockets. Though at the time of this writing it is too early to assess the policy impact of Ambedkarization or reveal how many people have benefitted from the programme, there is no denying that the initiative generated considerable enthusiasm among BSP cadres and the masses, even as it kindled the hostilities of other castes, particularly those who are just as poor as the dalits. Though modest, some of these measures—such as doubling the amount of scholarship money to high school students belonging to the Scheduled Castes, or the decision to double the scholarship admissible to children belonging to the families engaged in unhygienic occupations—have boosted dalit confidence simply by the preference given to them by a dalit-led government.

Within the larger administration of the state, Mayawati offered her constituency the greatest possibilities of obtaining access to jobs, offices, and power. In a state where caste politics is deeply entrenched, BSP's caste-based analysis of dalit deprivation was bound to appeal to them. Benefits in U.P. were distributed on the basis of patronage, consequently, dalits supported their 'own' élites in the expectation that they would share the spoils of power and wealth once they obtained government positions. But the BSP has succeeded in retaining dalit support without always delivering material benefits or political office.[20] It could be argued that its success owed much to the radical emphasis placed by the party on contesting upper caste oppression. This aspect of its mobilization programme is critical because the party did not subscribe to any economic programme or ideology and hardly ever proposed new policies. In these circumstances, the politics of symbolism and recognition has been given priority to encourage the growth of their own constituency. An enormous amount of its energy has been spent in the politicization of dalits through symbolic acts of dalit empowerment and resisting upper caste hegemony, rather than in securing material benefits. As one IAS officer put it, 'The dalit fight is not for economic emancipation, it is a battle for social recognition. If the dalit assertion was for economic rights then we would back the Communist parties. We are struggling for dignity and participation in government which gives us social status.'[21] Toward this end, the BSP emphasized the themes of recovering dignity and status. In this connection, the most flamboyant gesture of Mayawati's government was to build a Parivartan Chowk in the centre of Lucknow that would have statues of the great anti-Brahmin leaders: Jyotiba Phule, Periyar E.V. Ramaswamy Naicker, Ambedkar, Shahu Maharaj. This was supplemented by the installation of Ambedkar statues in every village and town; organization of Ambedkar melas; development of Ambedkar parks in every district; carving out new districts and naming them after dalit leaders; and instituting awards in memory of a pantheon of dalit heroes. These symbolic measures were meant to challenge the upper castes' political and cultural hegemony. Indeed it had an electrifying effect on the collective social status of the dalits.

Although gains in dignity and self-respect were important, they made sense because they were linked to the more tangible promise of political empowerment for the Scheduled Castes, as well as some improvement in economic opportunities.[22] Ultimately the principle of proportional representation played a key role in helping the party retain its hold on dalit loyalties. Mayawati achieved an increased representation of Scheduled Castes by an overt focus on caste identity as the sole criterion for distributing tickets and posts. This resulted in the political empowerment of dalits in U.P. being greater than in any other state. It is certainly true that the stable vote of Scheduled Castes for the BSP was the principal reason why it could promote dalit empowerment. The preferential treatment given to dalits in turn contributed to its durability, and undoubtedly, this was because they had 'their' party and their 'own' chief minister, and power was exercised for their benefit. In other words, U.P.'s political experience indicates that dalits used their votes to, at once, affirm identities and avenge past humiliations, as well as to secure instrumental benefits.

IV

The significant political transformation brought about by the dalit assertion should not, however, be allowed to mask the in-

equalities that continued to exist for the majority of dalits within
U.P. Benefits have flowed to a privileged minority within the
lower castes; the dalits still remain the most dispossessed and
disadvantaged group.[23] A point worth noting is that low levels
of income and education, rather than just underrepresentation
and non-recognition, are the major constraint on access to and
spread of social opportunities. Yet, most of the newly mobilized
people in U.P. continue to see themselves as members of castes
and communities anxious to preserve their group, rather than
individual or class, interests. Even though political competition is intertwined with an intensification of social conflict at
the class level, the tendency is to use mobilization as a means
for winning political power, and not as a condition for intra-
group equality and development. Redressing disadvantage and
deprivation within this framework of empowerment from above
prevented the rectification of inequalities of class, especially at
the lower rungs of the social order. The strategy of the Samajwadi
Party and the BSP certainly enhanced the political power of the
OBCs/dalits and their ability to influence state politics, but this
cannot substitute for radical social and economic change that
is imperative in U.P. It is difficult to imagine how the abbrevia-
tion of the political power of dominant castes could be limited
to the government sector. It is hardly possible for the BSP to
preside over governance without addressing the land question
or without doing something about the economic and extra-eco-
nomic oppression of agricultural labourers, for example. The
BSP faces a strategic predicament: its autonomous politics have
raised the political profile of dalits at the local level, which requires the government to support local resistance. But tackling
local problems entails a class approach to pressurize the government for implementation of economic redistribution, which
a caste-based following cannot achieve and which the party
wants to avoid. Far from generating social and political dynamism, caste mobilization and sectional governance tend to block
much-needed structural change.

The failure to address inequalities in education, health and
employment opportunities, which are in fact a reflection of inequalities in the social and economic powers of different groups,
is not a unique feature of lower caste parties. Equity in distribution was never the priority of any government. The political

importance of the state notwithstanding, U.P. remains one of the poorest and least developed states in the Union. This is reflected in its high levels of mortality, fertility, morbidity, under-nutrition, illiteracy, social inequality, and the slow pace of poverty decline.[24] The most striking is the high degree of inequality experienced by women in terms of life expectancy, literacy, access to health facilities and property in land. Even the redistributional programmes introduced in the early 1970s, at the height of the garibi hatao campaign have produced insignificant results because the state lacked both the commitment and institutions required for their implementation.[25] These institutions include the Public Distribution System, the Integrated Rural Development Programmes, and the Integrated Child Development Schemes. These programmes—which involve transfers of various kinds to target groups and no redistribution of assets between different classes—are easier to implement and, yet, the gap between promise and delivery is very wide. There were no significant initiatives—comparable to health care in Kerala, social security in Tamil Nadu, land reforms in West Bengal, employment guarantee schemes in Maharashtra and panchayati raj in Karnataka—to promote social development. No serious social reform, after zamindari abolition in the early 1950s, ever made headway in U.P.

Social and economic development have been stymied by an unbridgeable chasm between the rhetoric of development and the ground realities of implementing socio-economic policies which required structural changes in the pattern of social relations. In this context an important impediment has been the nature of agrarian politics. These have revolved around the interests of surplus producers in receiving input subsidies and procurement prices for foodgrains. The leadership of political parties and farmers' movements has been firmly in the hands of this class. Distributive policies could not be sustained in the absence of significant public action from below. The state machinery, police and village-level bureaucracy were tilted in favour of landed groups, not least because the bureaucracy recruited from the upper castes shared the concerns of the rural rich. The privileges of governmental control have been exploited for sectional benefit of those with political and bureaucratic power, or those with the opportunity to influence political action to challenge the oppressive patterns of caste, class, and gender relations.

By contrast, trends in south India, and Kerala in particular, point to the major role of collective action and structural change in the advancement of lower castes and classes. In Kerala, the major beneficial impact of public policy has come from strategies directed to the whole population and not merely to specific groups.[26] This is true in relation to the greater life expectancy, increased literacy, and above all the dignity of dalits. It has the best social indicators of any state in India. Although indicators for the Scheduled Castes rank lower than the state average, they are better than their counterparts in other states, and even though Kerala has been derelict with regard to fulfilling the reserved quota, dalits have benefitted from the general welfare policies of the state. Furthermore, the experiences of Kerala and Maharashtra underscore the importance of collective public action for effectively implementing the provisions of reservation policies. Marginalized groups which are politically unorganized are even less effective in pressuring the state to fulfil its welfare commitments. More broadly, the effectiveness of reservations in favour of the OBCs in south India seems to indicate that a general improvement in education and a measure of land redistribution are important conditions for the rapid promotion of equality.

Historically, the new groups in U.P. have had a more difficult time achieving what non-Brahmins achieved in south India, at least partly because lower caste politics in U.P. lacked ideological content. In the south, the non-Brahmin movement institutionalized participation at an early stage, and developed gradually enough to allow upper castes time to adjust to their loss of power; this small minority moved into the commercial and industrial sectors. In U.P., the upper castes form a fifth and the Brahmins nearly 10 per cent of the population. Besides, the organized sector was not the monopoly of Brahmins alone. Diverse groups such as Kayasths, Banias and élite sections of Muslims shared power. The wider range and large proportion of upper castes made it harder to organize a non-Brahmin movement to displace them.[27] The upper castes dominated the government and political organizations. While the reservation of government jobs was the principal channel of upward mobility for the OBCs and the Scheduled Castes, government jobs remained the most attractive career option for the upper castes as well because, in contrast to the south, alternative avenues of employment in U.P.'s stagnant industrial economy were limited. An opportunity for political change in U.P. arose only when the upper castes abandoned the Congress in favour of the BJP. This led to the disintegration of the Congress vote, creating a crucial opening for the disadvantaged groups to rally behind caste-based parties committed to social justice for deprived groups.

Eventually, such a group-empowerment strategy cannot bring about substantive change. The two subjects that have the greatest capacity to influence the well-being of subordinate groups—land reform and education—cannot be addressed without structural reform. In fact, the BSP is the only party which can push land reform legislation in U.P. and accelerate the painfully slow process of mass education, since it draws support from the Scheduled Castes and lower sections of the OBCs. However, the BSP has rarely spelt out policies on these basic issues; they consider them irrelevant to the bigger project of winning power. Though the party has attempted to implement the existing policy of redistribution in favour of dalits, it cannot energetically and purposefully pursue this without a majority of its own. This is clearly ruled out in the fragmented party system of U.P., structured by rough parity in numbers between the most privileged upper castes, the bloc of backward castes, and dalits. In reality, both the strength and weakness of the BSP stems from its caste-bloc politics. Its strength is that the Scheduled Castes are evenly spread across the state and a dalit vote gives the party a chance in a large number of constituencies, but it also makes it logically impossible to win even a single seat without strong support from other groups. It has not, however, been able to attract significant support from backward castes and Muslims. It has received their support only when it fielded candidates and gave organizational responsibilities to cadres from among them.

V

Although the benefits of empowerment have been captured only by a small élite among the subordinate groups, yet U.P.'s political system has been transformed. The emergence of the BSP has added a vital dimension to the ground level economic and political development of the lower castes. The new entrants see electoral triumph as the necessary means to gaining power and challenging the domination of the established élite. I have argued elsewhere that with all its limitations, caste-based mobilization has proved to be a successful vehicle for the political empowerment of the populous backward castes.[28] It has generated a shift in the balance of political power in the government and legislature: the gap between the upper and lower castes has been steadily narrowing since 1989, when the Janata Dal came to power. This is evident from the significant increase in the number of lower caste legislators and senior civil servants in influential government positions. However, it remains to be seen whether the benefits of state control can be distributed to larger sections of the population. At the same time, the rise of the lower castes has provoked the hostility of upper castes, especially in U.P., where the Samajwadi Party and the BSP emerged as major political forces. In reaction, the votes of these castes were transferred en bloc to the BJP. Even before these controversies came on to the political centre stage, the predominant conflict was between the backward and upper castes. The rise of dalits and their consolidation behind the BSP intensified this conflict, but it is clear that caste-based mobilization alone cannot continue to win mandates for lower caste leaders.

Uttar Pradesh's political scene presents a paradoxical combination of lower caste party fragmentation and the consolidation of Hindu nationalist sentiment and political appeal. The 1998 elections marked a watershed, accelerating the BJP's growth. The party again won a majority of the Lok Sabha seats from U.P., increasing its electoral strength from fifty-two to fifty-seven seats. In fact, since 1991 a major component of its strength in the Lok Sabha has come from U.P. Between 1991 and 1996, its growth was obstructed by lower caste parties and it was argued that the party's strength had peaked due to its inability to garner the support of lower castes, who overwhelmingly voted for the Samajwadi Party and BSP.[29]

Caste divisions among Hindus and inter-caste hostility continue to play a critical role in determining political conflict. The BJP has not been able to downplay these divisions; however, it has managed to weaken them by winning over some backward castes to its side. Although it is still heavily dependent on the double appeal of Ayodhya and the continued resentments of upper castes towards Mandal, it has marshalled a respectable chunk of the OBC vote, especially of the middle castes excluded from the Mandal list. It is well known that Kurmis and Lodhas, the caste to which the BJP chief minister Kalyan Singh belongs, have previously backed the BJP. The new development that has contributed tremendously to the BJP's electoral success is the support of the Jats, an intermediate caste, in western U.P., and of the smaller backward castes throughout the state.[30]

An early attempt to mobilize the lower castes was made during the Ram Janmabhumi campaign, which in the words of L.K. Advani 'succeeded in sublimating caste tensions'. But the support gained then was lost after the Babri masjid was demolished in December 1992. Many among the lower castes looked at the assault as an upper caste backlash against the Mandal move initiated by the Janata Dal government. This resulted in an alliance of the Samajwadi Party and the BSP, which halted the BJP's advance in the 1993 assembly elections. It encouraged the BJP leadership to concentrate its attention on splitting the lowest castes. This strategy succeeded in 1995, splitting the Samajwadi–BSP alliance forged in the 1993 elections and bringing down the Mulayam Singh Yadav government. The BJP then put its support behind the BSP, which allowed Mayawati to come to power as chief minister. This proved important in checking the consolidation of the lower castes, since the cooperation of the backward and Scheduled Castes presents a formidable challenge to the BJP and can potentially prevent it from coming to power.

Working in small-town, upper caste milieus, the BJP has on the whole kept away from caste reform. However, in the years after the Mandal Commission, they have had to make gestures of accommodation towards the lower castes. Following a policy of social engineering, the BJP has been inclined to broaden its base, but its effort has been opposed by leaders of the RSS. This organization considers caste assertion as essentially divisive and remains logically irreconciled to affirmative action. There is thus a tension between the BJP leadership's advocacy of social engineering and the traditional RSS view based on the varna hierarchy. Owing to the compulsions of electoral politics, the BJP–RSS combine has had to make room for the lower castes, but it has not been able to assimilate these groups within the electoral and decision-making structures. The upper castes remain overrepresented not only among its supporters in the electorate, but also among MPs, MLAs, and ministers.

The BSP's withdrawal from the BJP–BSP alliance in October 1997 saw the break-up of parties, barring the SP, on caste lines. Almost all the upper caste MLAs from other parties defected to the BJP and reinforced its upper caste orientation. But in spite of being upper caste and openly identified with the socially privileged strata, the BJP has gained the votes of the backward castes. According to the CSDS post-poll survey, the BJP made crucial inroads into OBC votes in 1998. More OBCs have swung towards the BJP in this election than any other community.[31] It remains to be seen whether the BJP will change its character as a result of appealing to the OBCs and dalits. As for the BSP, it managed to consolidate the Scheduled Castes behind the party: according to the same survey, 63.4 per cent of them voted for the party, as against 26 per cent non-Yadav OBCs, 4.3 per cent Yadavs, 4.7 per cent Muslims and less than one per cent upper castes.[32] In this election it maintained its 1996 strength, but its strong performance was restricted to eastern U.P. A major setback was the defeat of Kanshi Ram in the Bahujan-dominated Saharanpur constituency. In fact, the Samajwadi Party is the only party besides the BJP that marginally improved its position (from seventeen to twenty seats) in the 1998 elections. But the Samajwadi Party, which is limited to Yadavs and Muslims, cannot alone thwart the BJP's chances of coming to power in the absence of backing from the Scheduled Castes, who solidly voted for the BSP.

Given the BJP's continued dominance in U.P. politics, there are two possible strategies available to lower caste leaders. One is a form of all-embracing distributional politics committed to channelling state resources towards the improvement of all, regardless of particularism. This is conspicuous by its absence from the U.P. scene. The difficulties of this policy under present political conditions is evident from the Congress performance in the 1998 elections, when the party failed to win a single seat from the state. In 1998, its vote fell below eight per cent and a majority of its candidates forfeited their deposit.

The second alternative is a coalition of the lower castes and minorities led by the Samajwadi Party–BSP combine. Such a broad-based social coalition, or even an electoral adjustment

between the Samajwadi Party and the BSP, would deny power
to the upper castes and the BJP in U.P., power that is critical to
its control of the Centre. In the process, they could bag many
more seats and emerge as important players in state and national politics. This was the lesson of the 1996 elections. In them,
the absence of an understanding between secular parties helped
the BJP to win fifty-two seats. The Samajwadi Party and BSP
together polled 45.6 per cent of the vote but only won eighteen
and six seats respectively. In thirty-four of the fifty-two seats
that the BJP won, its share of popular vote was less than the
combined vote of the Samajwadi Party and BSP. Yet, backward
and lower caste leaders are averse to the formation of a broad
alliance. Rather, they are engaged in a bitter struggle for power
as both compete for scarce state resources. The increasing importance of the BSP and the assertiveness of its leaders has complicated patterns of social conflict and the possibility of making such alliances. Their autonomy and independence have no
doubt increased the political consciousness of dalits and promoted their empowerment, but they have also brought them
into conflict with both the Samajwadi Party and the BJP. This is
also why the BJP was relatively successful in breaking the
Samajwadi Party–BSP alliance.[33]

Even after the BJP's seizure of power, the OBCs and the Scheduled Castes, the Samajwadi Party and the BSP, persisted with
their rhetoric over which one authentically represented the lower
castes. Although the break-up of the BJP-BSP alliance was a good
opportunity for the non-upper castes to come together, they did
not. This was due partly to ground-level OBC–dalit hostility,
and partly to the power struggle between the two groups which
has moved from being a contest between unequals to a struggle
for power between near equals, facilitated by the BSP's pursuit
of a dalit empowerment agenda since 1993.[34]

Even as caste interests proliferate, there is however no simple
dualism of upper castes versus lower castes; rather, the growing power of the BJP could subvert the hard-won gains of the
latter. Backward and lower caste parties can act as a brake on
Hindu consolidation only when they are united on a common
platform. Should the Muslims, more than half the backward
castes, and the Scheduled Castes be united behind the
Samajwadi Party, the BSP and what remains of the Janata Dal,

the BJP would not win electoral majorities in U.P. It has come
to power by capitalizing on the divisions between these competing castes and parties. This is the central point of the 1998
parliamentary elections, when the BSP won only four seats, despite winning more than 20 per cent of the vote. In reality, the
consolidation of dalits behind the BSP has been advantageous
for the BJP. By refusing to come to terms with the changed political situation and allowing their egos to clash, the leaders of
both the Samajwadi Party and the BSP have caused serious damage to their own interests. The predicament is that the BSP's
unreliability as an electoral partner stands in the way of an alliance with any party, particularly the Samajwadi Party; on the
other hand, the high vote of the BSP clearly establishes its electoral clout, making an alliance with it imperative. It is with this
clout that BSP leaders hope to be in a position to dictate outcomes at the national and state levels.

Presumably, the lower caste leaders recognize the damage
caused by these divisions but are not prepared to subdue them
because they can still obtain political office, and hence do not
feel an urgent need for coalitions. Undoubtedly, caste constituencies help them to bargain with national parties, but it also
limits their horizon, and especially the prospect of extending
their political influence to other states.[35] There must still be
room to navigate between these constraints to find new ways
that do not altogether abandon self-empowerment, and to pursue them within coalitions. Surely, lower caste parties need caste
constituencies to gain access to government, as well as a broader
coalition to uphold and stabilize their access. In the absence of
such coalitions they will remain stalemated and trapped within
the specific castes they seek to represent, while the BJP presses
ahead with its mobilization on ethno-religious lines.

Today, there is little doubt that the growth of political consciousness around caste issues and related strategies of empowerment has provided a discursive vehicle for the mobilization
of what has clearly been a progressive social and political force.
It has also underwritten a new argument for secularism, one
that opposes caste to communalism. But it has left behind a
legacy in which caste has been bolstered as a focus of political
identity and affiliation, one that may exclude broader social
commitment and collective action.

North India's recent history, and that of Uttar Pradesh in particular, indicates that for collective action to become a real force, political parties must go beyond caste. The challenge is to accommodate interests and identities which are electorally disaggregated into a negotiable frame of governance. In the meantime, lower caste parties have managed to fragment the legacy of the Congress; they have also rebutted the BJP's claim of Hindu unity by forcing it to negotiate separately with competing Hindu groups, rather than with Hindus as constituents of a single homogeneous community. Although the lower caste parties do not have an agenda of structural reform, they have managed to bring formerly marginal groups into the government and diverted public resources and flow of benefits to them. Unlike the past, it is now difficult for any government to ignore the interests of dalits. Significantly, this has opened new spaces for the lower castes to enter the urban middle classes. This could well be the beginning of a more radical democratization of north Indian society, as the majority of dalits and OBCs begins to realize that its economic and social condition has not improved much as a result of proportional representation in the state.

Notes

[1] *Constituent Assembly Debate*, vol X, Official Report (New Delhi), 1989, p. 979.

[2] Harishankar Parsai, *Selected Satire*, (Delhi: Manas Publications), 1996.

[3] *Primary Census Abstract for Scheduled Castes and Scheduled Tribes*, Paper 1, 1993.

[4] For example, in Palanpur female literacy varies from zero for Scheduled Caste females to 100 per cent for Kayasths. Jean Drèze and Haris Gazdar, 'Uttar Pradesh: The Burden of Inertia', in Jean Drèze and Amartya Sen (eds), *Indian Development: Selected Regional Perspectives* (Delhi: Oxford University Press), 1997, pp. 83–6.

[5] Barbara Joshi, 'Whose Law, Whose Order? "Untouchables", Social Violence and the State in India', *Asian Survey*, no. 7, (July 1982), p. 684.

[6] For a discussion of the impact of land reforms on different groups, see my *Quest for Power: Oppositional Movements in Uttar Pradesh* (Delhi: Oxford University Press), 1998, Chapter 2.

[7] For details of the democratic upsurge, see Yogendra Yadav in this volume.

[8] R.S. Khare, *The Untouchable as Himself: Ideology, Identity and Pragma-*

tism among the Lucknow Chamars (Cambridge: Cambridge University Press), 1984, p. 129.

[9] Gail Omvedt, Dalit Visions. Tracts for the Times 8. (Delhi: Orient Longman), 1995, p. 87.

[10] Quoted in Seema Mustafa's biography of V.P. Singh. The Lonely Prophet: A Political Biography of V.P. Singh (Delhi: Wiley Eastern, 1996), p. 191.

[11] The Bahujan Samaj Party's most popular slogan is: 'Brahmin, bania, thakur, chor, Baki sab DS4' (Dalit Shoshit Samaj Sangharsh Samiti). It has gone much beyond other dalit organizations by projecting itself not as a 'dalit party' but as a bahujan party of dalits, non-Brahmins and minorities. See Gail Omvedt, 'The Anti-Caste Movement and the Discourse of Power', in T.V. Sathyamurthy (ed.), Region, Religion, Caste, Gender and Culture in Contemporary India (Delhi: Oxford University Press), 1996, pp. 344–6.

[12] Translation: 'We vote you rule, this cannot go on. Through the vote we will take the posts of prime minister and chief minister; through reservations we will take the posts of district magistrate and superintendent police.'

[13] Oliver Mendelsohn and Marica Vicziani, The Untouchables: Subordination, Poverty and the State in India, (Cambridge: Cambridge University Press), 1998, p. 223.

[14] Gail Omvedt, 'Kanshi Ram and the Bahujan Samaj Party' in K.L. Sharma (ed.), Caste and Class in India (Jaipur: Rawat), 1994, p. 163.

[15] Interviews with dalit IAS officials in August 1997 in Lucknow highlighted this point.

[16] The OBC and dalits comprised 231 MLAs in the 422-member Uttar Pradesh assembly in 1993. By contrast, Brahmin MLAs declined from 23 per cent in 1980 to 10 per cent in 1993. Their participation expanded with the extension of reservations to the panchayats in 1993 after a rapid census ordered by Mulayam Singh Yadav to estimate the caste-wise configuration. Equally significant is the changing composition of the Cabinet. The percentage of upper castes which, according to a study conducted by a member of the Uttar Pradesh Backward Classes Commission, was as high as 64.7 per cent at the time of chief minister Sripat Misra, had come down to 50 per cent under Mulayam Singh Yadav in 1990, while non-upper caste representation increased from 35 per cent to 50 per cent. H.S. Verma, Ram Singh and Jay Singh, 'Power Sharing: Exclusivity and Exclusion in a Mega State', Monograph presented to a panel on Deprivation, Backwardness and Social Transformation of the Backward Classes, Twentieth All-India Sociological Conference, 1993, Mangalore, p. 14.

[17] On this see Marc Galanter, 'Group Membership and Group Preferences in India', in his Law and Society in Modern India (Delhi: Oxford University Press), 1989, p. 133.

[18] Kanchan Chandra, 'Why does the Bahujan Samaj Party Succeed? A Case Study of the BSP in Hoshiarpur', Paper presented at the annual meeting of the Association of Asian Studies, Washington D.C., March 1998.

[19] *The Times of India,* 18 September 1997.

[20] Interview, S.R. Darapuri, Inspector General of Police, Economic Intelligence Wing, U.P. government.

[21] This point was emphasized in a number of interviews with Scheduled Caste officers in Lucknow. The point was repeatedly made by S.R. Lakha, Cane Commissioner, U.P. government. Interview, Lucknow, 22 August 1997. He is also the Secretary of the Uttar Pradesh IAS Association.

[22] Interview, Rohit Nandan, Director of Information, U.P. government, 22 August 1998.

[23] Caste differences in educational levels are even now very marked. Widespread illiteracy makes it difficult for disadvantaged groups to ensure that their needs receive due attention in public debates and resource allocation. Education is an important tool for effective participation in democratic politics. Yet, there were no political campaigns or bold initiatives to improve basic education in the state. On the contrary, there is evidence of a serious decline in real per capita expenditure on education, by 20 per cent between 1991–2 and 1993–4. K. Seeta Prabhu, 'Structural Adjustment and Financing of Elementary Education: The Indian Experience', *Journal of Educational Planning and Administration*, no. 9 (1995), p. 37.

[24] For instance, child survival, mortality and literacy levels are below almost all other states. Jean Drèze and Haris Gazdar point to three social failures: low levels of education, the restricted role of women in society, and the poor functioning of public services. Jean Drèze and Haris Gazdar, 'Uttar Pradesh', op. cit., pp. 40–61.

[25] Ibid.

[26] Oliver Mendelsohn and Marica Vicziani, *The Untouchables*, op. cit., pp. 118–24.

[27] For a discussion of caste mobilization based on a critique of caste hierarchy, see Nandini Gooptu, 'Caste, Deprivation and Politics: The Untouchables in U.P. Towns', in Peter Robb (ed.), *Dalit Movements and the Meaning of Labour in India* (Delhi: Oxford University Press), 1993.

[28] See my *Quest for Power*, op. cit., especially Chapter 4.

[29] See Paul Brass, 'General Elections, 1996 in Uttar Pradesh: Divisive Struggles Influence Outcome', *Economic and Political Weekly*, 20 September 1997.

[30] Ibid.

[31] *India Today* commissioned CSDS to conduct a special post-poll survey to track the pattern of voting. *India Today*, 16 March 1998.

[32] Kanchan Chandra and Chandrika Parmar, 'Party Strategies in Uttar Pradesh Assembly Elections, 1966', *Economic and Political Weekly*, 1 February 1997, p. 215.

[33] Mulayam Singh Yadav argues that his party suffered too much under Mayawati's chief ministership for him to consider a patch-up with her. Mayawati feels that Yadav's open opposition to the Atrocities Against Dalits Act during her term in office would harm the party's attempts to consolidate its political base.

[34] Interview, Director Information, U.P. government, Lucknow, 22 August 1997.

[35] Kanchan Chandra and Chandrika Parmar, 'Party Strategies in Uttar Pradesh Assembly Elections, 1996', op. cit., pp. 219–20.

Negotiating Differences: federal coalitions and national cohesion

BALVEER ARORA

The difficulties of building and sustaining coalitions have been accorded considerable significance in the theorization on federal solutions to the problems of diverse societies. Federal coalitions differ in important ways from other strategies for power-sharing through coalitional means, such as caste/class or religious coalitions. They seek to reconcile territorially-based identities within a cohesive frame even in the absence of shared ideologies. For instance, Daniel Elazar, one of the leading exponents of federalism, considers 'shared rule' to be as important as 'self rule' in explaining the possibilities of federal power-sharing.[1] Similarly, Arend Lijphart, whose understanding of multi-party coalitions in the Netherlands led him to formulate the theory of consociationalism, has argued that India has evolved distinctive forms of power-sharing which can be better understood within this framework.[2] Comparative studies on the relationship between federalism and democracy also focus on the capabilities of federal systems to reconcile, recuperate and even reintegrate potentially secessionist movements with innovative accommodation.[3] Finally, a federal culture which tolerates difference and not only accepts but celebrates diversity is considered central to the consolidation and stability of federal coalitions.[4]

Comparisons between the coalitional practices of different systems are difficult, given variations in political history, culture, and tradition.[5] In addition, insights from unitary parliamentary systems can be misleading because federal structures significantly alter both the time-horizons and the contexts of political conflict.[6] Situating India's recent experience with coalition governments in a comparative perspective therefore presents some difficulties. They arise in part from the number and range of coalition partners, in turn linked to the number of parties and the size of the electorate. With these caveats entered, let us nevertheless look at some of the insights thrown up by a comparative study of minority and coalition governments. We shall subsequently attempt to evaluate their significance in the Indian context through an analysis of the coalitional experience that followed the 1998 Lok Sabha elections.

I

In explaining the success or failure of coalitions, political culture is generally considered an important factor. For instance, low levels of trust in opportunistic political cultures are held to reduce the time-horizons of coalition partners engaged in multi-level political combats. Another premise of coalition culture is that while each partner works towards an improved vote/seat share, efforts are simultaneously deployed to contain rivalry and prevent antagonisms that could be fatal to the coalition itself. Political cultures which accord a central place to accepting and negotiating differences are considered conducive to the consolidation and stability of federal coalitions. In such contexts, parties which understand and seize the possibilities offered by coalition building have an advantage, those who can make the system work are rewarded, while those who are unable to reconfigure it to their advantage are gradually marginalized.

The Indian experience offers suggestive evidence in confirmation of some of these propositions, and also throws up new dimensions which need to be integrated into theorization on coalition practices in federal parliamentary systems. While the struggle for power between castes and classes dominates political life in the primary arena of state and panchayat politics in India, regional aspirations are significant factors in the political calculations that parties make when they enter the secondary arena, which is more concerned with national policy cohesion and federal governance.[7] Such calculations play a determining role in forging coalitions and therefore have important institutional consequences. It must be further noted that ideological affinities and programmatic alliances do not preclude regional aspirations: the stability of coalitions, even between natural allies, must take into account the ambitions of territorial consolidation and expansion of its partners.[8] These power-sharing arrangements of the political class cannot be dismissed as mere 'élite accommodation', for they are constitutive elements of tactical calculations based on ground-level cleavages. Elsewhere it has been shown that coalitions based on ideological affinity frequently end in splits or schisms after quarrels over turf between covetous allies, and the bitterest contests are often between like-minded parties seeking a reconfiguration of political space. On the other hand, federal coalitions based on the accommodation of regional aspirations can arguably be converted into stable arrangements with greater ease.[9]

Each polity has evidently to evolve its own ground rules for managing coalitions. However, it is instructive to take a brief look at some of the practices and conventions evolved in other parliamentary democracies with multi-party systems. For instance, in Fourth Republic France, the spoilers and wreckers of coalitions were generally not rewarded by the electorate, especially if they were seen to have been motivated by personal power ambitions.[10] This ground rule was summed up as: 'If you can't make it, don't break it.' While cornering credit and evading blame was the name of the game, expanding at the expense of coalition partners required consummate skill. The trick was to break the coalition without appearing to do so, *and* to succeed in moulding public perception of the collapse. This logic seems to find evidentiary support in recent Indian experience. When the Congress flouted this basic tenet and triumphantly brought down the Gujral government in November 1997, it appeared to have made a serious miscalculation. There is some evidence from opinion surveys to suggest that the electoral verdict on its role would have been far more damaging had Sonia Gandhi not intervened to salvage the situation, with what her grateful party was later to describe as a 'Herculean effort'.[11]

Other insights from comparative analysis relate to the role of independent institutions and agencies, particularly during periods of governmental instability and transitions. While some ground rules are self-enforcing, the observance of others is in large measure ensured by the permanent civil service, reinforced by a free press which can shape perceptions. More transparency and rule-bound governance can also minimise some of the friction that is inevitable in coalition governments. For this, it may be necessary to sacrifice some of the maneuverability and discretion that permissive, flexible arrangements provide to parties in power, but which can become a liability in coalitional situations.

The relationship between India's parliamentary federalism and coalition politics is in some significant ways *sui generis*, because there are no polities with a comparable configuration of party systems at multiple levels. The distinction between national and state parties is not on the basis of the arena in which they compete, since most of them contest in both assembly and parliamentary elections. Some national parties are in fact coalitions of state parties, especially those whose support base is restricted to a few states. Similarly, state parties are sometimes localized in a few districts, having their support base in specific castes or communities.

Since the states of India differ vastly in terms of population and size, they play for different stakes in the national parliament. Small states often perceive themselves as being on the periphery of national agendas, and seek to maximise the returns from their minuscule representation. The dominance of local concerns in the calculations of smaller state-based parties is therefore not unexpected. National level tie-ups are negotiated and justified primarily by their beneficial impact on state-level struggles. What appears to be political opportunism in fact has its roots in the compulsions of local political processes, which need to be taken on board as legitimate aspirations before they can be woven into a cohesive national fabric.

The institutional consequences of competing local logics are often neglected in the comparative analysis of coalition behaviour. In a federal polity, national governance is complicated by the existence of multiple majorities being concurrently made and unmade in the states. Different political waves occur during national elections, determined by power stakes at the state level with an eye to the next assembly elections. The interplay between state and central majorities is perforce complex, in a polity where regional plebiscites do not always add up to a majority in the Lok Sabha. It has been noted that while state parties may join federal coalitions for a variety of reasons, they invariably seek favourable policy outcomes which could enhance their local political prospects.

A certain degree of impermeability between espoused national causes and regional concerns has also been observed in recent electoral consultations. Because of the predominance of local concerns, leaders of state-based parties are shielded and insulated to some extent from the consequences of their actions at the national level.[12] Occasionally there is an overriding national event or issue capable of generating a 'wave', but the last such wave was arguably seen in 1984, after the assassination of Indira Gandhi. Local issues invariably prevail in non-wave conditions, especially when questions of identity and demands for space, voice and esteem in the wider polity dominate the electoral consultation.

One of the significant legacies of the Congress-dominance phase is that in most states, the Congress/anti-Congress cleavage continues to determine decisions relating to the choice of alliance partners. It provides the context for our analysis of the regionalization of the party system and the advent of coalition governments in India.

II

Reconciling regional aspirations and the imperatives of national policy cohesion has always been a major objective of federal political processes. Federal coalitions, within or between parties, have also been a constant feature of India's political development. Congress dominance began to wane as the party became less democratic and more centralized. Conventional wisdom confers watershed attributes on the 1967 general elections, as they marked the beginning of the end of Congress dominance and the advent of the first non-Congress governments in the states on a large scale. For our purposes, it is the Emergency of 1975–7 which has a stronger claim to this description because it permitted, or rather provoked, the forging of the first federal coalition to capture power at the Centre. It was a defining moment for state institutions, just as Partition was for civil society thirty years earlier.[13] Even though the Janata government (1977–9) included within itself strong centralist forces which pre-empted its further development as a durable federal alternative, it did mark the beginning of India's experience with coalition governments.

After this first experiment, which collapsed as a result of deft manoeuvring by the Congress, there was an apparent return to single-party majority rule during the Eighties. Simultaneously there was a consolidation of non-Congress alternatives in the states, largely due to Congress' inability to effect this reconciliation within itself. Though it had substantial majorities in two successive full-term Lok Sabhas and provided stable governments for an entire decade, the state of the nation at the end of this period of central stability was far from edifying. Internal strife and unrest attained unprecedented levels because the Congress failed to respond adequately to demands for a more federal and decentralized dispensation which would allow participative power-sharing. It continued to neglect inner-party democracy and to ignore regional sensitivities.

The Nineties have witnessed a succession of minority or coalition governments which, though reflecting the intense democratic churning in the states, were not able to generate confidence in their governance capabilities. Both the National Front (1989–91) and the United Front (1996–8) were minority governments, precarious from the start and short-lived.[14] They were stigmatized by their opponents as dominated by regional leaders preoccupied with regional interests, and the sceptre of disintegration was freely brandished.[15] This experience gave rise to apprehensions that coalitions might not constitute a viable mode of governance for India. Some even went to the extent of suggesting a regime shift which would 'insulate' the executive from the vagaries and uncertainties of shifting alliances in Parliament.

In interpreting India's coalitional experience which is long and rich at the state level, it is important to remember that most state-based parties have risen to prominence by building anti-Congress coalitions.[16] In most federal systems, state-based parties have historically preceded the development of powerful national parties.[17] However, given the range and magnitude of diversities, it should not come as a surprise that a polity-wide two-party system has not emerged, despite the 'first-past-the-post' electoral system. Interestingly, the hankering for such an orderly arrangement of alternation in power is deep-seated, particularly in the face of uncertain majorities and 'hung' parliaments. Some observers interpret the forging of coalitions as a first step towards the consolidation of a stable bipolar arrangement, as close as one can get to the seemingly irresistible ideal of a two-party system.

The fragmentation of parties for reasons which are sometimes ideological but frequently not is one of the major developments of the last few decades. One of the mainsprings of this fragmentation has been the articulation of interests by state-based parties. The combined effect of 'Mandalization' and the politics of Hindutva has given rise to new parties, notably in U.P. and Bihar, which are dedicated to the advancement of the backward classes and the protection of Muslims.[18]

Table 1: Lok Sabha elections 1977–1998: results for five main National Parties

Election Year	1977	1980	1984	1989	1991	1996	1998
Total no. of seats	542	529	542	529	511	543	543
Indian National Congress	154	353	415	197	227	140	141
Bharatiya Janata Party	@	@	02	85	119	161	182
Janata Party/Janata Dal	298	31	10	143	56	46	06
Communist Party (Marxist)	22	36	22	33	35	32	32
Communist Party of India	07	11	06	12	13	12	09
Total five national parties	481	431	455	470	450	391	370
% of total seats	88.8	81.5	84.0	88.9	88.1	72.0	68.1

Sources :For the 1977–91 results: Subrata K. Mitra and James Chiriyankandath (eds), *Electoral Politics in India* (New Delhi: Segment), 1992, and Election Commission Reports for 1996 and 1998.
@: The BJP was a constituent of the Janata Party in these elections.

The 1998 elections to the Lok Sabha were held against the backdrop of the collapse of the United Front minority coalition, led initially by Deve Gowda and then by Inder Gujral, as a result of the abrupt withdrawal of Congress support.[19] We begin our analysis of the election results by comparing the performance of the two main national parties, the Indian National Congress (INC) and the Bharatiya Janata Party (BJP), relative to the tallies of single-state and multi-state parties.[20] (Table 2)

Table 2: State-wise distribution of seats between parties in the twelfth Lok Sabha

Zone I: 245 Seats: North and Northwest [8 States + Delhi NCT + Chandigarh UT]

Zones/States	Seats	INC	BJP	Other	Details of other parties
1. Uttar Pradesh	85	00	57	28	Samajwadi P 20/BSP 04/Samata 02/ SJP 01 (Chandra Shekhar) / Ind. 01(Maneka Gandhi)
2. Bihar	54	05	20	29	RJD 17/Samata 10/JD 01/RJP 01
3. Madhya Pradesh	40	10	30	00	00
4. Rajasthan	25	18	05	02	AIIC(S) 01(Ola)/Ind.

Zones/States	Seats	INC	BJP	Other	Details of other parties
					01 (Buta Singh)
5. Punjab + Chandigarh	14	00	04	10	S.Akali Dal 8/JD1(Gujral)/Ind1(Satnam)
6. Haryana	10	03	01	06	H LokDal 04/H Vikas P 01/BSP 01
7. Delhi NCT	07	01	06	00	00
8. Jammu & Kashmir	06	01	02	03	J&K National Conference 03
9. Himachal Pradesh	04	01	03	00	00
Total North N-West	**245**	**39**	**128**	**78**	
Zonal Percentage	**100**	**15.9**	**52.3**	**31.8**	

Zone II: 88 Seats: East and Northeast [10 States]

Zones/States	Seats	INC	BJP	Other	Details of other parties
1. West Bengal	42	01	01	40	CPM 24/Trinamul Congress 07/RSP 04/ CPI 03/Forward Bloc 02
2. Orissa	21	05	07	09	Biju Janata Dal 09
3. Assam	14	10	01	03	ASDC 01/UMF 01/Indep.(Bodo SMC) 01
4. Seven North Eastern states (see Table 6)	11	03	00	08	CPM 02/Arunachal Cong 02/CPI 01/Manipur Cong 01/Citizens Common Front 01/Sikkim Demo Front 01
Total East North-East	**88**	**19**	**09**	**60**	
Zonal Percentage	**100**	**21.6**	**10.2**	**68.2**	

Zone III: 78 Seats: West: [3 States + 2 UTs]

Zones/States	Seats	INC	BJP	Other	Details of other parties
1. Maharashtra	48	33	04	11	Shiv Sena 06/RPI 04/PWP 01
2. Gujarat+D&D,D&NH	28	07	21	00	00
3. Goa	02	02	00	00	00
Total West	**78**	**42**	**25**	**11**	
Zonal Percentage	**100**	**53.9**	**32.0**	**14.1**	

Zone IV : 132 seats : South : [4 States + 3 UTs]

Zones/States	Seats	INC	BJP	Other	Details of other parties
1. Andhra Pradesh	42	22	04	16	TDP 12/CPI 2/JD 01/MIM 01
2. Tamil Nadu + Pondicherry	40	00	03	37	AIADMK 18/PMK 04/MDMK 03/ TRC 01 (V. Ramamurthy)/JP 01(S.Swamy) DMK 06/TMC 03/ CPI 01
3. Karnataka	28	09	13	06	Lok Shakti 03/ Janata Dal 03
4. Kerala	20	08	00	12	CPM 06/ CPI 02/ Muslim League 02/Kerala Cong (M) 01/RSP 01
5. Lakshadweep+Andaman & Nicobar Islands	02	02	00	00	
Total South	**132**	**41**	**20**	**71**	
Zonal Percentage	**100**	**31.1**	**15.1**	**53.8**	
TOTAL SEATS	**543**	**141**	**182**	**220**	
TOTAL PERCENTAGE	**100**	**26.0**	**33.5**	**40.5**	

Sources: Compiled from Election Commission, *Statistical Report on the General Elections 1998 (Vol. 1<Ver.1 for 539 seats>) National & State Abstracts*, supplemented by media reports for alliances and subsequent changes, for 543 elective seats. Two Congress seats in Rajasthan were vacant when the Lok Sabha was dissolved on 17 April 1999.

It may be noted that in our definition of zones we have departed from other classifications which, for example, place Bihar in the east and Madhya Pradesh and Rajasthan in the west.[21] The guiding factors in adopting such a classification have been linkages between party systems arising from ethno-linguistic continuities and the historical intertwining of polities. Similarly, in our classification of parties, we have preferred the term single-state or multi-state parties to designate those which are commonly clubbed under the 'regional' label. The smaller national parties are in reality multi-state parties, because the Election Commission accords them this status if they are recognized in at least four states.[22]

There are striking zonal differences in the support base of parties: while electoral contests are dominated by the Congress and the BJP in the north and the west, state-based parties dominate elsewhere. It is important to remember that most state-based parties that account for 40.5 per cent of the seats are not new political formations: they have stood the test of time and successive elections. The November 1998 state assembly elections were atypical because the Congress and BJP confronted each other directly in only five states, and three of them were involved in that contest.[23]

The party system today consists of the two main polity-wide parties that could organize coalitions, and the 'coalitionable' parties, an amalgam of over forty state-based parties that constitute the pool from which federal coalitions can and must be

Table 3. Polity-wide and state-based parties in the twelfth Lok Sabha

Zones	Seats	Congress		BJP		Others	
	No	No	%	No	%	No	%
North & North-western states	245	39	15.9	128	52.3	78	31.8
East & North-eastern states	88	19	21.6	09	10.2	60	68.2
Western states	78	42	53.9	25	32.0	11	14.1
Southern states	132	41	31.1	20	15.1	71	53.8
Grand Total	**543**	**141**	**26.0**	**182**	**33.5**	**220**	**40.5**

Sources: As for Table 2.

Table 4. The Indian National Congress-led group of parties

Parties	Type	Seats	Distribution
1. Indian National Congress (INC)*	National	141	All states except Uttar Pradesh, Punjab, and Tamil Nadu
2. Republican Party of India (RPI)	Single-state	04	Maharashtra
3. Muslim League	Single-state	02	Kerala (IUML)
4. Kerala Congress (Mani)	Single-state	01	Kerala
5. Majlis-i-Muslimeen	Single-state	01	Andhra
6. United Minorities Front	Single-state	01	Assam
7. All India Indira Congress **	Single-state	01	Rajasthan (Sisram Ola)
Total		**151**	

Sources: As for Table 2, supplemented by media reports.

* When the Lok Sabha was dissolved on 26 April 1999, two Congress seats from Rajasthan were vacant due to the demise of G.R.Yadav and the resignation of Ashok Gehlot on his appointment as chief minister. Orissa chief minister G.Gamang had not yet resigned his seat and cast a controversial vote against the Vajpayee government.

** Merged with the INC on 1 September 1998.

forged. As Table 3 shows, single-state and multi-state parties account for as many as 220 seats, and dominate political life in the eastern and southern states. In the sections that follow, we examine successively the attitudes of the Congress party and the United Front/Third Force parties towards coalition governments. We then examine the BJP's strategic shifts, both before and after the 1998 Lok Sabha elections, which enabled it to forge a majority and come to power.

III

The electoral strategies and governance policies of the Congress party over the past two decades provide the context which has shaped and determined the development of coalition politics. As the political system demanded more federalism, the Congress responded with less. There is by now sufficient evidence of its inability to secure a majority on its own strength for the last two decades.[24] It can be argued that it has not obtained a convincing majority since the 1980 Lok Sabha elections, for political assassinations scrambled voter preferences in 1984, and again in the second round of the 1991 elections. Deluded by the fortuitous and patently artificial majority it was able to muster then, the Congress persisted with its policy of combating regional parties as the principal obstacle to single-party majority.

The Congress' decision not to participate in coalition governments that it supported was based on this refusal to accept the need for new forms of power-sharing at the national level. Even though it repeatedly denounces the 'evil forces of regionalism' in its election manifestoes, the Congress has in fact had a long history and a rich tradition of coalition building at the state level. As a party with a unifying vocation, it perfected with considerable finesse its rallying skills during the national movement, and developed a coalitional strategy based largely on assimilation through co-optation. After Partition, it gradually slipped into a centralist mould, and its federal mainsprings were pushed into the background.

The question of an attitude shift towards coalitions was debated within the Congress party after the 1996 elections, when there was some pressure to abandon the 'support from outside' strategy and participate in governance. The arguments against participation were forcefully articulated by V.N. Gadgil, who prefaced his statements with Ramsay MacDonald's quip: 'Coalitions are detestable and dishonest.'[25] He defined a coalition as 'an alliance between two or more hitherto separate or even hostile groups or parties formed in order to carry on the government and share the principal offices of the State', and proceeded to advance three main arguments against Congress participation.

The first was a principled objection based on the immorality of entering into a 'dishonest' arrangement. Critics pointed out that it ignored the possibilities of 'honest' alliances and drew sustenance from a typically British aversion, which could be an unreliable guide to governance alternatives for a federal polity. They also added that the United Kingdom's record of negotiating and resolving differences through methods other than partition was unimpressive. The second argument against coalitions was the negative impact on governance, notably on the principle of collective responsibility and on the powers of the office of prime minister. Protagonists of coalition governments pointed out that while there was undeniably a difference in this respect because of the absence of party discipline mechanisms, the contrast was perhaps not as sharp as made out. It is widely recognized that heads of government do not really have absolute freedom to choose, shift and remove colleagues. Some impose themselves by virtue of their political weight, while others cannot be removed with impunity. We also know that regional, caste and minority representation have always played a role in cabinet formation. All these factors only become accentuated in coalition government situations. The third and most important reason cited was the impact on party prospects in future elections, and on the morale of state party cadres. This was the determining calculation, particularly as the problematic was situated within the framework of repeated attempts at the same goal, that is, single-party majority. Ultimately, this was the option that was retained, and the party stayed out. The calculation that control over oppositional space was more beneficial, electorally, than participation, prevailed.

It is striking that the BJP and the Congress drew diametrically opposite conclusions from the results of the April 1996 general elections. While the BJP moved to a vigorous search for allies and coalitions, the Congress party under president Sitaram Kesri chalked out a totally different strategy. Rejecting the inevitability of coalitions and reaffirming the attainability of single-party majority rule, the line adopted at the Calcutta plenary session of the Congress in August 1997, was clear and unambiguous:

This session firmly believes that the Congress party has the will and capacity to ensure and acquire the support of the people of this country for a viable and stable one-party government in the country.[26]

Kesri further developed this point in his presidential address:

According to a school of thought, we have reached an era of coalition and the days of single-party majority are over. This thesis, (which) is anchored to a philosophy that co-operative federalism can be operationalized in a better manner through a coalition government of regional parties, is erroneous, dangerous and factually incorrect.[27]

Elaborating, he maintained that 'it is too simplistic to come to such a conclusion from the results of one or two general elections', and declared: 'The voting behaviour of the Indian electorate completely rejects the thesis that they have lost faith in single-party majority rule.'[28] Denouncing the very idea of coalition politics, he said that it was a 'propaganda (that) is vigorously carried on by those parties who can never come to power at the Centre on their programme or their own strength' to gain legitimacy. It was in pursuance of this line that the Congress party provoked and went to the polls in February 1998, without forging much-needed electoral alliances with regional parties. [29]

It is indeed paradoxical that the Congress, trapped in its own shrill electoral rhetoric which accentuates the dichotomy between national and regional parties, should have persisted on a course which had shown disastrous electoral results. While preparing for victory, it did not plan for defeat. On the other hand, the BJP seized the opportunity and very swiftly moved into this space. Responding to whether the BJP was now joining the mainstream, Vajpayee declared: 'We are going to become the mainstream. The Congress is vacating the space. Apart from the BJP no one can fill this vacuum.'[30]

Though the INC won 141 seats with 25.9 per cent of the vote, as against 140 seats with 28.8 per cent votes in 1996, its overall position did not really improve. Whereas it was second in 247/535 seats in 1996, it was the runner-up in only 154/533 seats in the 1998 elections.[31] This decline prompted some analysts to speak of a post-Congress polity, but it is important to remember that its control over oppositional space in a large number of states constitutes an electoral asset which cannot be easily ignored. If one compares this to the earlier occasions when it failed to gain a majority, its vote share was 34.5 per cent in 1977, 39.5 per cent in 1989, and 37.6 per cent in 1991. Beyond representation in terms of seats, it is to be noted that the traditional support base of the Congress among the minorities, which earlier cut across regions, has been eroded. For instance, only 37 per cent of the Muslims voted for the Congress in 1996, as compared to 59 per cent in 1971.[32] Finally, the decimation of the Congress in its traditional bastions of the Gangetic Plain is indeed striking: it obtained merely 6.02 per cent of valid votes polled in Uttar Pradesh, and 7.4 per cent in Bihar. In Tamil Nadu, where the two dominant DMK/AIADMK-led alliances continue to hold sway, it could only muster 4.78 per cent.[33]

In its attitudes and policies towards state-based parties, the Congress proceeded on the assumption that it could have no stable alliances with them if they chose to retain their distinctive identities. All that it offered them were electoral adjustments, even when its own state units were in poor shape. It seemed to be averse to a strategy of crafting an alternative majority that required sharing contested spaces. Consequently, the big question that emerged was whether the Congress was still capable of putting together and leading a winning federal coalition.

Interestingly, President K.R. Narayanan characterizes the present national situation as dominated by 'parties based on fragmented interests, narrowly organized on the basis of castes and sects, or on personalities and personal ambitions of leaders', and suggests that coalitions can succeed under certain conditions:

> The Kerala experience has shown that coalition governments can provide political and administrative stability and indeed produce remarkable results for the benefit of the people.(. . .) The Kerala pattern of two Fronts organized around one major party, with smaller but stable allies in a multi-party situation, with each Front having an even chance, more or less, of being elected to power is, perhaps, the emerging model for the governance of India from now on. (. . .) Considering the multi-party phenomenon in India and the luxuriantly pluralist nature of our society, one has to look upon this kind of coalition as a provider of stable governments.[34]

A few conditions appear to be essential for the success of such experiments. While government formation via distribution of ministerial berths between partners is an integral part of the accommodation that sustains coalitions, the powers of the head of government are necessarily circumscribed with regard to the appointment and dismissal of ministers, or even the reallocation of portfolios. Moreover, clear ground rules become necessary for the conduct of government business. For instance, it is important to specify clearly those matters which require the prior approval of the council of ministers, as also the norms applicable to independent policy statements by ministers. While a common programme and a code of conduct for ministers are no doubt important, at the end of the day what really sustains a coalition is the successful negotiation of differences.

IV

The parties of the United Front (UF), which shared power with outside support from the Congress during the Eleventh Lok Sabha (1996–8) took a serious beating during and after the 1998 elections. The secularism cement proved inadequate when pitted against the compulsions of anti-Congressism. The losses suf-

Table 5: The United Front / third force / unattached parties in the twelfth Lok Sabha

Table 5.1 Left Parties

	Parties	Type	Seats	Distribution
1.	CPI(M)	Multi-state	32	W.Bengal 24/Kerala 06/ Tripura 02
2.	CPI	Multi-state	09	W.Bengal 03/Kerala 02/ Andhra Pradesh 02/Tamil Nadu 01/Manipur 01
3.	Revolutionary Socialist Party	Single-state+	05	W.Bengal 04/Kerala 01 (RSP)
4.	Forward Bloc	Single-state	02	W.Bengal (AIFB)
5.	Auton. State Demand. Cttee.	Single-state	01	Assam (J.Rongpi)(ASDC)
7.	Peasants & Workers Party	Single-state	01	Maharashtra (PWP)
	Total		**50**	

Table 5.2 Non-Left Parties

		Type	Seats	Distribution
1.	Samajwadi Party*	Single-state	20	Uttar Pradesh
2.	Rashtriya Janata Dal*	Single-state	17	Bihar
3.	Janata Dal	Multi-state	06	Karnataka 03/Punjab 01/ Andhra 01/Bihar 01
4.	D.M.K.**	Single-state	06	Tamil Nadu 05/ Pondicherry 01
5.	Bahujan Samaj Party	Single-state+	05 01	Uttar Pradesh 04/Haryana
6.	Tamil Maanila Cong	Single-state	03	Tamil Nadu
7.	Samajwadi Janata Party *	Single-state	01	Uttar Pradesh (S.Chandrashekhar)
8.	Janata Party	Single-state	01	Tamil Nadu (Subramaniam Swamy)
9.	Independent*		01	Buta Singh (Rajasthan)
	Total		**60**	

Sources: As for Table 2. Single-state+ denotes parties which have marginally exceeded the confines of a single-state. Small/single member parties and independents are often identified via the name of the leader/MP.

* Members of the short-lived Rashtriya Loktantrik Morcha (National Democratic Front) formed in June 1998 to work for a non-BJP alternative majority. The RLM, which also included the RJP, split up after the fall of the Vajpayee government over the leadership of an alternative government, and Buta Singh rejoined the Congress party.
** Voted for the Vajpayee government in the April 1999 confidence motion.

fered by the non-Left segment of the UF showed that it was not able to derive political advantage from the manner in which it was first destabilized and then toppled by the Congress. In fact, UF leaders turned their attention away from national politics to

constituency-related concerns, and no alternative leader was projected.[35]

While the Left parties managed to substantially retain their
earlier tally, there was a sharp decline in the political fortunes of
some key non-Left members of the Front, with others detaching
themselves and moving towards a closer understanding with
the BJP-led majority.

The defection of the Telugu Desam party and the National
Conference left the United Front badly truncated. The final blow
came on 17 April 1999 when the DMK broke ranks and the
Samajwadi Party subsequently decided to block the emergence
of an alternative Congress-led majority. While the Left parties
remain united in their opposition to the BJP, they are divided in
their attitude towards the Congress. The RSP and the Forward
Bloc also balked at the idea of a Congress-led government and
sealed the fate of Sonia Gandhi's bid for power after the fall of
the Vajpayee government.

Before we move to the coalitional strategies of the BJP, it would
be useful to factor in the special situation of small parties and
states in the forging of federal coalitions. The parties of the seven
small states of north-east India provide a good example of the
compulsions of unequal size. They have traditionally demonstrated flexibility and have readily adapted to changes in the
power structure at New Delhi by supporting or even affiliating
themselves with the ruling party of the moment. Viewing their
representation in the Lok Sabha primarily as a means of draw-

Table 6: Parties in the north-eastern states : 11 seats

	State/UT	Seats	INC	BJP	Others	Details of other parties
1.	Tripura	02			02	CPI (M) 2
2.	Manipur	02			02	Manipur State Congress 1/CPI 1
3.	Meghalaya	02	02			
4.	Arunachal	02			02	Arunachal Congress 2*
5.	Nagaland	01	01			
6.	Mizoram	01			01	Mizoram Citizens Common Front (Indep.)
7.	Sikkim	01			01	Sikkim Democratic Front
	Total	**11**	**03**	**00**	**08**	

Source : As for Table 2.
* The Arunachal Congress subsequently split into two and the Mitthei faction captured
power in the state. It has since merged with the Indian National Congress.

ing attention and resources to the region, they constitute a prime catchment area for federal coalition building.

As we noted earlier, the dominance of local concerns in the calculations of smaller state-based parties is not unusual. It is worth recalling that the Congress/anti-Congress cleavage remains a dominant factor in decisions relating to the choice of alliance partners in most states. Even larger state parties openly justify national level shifts by their beneficial impact on state-level electoral prospects. For instance, at a post-election review conference, the Telugu Desam reiterated its basic philosophy of anti-Congressism while justifying its decision to leave the United Front. It declared that 'conditional and issue-based' support to the BJP-led coalition was extended because, ' except for the TDP, the National Conference and the Asom Gana Parishad, other constituent parties adopted a pro-Congress approach'.[36] Explaining a similar decision, the Sikkim Democratic Front said it 'is backing the BJP-led Government at the Centre for the same reason as Mr Naidu of Telugu Desam, despite the fact that Sikkim has a lone MP to offer in the bargain'. [37]

V

While the participation of the BJP in the Janata government (1977–9) in the aftermath of the Emergency was the outcome of an extraordinary situation, the 1989–90 rapprochement with the National Front/Left Front government ended in a rupture whose after-effects are still being felt. The BJP, with its specific agenda and carefully nurtured support base, had never really been comfortable with the idea of federal coalitions. Being essentially an ideological party in its core, its first preference was understandably for like-minded parties with whom it has shared power at the state level, viz., the Shiv Sena and the Akali Dal. Determined initially to tread a lonely path as a party *unlike* any other, it moved with astonishing rapidity towards demonstrating that it could be a party *like* any other.

The BJP drew important lessons from its failure to secure a majority, both at the polls and in parliament during those thirteen fateful days in May 1996 when Vajpayee stood alone. Despite his best efforts at moderation and conciliation, the prime minister-designate was unable to muster the requisite support for a minority government and had to resign. In the 1998 elections, while its own tally increased only marginally, it moved towards a parliamentary majority on the strength of its alliances.

Its climb to power began in June 1989, when it decided to make Hindutva and the Ram mandir issues its main electoral planks. Though it scored impressive initial gains, a plateau was reached fairly rapidly. The social profile of its electorate also revealed constraints on expansion.[38] While stressing that the rapid advances made by the party during the period 1989–96 were due largely to ideological factors, party president L.K. Advani admitted the limits of the Hindutva agenda: 'But since (the) 1996 elections, it is not the same ideological factors which have sustained our growth. Equally emphatically, it is not these ideological factors which have brought us new political allies in different states.'[39]

The story of how the majority of 28 March 1998 was constructed is a tortuous one, capped by an eleventh hour deal with Andhra Pradesh chief minister Chandrababu Naidu, who got the speaker's chair for a TDP nominee. It is evident that the distribution of ministerial berths is an integral part of the power-sharing which sustains coalitions. The AIADMK-led group of parties, with 27 seats, engaged in stiff bargaining prior to government formation.[40] With the notable exception of the Trinamul Congress, most other major pre-election allies were included in the government. As Table 7 shows, the movement led by A.B. Vajpayee attracted some important post-electoral adhesions, too.

How did the BJP interpret the mandate of the 1998 election? Its leaders felt that the electoral verdict 'vindicates our stand on national issues and gives us the responsibility of setting right the grievous wrongs of the past'.[41] L.K. Advani spoke of the aspiration of becoming the new 'natural party of governance' and of the demands of coalitional situations:

(. . .) the interests of the coalition at the Centre are paramount. The party's strategies in the states must be subordinate to its national strategy. As a broad policy, it should be our endeavour to develop the right coalition chemistry with our allies by constantly enlarging the area of common interests and shrinking, or at any rate inactivating, the area of differences.[42]

However, keeping in view the composition of the majority put together by the BJP, it is possible to argue that the verdict was

Table 7: The Bharatiya Janata Party-led majority.

Parties	Type	Seats	Distribution
7.1 Pre electoral arrangements			
1. Bharatiya Janata Party	National	182	All states except Kerala & North east
2. AI Anna DMK (O)	Single-state	18	Tamil Nadu (AIADMK)
3. Samata Party (O)	Single-state+	12	Bihar 10 / UP 02 (SP)
4. Biju Janata Dal (O)	Single-state	09	Orissa (BJD)
5. Shiromani Akali Dal (R+)	Single-state	08	Punjab (SAD)
6. Trinamul Congress (O)	Single-state	07	West Bengal (TC)
7. Shiv Sena (R+)	Single-state	06	Maharashtra (SS)
8. Pattali Makal Katchi (O)	Single-state	04	Tamil Nadu (PMK)
9. Marumalarchi DMK(O)	Single-state	03	Tamil Nadu (MDMK)
10. Lok Shakti (O)	Single-state	03	Karnataka (LS)
11. Haryana Vikas Party (R+)	Single-state	01	Haryana (HVP)
12. Tamizhaga Rajiv Cong(O)	Single-state	01	Tamil Nadu (V. Ramamurthy)
13. Independents		02	Maneka Gandhi (UP), Satnam Singh Kainth (Punjab)
7.1 Sub-total		**256**	
7.2. Post electoral adhesions			
14. Indian National Lok Dal (O)	Single-state	04	Haryana (INLD)
15. Arunachal Congress *(R)	Single-state	02	Arunachal Pradesh (AC)
16. Sikkim Democratic Front (R)	Single-state	01	Sikkim (SDF)
17. Manipur State Congress Party (R)	Single-state	01	Manipur (MSCP)
18. Citizens Common Front (O)	Single-state	01	Mizoram (Independent)
19. Bodoland State Movt. Cttee. (O)	Single-state	01	Assam (Independent) (BSMC)
20. Telugu Desam (R)	Single-state	11	Andhra (excludes Speaker) (TDP)
21. J&K National Conference **(R)	Single-state	03	Jammu & Kashmir (J&K NC)
22. Anglo-Indians ***	Nominated	02	
23. Unattached ****	Defection	01	Bihar (Anand Mohan Singh)
7.2.Sub-Total		**27**	
Total T 7.1 + T 7.2		**283**	

Sources: As for Table 2.

Note 1: (O)= Opposition; (R) = Ruling party and (R+)= Ruling coalition with BJP at the state level. Single-state+ denotes parties which have marginally exceeded the confines of a single-state. Small/single member parties and independents are often identified via the name of the leader/MP.

Note 2: Two other MPs were originally members of this majority: (a) Subramaniam Swamy, who absented himself during the March 1998 confidence motion and was subsequently instrumental in engineering the defection of the 18-member AIADMK group, precipitating the fall of the Vajpayee government; (b) Buta Singh (Ind), who defected to the Rashtriya Loktantrik Morcha and ultimately rejoined the Congress.

*Split into two at the state level: the AC (Mitthei) came to power and subsequently merged with the INC. One MP crossed over and voted against the Vajpayee government.
**The National Conference abstained during the confidence motion vote on 28 March 1998 and initially offered only issue-based support to the BJP-led majority. It subsequently moved closer and even expelled its MP, Saifuddin Soz, who voted against the April 1999 confidence motion.
*** On the recommendation of the Vajpayee government, two members from the Anglo-Indian community were nominated by the president under Article 331 of the Constitution: Lt. Gen. Foley and Dr (Mrs) De Souza. Both voted for the government in the March 1998 and April 1999 confidence motions.
**** Elected as the Gujarat-based Rashtriya Janata Party's nominee, Anand Mohan Singh defected towards the Samata–BJP alliance and was expelled.

not as much a mandate for the BJP as a vote of confidence in its leader, Atal Behari Vajpayee, and his capabilities. Such majorities are not unknown in parliamentary systems: they rally round a leader, but do not necessarily transfer subsequently to the party.

During the election campaign, Vajpayee consistently skirted the issue of a programme-based coalition but spoke of the compulsions and constraints that might emerge:

> You have to make a distinction between our allies. There is one set of parties with whom we are already sharing power in (the) states such as the Shiv Sena, Akali Dal and HVP. In addition, we have found some new allies. They are part of a movement that we are leading and if we have to take their support for forming the government, we will have to work out a programme. Controversial issues will not come in the way.[43]

Having managed to put together a parliamentary majority, Vajpayee was confronted with the task of converting it into a coalition government. After some initial confusion, a co-ordination committee was set up to smoothen relations between the twelve pre-poll partners, representing eight states.[44] This committee however proved largely ineffective, mainly because it did not meet often enough. Major differences within the coalition were either resolved bilaterally or aired in parliament. For instance, an increase in the price of fertilizers included in the Union Budget for 1998–9 had to be reversed on the insistence of the Akali Dal and the AIADMK, who also demanded and obtained major changes in the proposed reform of the electric power sector to 'protect' the interests of their farmers.[45] The AIADMK also pressured vociferously for the dismissal of the government in Tamil Nadu, while the Trinamul Congress even suspended its support to the coalition for a week to express its dissatisfaction with government policies concerning West Bengal. Throughout its thirteen-month tenure, the Vajpayee government was beset with internal crises caused by fractious and disputatious allies. Despite these irritants, it is remarkable that, when it fell, the Vajpayee government managed to retain the support of most of its alliance partners. It lost 20 MPs (AIADMK 18, J&K National Conference 1, Arunachal Congress 1) but gained 6 (DMK) to finish with a tally of 269 against 270 that the opposition was able to muster.

It is said that while the fox knows many things, the hedgehog knows one big thing. Has the BJP made the transition from fox to hedgehog in its quest for political power? Is there metamorphosis or only camouflage? The answers to these questions are central to the interpretation of trends in the further development of federal coalitions.

VI

Is India becoming ungovernable? The twelfth Lok Sabha lasted barely thirteen months and the country will go to the polls in September 1999 for the third time in four years to elect another government. A summary recapitulation of the last two elections clearly shows that the BJP and the Congress together only marginally increased their vote share and, between them, obtained 59.5 per cent of the seats. As Table 8, on the relative share of national and regional/state parties, reveals there is a marked in-

Table 8 : National and state parties in the 1996 and 1998 Lok Sabha elections

Parties	1996		1998	
	Seats %	Votes %	Seats %	Votes %
Congress	25.8	28.8	26.0	25.9
BJP	29.6	20.3	33.5	25.5
Sub-total	**55.4**	**49.1**	**59.5**	**51.4**
Other national parties *	18.8	20.0	11.8	16.6
Sub-total	**74.2**	**69.1**	**71.3**	**68.0**
State parties and others	25.8	30.9	28.7	32.0
Total	100.0	100.0	100.0	100.0

*1996 = CPI (M), CPI, Samata, Janata Dal, AIIC (Tiwari) and Janata Party;
1998 = CPI (M), CPI, Samata, Janata Dal, and BSP.
Sources: As for Table 2. N = 543 seats for 1996 and 1998 per cent seats, but N = 539 seats for 1998 per cent votes.

crease in the representation of single-state parties, at the expense of smaller multi-state 'national' parties notably the Janata Dal, which seems to be on its way to political oblivion as it has in effect become a loosely-knit front of state parties pursuing often conflicting alliance strategies.

With the erosion of its credibility on the nationalism and socialism projects it earlier espoused, the Congress today is in search of mobilizing strategies capable of enthusing the electorate. Electoral statistics and trends of the past two decades show that a single-party majority is outside its reach. Nevertheless, its polity-wide organizational spread still makes it a formidable political force, capable of mobilizing an alternative majority. Congress party leaders met at a 'brainstorming camp' at Pachmarhi to take stock and map out a strategy for the November 1998 state assembly elections in Madhya Pradesh, Rajasthan and Delhi. One of the background papers admitted that 'the Indian political scene has reached a point where one-party dominance appears to be a thing of the past'.[46] In her inaugural address, party president Sonia Gandhi outlined the tasks before the party:

> We must acknowledge that we have not successfully accommodated the aspirations of a whole new generation of dalits, adivasis and backward people, particularly in the northern parts of the country. Could this be one of the reasons for our decline in states like Uttar Pradesh and Bihar ? (. . .) What is disturbing is the loss of our social base, of the social coalition that supports us and looks up to us.[47]

In her concluding remarks she alluded to the 'hot topic' of coalitional strategy:

> Friends, there has been much talk about the Congress' attitude towards a coalition government. The fact that we are going through a coalitional phase at national level politics reflects in many ways the decline of the Congress. This is a passing phase and we will come back again with full force and on our own steam. But in the interim, coalitions may well be needed.[48]

The context for these discussions was provided by the growing unpopularity of the BJP government for its inability to check rising prices of food staples, notably onions. Further, since the upcoming assembly elections were mostly straight contests between the Congress and the BJP, there was no urgency to take a more categorical stand. The question resurfaced with the abrupt collapse of the Vajpayee government on 17 April 1999. Rejecting the idea of a governmental coalition, Sonia Gandhi staked her claim for heading a minority government with outside support. When she failed to muster the necessary numbers, she withdrew and declared: 'We are not ready to support a Third Front, Fourth Front or whatever it is called. We will not give our support to anybody else.'[49]

Recent experience with the instability of minority and coalition governments has undeniably generated misgivings. Support to minority governments has been proffered and withdrawn with bewildering frequency, and often for reasons which strain credibility. Political malpractices and even downright corruption have further aggravated the malaise. The Congress perceives an anti-coalition mood in the electorate and is therefore averse to any power-sharing commitment at the national level which would implicitly legitimize the coalition idea. The choice it offers is again between the stability of one-party rule and the instability of coalitions. Sonia Gandhi has spelt out the strategy for the 1999 elections in these terms: 'When the electorate sees us strong, united and single-minded, and contrasts us with the multi-headed monster the BJP is fielding, there is no doubt that their vote will go to the solid, reliable, time-tested stability which the Congress has on offer.'[50]

Summing up the situation which led to the dissolution of the twelfth Lok Sabha, President K.R. Narayanan observed that 'the ruling alliance had lost its majority because of a lack of cohesion within its ranks, and those who voted out the alliance showed the same lack of cohesion when trying to form an alternative government'.[51]

While Vajpayee was able to muster a majority, whether he succeeded in forging a viable coalition remains a moot point. His experience underscored not only the need for credible public pacts but also the importance of taking sub-agendas seriously. The absence of effective co-ordination to resolve intra-coalition spats was one of the notable failures of the Vajpayee government. Its partners repeatedly complained of being ignored or not being consulted often enough on major policy issues. They felt that sharing power had not resulted in their being able to influence policies. On the other hand, efforts by the dominant party to push forward its own reserve agenda provoked sharp protest, notably its policy towards religious minorities and the resultant attacks on Christian missionaries. The BJP crafted a majority but had not yet evolved a strategy of living in peace with minorities. The traditions of the Sangh Parivar and its un-fulfilled projects arguably prevent it from seriously negotiating differences.

When the BJP executive met at Bangalore in January 1999 against the backdrop of the party's dismal performance in the recent state assembly elections and the attacks on Christian places of worship, there was an attempt to redefine government–Sangh Parivar relations. Vajpayee succeeded in getting his moderate line partially incorporated in the political resolution which said: 'Any attack on a place of worship, whether a church or temple, is deplorable and cannot be condoned.'[52] This trend towards granting greater manouverability to the government wing is also reflected in the strategy approved by the BJP national executive for the 1999 Lok Sabha elections. Recognizing that its organiza-tional base is still inadequate in many states, it decided to extend a power-sharing offer to all regional parties engaged in state-level contests with the Congress and declared: 'India's interests can be served best by involving regional parties in the process of governance.'[53] What is even more significant, the party decided not to issue its own election manifesto afresh but to work towards a joint manifesto based on the national agenda for governance evolved earlier.[54] Contrasted with the Congress' continued resistance to coalitions, the BJP appears to have em-braced them wholeheartedly.

The Vajpayee experiment in coalition government has thrown up some important lessons. When coalitions are viewed as a dharma to be suffered till better karma brings the rewards of undiluted power and dominance, broader questions of federal power-sharing and the participation of states in national policy-making are not addressed in any serious way. Robust federal coalitions which reconcile the demands of regional interests with the need for national cohesion can emerge only if coalition leaders are committed to developing it as a form of governance. For this, they must see in it not merely necessity but also some virtue.

If state-based parties assert themselves to defend their vital inter-ests, they are invariably castigated for being parochial. In reality, the polity has still to evolve appropriate institutions and processes for the effective articulation and aggregation of these interests. This grave lacuna has its inevitable consequences for governmental stability and periodically plunges the country into political turmoil. The political gridlock in which the party system finds itself today is probably the greatest challenge the Indian political class has faced so far. Never before have power-sharing deals been struck under such intense media coverage. Smaller parties seeking to extend their influence and defend their interests in the national policy arena use every possible leverage, even at the risk of being charged with opportunism and inconsistency.

Few things are inevitable in politics. Nevertheless, in the context of India's diversity, coalitions may well be one of them. To hold that coalition politics is not only here to stay but can also become a viable alternative to earlier arrangements is not merely the triumph of hope over experience. It is based on an understanding that democratic accountability is best achieved in plural societies through parliamentary federalism. Those who bemoan the costs of coalition governance ignore similar deals cloaked in the secrecy of dominant party discipline. The multiplicity of partners and sub-agendas obviously brings about greater transparency, but the policy outcomes are not necessarily different or even inferior to those emerging from single-party dispensations.

In sum, coalitions are likely to remain unstable till such time as one of the core coalition-making parties adopts the coalitional strategy on a durable basis as a deliberate political option. As long as both view them as transitory arrangements in the chimerical quest for single-party majority, they will fall prey to the power maximization calculations of smaller partners who will quite naturally take full advantage of the situation. The cycle of repeated elections and elusive majorities can only be broken by bold reorientations. As of now the BJP has opted for consolidating its existing coalition and facing the electorate on a common platform. An alternative coalition is nowhere in sight, but may yet emerge.

I am indebted to Douglas Verney for his detailed comments on an earlier version of some portions of this paper, which appeared as 'Regional Aspirations and National Cohesion: Federal Coalitions in the 1998 Lok Sabha Elections', in West Bengal Political Science Review (Calcutta), vol. 1, 1998.

Notes

[1] Daniel Elazar, *Exploring Federalism* (Tuscaloosa: Alabama University Press), 1987.

[2] Arend Lijphart, 'The Puzzle of Indian Democracy: A Consociational Interpretation', in *American Political Science Review*, vol. 90, no. 2 (June 1996).

[3] Cf. Alfred Stepan, 'Democracy and Federalism', *Seminar*, November 1997. See also his case for the parliamentary variant 'Constitutional Frameworks and Democratic Consolidation: Parliamentarism vs Presidentialism', *World Politics*, vol. 46, no. 1 (October 1993).

[4] Rasheeduddin Khan, *Bewildered India: Identity, Pluralism, Discord* (New Delhi: Har–Anand), 1994.

[5] A notable attempt is E. Sridharan, *Coalition Politics in India: Lessons from Theory, Comparison and Recent History* (New Delhi: Centre for Policy Research), 1997.

[6] The impact of multi-level governmental structures is not adequately reflected in theorization on coalitional stability in parliamentary systems, since most of them are unitary states. Cf. David P. Baron, 'Comparative Dynamics of Parliamentary Governments', *American Political Science Review*, vol. 92, no. 3 (September 1998), pp. 593–609.

[7] Francine Frankel and M.S.A. Rao (eds), *Dominance and State Power in India* (New Delhi: Oxford University Press), 1990, 2 vols.

[8] Examples of such tensions are to be found in the Shiv Sena–BJP alliance in Maharashtra. Cf. Mahesh Vijapurkar, 'BJP Forces Sena to Concede Its Demands', *The Hindu*, 20 August 1998.

[9] This is particularly applicable to coalitions with a predominance of parties in power at the state level. On the other hand, coalitions with parties in opposition seeking alliance to capture power with the help of central intervention as pivotal members could prove unstable. The power to dislodge state governments under Article 356 is now subject to judicially determined norms, and current levels of federal development would impose heavy political costs on overtly discriminatory practices. For a ruling /opposition classification of allied parties in the BJP-led coalition see Table 7.

[10] Cf. Philip Williams, *Politics in Post-War France: Crisis and Compromise* (Harlow: Longmans), 1964, 3rd edn.

[11] V. Athreya, 'Sonia Effect Checks BJP Advance', *Frontline*, 6 March 1998 and A.C. Nielson, 'Congress Resurgence', *Outlook*, 16 February 1998. A similar fall out was sought to be averted by disclaiming responsibility for the fall of the Vajpayee government. The counter-campaign of the BJP portrays Vajpayee as a hapless victim of intrigue ('What wrong did this man do?') and vows 'Let us teach them (Sonia Gandhi, Laloo Yadav, Jayalalitha, Harkishan Surjeet and Mayawati) a lesson, and bring back the true leader of India', *Indian Express*, 27 April 1999.

[12] Cf. James Madison, 'Men of factious tempers, of local prejudices, or of sinister designs may, by intrigue, by corruption, or by other means, first obtain the suffrages, and then betray the interests, of the people', in Alexander Hamilton, James Madison, John Jay, *The Federalist* (Bombay: Popular Prakashan/Harvard University Press), 1961, p. 53.

[13] Nirmal Mukarji and Balveer Arora (eds), *Federalism in India: Origins and Development* (New Delhi: Vikas), 1992.

[14] V.P. Singh (4.12.89–10.11.90) quit when the BJP withdrew support, and Chandrashekhar (11.11.90–21.6.91) resigned in March 1991 when the Congress pulled the plug. The 1991 Lok Sabha elections were conducted in two stages, and Rajiv Gandhi's assassination in the intervening period demonstrably improved the Congress tally. The United Front prime ministers, Deve Gowda (1.6.96–21.4.97) and Inder Gujral (22.4.97–18.3.98) were both victims of the abrupt withdrawal of support by the Congress.

[15] Cf. 'Naïve federalists think the rise of regional parties heralds a more federal India that will be more unified. (. . .) The entire ethos of regional parties is to magnify local interests and ignore those of the rest of the country. So, far from creating a happier country, the rise of regional parties could spell more tension.' Editorial, 'Unity in Unhappiness', *The Economic Times*, 13 August 1996.

[16] On the origins and growth of parties based on local particularisms during the phase of Congress party dominance, see Christiane Hurtig and Balveer Arora, *Les Partis Politiques Indiens* (Paris: Documentation Francaise), 1972.

[17] James Manor, 'Regional Parties in Federal Systems: India in Comparative Perspective', in Balveer Arora and Douglas V. Verney (eds), *Multiple Identities in a Single-state: Indian Federalism in Comparative Perspective* (Delhi: Konark), 1995.

[18] The Mandal Commission recommended job reservations for backward classes: it was implemented by the V.P. Singh government in 1990. Hindutva is the credo of the BJP and acquired political salience at the same time. It led notably to the demolition of the Babri masjid at Ayodhya in 1992.

[19] For an analysis of trends leading upto the 1996 Lok Sabha elections see Paul Brass, 'Regionalism, Hindu Nationalism and Party Politics in India's Federal System', (pp. 137–165), in Ian Copland and John Rickard (eds), *Federalism: Comparative Perspectives from India and Australia* (New Delhi: Manohar), 1999. On the regionalization of the party system, see Zoya Hasan, 'Region and Nation in India's Political Transition', ibid., pp. 166-83.

[20] The Election Commission lists seven national, 30 state and 139 registered and unrecognized parties which actually contested the 1998 elections. It terms national, any party which is recognized as a state party in at least four states. This categorization is reviewed after each election. For instance, the Samata Party was de-recognized as a national party by

the Election Commission in the light of the 1998 results, as it met the minimum criteria in only three states: Bihar, Haryana and Manipur. On the proliferation of parties and a proposal for curbing fragmentation through disincentives, see Douglas Verney, 'Improving Coalition Government in India', *Denouement* (New Delhi) Jan–Feb 1999.

[21] As for instance in David Butler et al, *India Votes 1952–91* (New Delhi: Living Media), 1991, p. 73.

[22] In common parlance, all parties except the INC and the BJP are dubbed 'regional parties' with the possible exception of the two communist parties. We have borrowed from Alfred Stepan the term 'polity-wide' for the INC and the BJP, since 'national' could have normative or ideological connotations which are not intended when we use it.

[23] Apart from Madhya Pradesh, Rajasthan and Delhi where elections were held, there is a Congress–BJP face-off in Gujarat and Himachal Pradesh. The sixth state where the BJP has sizeable support is Uttar Pradesh, where the Congress has been replaced by the Samajwadi Party and the Bahujan Samaj Party. These six states accounted for two-thirds of the BJP contingent in the twelfth Lok Sabha.

[24] The last genuine majority was arguably in 1980, since political assassinations scrambled voter preferences in 1984 (Indira Gandhi) and in the second round of the 1991 elections (Rajiv Gandhi). On the progressive consolidation of the non-Congress alternative during the Eighties and how the idea of a Federal Front took shape see Balveer Arora, 'India's Federal System and the Demands of Pluralism: Crisis and Reform in the Eighties', in J. Chaudhuri (ed.), *India's Beleaguered Federalism: The Pluralist Challenge* (Tempe: Arizona State University Press), 1992, pp. 5–25.

[25] V.N. Gadgil, 'Coalition Politics: Congress Must Stay Out', *Times of India*, 13 July 1996.

[26] Political Resolution of the 80th plenary session of the Indian National Congress held at Calcutta on August 9–10, 1997.

[27] Cited by Vijay Sinha in *Indian Express*, 10 August 1997.

[28] Ibid. Sitaram Kesri was removed from his post on 14 March 1998 and formally replaced by Sonia Gandhi at the New Delhi AICC session on 6 April 1998. Subsequently, party statutes were amended to enable her election as leader of the parliamentary wing, even though she was not a member of either House.

[29] There was an electoral understanding with the Samajwadi Party in Maharashtra. The relationship with Laloo Yadav's RJD and Mulayam Yadav's SP have been hotly debated within the Congress, as state party units seek to regain a foothold. On changes at the state level see Yogendra Yadav, 'Reconfiguration in Indian Politics: State Assembly Elections, 1993–95', *Economic and Political Weekly*, vol. XXXI, nos. 2–3 (13–20 January 1996), pp. 95–104.

[30] Interview citation in *Indian Express*, 25 January 1998.

[31] While the 1996 figure is mentioned by Gadgil, (art. cit.), the 1998 figure excludes two states (J&K and H.P.) and is compiled from Rajiv Jain (ed.), *Directory of 12th LS & RS Members 1998* (New Delhi: India Investment Centre), 1998.

[32] This rose to 39 per cent in the 1998 elections. Cf. Yogendra Yadav, 'Post-Poll: Who Voted for Whom?' *India Today*, 16 March 1998. Its tally in the reserved SC/ST constituencies has also decreased over the years.

[33] Election Commission, *Statistical Report on the General Elections 1998*, (Vol. 1, Ver 1 for 539 seats), p. 50.

[34] K.R. Narayanan, speech at the inauguration of the new state legislature complex at Thiruvananthapuram, 22 May 1998.

[35] While I.K. Gujral withdrew to nurse his Jalandhar constituency with the support of the Shiromani Akali Dal, other UF leaders rarely campaigned outside their states. Laloo Yadav had earlier broken away from the Janata Dal to form his own party (RJD) in Bihar, and advocated a tie-up with the Congress.

[36] Political resolution adopted at the annual conference (Mahaanadu) held on 27 May 1998. The resolution further recalls the contribution of its founder N.T. Rama Rao to building the (1989) anti-Congress National Front coalition. (*The Hindu*, 28 May 1998). Even the Samata party, an avowedly non-regional BJP ally, voices primarily Bihar-related demands within the coalition, viz., dismissal of the Rabri Devi government and financial compensation for the proposed Jharkhand/Vananchal state. More recently, the DMK moved to the BJP camp because the AIADMK had moved out.

[37] Mohan Dungmali, General Secretary, SDF, in a letter to *Hindustan Times*, 31 May 1998. The North-Eastern Council meeting of 8 May 1998 decided to admit Sikkim as its eighth member. Legislation for restructuring the Council is on the anvil, and the deputy chairman of the Planning Commission would replace the senior-most governor of the region as its head. *The Hindu*, 9 May 1998.

[38] On this point, see James Chiriyankandath, 'Tricolour and Saffron: Congress and the Neo-Hindu Challenge' in Subrata Mitra and J. Chiriyankandath (eds) *Electoral Politics in India* (New Delhi: Segment), 1992 and Yogendra Yadav, 'Who Voted for Whom?', op. cit.

[39] Presidential address at the meeting of the National Executive on 11 April 1998, cited in *The Hindu*, 12 April 1998.

[40] This group comprised four other local parties (PMK, MDMK, TRC and JP). The letters of support that President Narayanan required before inducting A.B. Vajpayee as prime minister were not forthcoming immediately and were obtained only after protracted negotiations. When the AIADMK finally withdrew support after thirteen months of uneasy co-

habitation and repeated threats, the PMK, MDMK and TRC remained with the Vajpayee government.

[41] Political Resolution adopted by the National Executive at its meeting of 11–12 April 1998.

[42] Speech at the National Executive Meeting, cited by Anil Saxena, *The Times of India*, 12 April 1998. Sonia Gandhi had earlier spoken of the need to restore the Congress to its earlier position of 'the natural party of governance' after assuming the presidency of the party at the AICC session of 6 April 1998.

[43] Interview with P.R. Ramesh, *The Economic Times*, 26 January 1998.

[44] Jaswant Singh was initially appointed convenor, with Advani representing the BJP on the committee. George Fernandes assumed the convenor's role in October 1998 because Jaswant Singh's services were commandeered for the delicate post-Pokhran II diplomatic talks with the United States. Of the post-poll adherents, only the Arunachal Congress received representation in the ministry.

[45] 'Power Reform: Stalled Again?' *Economic and Political Weekly*, 23 May 1998, p. 1215.

[46] 'Political Scene and the Indian National Congres', cited by Harish Khare in *The Hindu*, 31 August 1998.

[47] AICC, *Brainstorming Camp at Pachmarhi: September 1998*, p. 7. On the strategy vis-à-vis the BJP led coalition she said, 'Internal contradictions are being exposed day by day. (. . .) Our stand of not rushing into bringing this government down has been appreciated all round.'

[48] Ibid., p. 29. The political resolution adopted considered 'the present difficulties in forming one-party governments a transient phase' and decided 'that coalitions will be considered only when absolutely necessary, and that too on the basis of agreed programmes which will not weaken the party or compromise its basic ideology'. p. 17.

[49] Cited by Arati Jerath, 'Poll Clouds Gather', *Indian Express*, 26 April 1999. Parties which were resolutely opposed to a Congress minority government included Mulayam Singh's Samajwadi Party and two members of the Left Front, the Forward Bloc and the RSP.

[50] Address at the meeting of state party presidents, chief ministers and heads of legislature parties at New Delhi, 6 May 1999. Electoral understandings and adjustments at the state level were not ruled out. *The Hindu*, 7 May 1999.

[51] Rashtrapati Bhavan, *Press Communiqué*, 26 April 1999 (President's Secretariat).

[52] Mosques were significantly not mentioned! *The Economic Times*, 4 January 1999.

[53] Political Resolution adopted at the New Delhi session on 2 May 1999, *The Hindu*, 3 May 1999. Advani justified the need for a broader coalition

which would be a rallying point for all parties which have wrested political space from the Congress: 'The decline of the Congress was more rapid than the growth of the BJP and the vacuum was filled by other parties.'

[54] It would thus steer clear of controversial items on its earlier agenda, i.e., Ayodhya, a common civil code and Article 370, regarding which Advani said: 'We have not changed our views but the issues have been kept in abeyance as per requirement of coalition politics.' *Indian Express*, 3 May 1999.

Economic Policy and the Development of Capitalism in India: the role of regional capitalists and political parties

SANJAYA BARU*

An important aspect of the democratic transformation of India over the last half century has been the development of private enterprise and the movement of private surplus from agriculture to industrial enterprise. In many parts of the country, a new generation of industrial entrepreneurs has emerged since Independence and has begun to successfully challenge established business houses, many of which had merchant capitalist origins and came into being in the earlier part of this century.

Political economists have not paid the same attention to these contemporaneous trends in the development of capitalist enterprise as economic historians have to historical trends in this regard. While there is a rich and varied literature on the origins of business enterprise in British India, there is as yet scanty literature on the changing nature of capitalist enterprise in post-Independence India.[1] Moreover, even this limited literature is devoted largely to the analysis of 'big business' or 'monopoly capital', with relative neglect of the 'non-monopoly', 'regional' capitalist class.[2] Indeed, even the academic literature on Indian 'big business' or 'monopoly capital' is considerably out of date since most of it is based on obsolete analytical concepts developed by the various official committees of inquiry which studied the 'concentration of economic power' in the 1960s and 1970s. There has been considerable change in the structure of owner-

* Acknowledgment: I would like to thank Francine Frankel, Mario Rutten, D. Narasimha Reddy, Rama Vaidyanathan Baru, A.K. Bagchi and E. Sreedharan for comments on an earlier draft. I am also grateful to a referee for editorial changes and comments.

ship in the private corporate sector, the ranking of business houses, their control over various markets and industries, the nature of their operations, and so on.[3] Much of this has been written about in the financial media, but there is very little detailed academic analysis of these trends, and of the latter's significance for an understanding of the nature of Indian capitalism.

Given this academic neglect of the changing nature of Indian 'big business', it is not surprising that trends in the growth of the 'non-monopoly', 'regionally-based' business class have attracted even less academic attention, especially from economists.[4] Interestingly, of the published research on 'regional' business enterprise most of it has been authored by sociologists, largely non-Indians![5] A detailed analysis of the emergence of a new, post-Independence generation 'non-monopoly', regional business class is required to understand the dynamics of capitalist development in India. If economists have ignored these dynamics, political scientists have also been guilty of neglecting the analysis of the politics of regionally differentiated capitalist development, and the implications of the emergence of a new regional business class for state-level politics. Thus, the nature of the link between different segments of the business class and different layers of the political leadership has also not been adequately analysed.[6]

In this paper, I discuss the implications of the emergence of new entrepreneurial groups and regional differentiation in capitalist development for national economic policy, as well as some of the emerging links between these processes of economic change and political power in India.

Regional Differentiation in Capitalist Development

Economic historians have for long recognized the existence of regional variations in the development of capitalist enterprise in the Indian subcontinent.[7] However, in the post-Independence period the desire to discern national trends in capitalist industrialization may have discouraged a more detailed inquiry into the dynamics of state-based capitalism. The fact that the subcontinent had been united under a single national government which was now responsible for formulating national policies partly shifted the focus of attention to national trends. Perhaps ideology also played a role. The need felt by some analysts to discover 'all-India' trends and tendencies in order to show that the national economy had a dynamic of its own, that a 'national bourgeoisie' had come into existence, that national policy must be aimed at supporting such a national capitalist class, and so on, may also have encouraged glossing over these differences.

There is no doubt that the integration of the home market was an important objective of planned industrialization in India, and that a considerable degree of such integration had taken place even at the time of independence. Indeed, even historically we know that merchant capitalists from the West had travelled to both the East and the South, and subcontinent-wide networks of trade and investment had been established. At Independence, domestic 'big business' had nationwide operations. Thus, Marwari enterprise had acquired a base in such far-off places as Calcutta, Madras, Hyderabad, and Kanpur. Gujarati enterprise was well settled in Bombay, although Parsi enterprise was mostly localized in western India. What the process of planned industrialization did was to deepen this process of integration of the home market.

The new opportunities for private investment that planned industrialization created were naturally exploited mostly by those best positioned to do so, namely, either foreign companies or the already entrenched domestic business groups. By the 1960s, after almost two decades of industrial development, most private investment was controlled either by multinational companies or by the Marwari, Gujarati and Parsi enterprise that had made the best use of the new opportunities that came along. It is not surprising, therefore, that there was concern about the 'concentration of economic power', of the growth of 'monopoly capitalism' and so on. While this led to new legislation that sought to curb this tendency, it also led to political mobilization against 'monopoly capitalists'.

Interestingly, in some parts of the country, such mobilization acquired a 'regional' dimension, a fact not adequately researched. For instance, in Maharashtra in the 1950s, the state government consciously discriminated against Parsi and Gujarati capitalists and encouraged Maratha capital in newly emerging industries like sugar, as well as in traditional industries like cotton textiles. So was the case in Uttar Pradesh, where Charan Singh commissioned a study in 1969 on 'non-local' capitalists in the sugar mill industry and demanded the nationalization of their assets and its transfer to 'local' growers on the grounds that 'national capitalists' had not re-invested the surpluses they had extracted from their investment in sugar mills back into the industry. Instead, they had siphoned off these surpluses and invested them elsewhere.[8] However, what is interesting is that in Maharashtra, Gujarat, Tamil Nadu, and Andhra Pradesh regional capitalists were able to enter the sugar mill industry in a big way, marginalizing some of the older, national big business houses, while in Bihar and Uttar Pradesh, the absence of a regional business class meant that either the national big business survived the political onslaught of state politicians or allowed their mills to be nationalized.

Indeed, the sugar mill industry offers an excellent illustration of a wider phenomenon, since observed in textiles, steel, cement, and chemicals and fertilizers, wherein regional business groups have been able to make substantial headway, reducing the relative presence of national big business groups. Some regional groups, like Nagarjuna of Andhra Pradesh, have in fact been able to expand and acquire a national position. In the sugar mill industry, most of the expansion of capacity has occurred within the cooperative sector, facilitating the emergence of an agrarian capitalist class in Haryana, Punjab, western Uttar Pradesh, Gujarat, Maharashtra, Andhra Pradesh, Karnataka, and Tamil Nadu. At the same time, the growth of the private, joint-stock sector, to the extent new mills have been set up, has enabled regional capitalists like Mahalingam (Tamil Nadu Sugars) and Rajshree in Tamil Nadu, the KCP Group, Harischandra Prasad (Andhra Sugars) and Nagarjuna in Andhra Pradesh to expand their business activity. Interestingly, the new opportunities for foreign investment in sugar are increasingly being exploited by these regional business groups (Nagarjuna and Rajshree have recently set up sugar mills in Vietnam) rather than the national big business groups like Shriram and Birla.

While some sociologists have studied the conflict between regional and national capitalists, economists studying the development of capitalist enterprise in India have largely ignored this aspect of capitalist development. The fact that the industrial licensing system had been used to pre-empt capacity was well recognized by economists. This recognition did not, however, encourage much inquiry into the kind of conflict of interest between 'monopoly capital' or 'big business', with influence in Delhi, and the 'non-monopoly' capitalists with localized influence in some regions, as a consequence of such a partisan system. By the 1970s, however, it became difficult to ignore either the sharp inter-regional variations in capitalist development or the lines of tension within the domestic business class between the so-called 'national, monopoly' capitalists and the 'regional, non-monopoly' capitalists. In a fascinating essay on industrial development in India published in 1976, K.N. Raj called for a

> different kind of planning from the sort we have had so far—much more aware of the inter-regional differences within the country, hence more decentralized, and more genuinely experimental and innovative with fewer models, directives and guidelines imposed from above. This in turn would naturally require a more decentralized system of decision-making and therefore of political arrangements.[9]

What are the factors that may have played a role in regionally differentiated or state-based capitalist development in post-Independence India? Most commentators on the subject are agreed that history was the single most important determinant of this process. That is, the regional pattern of development that was shaped by two centuries of colonial rule, the differential impact of land settlement systems, development of urban markets, proletarianization of peasantry, and so on, were so enduring that post-Independence planning and state intervention could do little to alter the historical bias in regional development.[10]

While there is no doubt that long-run historical factors remained influential, state intervention and planning also played their part. The uneven progress of the Green Revolution, very much a product of a nationally planned intervention, further accentuated this historical differentiation. Banerjee and Ghosh make the point that state and central governments have intervened more effectively to support capitalist private enterprise where the regional capitalist class was already influential (as in Punjab, Haryana, Gujarat, Maharashtra, Karnataka, Tamil Nadu, and Andhra Pradesh), and where it has traditionally played a more important political role along with the rich peasantry.[11]

Conversely, they argue, the support given to private enterprise has been weak in eastern India, where the indigenous capitalist class is weak. This argument does not address the question as to why the 'national, monopoly' capitalist class, with a significant historical presence in eastern India, was unable to secure greater support for its growth in this region, but it does draw attention to the fact that capitalist development has been strongest where a local business class came into its own and had access to state power.

Exploring the influence of differential agricultural growth on industrialization, or growth of non-farm enterprises, Raj (1976) argued that regional variations in output growth and surplus-generation are bound to influence the potential for capitalist development in different regions. To quote him:

> When the incomes of the rural community fluctuate considerably, the purchasing power left for buying industrial products will also naturally vary a great deal. This is bound to affect the emergence and growth of industrial enterprises, particularly of small enterprises in the rural and semi-urban areas. And, without the rapid growth of such industrial enterprises, industrial growth in the larger enterprises can have but a limited impact on a relatively small section of the country's population.
>
> Viewed from this angle, it would appear that conditions are favourable for the more extensive and rapid growth of small-scale industries in only some regions of India (that is, those which have recorded moderate to high rates of growth of agricultural output without being subjected to serious fluctuations). It is probable that a large part of the favourable linkage effects have been taken advantage of more by large than small enterprises through their superior market power. Nevertheless, the linkages which already have been or could be established in states like Punjab, Haryana, Karnataka, Tamil Nadu and Kerala, need to be closely examined in the light of this analysis. . . . [The available data] do support the hypothesis that the rate of growth of small-scale enterprises. . . is generally higher in states which are characterized by high or even moderately high rates of growth of agricultural output and which are at the same time not subject to sharp year-to-year fluctuations.[12]

Raj can be excused for his over-optimism about Kerala, but the non-inclusion of Andhra Pradesh points to the limitations of using state averages. Coastal Andhra had already exhibited all the potential for the growth of non-farm enterprises which Raj refers to. Thus it is Punjab, Haryana, Gujarat, Maharashtra, Karnataka, Tamil Nadu, and Andhra Pradesh which emerged, by the late 1970s, as the main centres of a more broad-based capitalist development in the post-Independence period.

While Raj's seminal essay was followed by several studies on the macro-economics of regional differentiation in economic growth,[13] few examined the implications of such differentiation for capitalist development and public policy. Krishna Bharadwaj came close to exploring this relationship, stating:

> Certain parts of Andhra Pradesh, Kerala, and Karnataka in the south, Haryana in the north, and Gujarat and parts of Maharashtra, have shown prominently dispersed growth. . . . We note the importance of agricultural surpluses in adequate quanta to sustain industrial expansion. The regions sharing some industrial vitality appear to be the ones where agricultural growth has also been promising.[14]

While Bharadwaj expressed concern at what she called the 'dichotomous dynamics of growth', she did not examine the implications of these dynamics for regional variations in the growth of capitalist enterprise. In a perceptive essay on the emerging politics of regionally differentiated economic development, Ravi Srivastava argued that the 'central feature of recent changes [in policy] has been an increase in the influence of the newly emergent classes on the state at the national as well as the regional levels'.[15] Regrettably, however, Srivastava does not elaborate on an interesting observation he makes:

> There is a new rural élite which has benefited from the siphoning off of the increased flow of resources from the state. . . . There is an objective basis for a sharpening of the contradictions between the interests of the regional bourgeois–landlord classes and the aspiring sections of the petty-bourgeoisie in the states, on the one hand, and the interests represented by the Centre, on the other.[16]

Presumably the 'Centre' represents the interests of the national big business class.

There is, in this literature, recognition of at least two features of the regional differentiation of capitalist development. First, that historical factors have had an enduring impact on this phenomenon; and second, that post-Independence trends in agrarian change and agricultural growth have played an important role in shaping the process of capitalist development across regions, and in creating a new class of 'regional' capitalists.[17] I suggest that other factors may also impact on inter-state differences: for instance, (*a*) the policies pursued by individual state governments, some more supportive of local enterprise than others; (*b*) the impact of central government decisions, especially the location of public sector enterprises (sub-contracting and ancillarization have been important stimulants of new enterprise); and (*c*) the investment decisions of national big business which catalyze local business activity, much like public sector enterprises do through sub-contracting, ancillary development, demand for support services, dealerships, etc.

These factors individually or in combination have influenced the differential development of capitalist enterprise in different regions of India. Consequently, a new generation of capitalists, as distinct from national big business with origins dating back to the pre-Independence period, came into existence in some regions. It is to the analysis of this phenomenon that I now turn.

The Regional Capitalist Class

This paper concerns itself only with the role in industrialization of 'regional capitalists' with rural roots or agrarian links going back not more than one generation. The core business of the owner/promoter is confined largely to his state of domicile. Typically, such businessmen are born in agrarian, merchant/trading, money-lending or professional middle-class families. They have had no prior family-based experience in running an industrial enterprise, and acquire this first while working for another private or public sector enterprise, or in a completely different occupation ranging from farming to government service. In an increasingly visible phenomenon, nearly a quarter of the top one hundred private companies in India today, is owned by first-generation businessmen. There are regional capitalists who have had no links with the agrarian economy for several generations and have moved into manufacturing business from commerce or other professions. I have not considered such examples in this paper. Further, no distinction has been made within the category of 'regional business' class between small-scale and medium or large companies. Admittedly such a distinction is necessary, especially to comment on the survival of firms, their access to political power, and so on. However, for the purposes of this study I have not explored the importance of this distinction. One of the consequences of this is that while the businessmen in Rutten and Upadhya are mostly small-scale industrialists, our own case studies refer to medium and large businesses.[18] Gorter's examples are drawn from both groups.[19]

The literature on regional capitalists is limited largely to sociological inquiries pertaining to particular states, caste groups or industrial centres; no attempt has been made so far to quantify the phenomenon of industrial entrepreneurship at the national level. This is surprising, since in many industries capacity enhancement has come both through the expansion of already existing national big business, as well as through the entry of new business groups. In such diverse industries as textiles, cement, sugar, chemicals, fertilizers, pharmaceuticals, electronics, steel and engineering goods, industrial expansion in the 1980s has facilitated the growth of new business groups, often first-generation entrepreneurs, in states like Punjab, Haryana, Maharashtra, Rajasthan, Gujarat, Karnataka, Andhra Pradesh, and Tamil Nadu.

In Andhra Pradesh, for example, most of the large-scale manufacturing establishments set up during the 1950s and 1960s were either in the public sector or owned by national big business houses like Birla, Thapar, Shriram, etc. However, in the 1980s, a substantial share of the new capacity in cement, sugar, pharmaceuticals and electronics was controlled by regional first- or second-generation business families like R.S. Raju (Raasi Cement), K.V.K. Raju (Nagarjuna group), and so on. The same was true in Gujarat, Maharashtra, and Punjab. Regional capitalists moved confidently into new avenues of investment supported by state governments, public financial institutions and their inherent ability to act quickly. The inertia of large business houses, internal family quarrels and their fear of losing control over their corporate fiefdoms may have slowed them down in this race.

I now offer some case studies from a few states to illustrate the process of transformation underway.

Andhra Pradesh

Following from Baru which drew attention to the phenomenon of 'capitalist farmers' and 'landlords' moving into manufacturing activity in Andhra Pradesh in the 1970s,[20] Upadhya examined in some detail the characteristics of one such 'rural–urban entrepreneurial class', the Kammas of coastal Andhra.[21]

Upadhya traces the history of the 'regional capitalist class of coastal Andhra region' to the late nineteenth and early twentieth centuries. The construction of the Godavari and Krishna anicuts and the introduction of canal irrigation in these deltas during this period, increased the prosperity of paddy farmers in the region. The main beneficiaries of these changes, according to Upadhya, were the Kammas, a peasant caste on par with Reddys and Velamas. The rich Kamma peasantry utilized this surplus first to invest in education and the acquisition of urban property. This was followed by movement into business and commerce, especially agri-business. Rice mills, sugar mills and the rice and tobacco trade were typically the avenues for Kamma capital to move from farming into non-farm business. Upadhya draws attention to the supportive role of 'caste affiliations' in enabling Kamma peasant families to move into business. Says Upadhya:

> To establish and run an enterprise successfully, an entrepreneur requires a network of acquaintances, friends and relatives holding important positions in the right places, especially when starting out in a new town. In this regard, caste becomes significant as a potential source of new social connections. Thus, business entrepreneurship depends in part on the ability to build extensive and useful social networks, which may be based on caste, kinship, or other relationships.[22]

Upadhya's study, which is limited to Kamma businessmen alone, shows how the Kamma businessmen of Vishakapatnam have used these networks to establish their pre-eminent position within this nascent industrial township. Other caste groups have also made use of such kinship networks to help make the transition from agrarian to industrial capitalists. For instance, the example of the late K.V.K. Raju of the Nagarjuna group illustrates how even Rajus have used the caste network to establish their businesses.

K.V.K. Raju came from a family of landowners from north coastal Andhra. They belonged to a landowning caste regarded as superior to the Kammas in the caste hierarchy. His family invested in his education in order that he might acquire a professional degree. This enabled him to go to the United States for further education and to secure a job with a U.S. multinational firm. After working with Union Carbide for several years, in

India and abroad, Raju returned to Andhra Pradesh and decided to set up his own business. He travelled extensively in the coastal districts, and through his kinship network was able to mobilize a substantial sum of money. Hundreds of rich peasant families lent him sums as fixed deposits. Raju used this money, along with his own funds, as 'equity' capital. He then borrowed funds from public financial institutions to get into the chemicals and fertilizer manufacturing business. The Nagarjuna group was able to expand its activities into steel, engineering, and finance. Recently it has shown interest in the power sector.

When the Government of India decided to license a new fertilizer plant in Andhra Pradesh in the early 1980s, Raju saw himself competing with the Birlas for the license. He entered into a financial and technical collaboration with Snamprogetti of Italy, and this ensured that he secured the license! The lobbying for the fertilizer license showed how Birla, a national big business group, began with a headstart and, fairly early in the race, entrenched its position by securing the support of the Congress Chief Minister, Chenna Reddy. However, Raju beat Birla by linking up with Snamprogetti and securing access to Indira Gandhi through her family. The fertilizer deal was important for Raju, taking him into the 'big league'; but it also showed how regional business groups were increasingly able to compete against national big business, with support from a range of new political power centres.

The second example is Ramoji Rao, a Kamma. Rao belonged to a rich peasant family from the Krishna district of coastal Andhra Pradesh. In his youth he was an active member of the Communist Party of India, a party popular among the Kammas. (The Kamma dominance of the CPI [and later CPM] has attracted such barbs as the CPI being called the 'Kammanist Party of India'). Rao began his career in business by floating a chit fund company (similar to a U.S. 'savings and loan' company), Margadarsi Chit Funds, that operated from a small office in Hyderabad in the 1960s. By the 1970s, Rao was expanding into newspaper publishing (*Eenadu*), hotels, and real estate. He subsequently branched out into food processing, ship-breaking (breaking down of old ships for scrap) and films.

A third example is G.V. Krishna Reddy (GVK). The Reddys are a differentiated caste among the Telugus. In Telengana there are rich peasant Reddys as well as feudal landlord Reddys (the latter often use the suffix of Rao rather than Reddy, like Rameshwar Rao, the erstwhile Raja of Wanaparthi). In coastal Andhra, Reddys are mainly rich peasants. G.V. Krishna Reddy, like his kinsmen Kasu Brahmananda Reddy and T. Venkatram Reddy (former publisher of the *Deccan Chronicle*), is from south coastal Andhra Pradesh. As a civil contractor he made his money in public works—the construction of the Nagarjunasagar Dam, for instance—and moved into manufacturing business only in the 1980s. GVK moved from construction and real estate into hotels (the Krishna Oberoi) and into the power sector. GVK Power is one of the earliest private power companies to have been commissioned from among the recent projects approved by the government under its new power policy.

A fourth example is Anji Reddy, CEO of Dr Reddy's Laboratories. Dr Reddy is a first-generation professional who was employed by the public sector pharmaceutical company, Indian Drugs and Pharmaceuticals Limited. He quit IDPL, taking the technology that IDPL had secured on license from drug multinationals, to start his own company. Dr Reddy's Labs emerged as a major manufacturer of bulk drugs and soon became a manufacturer and an exporter of Ibuprofen. It is Dr Reddy's Ibuprofen exports to the U.S. that attracted legal action in U.S. courts for product patent violation in the 1980s. This became a *cause célèbre* during the early 1990s when India was named under the U.S. trade law Super and Special 301, a U.S. law that restricts imports from countries identified as violating U.S. principles of fair trade. While Dr Reddy won his case in the U.S. courts, he read the writing on the wall and decided to globalize his operations. Dr Reddy's has since set up a production base in Russia, being one of the first Indian companies to manufacture drugs outside India. Dr Reddy's raised U.S. $50 million in the global depository receipts (GDR) market in 1995 and has invested heavily in medical research and health care.

Apart from pharmaceuticals, regional business has moved in a big way into private corporate hospitals. All the major private corporate hospitals in Andhra Pradesh, as well as in Tamil Nadu and some other states, have been set up by first-generation medical professionals with agrarian roots. R. Baru shows how Kamma cultivators invested in the professional education of their children. They then became medical doctors, accumulated capital working abroad (mostly USA), returned home to mobilize additional finance locally and from the state government, and then set up corporate hospitals. The expansion of this sector and the emergence of some of these corporate entities, such as Apollo, into national business enterprises with foreign collaboration is a story that R. Baru has clearly documented.[23] There are scores of such examples of first generation 'regional' businessmen, some of whom have even been able to globalize their operations. They show that Andhra Pradesh has become a fertile breeding ground of capitalist enterprise. It is not an accident that the political dynamics of the state have produced a first generation businessman, Chandrababu Naidu, as its new political leader. He began life as a small farmer who later diversified into poultry and dairy products.

The examples I have cited above are of first-generation regional entrepreneurs who have now become big players in the market. An equally important phenomenon in Andhra Pradesh, as in other Green Revolution states, notwithstanding Ranji Sau's skepticism, has been the proliferation of small-scale enterprise. I examined this phenomenon and showed how urban centres like Hyderabad, Vijayawada, Vishakapatnam, and Tirupathi had witnessed a sharp increase in the number of small- and medium-scale enterprises in the early 1980s.[24] Rutten made a detailed analysis of the movement of agrarian capitalists into small-scale manufacturing activity in Gujarat.[25]

That this process is intrinsically linked to the rise of regional politics in states like Andhra Pradesh has been widely commented upon. It is not an accident that the Telugu Desam Party is dominated by Kammas and its chief financiers, as well as key leaders, remain Kamma businessmen.

Gujarat

Rejecting the traditional urban–rural dualism, Mario Rutten sees a continuum emerging between agrarian surplus and industrial investment.[26] Rutten's study finds a 'tendency among large farmers and rural industrialists in central Gujarat to make investments in a multiplicity of areas and to participate in a variety of activities simultaneously'. Just as Upadhya saw caste and kinship

networks used extensively among the Kammas of Andhra
Pradesh, Rutten sees evidence of them in building business links.
In a detailed study of small-scale industrial enterprise in two
villages—named for the purposes of the study as Vepargam and
Udyoggam—along the Bombay–Ahmedabad highway, Rutten observes: 'Economic diversification based on the accumulation of
local capital deriving from agriculture is the typical feature in
these two villages.' He calls the large farming families of these
villages the 'agrarian capitalist entrepreneurs' who have branched
out into manufacturing business from farming.

Pieter Gorter extended Rutten's work to cover urban first-
generation entrepreneurs, and supports the findings of Baru and
Upadhya. He offers further evidence from Gujarat of the growth
of a 'stratum of small- and medium-scale industrialists who are
striving for political influence'. Gorter's examples from Vapi
industrial estate are first-generation industrialists with an urban, middle class background. Based on his case studies, Gorter
comes to a remarkable political conclusion:

> The planning system is dismantled, lower castes and classes are mak-
> ing a bid for political power, and as a response to this threat from
> below the upper castes and middle classes support right-wing, com-
> munalist political parties. These changes force the industrial middle
> groups to take a stand. They are committed to an ideology of free
> enterprise (even if this is not always in their interests) and embrace
> the ideal of the self-made man, together with a moralistic call for
> clean politics. With their business organizations, product- or estate-
> based, and the financial resources at their disposal, they promise to
> become a political force in Indian society.[27]

This conclusion is relevant in the context of the transformation
of the BJP government in Gujarat into a 'regional' party government. It now has a first-generation industrialist as chief minister, mirroring the emergence of the Telugu Desam Party as a
regional political party dominated by Kamma capitalists.

Maharashtra

The contrast between regional and national big business has
nowhere been as sharp as in Maharashtra, where Bombay (now
Mumbai) was the centre of national big capital. This was dominated by Parsi, Gujarati, Jain and Marwari enterprise. The first

battle between non-local metropolitan business in Maharashtra, and regional capitalists took place within the sugar mill industry.[28] Initially, all the private joint-stock sugar mills in the Bombay Presidency were owned by Marwari or Gujarati businessmen. Even before Independence, political leaders in the Bombay Presidency had campaigned against private sugar mills and demanded the setting up of sugar cooperatives run by local peasantry. The Indian Sugar Mills Association (ISMA), controlled as it was by national big business, opposed the policy of giving cooperatives preference over joint-stock mills. Government of India policy, under pressure from state governments, supported peasant cooperatives. The role played by sugar cooperatives in the emergence of agrarian capitalism in Maharashtra and the subsequent branching out of sugar millers into other business ventures, has been extensively analysed.

Going beyond sugar, we find the emergence of first-generation Maratha enterprise even in the cotton textile (power loom sector) and the food-processing industries. They have demonstrated increasing clout in Mumbai. Indeed, at one level it is possible to view the politics of Maharashtra, as in the case of Gujarat and the southern states, as a process of the rise to prominence of a regional party with the support of regional capital. The conversion of the Hindutva alliance between the BJP and the Shiv Sena into a regional alliance of a Maharashtra Congress and Shiv Sena, espousing the cause of regional capital, cannot be ruled out.

Tamil Nadu

Despite the history of capitalist development associated with the Madras Presidency, Tamil business was never viewed as part of national big capital. This was mainly because there were very few Tamil business groups that had made it to the apex of the business pyramid constructed by the Hazari and other committees inquiring into monopoly capital. Even groups like T.V. Sundaram (TVS), Madras Rubber Factory (MRF) and Lakshmi were not part of the top twenty business houses. However, a distinction can be made between the national big businesses based in Tamil Nadu, like the Kotharis, TVS, MRF and so on, and the new regional capitalist class, products of the post-Green

Revolution phase of development. Interestingly, many of the latter come from intermediate and backward castes, the equivalent of the Kammas, and have generously supported Dravidian political parties. The sugar industry in the state has a fair share of first-generation entrepreneurs, so have textiles, electronics, chemicals, and engineering goods.

Political scientists have yet to analyse the significance of the ideological transformation of the Dravida Munnetra Kazhagam. From being a party that espoused Tamil nationalism largely in its cultural and social form, it has today become a powerful advocate of Tamil business interests. The pro-active role played by the former Union Industry Minister Murasoli Maran in promoting Tamil business (much like Andhra's Vengal Rao promoted Andhra business when he was Union industry minister in the mid-1980s), shows that regional capital has come to the fore in Tamil politics as well. The account of agrarian capitalism in Tamil Nadu by Athreya, Djurfeldt and Lindberg substantiates the work of Rutten and Upadhya and offers more evidence of the rural roots of emerging business enterprise.[29]

Regional Capital, Regional Politics and National Policy

The above are just a few case studies or examples. Similar studies for states like Punjab, Haryana, and Karnataka also reveal the emergence of regional capital in the post-Green Revolution period and its movement into industry.[30] K.N. Raj had in fact predicted that these three states would be the first to exhibit this tendency.

It may be asked whether the distinction I draw between 'regional' and 'national big' is useful to understand the dynamics of capitalist development in India. May this not be a transient distinction, with some 'regional' capitalists joining the ranks of the 'national big' and vice-versa? Does the distinction throw any additional light on the potential for capitalist development that a more generalized study of 'Indian business' cannot? Was this distinction all that relevant historically, when Indian business was struggling to come into its own in the face of competition from foreign capital?

First, the relevance of the distinction between 'regional' and 'national' is premised on the hypothesis that there is indeed a conflict between the two, which is in fact defined as such. There is evidence to support this hypothesis. The centralization of political authority under the 'license-permit raj' created a rift between those who could effectively lobby the central government, and others whose political and business influence was restricted to a state or a region within that state. Second, unlike the merchant capitalist and largely metropolitan origins of the 'national big' business groups, the new generation of businessmen we call 'regional' have agrarian origins and rural roots. The dynamics of this regional capital is linked to agrarian change, which has been uneven across states. Primarily for this reason, the growth of such regional capitalists has accentuated already existing inter-regional variations in capitalist industrialization in India. The ability of states like Gujarat, Karnataka, Andhra Pradesh, Haryana, and Punjab to catch up with Maharashtra, and to overtake West Bengal and the Kanpur region of Uttar Pradesh as the new industrial centres, is linked to the varied patterns of agrarian change. Finally, there is something called the self-consciousness of businesspersons: how do they see themselves? Indian national big business, which supported the national movement, funded the Congress party, authored the Bombay Plan, and influenced national policy for over four decades, had an image of itself as related to the central government and national political parties. This can be contrasted with the self-identity of the newly emergent regional groups. The latter went through a phase in their growth when Government of India support was regarded as inadequate and national policies as discriminating against them. They invested in regional political parties to gain political support at the state level and entered into collaborations with foreign investors to gain market leverage over national big business.

Both from the literature I have cited above, as well as from my own random and occasional interviews with regional businesspersons,[31] a clear perception emerges with respect to the attitude of regional business towards national industrial policies. It is clear that they have felt less able to influence national-level decision-making directly. It is true that there have been instances where regional business groups have secured industrial licenses in competition with national big business, like Nagarjuna's battle with the Birlas for the award of the license for a fertilizer factory in Andhra Pradesh. Generally speaking, however, the licensing system was considered inequitable, benefiting big business. This system, as well as cumbersome bureaucratic procedures, became effective barriers to entry for new firms and increased the cost of establishment. Hence, regional business groups became increasingly opposed to the erstwhile 'license-permit raj'. Of course, big business was also interested in ending the licensing system because it restricted their growth. With this system being terminated, many firms owned or controlled by big business houses have been able to expand capacity freely, and this would have helped them face the 'competition from below' from smaller firms owned by regional business groups. However, the fact is that entry barriers have eased for new groups. Thus the termination of the licensing system has benefited both national big and regional businesses.

From actual experience it also became clear to regional business groups that any system which increased the leverage of the state government over the central government would increase their relative strength vis-à-vis national big business. The experience with state- and national-level public financial institutions was an important factor in this understanding. Complaints from regional businesspersons against the pro-big business bias of national public financial institutions like Industrial Development Bank of India, Industrial Finance Corporation of India, etc., and their easier access to state finance and industrial development corporations (SFCs and SIDCs) have often been reported in the media. A strong development of these institutions at the state level has been a necessary condition for the growth of regional businesses.

Equally important has been the deepening and widening of the capital market, both primary and secondary. It is not a coincidence that states like Gujarat, Maharashtra, Punjab, Andhra Pradesh, Tamil Nadu, and Karnataka have had the most active primary capital markets, with a large number of public issues being subscribed here. The rapid development of the Bangalore stock exchange in Karnataka and the Hyderabad exchange in Andhra Pradesh testify to this phenomenon. Nine states now have stock exchanges (Maharashtra, Gujarat, Karnataka, Tamil Nadu, Kerala, Andhra Pradesh, Uttar Pradesh, West Bengal, and Delhi). Andhra Pradesh has had a significant number of new businesses set up with funds mobilized from both the primary and secondary markets.[32]

The emergence of regional business, its ability to grow in the face of both market and non-market barriers to entry imposed by national business and national policy, was undoubtedly aided by the supportive role of the state governments and political leadership. However, in most states it is now clear that the inability of the national political party—that too, a highly centralized one like the Congress party of the Indira–Rajiv era—also encouraged regional business groups to turn increasingly to regional political parties, to fund them and ensure their access to them. It is not a coincidence, for example, that the key economic ministries in the 1996–8 United Front government were held by the DMK (industries) and TDP (commerce), and even Finance Minister P. Chidambaram became increasingly receptive to the demands of regional business.

Recent trends in private investment since the implementation of the new economic policy, show an increased level of activity by regional business groups as opposed to the older, big business houses. In the power sector, for instance, most of the 'fast-track' private power projects have been set up by regional business houses. Both Spectrum and GVK Power in Andhra Pradesh belong to this category. Though Nagarjuna ventured into power, it has since decided to call off its proposed project in Mangalore. Regional groups have also been active in setting up enterprises abroad. Dr Reddy's Labs has set up a production facility in China (near Shanghai), from where it exports drugs to the U.S.! Nagarjuna has set up fertilizer and sugar units in South East Asia.

The increasing corporate presence of regional business groups has also been articulated in the membership and organizational structure of regional branches of national chambers of commerce and industry. Gorter reports the case study of how a business association in Vapi, Gujarat, was 'taken over' by regional businessmen, wresting control from national big business.[33] At the national level, this process is reflected in the growing profile of regional business groups in the Confederation of Indian Industry and in Associated Chamber of Commerce, while the Federation of Indian Chamber of Commerce and Industry continues to be dominated by the national big business groups.[34]

Conclusion

Contrary to long-held notions of Indian capitalism being 're-tarded', 'stunted', or 'dependent', the process of agrarian change in many parts of the country has laid the foundations for capital-ist development in the non-farm sector. This process has allowed a new generation of agrarian capitalists or other middle-class professionals to make the transition to capitalist entrepreneurs. In states like Punjab, Haryana, Gujarat, Maharashtra, Tamil Nadu, Andhra Pradesh and Karnataka, a dynamic first-genera-tion business class has emerged over the last two decades. This class remains distinct from the traditional 'national' business class in a variety of ways. First, while the origins of the latter are mostly traced to trade, commerce and moneylending, the majority of the new regional business class is drawn from the agrarian economy. Second, the failure of national political par-ties and the central government to address the needs of emer-gent regional business groups encouraged the latter to seek po-litical and material support from state governments and regional political parties. It is not surprising that regional political par-ties have been most active in States where regional business groups have been more dynamic and assertive. The link between the emer-gence of regional capitalism and regional parties is too stark to be ignored. Finally, while regional business groups initially began in food-processing or low technology intensive areas, they have been quick to move into new industries and also enter into joint ven-tures with foreign companies, sometimes with the purpose of tak-ing on competition from national big business groups.

This paper offers anecdotal evidence, the results of prelimi-nary or micro-level studies, to draw attention to an important economic and political process under way. The phenomenon of capitalist development in India deserves a closer look than has been on offer so far. State level studies must be encouraged to study the dynamics of agrarian change and industrial develop-ment. Political economists have not adequately recognized the potential for capitalist industrialization in India. While legitimate concerns can be expressed about growing regional disparities, the fact remains that some states in India have exhibited the po-tential for high growth. If market forces are left unfettered, re-gional differentiation can generate political tensions. However,

for this reason, state intervention should not inhibit rapid capitalist development; rather it should address the problems of unequal and unequalizing growth and intervene to resolve such
problems. This is the model China has followed in the recent
past—allowing growth to take off in some regions and then intervening to redress the problems of inter-regional inequality in
development. This calls for new and market-friendly instruments
of planning, based on greater decentralization of political authority, rather than the blunt instrument of centralized planning and
bureaucratic intervention by the central government.

Notes

[1] On the economic history of indigenous enterprise in India see for example, A.K. Bagchi, *Private Investment in India, 1900-1939* (Cambridge:
Cambridge University Press), 1972; Rajat K. Ray, *Industrialisation in India*
(Delhi: Oxford University Press), 1979; R.S. Rungta, *Rise of Business Corporation in India, 1851–1900* (Cambridge: Cambridge University Press),
1970; and Dwijendra Tripathi, *Business Communities of India: A Historical
Perspective* (Delhi: Manohar), 1984. There are also several studies in the
economic history of capitalist enterprise in specific regions or for specific
groups as, for instance, James G. Berna, *Industrial Entrepreneurship in
Madras State* (Bombay: Asia Publishing House), 1960; Raman Mahadevan,
'The Origin and Growth of Entrepreneurship in the Nattukottai Chetty
Community of Tamil Nadu', Unpublished M. Phil thesis, Jawaharlal Nehru
University, New Delhi, 1976; Thomas Timberg, *The Marwaris: From Traders to Industrialists* (New Delhi), 1978; D.H. Buchanan, *The Development
of Capitalist Enterprise in India* (New York), 1934; and Dwijendra Tripathi
(ed.) *Business and Politcs in India: A Historical Perspective* (Delhi: Manohar),
1991.

[2] For example, R.K. Hazari, *The Structure of the Corporate Private Sector*
(Bombay: Asia Publishing House), 1966, L.A. Joshi, *Central of Indus-
try in India: A Study in Aspects of Combination and Concentration*
(Bombay: Vora and Co.), 1965. N.K. Chandra, 'Monopoly Capital, Pri-
vate Corporate Sector and the Indian Economy: A Study in Relative
Growth, 1931-1976' in A.K. Bagchi and N. Banerjee (eds), *Change and
Choice in Indian Industry* (Calcutta: K.P. Baghi and Co.), 1981.

[3] For instance, half of the top twenty business houses listed in 1969,
ranked by asset size, are no longer anywhere near the top (Bangur,
Scindia, Bhiwandiwala, Kirloskar, Walchand, Modi, Sarabhai, Macneil
& Magor, Lalbhai and ICI), having broken up through partitioning of
assets, or being absorbed into other corporate entities, etc. On the
other hand, several new business houses have moved into the top

twenty, including, Reliance, Nagarjuna, Abhay Oswal, Mittals, and Ruias (Essar). Others on the threshold include Bajaj, Mallya and ITC. New entrants to the top 100 include Ranbaxy, Hero, Videocon, TVS Sundaram, etc.).

Tyabji was an exception. The paper not only recognized the importance of the 'non-monopoly' business class but also drew attention to the notion of a 'regional' capitalist class. Says Tyabji: 'In more specific terms we might say that the 'unintegrated' nature of the economy leads to distinct cycles of reproduction of capital, one of which might be defined as national and the others as regional; and initially define big business to be that which operates at an all-India level both for its sources of capital and the market for its products; small or regional business is localised in both aspects'. See Nasir Tyagi, 'Stratification of Indian Business', in Bagchi and Banerjee (eds), *Change and Choice*, op. cit.

However, corporate sector analysts today question the validity of the notion of 'monopoly' capital, given the structural changes that have taken place, and the traditional classification of Indian business into 'monopoly' and 'non-monopoly' itself may have to change. We prefer to use the more neutral concept of 'national big business' and 'regional business'.

5 For example, Berna, *Industrial Entrepreneurship*, op. cit., (1960), Mario Rutten, *Farms and Factories: Social Profile of Large Farmers and Rural Industrialists in West India* (Delhi: Oxford University Press), 1995 and Mario Rutten and Carol Upadhya (eds), *Small Business Entrepreneurs in Asia and Europe: Towards a Comparative Perspective* (New Delhi: Sage), 1997. Carol Upadhya 'The Farmer-Capitalists of Coastal Andhra Pradesh', *Economic and Political Weekly*, vol. XXIII, nos. 27–28 (1988).

6 Political scientists have examined the link between business and politics at the 'national' level, as well as the link between the 'national bourgeoisie' and political leadership, for example see Stanley Kochanek, *Business and Politics in India*, (Berkeley: University of California Press) 1974, but there is scanty literature on the link between 'regional' capital and 'regional' political parties. Kochanek is now engaged in a study of the role of 'regional' business groups within 'national' business lobbies like the FICCI and CII; the changing regional composition of FICCI/CII membership, and its implications for the policy stance adopted by these business chambers.

7 See, for instance, A.K. Bagchi, *Private Investment in India*, op.cit. and Bagchi, 'Reflections on Patterns of Regional Growth, in India during the Period of British Rule, *Bengal Past and Present*, January–June, (1976).

8 See Government of Uttar Pradesh, *Report of the Committee on Take-over of Sugar Mills*, June 1970.

[9] K.N. Raj, 'Growth and Stagnation in Indian Industrial Development', *Economic* and *Political Weekly*, vol. XI, nos. 5, 6 & 7 (Annual Number, February 1976) pp. 223–36.

[10] For example, Bagchi, 'Reflections on Patterns of Regional Growth' and Krishna Bharadwaj, 'Regional Differentiation in India', in T.V. Sathyamurthy (ed.), *Industry and Agriculture in India since Independence* (Delhi: Oxford University Press), 1995.

[11] D. Banerjee and A. Ghosh, 'Indian Planning and Regional Disparity in Growth' in A.K. Bagchi (ed.) *Economy, Society and Polity: Essays in the Political Economy of Planning* (Delhi: Oxford University Press), 1988.

[12] Raj, 'Growth and Strategies' op. cit., pp. 200–1.

[13] Bharadwaj, 'Regional Differentiation', op. cit. and Amitabha Kundu & Moonis Raza, *India Economy, the Regional Dimension* (New Delhi: Centre for the Study of Regional Development, Jawaharlal Nehru University), 1982.

[14] Bharadwaj, 'Regional Differentiation', op. cit., p. 209.

[15] Ravi Srivastava, 'India's Uneven Development and Its Implications for Political Processes: An Analysis of Some Recent Trends in T.V. Sathyamurthy (ed.), *Industry and Agriculture since Independence*, vol. 2, (New Delhi: Oxford University Press), 1995, p. 212.

[16] Ibid., p. 241.

[17] There are some skeptics who question the positive relationship between the Green Revolution and industrial development. For instance, Sau (1988) says, 'The green revolution helped create a class of rich farmers with sizeable income and investable resources. Why did they not transcend themselves to the rank of industrial capitalists? . . . (because) the outlets (for investable surplus) seem to be few and precarious'. See Ranjit Sau, 'The Green Revolution and Industrial Growth in India: A Tale of Two Paradoxes and a Half', *Economic and Political Weekly*, vol. XXIII, no. 16 (1988). This is an excessively pessimistic view of the process. The outlets did exist, but not every rich farmer could make the transition, but that is not unnatural.

[18] Rutten and Upadhya, *Small Business Entrepreneurs*, op. cit.

[19] Pieter Gorter, "The Social and Political Aspirations of a New Stratum of Industrialists: Local Politics on a Large Industrial Estate in West India" in Rutten and Upadhya (eds), *Small Business Entrepreneurs*, op. cit.

[20] Sanjaya Baru, 'Capitalism in Agriculture and Growth of Manufacturing: Some Issues with Reference to Andhra Pradesh', in Y.V. Krishna Rao et al. (eds), *Peasant Farming and Growth of Manufacturing in Indian Agriculture* (Vijayawada: Visalandhra), 1984.

[21] Upadhya, 'The Farmer-Capitalists of Coastal Andhra, op. cit.

[22] Ibid.

[23] Rama V. Baru, 'Some Aspects of the Private Sector in Medical Care and Its Interrelationship with the Public Sector: A Study of Hyderabad–Secundrabad', unpublished Ph.D. thesis, Jawaharlal Nehru University, New Delhi, 1994.

[24] Baru, 'Capitalism in Agriculture', op. cit.

[25] Rutten, *Farmers and Factories*, op. cit.

[26] Ibid.

[27] Gorter, 'The Social and Political Aspirations' op. cit., p. 108.

[28] This has been documented in Sanjaya Baru, *The Political Economy of Indian Sugar* (Delhi: Oxford University Press), 1990, Chapter IV.

[29] V. Athreya, G. Djurfeldt and S. Lindberg, *Barriers Broken: Production Relations and Agrarian Change in Tamil Nadu* (New Delhi: Oxford University Press), 1987.

[30] A study of Karnataka that looks at recent industrial development of the state without appreciating the significance of the regional dimension of capitalist development is Kyoko Inoue Industrial Development Policy of India (Tokyo: Institute of Developing Economics), 1992.

[31] We have interviewed regional businesspersons from Andhra Pradesh and Tamil Nadu at random. The interviewees include K.V.K. Raju (in 1986), K.S. Raju, Ramoji Rao, Rajshree Pathy, Sakuntala Gnanamgari, and B.B. Ramaiah.

[32] A direct consequence of this phenomenon is observed in the marketing strategy of the premier financial daily, *The Economic Times*, which ran editions only from Bombay, Delhi, Calcutta and Ahmedabad until the 1980s. The first foray into south India was made with a Bangalore edition, followed by Madras and Hyderabad in the early 1990s. Chandigarh and Cochin editions are on the anvil.

[33] Gorter, 'The Social and Political Aspirations', op. cit.

[34] Stanley Kochanek is currently engaged in a study of the changing membership pattern of the FICCI, CII and ASSOCHAM. He makes the point that the representation of the southern states and involvement of new business groups has increased in these organizations. This is particularly true for CII, where despite the continued dominance of Tata, Bajaj and Godrej, several regional groups from the Punjab, Haryana, Bengal and the southern states have acquired a higher profile.

Economic Policy and Its Political Management in the Current Conjuncture

PRABHAT PATNAIK

I

Different political parties and movements are usually distinguished from each other by the difference between their social programmes, of which the economic programmes constitute an important component. What is striking about the contemporary world, however, is that apparently dissimilar political movements, whether within a particular country or across countries, are adopting identical economic programmes. Three successive governments in India, the Congress, the United Front, and the BJP-led coalition, have sought to pursue such a programme, also in vogue elsewhere, irrespective of the professed ideologies of the governing formations. How long it will continue to be widely espoused is a moot but separate point; its present currency however is indisputable.

The main characteristics of this common programme are well known: removal of internal controls over the freedom of operation of private (including foreign) capital; trade liberalization; gradual removal of restrictions on capital flows into and out of the country; reduction in the role of the state as producer and investor; energetic wooing of multinational corporations (MNCs) for undertaking direct foreign investment; unification of the exchange rate; reduction of direct tax rates; reduction of subsidies and transfer payments to the poor; severe restrictions on the size of the fiscal deficit; and the privatization of state-owned assets.

It is futile to pretend that this apparent unanimity among dissimilar political movements is the result of all of them suddenly 'having seen the light'. Over much of the developing world (and the former socialist countries) it is, in a proximate sense, the result of coercion exercised by the Bretton Woods institutions, though of course there are always important domestic sectors providing social support for such measures. But the word coercion immediately raises two questions: first, what is its *modus operandi,* and second, what are the social forces, the constituency, on behalf of which the Bretton Woods institutions exercise it?

II

The commonly-held view about the *modus operandi* of this coercion is as follows: thanks to populist measures undertaken by third world governments under pressure from diverse and competing social groups, these economies go into fiscal crises which, if their consequences are not to become 'intolerably' inflationary, necessitate increasing amounts of external borrowing;[1] this cannot go on indefinitely, so the terms of borrowing get stiffer at the margin, and its maturity shorter; at some point, therefore, there is an inevitable balance of payments crisis, usually triggered off by speculative capital flight that forces the country to go to the International Monetary Fund and accept its 'conditionalities' which usher in the programme outlined above. Central to this view is the belief that IMF coercion is the result of an internally-caused mismanagement of the economy. Not surprisingly, this view is held by both those critical of the IMF-programme as well as those who support it as a means to 'set the house in order', and create the basis for rapid and more sustainable growth than the *dirigiste* regimes had achieved.

There are at least two ways in which this view is misleading. First, the main reason for the balance of payments crisis in third world countries is import liberalization, in the context of a world economy where growth in their export revenue is necessarily sluggish. The reason for Africa's growing debt was an external shock: the collapse of primary commodity prices. The reason for Latin America's and Eastern Europe's burgeoning debt was import liberalization, undertaken on the argument that it would help exports, but which ended up financing a pent-up demand for imported luxury goods instead. Fiscal deficits, rather than being the 'original sin', were often resorted to to sustain this consumption splurge, in the absence of which the economies would have slipped into massive recessions[2]. In short the cause for the crisis, which in turn makes for the imposition of IMF-style liberalization, is some initial liberalization itself, rather than the sins of the *dirigiste* regime. To say this is not to deny these 'sins', including fiscal deficits (which in my view are a manifestation of 'primitive accumulation of capital' rather than a result of 'competing claims'); but to focus on them alone is to remain blind to the whole international context which produces a liberalization dialectic: some initial liberalization giving rise to a crisis which is used for further liberalization, and so on.[3]

Second, the reason for the crises which arise along the liberalization route may not necessarily be the spontaneous behaviour of speculators, giving rise to capital flight; rather their panic reaction is quite often stimulated by the actions of the Bretton Woods institutions themselves, so that we have a 'signalled' crisis. This serves to undermine the autonomy and resilience of the economy and pushes it further under the tutelage of these institutions.

Examples of such 'signalling' can be cited from several countries, but we shall confine ourselves to the Indian case. India went in for import liberalization in the latter half of the Eighties to obtain capital goods and components for the automobile and electronics sectors. A large fiscal deficit sustained the boom in these sectors while foreign commercial borrowing—which India had been very reluctant to undertake earlier—sustained the current account deficit incurred as a result of import liberalization. This borrowing, which was approved of by the World Bank (as well as its ex-employees manning the Indian ministry of finance), inevitably involved stiffer terms and shorter maturity at the margin, as it kept increasing. But in 1991 even though the strain on the balance of payments owing to the Gulf War was well on the way to being managed (and could have easily been managed) through non-conditionality borrowing from the IMF, the World Bank wanted a 20 per cent depreciation in the value of the rupee. This demand found its way to the press. Not surprisingly it triggered off capital flight in anticipation of a currency depreciation, with non-resident Indians clamouring to take their funds out of the country. To meet this crisis the government approached the IMF which came up with a stabilization-cum-structural adjustment programme. In short the Bretton Woods package was adopted by the country without any debate or discussion in a situation of crisis, even as the crisis itself arose because of 'signals' from the Bretton Woods institutions themselves.[4]

These are therefore not just two disinterested institutions, which third world countries turn to for succour when pushed beyond tolerance by the contradictions of *dirigiste* regimes; on the contrary they are keen on prising open third world economies for the free movement of commodities and capital, including speculative finance capital. Their ex-employees, who also freely migrate back when they choose, are placed in economic policy-making positions, in finance ministries in particular, in all third world countries even during the *dirigiste* phase. Whenever an opportunity arises for intervention by these institutions, whether because of external shocks or the pitfalls of import liberalization, or because of some internal strains, they use it for enforcing further liberalization, and every crisis along this route, often triggered by their own actions, is used by them for still further liberalization. The term 'coercion' used above has to be understood in this broader sense, and not just as referring to 'conditionalities'.

III

This brings us to the question: whose interests do programmes imposed by the Bretton Woods institutions represent? Leaving aside those who see 'liberalization-cum-structural adjustment' as the embodiment of pure reason, the tendency has been to point to the MNCs. Trade liberalization no doubt enables MNCs to capture third world markets at the expense of local producers by providing or arranging for loans or export credit. Likewise the wooing of MNCs to undertake investment in third world economies opens up very profitable investment opportunities for them; and the sale of public sector assets as well as the removal of restrictions on taking over local companies enables them to buy their way cheaply into business empires in third world economies. There is therefore no denying the fact that the interests of the MNCs are well served by the Bretton Woods prescription which achieves what Marx called 'centralization of capital' on a global scale.

It is also the case that the undermining of food security in the third world by institutionalizing export agriculture serves both to make a number of tropical products available cheaply to metropolitan consumers, and to increase the leverage of metropolitan countries on an increasingly food-import-dependent third world. In this sense the Bretton Woods programmes can be seen as a means of perpetuating the overall structural dichotomy in the world economy, quite apart from serving specific interests.

While all this is true, the overriding characteristic of such programmes is that they serve above all the interests of what I shall call international finance capital. This entity is not synonymous with the finance capital that Hobson, Hilferding and Lenin had written about. Their concept of finance capital was nation-state based; referred in varying degrees to a coalescence between industry and finance (less true of Hobson); and envisaged a confrontation between rival blocs of it. What we have today, however, is a remarkable degree of unity, rather than rivalry, among the metropolitan powers and their finance capitals; a remarkable degree of fluidity and hence non-rootedness (in industry or in any other sectors) of this capital; and its unparalleled international reach. In other words, what we have is a huge bloc of finance, dominated no doubt by finance from the metropolis but devoid of any national character. Of this, the finance from individual countries is increasingly becoming an aliquot part; and it moves around the globe in quest of opportunities for quick profits—essentially speculative gains. The rise to ascendancy of this international finance capital from the position to which finance capital generally had been reduced in the immediate post-war world, dominated by Keynesianism with its call for the 'euthanasia of the rentier',[5] is a matter that need not detain us here. The point is that the Bretton Woods programme, with its emphasis not just on trade liberalization but on the removal of restrictions on capital flows, on 'financial liberalization' and on currency unification and convertibility, serves above all the interests of international finance capital by prising open third world economies to its unhindered access, exit, and operation. True, the programme represents a convergence of interests between MNCs; international finance capital; sections of the domestic third world bourgeoisie anxious to break out of the straitjacket of the national economy; kulak and landlord elements lured by the promise of export agriculture (a promise that is not necessarily realized subsequently as prices crash); and sections of the third world élite that benefit from 'globalization' in terms of access to opportunities and commodities. But it bears the unmistakeable stamp of international finance capital.

IV

Conformity to a certain programme, apparently enforced by the Fund and the Bank, is in reality produced by certain fundamental features of contemporary capitalism, marked *inter alia* by the ascendancy of finance capital. This ascendancy is of relevance not only in countries like India. It also underlies the retreat in the advanced capitalist countries from the Keynesian programme of state intervention for achieving near-full employment, as well as from the commitment to maintaining a welfare state. Basically this ascendancy undermines the 'control area' of the state, within which its intervention can be effective. If Keynesian policies of stimulating demand lead to a flight of 'hot money' and hence a balance of payments crisis, in which the traditional instrument of exchange rate depreciation becomes either ineffective (since it may give rise to expectations of further depreciation) or extremely costly (since the requisite depreciation may entail large increases in the domestic price-level), then clearly the state's ability to control the level of activity is greatly reduced.

If the state could cordon off the domestic economy against the capricious movements of finance capital, then it might well be able to regulate the level of economic activity in the manner that Keynes had advocated. But in the absence of such cordoning off, Keynesian demand management of the sort that was in vogue in the period up to the mid-Seventies becomes untenable. Since fiscal deficits fuel fears of inflation and balance of payments difficulties, the pressure to keep these under control increases and the welfare expenditures of the state become an immediate target of fiscal conservatism.

Thus if the so-called 'triumph of neo-liberalism' is more general and not just confined to third world countries, the reason for it is obvious: the same conjuncture confronts both sets of countries, a conjuncture marked by the ascendancy of finance capital and the difficulty of sustaining state-interventionist programmes. This explains why the uniformity of programmes referred to at the beginning in a sense straddles both the advanced and the backward capitalist worlds.

Some have concluded from this that the structural dichotomy between the advanced and backward segments has itself lost all relevance. If both segments are at the mercy of the same force, namely an internationally-mobile finance capital which knows no national boundaries and whose national origins have no significance, then clearly this traditional dichotomy has been rendered obsolete for comprehending capitalist dynamics (though of course it remains a *fact* of undeniable importance). This view is erroneous however, since it looks at finance in isolation. The neo-liberal programme is not just a one-point programme relating to mobility of finance; the latter, though of great importance, is superimposed on a host of other measures. Their end result, as mentioned earlier, is centralization of capital on a global scale, combined with the re-imposition (via the promotion of export agriculture and, in general, of primary commodity exports) of the old international division of labour from which the third world has been trying to break out since de-colonization. Thus, in a structurally unequal world, the apparent equality of the uniform application of neo-liberal programmes is in fact a means of perpetuating and compounding structural inequalities. (This is quite apart from the fact that assertions about the uniform application of trade liberalization measures and the irrelevance of the national origins of finance capital are not even factually true.)[6]

V

The consequences of the adoption of the 'neo-liberal' programme in third world economies have been widely discussed, and it is unnecessary to repeat that discussion here.[7] Three consequences, in particular, can be postulated. First, it would entail a loss of economic sovereignty; second, it would make for greater inequalities in income and wealth in society; and, third, it would not, on average and on a sustained basis in each country, achieve rates and patterns of growth that would (given the increase in inequalities) cause any reduction in the problem of poverty, such as the *dirigiste* regime with all its failings had effected. While the first two assertions would be generally accepted even by the advocates of 'structural adjustment', it is the third—the one that considers neo-liberalism retrograde (whether or not it is inevitable is a separate issue to be discussed later)—that arouses fierce opposition.

The ascendancy of internationally-mobile finance capital and the associated decline in Keynesian demand management has the effect of slowing the growth of world economy as a whole. The adoption of neo-liberal policies in the third world at this very time, therefore, has the effect, *ceteris paribus,* of importing crisis and stagnation rather than achieving export-led growth. Advocates of structural adjustment may argue that the slowdown in world capitalism provides an ideal setting for capital to move into low-wage third world economies to locate plants in the latter for meeting global demand, and that this will provide a new basis for growth. But a neo-liberal regime, by its very nature, cannot discriminate between speculative capital inflows and productive capital inflows and, within the latter, between inflows for producing for the domestic market (and supplanting already-existing home producers) and those that produce for the global market; it cannot keep out one sort of capital and encourage the other. Consequently, it is bound to be concerned with maintaining the confidence of speculators, to which end it pursues generally deflationary policies that adversely affect growth, even when there is no actual capital flight. Since productive capital (DFI) inflows into the third world are both small, and of the de-industrializing kind (aimed at meeting local demand by supplanting local producers whose production generally has a lower import-content), the contractionary consequences of neo-liberal policies are further reinforced.[8]

VI

The Indian experience under liberalization confirms this. The industrial revival, starting from 1993–4, after an initial drop in the growth rate of the index of industrial production in 1991–2 and 1992–3, gave a contrary impression, but that revival itself has proved to be transitory. After 1995–6 when the growth rate reached a peak of 12.8 per cent, there has been a decline to 5.5 per cent and 6.6 per cent respectively in the next two years. This is not surprising. The pick-up in industrial growth was initially a result of an increase in the fiscal deficit in 1993–4 and, after that was lowered in the subsequent years, of the pent-up demand for a variety of hitherto-not-available luxury consumption goods.[9] The latter, however, is only a transient stimulus, whose petering out has also coincided with the dumping of a range of manufactured goods in the Indian market by recession-hit foreign producers. For the entire seven-year period, 1990–1 to 1997–8, the average industrial growth rate works out to 5.9 per cent which is lower than the 8.4 per cent for the preceding quinquennium.[10]

A slowdown is also in evidence in the agricultural sector.[11] Real value added (1980–1 prices) in agriculture increased at an average annual rate of 2.5 per cent between 1990–1 to 1996–7, compared to 3.1 per cent during 1983–4 to 1990–1 (all comparisons are peak-to-peak). The growth of foodgrain production in particular has declined sharply, and has even fallen below the population growth rate. During the 12-year period 1978–9 to 1990–1 the average annual growth rate of foodgrain production (in tonnes) was 2.4 per cent. Between 1990–1 to 1996–7 this dropped to 1.4 per cent, well below the population growth rate. (Even the growth rate based on the index number of foodgrain production only reaches 1.7 per cent for the latter period.) The fact that despite this there has not been any actual food shortage till now is partly due to a series of good harvests (i.e., low peak-to-peak growth rates have not meant low absolute outputs), and partly to the limited increase in real terms in purchasing power among workers, especially rural workers (i.e., when deflated by an index of administered food-grain prices). There are several reasons for this limited increase: the steep escalation of administered food prices that occurred in the aftermath of liberalization; the cutback in government expenditure in rural areas which has curtailed non-agricultural employment; and the shift from food to export crops that are, on average, less employment-intensive.

To be sure, the decline in per capita foodgrain production cannot be attributed to liberalization alone. Several factors have contributed to it, some of them rather long-term, e.g., the decline in real gross capital formation in agriculture by the government. Liberalization, however, has also contributed, first, through a shift of acreage away from foodgrains, especially coarse grains, to export crops, and second, by perpetuating the lack of government investment (the rise in private investment in agriculture that has occurred in this period does not make up for this since it is not in the traditional foodgrain sector).

This slowdown in commodity-producing sectors has not been accompanied by any notable gains on the trade front. It appeared for a while that exports were on a high growth trajectory, but the growth rate (in USD) has slumped from 20.3 per cent in 1995–6 to 4.5 per cent and 2.6 per cent respectively in the following two years. While the decline in the last two years may be attributed, partly at least, to the slowdown in world trade, import growth, at 10.1 and 5.8 per cent respectively, has been comparatively higher in this very period, despite the slowdown in industrial growth. The consequent enlargement of the trade deficit that has occurred poses a serious threat in the context of large hot money inflows (outstripping DFI inflows) that have taken place during the 1990s. Under pressure to increase exports, the government has been turning increasingly to agricultural and other primary commodities. Exports of the latter have been resorted to even at the cost of domestic shortages, a fact which underlies the acceleration of inflation in 1998. There was an inflationary upsurge in the immediate post-liberalization period, owing mainly to administered price-hikes (especially of foodgrains), which gradually subsided after 1994–5. The acceleration in 1998 marks a return to high inflation.

Estimates of rural poverty for the post-liberalization years show, on average, an increase compared to the immediate pre-liberalization period;[12] but the post-liberalization years are too few, the estimates are derived from 'thin samples', and causation is always a matter of controversy. The fact that the average net daily per capita availability of cereals and pulses for the six years 1992–7 (i.e., prior to the impact of the latest inflation) was nearly the same as for the preceding six years, 1986–91 (485 gms compared to 480 gms), despite the much larger diversion of foodgrains towards processed and junk food consumed by the urban affluent in the later period, lends some credence to claims of a slight increase in poverty. In any case the process of declining poverty witnessed during the Eighties has come to an end.

The Indian liberalization experience of course has not been as bad as that of several other third world countries,[13] partly because the process itself has been incomplete and partly because of the absence of any major crop failure or capital flight till date. Even so, the tendency towards an accentuation of economic inequalities in the midst of undiminished mass poverty, characteristic of a neo-liberal regime, is evident. Since such a tendency sharpens social contradictions, the question that arises is: how would such a regime sustain itself *politically*? That it would entail an abridgement of democracy is clear, but what are the forms that such an abridgement might take? A shift to a presidential form of government, such as is being mooted in India, is one obvious possibility, but even if this does not happen, there are other kinds of abridgement and these merit discussion.

VII

Before proceeding, however, we have to consider a preliminary question. Mass poverty after all has continued, and inequality has increased in India in the past, even when reasonably effective institutions of political democracy prevailed. Why then should any fall-out of neo-liberal economic policies also not co-exist with political democracy, without requiring any abridgement of it?

To answer this question, a more general issue needs to be investigated: how can abysmal poverty in India continue to be perpetuated even under conditions of political democracy? The answer lies in the fact that the country *has* made notable advances since Independence, not only in such things as developing an industrial base and achieving not insignificant increases in per capita GDP, but in averting famines which were a recurrent phenomenon in the colonial period; in increasing per capita foodgrain availability; in lowering somewhat the poverty ratio; in almost doubling life expectancy at birth; in raising the literacy rate to some extent; in lowering the infant mortality rate, and so on. The fact that the achievements *should* have been far greater should not mean that we deny them altogether. The fact that there have reportedly been 'miracles' in East and South East Asia, relative to whom India has performed poorly, should not lead us to believe that India has retrogressed in absolute terms. The fact that the benefits of India's economic progress have been distributed in an extremely uneven manner should not persuade us to think that people at the bottom of the ladder have had zero or negative gains. To think so would not only be a retrospective apology for colonialism, but a real insult to the struggles of the people before and after independence, which alone have enabled them to obtain some improvement in their condition.

Even more significant than these achievements, however, is something else, namely the opportunities for upward mobility that have been made available, in varying degrees no doubt, to the population at different levels. This is due not just to the exit of foreigners who had monopolized top positions in every sphere, or to the expansion of opportunities arising from the significant rate of growth that came with independence, or even to the enormous opening up of educational opportunities, regardless of whether its quality and quantity have been adequate or not. All these have been important factors; above all, however, there has been a tremendous social churning which has characterized the practice of political democracy in the country. From the abolition of *zamindari* to the *Garibi Hatao* populism of the Indira Gandhi era; to the Other Backward Classes (OBC) movement and the dalit upsurge, not to mention the very significant and unique experiments in rural development and empowerment undertaken by Left-ruled states in the country, India has been in the throes of continuous, rapid and significant social change. One commonly encounters a debunking of 'populism', 'political patronage', 'Mandalization', etc., but these precisely have been the mechanisms of this social change.

While this change, and the upward mobility that ensued, have not reduced income and wealth inequalities (which, especially the latter, have actually been accentuated since Independence), they have kept alive the hope, even among the poor and to some extent, of the possibility of improvement in their economic status—if not for themselves, then, at least, for their children. In other words in post-Independence India, although there has been a process of 'primitive accumulation of capital', this process itself has been affected, shaped, modified and even restrained by a parallel and complex process of social change. The net result has been a broadening of the social composition of the bourgeoisie as well as keeping alive hopes of economic betterment among sections of the poor. The co-existence of substantial deprivation on the one hand, with political democracy on the other, has been possible because this deprivation has been accompanied by social flux and upward mobility.

A neo-liberal economic policy, however, not only entails economic stagnation for the mass of the people (and even retrogression owing to shrinking world trade or in the event of capital flight), but also curtails the opportunities of upward mobility hitherto available to those outside the circles of the urban élite, because of its 'western orientation' and restrictions on the size of government employment. Its coexistence with political democracy therefore becomes more problematical. In other words, it greatly enhances both vertical (rich–poor) and horizontal (rural–urban) dichotomies in society. The fact that, as far as landlords and kulaks are concerned, the promise of export agriculture does not necessarily materialize owing to price crashes, is germane to this second dichotomy. This is why neo-liberal economic policies are invariably associated with an abridgement of democracy. There are several ways in which this occurs; of these, three in particular, relevant to the Indian context, are discussed below.

VIII

The first relates to the strategy of influencing policy making and public opinion. It is common to think of the influence of Bretton Woods institutions over policy making solely in terms of 'conditionalities'. But influence would be far more difficult to exercise if it had to be exerted through 'conditionalities' alone or even principally, since the charge of 'outside interference' then would be too strong to permit smooth passage of the favoured policies.[14] The placing of World Bank and IMF employees who happen to be nationals of the country concerned to key positions in the economic bureaucracy, especially the finance ministry, is a key element of the strategy, and is pervasive all over the third world. These bureaucrats remain entitled to handsome pensions from these institutions and even go back there from time to time. Imbued with the outlook of the Fund and the Bank, and having personal links with the bureaucracy of these institutions, they help implement neo-liberal policies as the government's own policies, even without any explicit Fund–Bank 'conditionalities'. Along with this, however, there is a process of introducing greater opacity on economic issues. Increasingly, such issues are excluded from public debate; facts concerning them are a closely-guarded secret and, whenever necessary, a few hand-picked persons are appointed to a committee whose predictable recommendations give the imprimatur of 'expertise' to neo-liberal policies, so that any opposition to them can be dismissed as 'uninformed'.

The influencing of public opinion in other ways is equally important. Individual media-persons and academics are shown favours and given assignments which are very lucrative when compared to local salaries. The privatization and 'denationalization' of media, especially electronic media, also plays a vital role. All this is well-known; what is less well-known is the following. Since deflation, in particular a reduction in government expenditure, is an important component of neo-liberal policy, research and higher education invariably experience a cut in funding. This is usually justified on the grounds that more funds should be given to primary education, or that research must support itself by raising its own resources. The net result is a decimation of any intellectual base for opposition to neo-liberal policies and to the MNCs, or at a different level, for national self-reliance. Privatization of education and research means the saleability of their products as commodities; in a world where the 'market' is dominated by neo-liberalism, or where buyers are the MNCs themselves, conformity becomes the order of the day.

The ramifications of this go very far. It is not only educational and research institutions that have to sell their wares but individual academics and researchers as well. On the one hand, deflation and government cuts entail a deterioration in the living and working conditions of academics and researchers; on the other, very lucrative offers are made to them from international agencies, Bretton Woods institutions and various private sources, provided they espouse the dominant ideological position of neo-liberalism that informs all these institutions. The oppositional challenge from academia and institutions of higher learning simply fades away under pressure of personal hardship in the event of a refusal to conform to neo-liberal orthodoxy. More generally, neo-liberal policies entail an accentuation of dualism in every sphere, including the intellectual, between a small prosperous élite on the one hand, and a mass of underpaid workers on the other; and an assimilation of this élite to the cause of neo-liberalism through large-scale patronage by a host of agencies led by the Bretton Woods institutions. This fractures any concept of a nation, or national interest and self-reliance, and apotheosizes 'globalization' in complete disregard of the conditions of the mass of people. A coherent theoretical articulation of the peoples' grievances and of an alternative socio-economic arrangement in which these grievances can be addressed is thwarted; also stifled is effective popular opposition to neo-liberalism—at best this takes the form of sporadic inchoate rebellions.

IX

The second factor which helps abridge political democracy consists of what was mentioned earlier: namely, the creation of conditions whereby differences relating to socio-economic programmes between alternative political formations disappear. The reason has to do with the fluidity of international finance capital. Any political formation that proposes a different programme runs the risk of frightening speculators into taking 'hot money' out of the country, thereby precipitating a balance of payments crisis. Such a crisis would result not only in stricter 'conditionalities' but in deflation, wage-cuts and harsh austerity measures which would make the government unpopular with the people. In other words, if people suffer under neo-liberal economic policies, they could suffer even more from attempts to break out of these policies, i.e., in the aftermath of the speculative outflow which would accompany any effort to change neo-liberal policies. All political formations therefore, are haunted by fears of alienating speculators, and consequently tend to converge on the neo-liberal programme that the latter approve of.

What we have here is a remarkable inversion of perspectives. The entire concern of governments focuses not on the welfare of the people but on keeping international finance happy, even if the latter entails the imposition of great privations on the people. This happens even when governments committed to the interests of the people are elected. In other words, it happens not because of some crude collusion between political formations and financial interests, but for structural reasons, for within the structure of the economy that neo-liberal policies conjure up there is no alternative to appeasing financial interests. Unless this structure itself is transcended (on which more later), appeasing financial interests makes sense because it is dictated by the logic of the structure. The queer logic whereby the imposition of hardships on the people is supposed to be in their best interests, does have an element of truth. The fact that it does so, however, only reflects the absurdity of the structure of a liberalized economy.

It follows from this that such a structure is directly antithetical to political democracy. The essence of political democracy is the sovereign right of the people to make choices between alternative programmes, alternative leaders and alternative political formations, each with its own *weltanschaung*. But if the programme, the leaders and the *weltanschaung* are dictated by speculators (in the sense of having to conform to their predilections), and if all the different political formations, masquerading as alternatives, have willy-nilly to adopt what the speculators want, then we have a denial of democracy in effect, even though it occurs within the framework of democratic forms. We have, in other words, a reconciliation of neo-liberal economic policies with political democracy which *simultaneously* amounts to a denial of democracy.

The most blatant instance of this denial is when the selection of the prime minister or the composition of the government are decided upon by the Bretton Woods institutions with the objective of 'instilling confidence among investors'. If Fujimori of Peru and Carlos Menem of Argentina provide us with examples of leaders elected on an anti-liberalization platform but switching sides to become champions of neo-liberalism (thus underscoring our contention that the scope for choice by the people does not exist), then Turkey and Pakistan are examples of Bretton Woods ex-employees being chosen as prime ministers under the influence of these institutions.[15]

X

The third element in the political management of structural adjustment is a discourse shift that occurs as a result of the adoption of structural adjustment policies themselves, and this has to do with the growth of divisive forces like communalism, fundamentalism and secessionism. This growth is usually seen in *sui generis* terms, as unrelated to the pursuit of neo-liberal policies. This is a misconception. The 'globalization' ushered in by the pursuit of neo-liberal policies promotes fundamentalist and secessionist tendencies in various ways. In general terms, one can say that with the fracturing of the 'national' consciousness, which 'globalization' under capitalism entails, the consciousness of particular groups tends to come to the forefront. It is not that the consciousness of particular groups had ever been obliterated; only that it had been overlaid by an overarching national consciousness during the struggle for decolonization which welded diverse groups into a nation-in-the-making. As this overarching national consciousness recedes, these particular consciousnesses emerge to prominence. Paradoxically, the espousal of 'globalization', which apparently transcends nationalism, has the effect of strengthening sub-national consciousnesses.

However, it is not just in such general terms that globalization contributes to the growth of divisive movements; it makes very specific interventions. For instance, it promotes secessionist tendencies in regions belonging to either end of the development spectrum. The advanced regions within a third world economy develop a secessionist tendency, because they think they have a better chance of attracting foreign investment from the MNCs if they are unencumbered by the company of backward regions. The first state to secede from the former Soviet Union, significantly, was the richest, Lithuania, and the first to do so from the former Yugoslavia was Slovenia, also the richest. Though neither the Soviet Union nor Yugoslavia were third world economies, nonetheless the examples are instructive. 'Backward' regions on the other hand, develop a secessionist tendency since they feel they are getting a 'raw deal', accounting for the perpetuation of their 'backwardness'.

Likewise 'globalization' creates conditions that are conducive to the growth of different kinds of 'fundamentalist' movements in various ways. Insofar as 'globalization' means a worsening of the lot of the common people while a section of the domestic rich not only becomes richer but is increasingly identified with the 'West' and indulges in lavish consumerism, there develops among the people an anti-'Western' and anti-élite feeling, which is a refracted form of anti-imperialist consciousness. In certain circumstances, this feeling takes on a fundamentalist colour, especially where there has been a previous history of the suppression of progressive and democratic movements. Iran provides a classic example both of such a fundamentalist movement, as well as of its limitations—after all it eventually turned to the IMF for help despite all the rhetoric of the Khomeini years. A second kind of 'fundamentalism' (of which Hindutva is an example) uses popular distress and a sense of being belittled by history not for any anti-élite, anti-'West', or anti-consumerist platform, but for singling out some minority group as the source of this distress. In fact, it attempts to come to power by simultaneously appeasing multilateral agencies and the advanced capitalist countries and organizing pogroms and riots against hapless minorities.

One can of course see combinations of such movements—there may for example be divisions within forces of 'comprador fundamentalism' just referred to, with some sections opposing some aspects of neo-liberal economic policies—and there may, in a particular situation, be the simultaneous coexistence of more than one such movement. The important point is that the emergence of these divisive movements leads to a shift in political discourse away from the issue of economic programmes towards those raised by the agenda of these forces; a polarization of political forces occurs around such movements as a result of which whatever differences may exist on the economic programmes (already narrowed down as we have seen) are further obscured. We have thus a remarkable scenario in which the domestic political forces appear to be agreed on the need for neo-liberal economic policies but differ solely on internal matters relating to the agenda of divisive forces. The people are offered a choice no doubt: between divisive forces and the rest, a choice of the utmost importance, but one which does not extend to a real choice between alternative economic programmes. This makes the task of imposing an economic programme suited to the interests of the MNCs and international finance much easier.[16]

Indeed some sections, including among progressive and democratic intelligentsia, even welcome such a programme on the grounds that the 'modernization' it entails will help in transcending the 'backwardness' which produces 'fundamentalism' and communalism. In other words, the very emergence of these tendencies encourages a belief in a simple 'dualism' reminiscent of early development economics in which there are two separate sectors: the 'modern' and the 'traditional', and 'progress' is seen in terms of a rapid development of the former; by drawing labour from the latter, this is supposed to gradually reduce it to insignificance. The erroneousness of this assumption arises from two distinct facts: first, the two sectors are dialectically related, and the 'backward' is what it is because the 'modern' is what *it* is; second, the 'modern' does not exist in isolation from the rest of the world, it is integrated with the metropolis in a manner that gives it a specific dynamics. The inability to see these relationships fosters the illusion that neo-liberal policies will help in overcoming 'backward' tendencies whereas, in fact, they contribute towards their strengthening.

XI

The foregoing must not be taken to mean that an abridgement of democracy will inevitably occur, that nothing can be done about it. On the contrary, the worsening conditions of the people also call forth resistance. Where authoritarian regimes exist, popular resistance creates pressures for democratization, as has happened in Indonesia. Where the framework of democracy is preserved but its content is diluted through apparent agreement among political formations on neo-liberal economic policies, popular resistance takes the form of regularly voting out incumbent governments. In India, for example, not only did the Congress which ushered in liberalization get an electoral drubbing, the BJP too lost popular support within months of coming to power because of its inability to tackle inflation which was a fallout, *inter alia,* of neo-liberal policies.

Strategies of political management , in other words, have to be seen not as creating a 'no exit' situation but in the context of a tussle: efforts to abridge democracy being countered by popular resistance, not necessarily to these efforts but to some fallout of neo-liberal policies. The question then arises: are countries like India doomed to be victims of this paralyzing tussle until this conjuncture (i.e., of the ascendancy of international finance capital) itself undergoes a decisive change? Not necessarily, in my view. The size of a society like ours is so enormous; the range of goods it can potentially produce so large; its dependence on the rest of the world so minimal; and its vulnerability to the caprices of international finance capital is so manageable, at least till now, that a shift away from neo-liberalism can both occur here, and contribute substantially to a change in the international conjuncture itself. In other words, even in a context where the scope for autonomy in national decision-making has been significantly eroded, countries like India and China still retain sufficient capacity for it. What it requires, however, is a broad mobilization of internal class forces around an agenda alternative to what international finance capital is pursuing, and skilful and imaginative manoeuvres on the external front, including mobilization of external support for facilitating a change in the conjuncture.

The details of this alternative agenda need not detain us here;[17] suffice it to say that, far from entailing a return to the earlier *dirigiste* development strategy, it must begin with an alternative critique of it. Such a critique would focus on the failure of that programme to base itself upon egalitarian land reforms, and its complicity in a process of primitive accumulation, whose obverse was a meagre achievement in spheres such as literacy, education, health, sanitation and rural infrastructure. An alternative agenda must make the rectification of these its cornerstone, which alone will enable it to mobilize the class support needed for its execution.[18] The real issue relates not to the state-versus-market dichotomy but to a strengthening of democratic interventions by the people so that they can exercise more effective control over the state and, through it, the market.

To be sure, the formulation of such an agenda and mobilization around it are no easy tasks; but then retaining economic sovereignty and using it to improve the living conditions of the mass of people are not, if one may paraphrase Oskar Lange, 'tasks for the timid'.[19]

Notes

[1] This, for instance is the view articulated in the context of India by Bimal Jalan, *India's Economic Crisis* (Delhi: Oxford University Press), 1994.

[2] The argument that the current account deficit in the Indian balance of payments prior to 'liberalization' in 1991 was caused by independent factors unrelated to the fiscal deficit has been put forward by Mihir Rakshit, 'The Macroeconomic Adjustment Programme: A Critique', *Economic and Political Weekly*, vol. 26, no. 52 (28 December 1991) pp. 2995–6.

[3] For an elaborate discussion of the internal and external factors that formed the backdrop for the introduction of 'structural adjustment' in the context of the Indian economy, see Prabhat Patnaik and C.P. Chandrashekhar, 'The Indian Economy Under Structural Adjustment', *Economic and Political Weekly*, vol. 30, no. 47 (25 November 1995) pp. 3001–13 and C.T. Kurian, *Global Capitalism and the Indian Economy* (Delhi: Orient Longman), 1994.

[4] Even the import liberalization of the late Eighties that sustained the boom of the Rajiv era and contributed, in the first instance, to making the balance of payments vulnerable, had the blessings of the World Bank. Many have dated India's liberalization to 1985; while Left critics consistently underscored the pitfalls of import liberalization even in this period, drawing special attention to the emerging balance of payments vulnerability, the World Bank equally consistently supported it.

[5] John Maynard Keynes, *The General Theory of Employment, Interest and Money* (London: Macmillan), 1949, p. 376.

[6] For a fuller discussion of this issue, namely the extent to which traditional theories of imperialism have been rendered obsolete by the commonality of experience of the advanced and backward capitalist economies in the current conjuncture, see Prabhat Patnaik, 'Globalisation of Capital and the Theory of Imperialism', *Social Scientist*, 283–4, November–December 1996, pp. 5–17.

[7] For a comprehensive discussion with country studies, see G. Cornia, R. Jolly and F. Stewart, *Adjustment with a Human Face* (Oxford: Oxford University Press), 1987, 2 vols.

[8] The distinction between productive and speculative capital inflows is sometimes rejected on the grounds that both add to the availability of resources for the domestic economy. But, for the latter to be used for investment and growth, there must *additionally* be adequate inducement to invest in the domestic economy (otherwise it would merely add to reserves or, if the exchange rate is allowed to appreciate, have a de-industrializing effect). Since the adoption of neo-liberal policies, notably public expenditure cuts and import liberalization, has a contractionary effect on aggregate demand, the problem of inadequate inducement to invest acquires significance. This contractionary effect also makes the concept of 'efficiency gains' (and all calculations of

such gains) which assume full employment, untenable. See Prabhat Patnaik, 'On the Concept of Efficiency', *Economic and Political Weekly*, vol. 32, no. 43 (25 October 1997) pp. 2807–13.

[9] See C.P. Chandrashekhar 'Explaining Post-Reform Industrial Growth', *Economic and Political Weekly*, vol. 31, nos. 35–37 (Special Number, September 1996), pp. 2537–45.

[10] Against this comparison it is often argued that the growth rate of the preceding quinquennium was not sustainable for balance of payments reasons. But this argument would be valid only if the 5.9 per cent growth of the later period was all that the balance of payments situation permitted; i.e., if it was not a reflection of a demand constraint, as it actually is.

[11] For details of the argument in this and the following paragraphs, see Prabhat Patnaik, 'Post-"Reform" Growth Trajectory of the Indian Economy', *The Marxist*, vol. XIV, no. 3 (July–September 1998), pp. 7–23.

[12] Abhijit Sen and Utsa Patnaik, 'Poverty in India', Working Paper, Centre for Economic Studies and Planning, Jawaharlal Nehru University, 13 August 1997.

[13] Apart from Cornia, Jolly and Stewart, op.cit., see, for a review of African and Latin American experiences, R. van der Hoeven, 'Structural Adjustment, Poverty and Macroeconomic Policy', Seminar on Structural Adjustment and Poverty in India, organized under the Indo–Dutch Programme on Alternatives in Development, The Hague, November 1994; for Pakistan, see S. Akbar Zaidi, 'Health, Well-being and Adjustment', Conference on the Impact of Structural Adjustment on Health, Centre for Social Medicine and Community Health, Jawaharlal Nehru University, New Delhi, September 1997.

[14] This fact, however, has not prevented the Bretton Woods institutions from widening their sphere of direct interference, as is evident from the decision taken at their annual meeting held recently in Hong Kong, that issues of 'corruption' and 'good governance' will henceforth be included in the ambit of 'conditionalities'.

[15] The reference here is to Tansu Ciller of Turkey who was an employee of the IMF, and to Moin Qureshi of Pakistan, an ex-employee of the World Bank. In addition, Javed Burki, another employee of the World Bank became finance minister of Pakistan and enjoyed great influence in that position. For a discussion of the role of these institutions in policy making in Pakistan, see A. Zaman, 'The Government's Present Agreement with the IMF: Misgovernment or Folly?' *Pakistan Journal of Applied Economics*, vol. 11, nos. 1–2 (1995), pp. 77–94.

[16] This, in my view, describes the Indian situation today. It is instructive that on the broad parameters of economic policy, there is a common-

ality of views between the Congress, the BJP, and substantial sections of the UF.

[17] These details are given in Prabhat Patnaik and C.P. Chandrashekhar, op. cit.

[18] It is often suggested that a neo-liberal policy is compatible with the maintenance, or even increase, in the government's development and social expenditures. This is not true. Since there has to be some symmetry between corporate and personal income taxes, and in the treatment of foreign and domestic capital, governments in a neo-liberal regime committed to wooing foreign capital, are constrained in raising larger direct tax revenue. Likewise, symmetry between customs and excise duties in a world in which the former have to be lowered entails a constraint in raising indirect tax revenue. Finally, to retain speculators' 'confidence', the interest rate has to be kept high (which raises the interest payments on government debt) and the fiscal deficit, kept low. These constraints together ensure that development and social expenditures are cut.

[19] Oskar Lange, *On the Economic Theory of Socialism* (Minneapolis: University of Minnesota Press), 1938.

Depicting the Nation: media politics in independent India

VICTORIA L. FARMER*

Introduction

A vantage point offering broad vistas on India's fifty years of experience with democracy has informed earlier chapters in this volume. Insight is also to be gained, however, through an examination of changes in specific institutions, including the police, the media and the judiciary, that were constructed or altered during the first fifty years of independence. This chapter focuses on India's experience with the governance of mass media, particularly television. I examine the assumptions regarding the power of television, and resultant policy initiatives that led Indian political leaders to link the notions of state, nation, and socioeconomic development in the construction of India's national television system, Doordarshan.

One reason for studying India's electronic media is that its increasing variety of forms—radio, ground-based television broadcasting, cable and satellite transmissions—continuously renews public debates about national policy towards the media, shedding light on how the Indian government contends with the challenges of technological innovation. Doordarshan is also a critical case for examining the role of the state in issues related to cultural pluralism, multi-lingualism, and the concept of the nation. With the advent of television technologies, the Government of India found itself in a position to exercise cen-

* I thank Douglas Verney for extensive discussion on this chapter; and Amrita Basu, Francine Frankel, Desmond Nazareth and Eswaran Sridharan for comments on an earlier draft.

tralized control over this new medium, and to link television to its policies of national development.

Finally, studying the origin of institutions such as Doordarshan is useful for understanding the shape of, and constraints on, contemporary political institutions. This historical approach—particularly when a number of institutions are juxtaposed, as in the three analyses in this volume of the judiciary, the police, and media policy—highlights continuities between the colonial and independent periods in India, continuities that may be less apparent in other methodological or disciplinary analyses of contemporary India. Post-World War II scholarship on India, through the vagaries of academic organization and disciplinary divides, has often over-emphasized 1947 as a watershed. For example, historians have tended to study periods of Indian history prior to independence, while political scientists have tended to focus on the politics of independent India. Recent trends in social science theory have helped to balance this overly sharp dichotomization, but close examination of political institutions further helps to detail the precise linkages between these two periods.

The case studies in this volume demonstrate that India's political institutions often share a common origin in concepts, policies and laws from the latter half of the nineteenth century, rather than from post-Independence initiatives. This is not to make a deterministic argument, but simply to point out that these studies show how the colonial legacy shaped the range of political possibilities for the reconstruction of independent India's institutions of governance. For example, radio and television continue to be governed by laws based on the 1885 Telegraph Act; R.K. Raghavan (this volume) notes that laws regarding the police rest upon the Police Act of 1861; and Rajeev Dhavan (this volume) examines the colonial codification of Indian law and its later effects on jurisprudence.

For narrative simplicity, this chapter delineates three periods in the governance of Indian mass media. The first period begins with the 1885 Telegraph Act and concludes in mid-1983, when Indira Gandhi's government undertook the creation of a pan-Indian infrastructure for broadcasting television. During the second period, from approximately 1983 to 1991, the central government continued to hold a monopoly over both television hardware and programming. This period represented a rare, and perhaps unique, situation in which the ruling party of a thriving post-colonial democracy held sway over the airwaves of a phenomenally diverse country, facing the difficulties of broadcasting to an audience characterized by great diversities in language, cultural practice, religion, and living standards. Unlike government-run television infrastructures in industrialized societies, the legitimacy of the Indian government's monopoly was predicated on its use to promote socio-economic development; and, unlike national television systems in more homogeneous societies, the cultural link between programming and its audience was not clear. Instead of television naturally reflecting a relatively homogenous national culture, Indian programming was specifically designed to *create* such an identity. In addition, India's sheer size meant that most of its citizens only received transmissions from within India. The establishment of stations whose signals blocked transnational transmissions also made this true in many border areas. India's near monopoly was in contrast to the experience of smaller countries inundated by transnational television. It was also very different from the experience of impoverished, dependent countries in which most, or sometimes all, programming was provided by sources such as the Voice of America or multinational corporations. The third period under discussion dates from 1991–2, when the Government of India effectively lost its monopolistic control of the airwaves through the advent of transnational satellite television. Satellite channels became more lucrative, numerous and heavily capitalized after the popular demand for satellite news coverage of the bombing of Iraq during the Gulf War.

Justifying Public Television: The Implications of Doordarshan's Monopoly

India inherited a legal structure from the British that included centralized governmental control of telegraphs starting in 1885. Almost a century later, that precedent, along with the examples of many other state-operated television infrastructures in the Commonwealth, such as the British Broadcasting Corporation (BBC) and the Canadian Broadcasting Corporation (CBC), served to underpin centralized control of India's new television technology. In addition, political movements and social theories in the twentieth century shaped the assumptions regarding mass media held by political leaders, worldwide. Social theorists of the 1920s and '30s optimistically linked mass media and social engineering; for instance, a 1936 League of Nations convention examined the potential of broadcasting for international understanding. Propaganda during World War II powerfully solidified the belief, and fear, that mass media could transform societies,[1] and this assumption became an integral part of post-war development theories.[2]

In India, nationalist sentiments during the freedom struggle in the first half of the twentieth century fostered the notion that cultural nationalism could serve as a potent force for nation-building and as a tool for resisting cultural neo-imperialism. Through the interacting forces of legal precedent, cultural nationalism, and development theory, television in independent India evolved as an institution controlled by and emanating from Delhi. In this process, though, the Government of India took responsibility for the implementation of a complex set of policy goals that ultimately proved unachievable. Initially, social theories and nationalist objectives legitimated centralized control over radio and television; over time, however, the unfulfilled promise of these goals brought this legitimacy into question, and by extension raised questions about the motives and credibility of successive national governments perpetuating and consolidating a hierarchical centralization that was quite different from other media, notably newspapers.

In retrospect, it is apparent that television differed from other forms of media, including the press and cinema, in one respect that is of crucial importance to India's democratic experience. It was only what is termed 'electronic media' in India, including radio and television, that came under the direct purview of the Centre. Other media genres were, by and large, privately held and profit-driven. Many caveats are necessary here; the Centre has influenced these media forms in numerous, and sometimes nefarious, ways. Its influence has ranged from the largely accepted continuance of film censorship (at the state level under the British, centralized in independent India under the Cinematograph (Censorship) Act of 1952),[3] to the blatantly anti-democratic machinations against the press during the 1975–7 Emergency.[4]

Despite the ways in which the Centre has power over media other than radio and television, though, there is a basic, qualitative difference between its legal relationship to television and other media forms. The Centre builds, owns, promotes and governs India's television infrastructure, legitimating this control through the argument that it is needed to promote socio-economic and national development, and basing it on a century of legal precedent. The privately-owned press, on the other hand, evolved earlier in the heady, oppositional environment of the freedom struggle. Journalists, newspaper owners, and the general public were extremely unlikely to countenance direct governmental control of the press. This stance has become particularly entrenched since the excesses of the Emergency.

The dichotomy between ownership of television and other media also created differing expectations. For example, because state ownership of television was initially predicated on socio-economic development, achievement of such goals could be applied as a measurement of television's success. When these goals were not easily reached, the justification for continued state ownership turned increasingly to the rhetoric of cultural nationalism. By contrast, achievement of development goals was largely irrelevant for public assessment of print media. Magazine editors or film producers may be thought heartless if they do not foster development schemes for the poor, and social activists may call for greater responsibility on the part of wealthy media barons. But this does not necessarily bring into question the legitimacy of the ruling party, the state, or Indian democracy.

Doordarshan, on the other hand, is a different case. It has been a costly Centre-led government undertaking predicated on using television as an investment in socio-economic development, education, and national integration. Central governmental control of television has therefore rendered the Centre vulnerable to questions of the state's efficacy, credibility, and legitimacy. In responding to the advent of television technologies by linking central control with social betterment, it is now clear that the Centre took on a role in which little could be easily won, but much could be lost in terms of credibility.

A number of unintended consequences arose from justifying the construction of India's television network on the basis of television's potential for promoting 'development'. Development was defined broadly, in a way that included two very different types of goals. One was basic economic development, improving the living standards of India's poor. This I term 'material' development, as opposed to more culturally based 'national' development. Exactly how television was to accomplish material development was never entirely clear. The Satellite Instructional Television Experiment (SITE) of 1975–6 did show that some gains could be made through provision of information on topics such as new agricultural practices and basic health care. However, these gains proved to be of very limited scope. Providing information cannot remedy a lack of infrastructure. For example, lessons on the importance of childhood immunization are futile, at best, if clinics do not exist or sera are not available.

The second type of development implicit in media policy was the creation of a national identity, evident in the title of the third government-commissioned study of Doordarshan, *An Indian Personality for Television.*[5] The inability of television to foster significant material development was indeed unfortunate. However, the unintended consequences of linking television and national integration proved to be significantly more damaging to the fibre of Indian democracy. In attempting to inculcate a national identity through media depictions, the Centre entered into a game that simply could not be won. There are many different views of 'India'. No conception of its national identity, however overarching, will ever be uncontested, and no conception, however pluralist, will ever be deemed fair by everyone. Ultimately, both the medium and the message-maker lose credibility. It is one thing for a local newspaper, or a foreign-based television drama, or a made-for-profit advertisement to be seen as partisan or élitist. When the construction of the message is under the aegis of the central government, however, such perceptions are much more insidious.

The insistence on developmental goals for Doordarshan was sensible in many respects. The creation of a television infrastructure was costly, and the informational needs of India's citizens were great. By declaring that Doordarshan would provide an instrument to promote national unity, widespread education, and economic development, the Government of India was able to justify its huge investment. However, in due course it ren-

dered itself vulnerable to the criticism that neither the state nor
its television service could accomplish such goals. The government also opened itself to arguments that instead of promoting
'national unity' or 'development', it was promoting the interests
of the party at the Centre. The inability of television to fulfil
goals articulated in government policy thus ultimately brought
into question the very legitimacy of the state, in a manner and
to a degree that did not occur with respect to profit-driven media forms.

The most damaging aspect of this media policy, which closely
correlated the Centre's interests with its investment in television,
was therefore not Doordarshan's inability to bring about the
improvement of the economic situation of India's poor. After all,
there was already widespread cynicism regarding the government's
development programmes, after so many institutions, plans,
schemes and promises had come to so little. Instead, the aspect
of centralized control of television that proved to be the most
dangerous to the legitimacy of Indian democracy was linking
media technology with promoting a national identity. In a culturally plural, multilingual and multireligious country, no state-
sponsored depiction of the ideal national personality, character
or ethos could possibly be without controversy; and these controversies ineluctably both reflected and promulgated schisms
inherent in the inexact fit between 'state' and 'nation'. In independent India, the most damaging aspect of media policy proved
to be the impossibility of any state-sponsored depiction of the
'nation' to be fully devoid of religious, communal overtones. This
was particularly problematic in the implication of the state-
sponsored serialization of the *Ramayana* and other epics in the
general rise of a virulent Hindutva.[6] Though such charges could
never be conclusively proven, the hierarchical control of television from Delhi also meant that the government could never fully
clear itself from such accusations, and so the secular credentials
of the state were brought into question.

Hierarchical Centralization and the Colonial Legacy

How did hierarchical, centralized state control of television hardware and programming come to be seen as legitimate and necessary in India?

When television was first broadcast in India in a 1959 educational experiment in Delhi, a legal infrastructure to govern its vast potential had not been created. As is the case with any novel technology in a law-based society, the legal implications of scientific breakthroughs cannot be fully anticipated. Often, regulations initially rest upon extant laws, and additional administrative mechanisms are created, with lag time, through legal precedent, court decisions, or the creation of new laws. This accretionary process can be seen in the evolution of laws governing the electronic media in India, the genealogy of which can be traced to the 1885 Telegraph Act. This Act stated that 'the Central Government shall have the exclusive privilege of establishing, maintaining and working telegraphs'. Telegraph was defined to include virtually any electronic communications technology. Some forty years later, in the 1920s, radio became available. The British initially allowed the creation of an independent broadcasting corporation, but this attempt failed, in part because the licensing fees allowable within colonial legal structures were inadequate to keep it solvent. Eventually, the Raj somewhat reluctantly agreed to protect radio-related capital investments by putting radio under direct governmental control.[7] Later, based on the precedent of the 1885 Act, administration of television was joined with that of radio. The 1885 Telegraph Act thus serves as the origin of the evolution of the legal strictures governing India's electronic media.

The 1935 Government of India Act reaffirmed the hegemonic role of the state in broadcasting. However, while it reserved broadcasting for the Centre, it also stated that the Centre should not unreasonably prevent provincial administrators from constructing transmitters. Independent India's 1950 Constitution incorporated many features of the 1935 Act, including placing broadcasting under the Union (i.e., the Centre's) list of responsibility. The Union List of the Constitution's Seventh Schedule, item thirty-one, includes 'posts and telegraphs, telephones, wireless, broadcasting and other like forms of communication'. (This should not be confused with the inclusion of 'communications' on the State List, in which communications refers to 'roads, bridges, ferries, and other means of communication not specified in List I' [the Union List].) The Seventh Schedule inclusion of broadcasting on the Union List, however, did not include even

the minimal provision for decentralized broadcasting found in the
1935 Act. Thus, the legal basis for centralized control of broadcasting was continued, and actually strengthened, after 1947.
The 'fear of disorder' at Independence (Brass, this volume) pre-
cluded abrupt decentralization of the electronic media. While
Prime Minister Nehru did argue that broadcasting should be
made autonomous from direct central command, he also indi-
cated that this would have to be postponed due to the immediate imperatives of political stability.[8]

Although the first television broadcast was made in 1959,
Delhi did not become a full-fledged broadcasting station until
1970. The order in which subsequent stations were constructed
was based on two goals: covering major metropolitan areas, and
creating stations on border areas that might have access to
transnational transmissions. After Delhi, stations were created
in Bombay (1972), Srinagar, Amritsar and Pune (1973), and
Calcutta and Madras (1975). By the time of the Asian Games in
late 1982, there were approximately forty transmitters in the
Doordarshan network. Most were relay stations that did not have
production facilities, and many were relatively low-power (100
W) transmitters in remote or mountainous areas, including
Imphal, Shillong, Jammu and Shimla (full listings are updated
periodically in *Mass Media in India*). Significant expansion, creating a nearly pan-Indian infrastructure, occurred only after the
Asiad. India's growing television network thus came to be in-
exorably linked to the Centre through an accretionary, reactive
evolution based on the legislative precedent of the 1885 Telegraph Act. This does not, however, explain how state control of
television became linked to the more *proactive* project of constructing an Indian national identity. This came about as a fall-
out of scientific interest in space research and Indira Gandhi's
political ambitions.

In the early 1960s, the eminent scientist, Vikram Sarabhai
began to argue for national investment in cutting-edge scientific
research, particularly on space, communications, and energy
production. He conceptualized development as a total process
requiring not only increased *production*, but also modernized
administration of technological applications and the creation
of greater *demand* for public provision of advanced technologies and services. Planned scientific research would generate

both supply and demand for such large-scale technologies as nuclear power production and telecommunications satellites.[9] Hoping to strengthen political and public support for investment in advanced space research, and genuinely committed to using the most sophisticated technologies for rural development, Sarabhai argued that satellite-based television could be used to 'leap-frog' India into sustained economic growth and development.[10] Sarabhai was a confidant of Indira Gandhi, who was also not new to the notion that media could be a potent force in shaping societies. After Nehru's death in 1964, Shastri appointed Mrs Gandhi as minister of information and broadcasting, largely to pursue an appearance of continuity with the Nehru years.[11] This was initially not a particularly powerful appointment; Shastri had ignored suggestions that she be given a more senior portfolio. It was enhanced, though, through Mrs Gandhi's stature, and was elevated to cabinet status.[12] Mrs Gandhi began to explore her new appointment in 1964 by constituting a committee, led by Asok K. Chanda, to report on the status of Indian broadcasting and to propose policy guidelines for its expansion. The *Report of the Committee on Broadcasting and Information Media*, published in 1966, argued that broadcasting could promote compliance with government-led development schemes, including the Five Year Plans. Noting that visual depictions would greatly enhance the educational value of audio broadcasts, the Committee recommended that expansion of television should be undertaken alongside that of radio.[13]

Vikram Sarabhai's vision culminated in the largest, most successful, and most widely studied development communications experiment ever undertaken to date, the Satellite Instructional Television Experiment (SITE) of 1975–6. A NASA satellite broadcast educational programmes, produced mostly by All-India Radio, in four languages to schoolchildren in 2330 villages, spanning twenty districts in six states. Broadcasts for adults included educational and entertainment programmes, along with the national programme from New Delhi. In addition, relay transmitters broadcast the national programme in Hindi to 355 villages in Kheda district, Gujarat. The ground segment of the project was coordinated by the Indian Space Research Organisation (ISRO), using indigenously produced equipment.[14] Despite SITE's success, however, it did not serve as the prototype for subsequent growth in television, which, particularly after 1983, was more explicitly driven by political initiatives, and more focused on 'national' development for political ends.

Arguments of the 1960s and '70s that promoted investment in television drew on a modernization paradigm that correlated modernity, mass media, and development. This paradigm included ambiguities surrounding both the definition of development, and the role of the state in promoting it. At a minimum, this conflated what I term material development, a promotion of better living standards, with national development, which equated modernity with the creation of a national identity and the fostering of citizens' allegiance to it.

The major outcome of this development communications paradigm in India was a shift in the terms and parameters of political debate regarding the electronic media. State control over television had already been established as legitimate (with some dissent by small circles within the intelligentsia and opposition parties), but the realm of legitimate central initiatives has now been expanded to include active inculcation of a national identity. Possibilities for a critique of this control became increasingly limited, because a critique of government media policies came to require not only a stance of political opposition, but one that could easily be characterized as anti-development, anti-poor, and anti-national. By the early 1980s, then, television was largely considered to be legitimately under centralized state control. This legitimacy was justified through a rhetorical commitment to development, and development was defined to include promotion of a national identity.

Television Infrastructure in the 1980s

After Indira Gandhi's electoral comeback in 1980, she had a maximum of five years to ensure her re-election. Preparations had to be made in the context of increasing political opposition, both within and outside the Congress party, and the increasing awareness of Congress' inability to promote significant economic development. At this time it was also clear that coercive practices used during the Emergency would not be tolerated a second time. Finally, by this time the Congress was no longer capable of serving

as the network for communication between élite and grassroots
levels in the way it had before the Emergency, and particularly
during the freedom struggle. Facing these difficulties, Mrs
Gandhi had to find new methods for garnering votes, and turned
to the persuasive potential of television.

Following a recommendation of the Chanda Committee, the
administration of Doordarshan had been separated from that of
All-India Radio in 1976. It had not, however, been restructured
as an autonomous corporation, which the Chanda Committee
considered necessary for 'a broader outlook, greater flexibility,
and freedom of action which the corporate form alone can give'.[15]
Though separated from radio, television continued to be an attached department of the ministry of information and broadcasting. The post-Emergency Janata government had reiterated
the recommendation for granting autonomy to television in the
second major government-sponsored report on broadcasting,
*Akash Bharati: The Report of the Working Group on Autonomy for
Akashvani [All-India Radio] & Doordarshan*. The Working Group,
chaired by B.G. Verghese, wrote, 'We are of the opinion that all
the national broadcasting services should be vested exclusively
in an independent, impartial, and autonomous organisation established by law by Parliament to act as a trustee for the national interest.' It added, 'the autonomy of the corporation and
its independence from government control should be entrenched
in the Constitution itself'.[16] The Janata government was unable
to carry out these recommendations before its fall, however, and
so television remained a tool easily available to the ruling party.

Hosting the 1982 Asiad offered an opportunity for India to
showcase its technical capabilities and world-class facilities.
Television played a major role, as India cooperated with other
countries to provide satellite telecasts of the Games throughout
Asia. Broadcasts of the Asiad—the first Indian broadcasts in
colour—proved to be phenomenally popular within India, a fact
that did not go unnoticed by the former minister of information
and broadcasting, Indira Gandhi. After the Asiad, her government made a political decision to invest heavily in an unprecedented expansion of India's television system. S.S. Gill, who had
orchestrated the building of stadia, roads, and other infrastructure
for the games, was given the task of creating a near pan-Indian
network within a very short time-span. The tacit implication was

that this expansion should be completed in time for elections in 1985. Importation laws were changed to allow purchase of components necessary for the indigenous production of more viewing sets for the exponentially growing audience, and educational schemes were launched to train teams of engineers and technicians. Beginning in July 1983, an 18-month project to expand the network was sanctioned by the government, with a budget allocation of Rs 680 million.[17]

In early 1983, only about one-quarter of India's population was within signal range of a Doordarshan transmitter. While the oft-repeated claim that a new transmitter was raised almost daily in 1984 does not tally with published Doordarshan statistics, most sources agree that coverage was extended to more than half the population by mid-1985, and to three-quarters by 1990. As of 1999, this figure has been raised to 86 per cent of the population, covering approximately 68 per cent of Indian territory.[18]

In addition to fiscal allocations for expanding Doordarshan's hardware infrastructure, commercially sponsored serials were also commissioned, beginning in 1983. In part this was because increased broadcast hours not only outpaced Doordarshan's ability to create sufficient programming, but it was also a strategic decision to broadcast appealing, popular programming in order to build a wide audience for effective political communication. The first, *Hum Log*, a drama with a family-planning message, began airing in 1984. Serialization of the *Ramayana*, followed by the *Mahabharata*, aired for over three years beginning in early 1987.

The expansion of Doordarshan's reach and programming in the early 1980s, coupled with the advent of commercial sponsorship, created a nexus linking state control of television for electoral ends with the commercial pursuit of profit through advertising. The logical goal of both electioneering and advertising, however, is to reach the largest number of people possible, and in a country as diverse and as riven with potential cleavages as India, this logic is fraught with possibilities for unintended outcomes. Three major consequences arose from the increasing use of Doordarshan, throughout the 1980s, as a tool for promoting a national identity through the projection of an 'Indian' national character, closely identified with the ruling party.

One major consequence was the inadvertent implication of Doordarshan, and therefore of the state and the ruling party, in widening schisms between the majoritarian 'nation' as presented on Doordarshan and those outside this homogenized conception. Programming during the 1980s projected an India that was overwhelmingly north Indian, Hindi speaking, middle class, and Hindu.[19] Of greatest political import was the implication of Doordarshan in the increasingly venomous Hindutva of the mid- to late-1980s. The programming initiated when Mrs Gandhi decided to expand Doordarshan included serialization of the epics. This decision, to the chagrin of many of those involved, unintentionally served the growing forces of a dangerously communalist Hindutva.[20] The serialization of the *Ramayana*, and particularly its treatment as a Hindu, rather than an Indian, saga, constructed a symbolic lexicon that aided communalist mobilizations and formed the basis of the imagery used by L.K. Advani in his *rath yatras*. By the end of the 1980s, Advani and the BJP had emerged as media-savvy manipulators using Ram-related imagery, which had been given pan-Indian exposure by Doordarshan, to forge a sense of Hindu resurgence and unity.[21] Kancha Ilaiah offers an impassioned critique of this complex conflation of Hindu majoritarianism, cultural nationalism and advertising, in his critique of Brahmanical Hinduism, *Why I am Not a Hindu*:

> Suddenly, since about 1990, the word 'Hindutva' has begun to echo in our ears, day in and day out, as if everyone in India who is not a Muslim, a Christian or a Sikh is a Hindu. Suddenly I am being told that I am a Hindu. I am also told that my parents, relatives and the caste in which we were born and brought up are Hindu. This totally baffles me. In fact, the whole cultural milieu of the urban middle class—the newspapers I read, the T.V. that I see—keeps assaulting me, morning and evening, forcing me to declare that I am a Hindu. Otherwise I am socially castigated and my environment is vitiated. Having been born in a Kurumaa (shepherd caste) family, I do not know how I can relate to the Hindu culture that is being projected through all kinds of advertising agencies. The government and the state themselves have become big advertising agencies. Moreover the Sangh Parivar harasses us every day by calling us Hindus.[22]

The contradiction between state-professed secularism and media-abetted communalism has been the focus of much scholarly writing on Doordarshan's 1980s project in nation-building. Three additional contradictions also deserve note. First,

Doordarshan programming has been unable to overcome the schism between the Centre's sloganeering profession of 'unity in diversity' and the reality of tensions in Centre-state relations. Visually lush family dramas set in communally harmonious, timeless Kashmiri and Punjabi villages accomplished little except adding irony to the day's news headlines. In addition, the contradictions between dreadfully inadequate developmental programming and advertising-driven consumer fare made a farce of development as the rhetorical justification for continued centralized state control of television. Finally, requiring all stations to carry the prime-time National Programme in Hindi and English only added fuel to the fire of linguistic regionalism, and was vociferously rejected in Madras. This Hindi-centric approach was not entirely Doordarshan's invention. Hindi and (temporarily) English are defined as national languages in the Constitution (Article 343), and the Constitution directs the Union to promote the spread of Hindi, drawing primarily on Sanskrit vocabulary (Article 351). Nonetheless, the National Programme effectively banned regional language broadcasts during prime viewing hours, strengthening regional perceptions of an imperious Delhi. Discordance between Doordarshan's depiction of the 'nation' and the Centre's policy stances regarding secularism, federalism and development severely compromised the legitimacy of the Centre's control of Doordarshan by the end of the decade.

A second major consequence of Doordarshan programming in the 1980s was the erosion of the credibility of its news programming, through blatant use of the medium for publicizing Congress party leaders and initiatives. This became particularly severe in the period preceding the 1989 elections, when the conspicuous use of news broadcasts for electioneering earned for Doordarshan the derisive sobriquet 'Rajiv Darshan'. Mrs Gandhi had returned to power in 1980 knowing that persuasion might work where coercion had failed. Steeped in modernization theories linking communications and development, she had discovered in television a powerful tool at her disposal. In addition to commissioning the construction of a pan-Indian television hardware infrastructure, she fostered programming to create *An Indian Personality for Television*, the title given to the third major government-sponsored report on Indian television, commissioned in 1982.[23] Unlike the earlier

Chanda and Verghese Reports, the Joshi Committee did not recommend autonomy for Doordarshan. Instead, it focused on the
need for the creation of software (programming) for development, maintaining the tacit assumption that this is best conducted under the aegis of the central government.

In this quest, the Joshi Committee was buttressed by the report of the UNESCO-appointed MacBride Commission (of which
B.G. Verghese was a member), which called for a new international information order to undermine cultural neo-imperialism through the media.[24] The MacBride Report emphasized
international disparities in access to communications technologies and the free flow of information, more than it did disparities within individual countries. The Joshi Committee Report,
however, rather selectively drew only on the MacBride
Commission's statements regarding the need to prevent the
influence of western media in the developing world:

> Most relevant for our purpose is the Commission's observation that
> 'it is in the field of television, more than any other, that anxieties
> arise about cultural domination and threats to cultural identity'. This
> is because television has a 'strongly transnational face'. Being a hun-
> gry medium, it has to be fed all the time. The production of television
> programme [sic] is a highly expensive business for which the poor
> countries are not always able to provide adequate resources. As a re-
> sult 'in most developing nations the screens are filled for many hours
> with imported programmes, made originally for audiences in the de-
> veloped countries; these imports account for half of transmission time'.
> Further, 'the home produced material is often a poor second to im-
> ports in the daily programming of developing countries'. Another
> major threat to national culture arises from cheap and titillating
> programmes produced within a country which are projected through
> the television day in and day out in order to fill television time.
>   It is clear that the main source of danger to national cultural identity
> arises from the neglect of software planning by a developing country. To
> meet this threat at its source, developing nations must not allow the gap
> to widen between hardware and software, between programme transmit-
> ting and programme-making capacities, between the media and the mes-
> sage. Restriction of imported programmes is necessary but not sufficient.
> Positive software planning is the most effective way of strengthening the
> foundations of cultural independence and of national culture.[25]

While the statements culled from the MacBride Report are
cogent indictments of international inequities, it is not clear

that the Indian situation was as dire as the preceding paragraphs imply. The Joshi Committee Report itself said that in 1983 foreign programming was only 10.3 per cent of the evening National Programme.[26] This actually was comprised mainly of reruns of shows like *I Love Lucy* which, while definitely not of Indian origin, hardly seem likely to crumble the foundations of Indian civilization. This extreme concern in the early 1980s was somewhat premature. The real problems surrounding a flood of violent, salacious and consumerist programming—other than such messages found in ubiquitous Hindi films—arose only after the advent of cable transmissions and transnational satellite television in the 1990s. Nor did the MacBride Report necessarily lead to the conclusion of the Joshi Committee that programme production should not be autonomous from national governments. Even with this somewhat guarded, pro-Centre stance, however, the Joshi Committee Report was never fully embraced by the government, and the third volume was never even published. This was perhaps prompted by statements such as 'Doordarshan news needs to be gathered and presented from perspectives not only of the government, the ruling party and the urban well-to-do, but also of the many other economic, social, cultural and political groups who constitute the nation.'[27] The two published volumes nonetheless serve to document the beginnings of a shift in argument for continued central control which, given the obvious inefficacy of poverty reduction schemes, was increasingly justified through the language of cultural nationalism.

Following the tragedy of Indira Gandhi's assassination, the rewards of her investment in television accrued to her son, Rajiv. In the early years of his prime ministership, television was included in his general promotion of liberalization and openness. This was most apparent in the appointment of Bhaskar Ghose as Director General of Doordarshan in 1986, leading to a clear increase in the autonomy and quality of programme production. However, by 1987 the political climate had become more threatening to the prime minister, as the print media, and particularly the *Indian Express*, began to focus on issues such as the Bofors arms kickback scandal and deep disagreements among Congress leaders. In October 1988, Ghose was transferred from Doordarshan. Subsequently guided by stalwart Congress advisors enamoured of television's capabilities, including K.K.

Tewary and H.K.L. Bhagat, the Congress party's campaigning for the 1989 elections included virtually direct control of Doordarshan newscasts from the Prime Minister's Office. Seemingly every news broadcast began with the words '*aāj pradhān mantrī Rajiv Gandhi ne kahā ki.* . . .' (Today, Prime Minister Rajiv Gandhi said that. . .). Congress functionaries and party initiatives were depicted night after night, while leaders of opposition parties were ignored or presented in less-than-flattering ways. Poll broadcasts, time allotted on Doordarshan for campaign speeches by each national party recognized by the Election Commission, also became controversial. The demand by Doordarshan that each party submit its speech in advance, ostensibly so that Doordarshan technicians could be prepared for the length of the speech (stipulated by the Election Commission, in any case) or need for changes in camera angles, was widely seen as a thinly-veiled attempt at censorship. Ultimately, nearly every opposition party boycotted the poll broadcasts. In short, the use of Doordarshan for electioneering was onerous and clumsy; did not have any discernible benefits for the Congress party; and fundamentally undermined Doordarshan's credibility.[28]

The third major consequence of Doordarshan's nation-building experiment of the 1980s arose because both political communication and commercial advertising seek the largest possible audiences. Because of this, central control of television has thus far proved satisfactory to business leaders. Ironically, while television became less and less credible in the late 1980s, the ability to mount a realistic challenge to central control was undermined by television's value as an advertising medium. It was unlikely that the very political party that benefited most from its continued control by the state would implement reform. Voluntary organizations, grass roots activists, and actors in civil society held numerous social goals, many more pressing and few requiring solidarity around a struggle for media reform. This left, as likely sources of reform, only opposition parties, still in disarray after the Janata period, and the very real power of business interests. Commercial interests, however, had no reason to counter the creation of an 'Indian' national character, because this entailed the simultaneous creation of an 'Indian' market. Increasing the reach of television signals expanded the target audience for advertising, and having television advertising for the entire country under the direction of one agent, albeit the state, simplified advertising campaigns and negotiations over pricing and placement. Therefore, during most of the 1980s, significant reform of television administration was politically unlikely.

One opportunity for restructuring Doordarshan did arise, however, after the Congress party lost the 1989 Lok Sabha elections. Congress had faced a National Front coalition composed of parties spanning the political spectrum, fully united on only two goals. First, the Congress simply had to lose, due in part to its implication in corruption scandals such as Bofors. Second, television had to be wrested from Congress control. One of the first acts of the new National Front government was the December 1989 proposal of the Prasar Bharati (Indian Broadcasting) Bill, probably because this issue was easier to tackle than many others in the National Front's election manifesto. The Prasar Bharati Bill was modelled on the 1978 Akash Bharati Report of the Janata government, and recapitulated the call for the creation of an autonomous corporation to administer television, found in the 1966 Chanda Committee Report.[29] As was the case with recommendations in the Akash Bharati report, however, the changes called for in the Prasar Bharati Bill could not be implemented before the government fell.

Informed by the twin notions of development and cultural nationalism, Indian television evolved as an instrument for the state's construction of a national identity. The logics of development (at least in what I term its national, as opposed to material, form) and of cultural nationalism are dyadic. The first posits a national identity based on, or one that can be constructed out of, a presumed Indian cultural ethos. The second similarly posits a quintessential national identity that must be protected from external influence. Television predicated on these notions resulted in the 1980s project to construct a national identity for political ends. However, Doordarshan's nation was at best hollow, and at worst implicated in communal bloodshed. By the end of the decade, the credibility of both Doordarshan's news programming and its conception of the nation was severely compromised, and so the continued role of the government in television administration became increasingly difficult to justify.

End of an Era: The Invasion

At a time when state investment in and control of television seemed of dubious merit, the arrival of transnational television in the early 1990s provided renewed legitimation: the state must defend the nation!

Transnational satellite television programming made a splashy entrance into India in 1991, with CNN satellite broadcasts of the techno-colour spectacle of U.S.-led forces bombing Iraq. Since then, satellite broadcasting received through dishes and transmitted through cable systems has increased exponentially, as have debates about the impact and long-term effects of this new technological infrastructure.

The most notable feature of much of the debate surrounding transnational television in India has been the characterization of transnational satellite television as an invasion, and of cable systems within India as a threat. For example, the 1995 Cable Bill presented in the Lok Sabha stated:

> There has been a haphazard mushrooming of cable television networks all over the country during the last few years, as a result of the availability of signals of foreign television networks via satellites. This has been perceived as a 'cultural invasion' in many quarters since the programmes available on these satellite channels are predominantly western and totally alien to our culture and way of life. Since there is no regulation of these cable television networks, undesirable programmes and advertisements are becoming available to the viewers without any kind of censorship.[30]

More recently, in 1999, the *Discover India* website provided by the ministry of external Affairs continues to emphasize invasion, stating that 'India in the last five years has been invaded by TV channels from all over the world'.

The rhetoric of invasion is appealing. Western hegemonies in communications hardware and news gathering capabilities are well documented, as is their embeddedness in an international system shaped by the inequities of global capitalism and U.S. military might. It is not difficult to question the value of a global communications infrastructure in which Rupert Murdoch champions the voyeuristic pleasures of American soap operas such as *Santa Barbara* and *The Bold and the Beautiful*.[31]

That said, though, it is necessary to ask what, exactly, was being invaded. Successive governments, using this rhetoric of invasion, have conflated Indian broadcasting with a state-constructed conception of Indian culture. What was being invaded was not Indian culture per se, as much as the Centre's power to use television to construct its own sense of a national identity. In addition, successive central governments, including those that initially espoused autonomy for television, have eventually prioritized retention of the (dubious) value of television as a campaign tool.

The Government of India initially faced difficulties responding to this invasion. Indeed, virtually every country in the world was forced to re-examine the infrastructure available to regulate rapidly expanding communications technologies in the 1990s. The Indian case is not *sui generis*. Some countries, such as Singapore, used their legal and regulative capabilities to control reception of transnational signals through such methods as limiting ownership of satellite dishes. At the other end of the spectrum, the United States emphasized the value of open markets, and focused legislation on the allocation of the profits accruing from these technologies. The Telecommunications Act of 1996 amended extant law, the 1934 Communications Act (Federal Communications Commission). As one critic notes:

> The overarching purpose of the 1996 Telecommunications Act is to deregulate all communication industries and to permit the market, not public policy, to determine the course of the information highway and the communications system. It is widely considered to be one of the three or four most important federal laws of this generation. Even by the minimal standards of the 1934 Act, the debate surrounding the 1996 Telecommunications Act was a farce. Some of the law was actually written by the lobbyists for the communication firms it affects. The only 'debate' was whether broadcasters, long-distance companies, local telephone providers, or cable companies would get the inside track in the deregulatory race. Consistent with the pattern set in the middle 1930s, the primacy of corporate control and the profit motive was a given.[32]

Based in part on doubts that corporate control and the profit motive could promote a communications infrastructure suitable for Indian conditions, India's policy debates initially resembled the Singapore model more than the American. This 'anti-invasion' stance was predicated on the rhetoric of cultural nationalism, which called for the protection of Indian airwaves, and thus Indian culture, from foreign broadcasts. Early cultural nationalist arguments sought to prevent Indians from receiving foreign satellite broadcasts. However, virtually nothing could be done to force other countries to prevent satellite transmissions originating from their territories or using their satellites—the BBC was unlikely to cease its World Service, and Hong Kong was unlikely to oust highly profitable communications companies, simply because of an Indian nationalist, élite call for the protection of 'Indian culture'. Early proposals instead suggested blocking transnational transmissions, either by jamming the signals or controlling the technologies for their reception.

However, such repressive solutions were quickly discounted. For one thing, satellite and cable technologies became widely available in India at the same time that the government was undertaking a significant programme of economic reforms. Calling for a massive, repressive system of direct governmental control of new communications technologies was simply incompatible with efforts to gain public support for opening the Indian economy to global investment. Also, these new forms of communication, by their very nature, defy the kind of monopoly India held over television in the 1980s. Transnational satellite broadcasts are easily received through a satellite dish, and this programming can then be redistributed to many homes and other sites through cable networks. Both satellite reception and cable distribution can operate on very small scales, at local levels, and with minimal capital investment. To control reception of programming through satellite dishes or transmission through cable networks would thus require a phenomenally large and widespread repressive force that—even if technically or economically feasible—would be completely antithetical to India's democratic political culture. The more vociferous nationalist calls for preventing Indians from receiving satellite broadcasts were thus rejected because of the difficulty, if not impossibilities, of creating the policing systems necessary to control these new technologies in a country of the size of India. Assuredly, any such anti-democratic attempts in post-Emergency India would be met with aversion and opposition. Implicitly differentiating India's approach from those of China or Singapore, a spokesman for an inter-ministerial committee on cable television networks and dish antenna noted succinctly, 'It is practically impossible to monitor the misuse of a dish antenna in a country like India . . . Since India is not a totalitarian state, it is simply not possible to see whether everybody is observing the rider to the license: that the dish should be used to receive only Doordarshan signals via INSAT.'[33]

In the early 1990s, then, communications infrastructures grew exponentially while laws to govern them floated in legal limbo. After the fall of the National Front government, Congress was not eager to implement the 1990 Prasar Bharati Act. Official policy statements throughout the early 1990s were unable to transcend reiterations of the necessity of continued state control, still justified as an investment in development but increasingly buttressed by the oratory of cultural nationalism. In the meantime, Doordarshan embarked on a numbers game: Asiasat beamed five channels into India from Hong Kong, so Doordarshan announced plans to increase its number of channels to five. By 1999, Doordarshan had 19, including the Metro Channel (entertainment for urban audiences), the Movie Club channel, a channel for literature and arts programming, a channel for broadcast to international audiences, and a number of regional language channels. Proposals for a channel devoted to education have not yet met with success.[34]

Also during the early 1990s, untold numbers of local entrepreneurs wired India for cable, in a feat that bears comparison with Doordarshan's 18-month expansion of its network in the mid-1980s. By the mid-1990s, a consensus was emerging on the need for some form of regulation of cable systems. This was not only due to arguments of cultural nationalism and shock at the content of some satellite channels re-transmitted through cable, but also to internal, domestic considerations. By this time, the cable system had grown to such significant proportions that the common public image of a cable operator was no longer that of a young, science-minded entrepreneur so much as that of increasingly powerful syndicates commandeering uncharted technological frontiers. By 1995, there had still been no move to implement Prasar Bharati. However, the rapid growth of non-government communications systems did lead to the creation of legislation to address expanding cable and satellite systems. Reflecting the salience of media in Indian policy debates, the Cable Bill was enacted relatively early, in 1995. (The U.S. was still operating under 1934 regulations until 1996.)

The provisions of the 1995 Cable Television Networks (Regulation) Act, as was to be expected, did not meet with universal approval. Nonetheless, when viewed in comparison with other Indian and international broadcasting regulations, its provisions are, by and large, reasonable. The Act requires that cable operators be registered, that they keep a log of what programming has been transmitted, and that they transmit only programmes or advertisements that are in conformity with a prescribed programme and advertising code. The codes are similar to regulations governing Doordarshan programming, including prohibition of broadcasts that attack religious communities, criticize friendly countries, are obscene, encourage violence, or promote unlawful behaviour. While any such set of regulations cannot, once and for all, resolve disputes on the legality of any particular broadcast, they do at least codify a set of norms around which such disputes can be based. Furthermore, the Act clarified the legal responsibilities of cable operators regarding censorship of programming they transmit. Cable systems can transmit programming, such as a film, from a videocassette recorder. In this case, the operator has straightforward control over the programming: he can determine what is on the video, and whether or not it conforms to the broadcasting code. Cable systems can also re-transmit programming received from satellites through a dish. In this case, making the cable operator responsible for determining if the programming meets Indian broadcast criteria puts the cable operator into an untenable legal position. The cable operator is unlikely to know in advance the content of transnational channels. Even if the operator knows that a channel's programmes conform to another country's broadcasting codes (such as the CNN following U.S. censorship norms), those codes do not always match Indian standards. The Cable Bill was unable to resolve the concerns of some of India's policy élite regarding Indians having access to foreign programming that does not conform to Indian broadcasting codes; as noted above, blocking such transmissions is both technologically and politically unachievable. It does, however, relieve the cable operators of legal liability over programming which they cannot control. Instead, they are responsible only for those transmissions, such as films from video, that are under their control. Comparison with film censorship is apt here. While producers regularly push the limits of particular censorship norms, there is nonetheless an industry-wide acceptance that some general system for censorship is both necessary and legitimate. As film producer and scholar K. Hariharan notes, this acceptance results in part from the need to overcome a public goods problem. If no system of norms and method for adjudication exist, then each producer has an incentive—and perhaps an incentive that he would prefer not to face—to constantly push the envelope, pandering to the least common denominator for the shock value that may bring audiences.[35] The programming code of the 1995 Act is likely to serve a similar role.

A more controversial aspect of the Act is the requirement that every cable operator re-transmitting satellite or television signals (as opposed to transmitting solely from videos) re-transmit at least two Doordarshan satellite channels. While this does not seem terribly unreasonable at first glance, re-transmission of Doordarshan satellite channels means that a single satellite dish cannot simultaneously be pointed to satellites transmitting more popular foreign channels, thus requiring additional investment in a second dish and effectively undermining poorly-capitalized operators. Despite such concerns, however, the simple fact that some principles are now codified is preferable to the anxiety faced by cable operators when no laws existed, leading them to fear that their investments could be rendered illegal at any moment. And, though there may be disagreement about particular aspects of the Act, the simple fact of its existence can help to crystallize negotiation, adjudication and, if need be coordinated opposition to specific details.

Unfortunately, this degree of progress in codifying media regulations has not been paralleled in the administration of other aspects of television. A new window of opportunity was opened in 1997 with the commitment of the Minister of Information and Broadcasting, Jaipal Reddy to implement the Prasar Bharati, and with the formulation of a 1997 Broadcasting Bill. The Broadcasting Bill, which was meant to supercede the 1995 Cable Bill, attempted to create a legal structure to allow, and govern, private television channels. It required private channels to be licensed, and set a cap on foreign ownership in Indian companies of 49 per cent. It also, for the first time, allowed broadcasters to legally uplink to satellites from within India. Previously, only

Doordarshan had this right; other satellite channels received in India were uplinked elsewhere—Star TV signals, for example, were uplinked from Hong Kong. Only channels with no more than 20 per cent foreign equity were granted uplinking rights. These stipulations on foreign ownership received a negative response by some American analysts who characterized them as barriers to free markets,[36] including a March 1998 delegation to India from the U.S. India Business Council.[37] It should be noted, however, that the U.S. 1996 Telecommunications Act did not overturn the 1934 Communication Act's limitation of foreign ownership of broadcasting stations to 20 per cent (as in India), though the Federal Communications Commission does have leeway to grant exceptions.[38] Although the 1997 Broadcasting Bill attempted to grapple with new media technologies, it was not voted upon in parliament before the fall of the government, once again leaving administrators and investors in a precarious legal position.

Much the same has been true of the Prasar Bharati Bill. Initially enacted in 1990, it was never implemented until September 1997, when it was promulgated by ordinance, coming into effect on 15 September. This was no doubt done with the best intentions; Jaipal Reddy had made repeated promises to grant autonomy to Doordarshan and All-India Radio. It is indeed ironic, though, that this democratizing initiative could be undertaken only through the promulgation of an ordinance. As has been the case all too often, however, once again the government fell before legislation could be passed by parliament. Subsequently, the BJP named Sushma Swaraj minister of information and broadcasting, and the familiar cycle began anew: autonomy was promised, actions of clear benefit to the ruling party but of dubious value to Indian democracy were undertaken; and as of early 1999, no new legislation was passed by parliament. When the ordinance promulgated under the United Front government was to lapse, the BJP government renewed its commitment to the Prasar Bharati Bill. However, it returned to provisions of the 1990 Bill that had not been included in the 1997 ordinance. This was a thinly veiled, yet ultimately successful, attempt to use a clause regarding the retirement age for Prasar Bharati personnel from the 1990 Bill to oust S.S. Gill, who had been appointed Prasar Bharati CEO after promulgation of the 1997 ordinance. BJP leaders, including Minister of Information and Broadcasting, Sushma Swaraj, repeatedly decried the Prasar Bharati board as being 'packed with leftists'. Gill also antagonized Sangh Parivar cultural nationalists when, during the first speech as CEO, he denounced programming based on Hindu mythology, astrology or other topics regularly espoused by the Sangh Parivar. The BJP government did attempt to pass its revised version of Prasar Bharati legislation. However, the opposition parties made it clear that they would not approve the Bill. It did pass the Lok Sabha, but faced no chance of doing so in the Rajya Sabha, which had proportionately less BJP representation. Facing defeat, the BJP withdrew the legislation and instead re-promulgated Prasar Bharati by ordinance.

Electronic Media Autonomy: Prasar Bharati and Indian Democracy

The notion that those who work in the Indian media, and the population in general, are simply not ready for the electronic media to be autonomous from direct central government control has become a repeated refrain. Nehru faced the 'fear of disorder' discussed by Brass (this volume), although he hoped that ultimately broadcast media would become autonomous. The recommendations of the 1966 Chanda Committee Report were never fully implemented, and Indira Gandhi was more attracted to those aspects of modernization theory that called for a strong state rather than those emphasizing democratic practice, particularly with regards to the media. The Janata government's 1978 Akash Bharati Report succumbed to political paralysis, as did the 1989 Prasar Bharati Bill of the National Front government. Approximately six months after the National Front came to power, the Minister of Information and Broadcasting, P. Upendra, stated:

I admit that Doordarshan is not autonomous today. Autonomy is a promised thing, it's there in the Bill. Right now my ministry is responsible for the functioning of the media and we have to keep a watch over it. That doesn't mean we're controlling it on a day-to-day basis. A lot of functional freedom has been given. Things are not as they were under the previous government, when minute-to-minute instructions were issued to the radio and TV newsrooms from the

PM's office. Our general policy is to bring to their notice any lapses or shortcomings on their part *after* the event, not before. We've to prepare the organisation for autonomous functioning next year.

Frankly, they're not yet ready for autonomy—they are conditioned to being dictated to at every stage, they're not used to using their own judgement. They don't know how far they can go. They're confused, and it shows.[39]

These statements all indicate, whether in 1947 or 1990, that India is not ready for autonomous electronic media. However, they do all share the notion that autonomous electronic media are of value; that is, a goal worth pursuing. This has not been a value explicitly espoused by all political leaders throughout India's first half-century of independence. While a number of policy statements do call for autonomy, this concept has not become an effective, ingrained assumption within Indian political debate. For example, under the Congress government in 1985, the third major government-sponsored review of television shifts attention away from the question of autonomy. Instead of lauding autonomy as a goal that might be met in the future, it bluntly states that the conditions for autonomy had not been in place earlier, and still were not in 1985. The title of the report, *An Indian Personality for Television* (in the singular), emphasizes content and culture over legal structure. It's recommendations for Doordarshan state:

The Chanda Committee in its Report on Radio & Television, in April 1966, recommended the separation of Doordarshan from Akashvani, and the formation of autonomous corporations to run both. The first recommendation was accepted, and began to be implemented—the process is still not complete—with effect from 1st April 1976. As regards the second recommendation, the Government stated in Parliament in April 1970 that the time was not opportune for considering autonomy for the broadcast media. This position holds. Doordarshan continues to be run as an attached office of the Ministry of Information and Broadcasting.[40]

After 50 years of independence, no political initiative has fundamentally altered the administrative and legal infrastructure, created under colonial rule, that governs India's electronic media. New communications technologies have sometimes prompted remarkable creative innovation in both All-India Radio and Doordarshan. However, no governing party has had both the will and the longevity needed to loosen the strictures on Indian television that prevent it from achieving its potential—either in artistic creativity, or as a tool for improving the lives of India's citizens. Congress governments have remained in power long enough to enact such legislation, but they have not chosen to do so, preferring instead 'functional autonomy' within the ministry of information and broadcasting. The National Front and then the United Front governments initially championed new legislation, but their efforts diminished as their coalitions weakened.

It is overly simplistic to argue that freeing Doordarshan from political control necessitates abandoning it to the caprice of the market. Indeed, there is no such thing as a 'free' market; markets themselves are political constructs. The global communications market is shaped by inequitable hierarchies, which no effort on the part of Doordarshan—or any national television system—is likely to restructure in the foreseeable future. In recent years, however, Doordarshan and the Indian government have made great strides in contending with these challenges by, for example, increasing the type and quality of programming available, instituting its own transnational broadcasts, and codifying regulation of the cable industry. It should also be noted that transnational channels have adapted to the global market by learning that unaltered western fodder is not automatically the most successful transnational programming. MTV, for example, by 1997 had altered its Asian programming to include 60 per cent Indian programming.[41]

Restructuring Doordarshan to insulate it from domestic political whims, however, would also have a number of additional beneficial effects for Indian democracy. One is simply a renewed demonstration of democratic practice, following the old adage that democracy breeds more democracy. Autonomy would also buttress the credibility of the medium so that it could serve the information needs of India's citizens, which is a prerequisite for attaining any socio-economic development goals. Also, the benefits of insulation work both ways. Distancing television administration from the ruling party would serve to insulate the reputation of the government, and the broader concept of Indian democracy, from poor programming decisions, thus avoiding a repeat of at least one of the unintended consequences of the serialization of the epics. The provision for an autonomous body, insulated from the ruling party, for the adjudication of programming disputes will also further strengthen those aspects of Doordarshan administration that already serve as positive communications models. For example, the provision of airtime for poll broadcasts seems far superior to the purchase of airtime by candidates in the U.S., which has led to staggering increases in campaign costs. This effectively puts public office outside the realm of all but the very wealthy and well connected, and forces politicians to focus on fund-raising, which inevitably requires payback through political favours.[42] India's poll broadcasts can help to prevent this vicious cycle, provided there is no manipulation of the broadcasts as occurred during the 1989 elections.

Calling for autonomy for Doordarshan does not imply that there is no role for the state in broadcasting. However, the unintended outcomes of predicating investment in Doordarshan on fuzzy, and easily politicized, notions of development have undermined this justification for the state's hegemony. Given the multiplicity of media forms now available within India, state investment and involvement in television programming is likely to be seen as legitimate only if its goals are clearly delineated, and the needs identified are not likely to be met through other sources. One clear niche for state-run media is in the case of market failures, where market forces are unlikely to meet social needs. This is the logic by which Doordarshan could return to its roots, emphasizing state-sponsored programming for development—but now for development goals that are clearly defined, widely seen as socially beneficial, and insulated from a conflation of notions of national development with the immediate interests of the ruling party. One such area is literacy. It should be noted that despite the historic use of development theory to justify investment in television, literacy has never particularly been one of Doordarshan's goals. Television was used instead to *transcend* the need for literacy, making it more effective for political communication.

Clearly, no specific Doordarshan programming will ever be without controversy. However, the articulation of a clear rationale for continued state investment, coupled with the creation of an autonomous and insulated body for the mediation of disputes, would certainly help to improve Doordarshan's credibility, and so its efficacy in promoting developmental goals. This will require the political will to embed media autonomy in Indian law. The continuous promulgation of ordinances such as the 1997 Prasar Bharati ordinance, even though the impetus behind such promulgation may be democratizing, is not sufficient. Furthermore, even the enactment of the best-intentioned laws will not resolve issues surrounding television once and for all. Vigilance, and sometimes opposition, on the part of actors within civil society is, and will continue to be, needed to stem centralizing and hierarchical tendencies. Having codified laws, around which debates can crystallize, greatly facilitates the mobilization of interests to create the checks and balances required for democratic media practice. In addition, the codification of laws provides at least some assurance to potential investors, both foreign and domestic, that creating communications infrastructures is a worthwhile enterprise.

There is currently a window of opportunity for the reconstruction of Doordarshan to become a credible source of information, a widely accepted national investment, and an effective aid in promoting better living standards for India's citizens. According to the 1998 Indian Readership Survey, television has the largest reach of the various media forms available in both urban and rural India,[43] and Doordarshan has by far the largest reach of all television channels available within India. This window is not guaranteed to remain open forever, though. As recent history shows, new technologies quickly arise to challenge old monopolies.

It is often easier, both politically and analytically, to critique international communications inequities than it is to question national media policies. Despite this, a quotation from the MacBride Commission Report that did not find its way into the 1985 *Report of the Working Group on Software for Doordarshan* serves as a fitting closing remark:

Obstacles to freedom and distortions of democracy are dangerous symptoms in every society. It is sometimes argued that such criticisms constitute an interference in the legal or political affairs of nations, or in the natural processes of private enterprises, but such abuses of State power or monopolistic practices are still serious impediments to the free flow of information. Certainly, there is a margin in almost all systems to improve the existing situation and decrease restrictive measures to a minimum. There are ways, means and forces in each society to overcome and eliminate restrictions on the freedom of information. What is basically needed is the political will.[44]

Notes

[1] Joselyn Zivin, 'The Projection of India: Imperial Propaganda, the British State, and Nationalist India, 1930–1947' (Ph.D. Dissertation, Duke University), 1994.

[2] Biswa Nath Mukherjee, *Mass Media and Political Modernity*, Bhargava Research Monograph Series, Number 4. (Agra: National Psychological Corporation), 1979; Wilbur Schramm, 'Communication Development and the Development Process', in Lucien Pye, (ed.), *Communications and Political Development* (Princeton: Princeton University Press), 1963; Karl Deutsch, *Nationalism and Social Communication* (Cambridge: MIT Press), 1953.

[3] P.C. Chatterjee, *Broadcasting in India* (New Delhi: Sage Publications India Pvt. Ltd.), 1991, Second edition, p. 37.

[4] See for example Soli J. Sorabjee, *The Emergency, Censorship, and the Press in India* (New Delhi: Central News Agency), 1977.

[5] P.C. Joshi, *An Indian Personality for Television: Report of the Working Group on Software for Doordarshan* (New Delhi: Publications Division, Ministry of Information and Broadcasting), 1985.

[6] Victoria L. Farmer, 'Mass Media: Images, Mobilization, and Communalism', in David Ludden (ed.), *Contesting the Nation: Religion, Community, and the Politics of Democracy in India* (Philadelphia: University of Pennsylvania Press). Also published as *Making India Hindu* (New Delhi: Oxford University Press), 1996; Amrita Shah, *Hype, Hypocrisy and Television in Urban India* (New Delhi: Vikas), 1997, Chapter 6.

[7] H.R. Luthra, *Indian Broadcasting* (New Delhi: Publications Division, Ministry of Information and Broadcasting, Government of India), 1986, Chapters 2 and 6.

[8] Asok K. Chanda, *Radio and Television: Report of the Committee on Broadcasting and Information Media* (New Delhi: Ministry of Information and Broadcasting), 1966, paragraph 688.

[9] Vikram Sarabhai, 'Television for Development', Paper Presented at the Society for International Development Conference, Delhi, 14–17 November 1969. Also Mrinalini Sarabhai, interview, 28 February 1990, Ahmedabad.

[10] Itty Abraham, *The Making of the Indian Atomic Boms: Science, Secrecy and the Post-Colonial State* (London: Zed Books), 1998, pp. 129–44.

[11] Francine R. Frankel, *India's Political Economy, 1947–1977: The Gradual Revolution* (Princeton: Princeton University Press), 1978.

[12] Ibid., p. 289

[13] Asok K. Chanda, *Radio and Television*, op. cit.

[14] Binod Agrawal, *SITE: Television Comes to Village* (Bangalore: Indian Space Research Organisation), 1978.

[15] Asok K. Chanda, *Radio and Television*, op. cit., paragraph 779.

[16] See B.G. Verghese, major recommendation 9–10, *Akash Bharati, National Broadcast Trust: Report of the Working Group on Autonomy for Akashvani & Doordarshan* (New Delhi: Ministry of Information and Broadcasting), 1978.

[17] P.C. Chatterji, *Broadcasting in India*, op. cit., p. 31.

[18] For statistical compilations, see *Discover India*, (New Delhi: Ministry of External Affairs, Government of India). Website downloaded 31 January 1999. [Website: www.meadev.gov.in]; See also *Doordarshan. Annual*. (New Delhi: Audience Research Unit, Directorate General, Doordarshan; Produced by the Directorate of Advertising and Visual Publicity, Ministry of Information and Broadcasting, Government of India) and *Mass Media in India* (New Delhi: Publications Division, Ministry of Information and Broadcasting, Government of India).

[19] For further discussion see Amrita Shah, *Hype, Hypocrisy and Television in Urban India*, op. cit., chapters 3–6.

[20] S.S. Gill, interview, 8 February 1990, New Delhi.

[21] Victoria L. Farmer, 'Politics and Airwaves: The Evolution of Television in India', Paper presented at a panel on 'Mass Media and the Construction of the Indian Nation–State', Association for Asian Studies Annual Meeting, Boston, 27 March 1994, and 'Mass Media', op. cit.

[22] Kanchan Ilaiah, *Why I am not a Hindu* (Calcutta: Samya), 1996, p. x.

[23] P.C. Joshi, *An Indian Personality for Television*, op. cit.

[24] Sean MacBride, *Many Voices One World: Towards a New, More Just and More Efficient World Information and Communication Order* (The MacBride Commission Report) (Paris: UNESCO, International Commission for the Study of Communication Problems), 1980.

[25] P.C. Joshi, *An Indian Personality for Television*, op. cit., vol. 1, chapter 1, paragraphs 3–4.

[26] Sean MacBride, *Many Voices One World*, op. cit., part I, chapter XI, paragraph 18.

[27] P.C. Joshi, *An Indian Personality for Television*, op. cit., vol. II, chapter V, paragraph 1.

[28] Victoria L. Farmer, 'The Limits of Image-Making: Doordarshan and the 1989 Lok Sabha Elections', Paper presented at a conference on 'Democracy and Development in South Asia', Tufts University, 22 April 1990.

[29] *Prasar Bharati (Broadcasting Corporation of India) Bill, 1989: Text of the Bill as Introduced in Lok Sabha on 29.12.1989* (New Delhi: Directorate of Advertising and Visual Publicity, Ministry of Information and

Broadcasting, Government of India).

[30] Cable Bill 1995, Government of India.

[31] Victoria L. Farmer, 'Politics and Airwaves', op. cit.

[32] Robert W. McChesney, *Corporate Media and the Threat to Democracy*, Open Media Pamphlet Series 1 (New York: Seven Stories Press), 1997.

[33] *The Times of India*, 14 March 1991.

[34] *Discover India*, op. cit.

[35] K. Hariharan, interview, 29 October 1997, Philadelphia.

[36] Kenneth R. Donow, 'Globalization, Bureaucratic Politics, and the Deregulation of Indian Broadcasting', Paper presented to the Department of Sociology, University of Pennsylvania, 9 November 1998.

[37] *The Hindustan Times*, April 1998.

[38] Federal Communications Commission (FCC). Website homepage, downloaded 31 January 1999. [www.fcc.gov.] See 1934 Section 310[b][4].

[39] *The Times of India*, 3 June 1990.

[40] P.C. Joshi, *An Indian Personality for Television*: op. cit., vol. I, chapter III, paragraphs 3–4.

[41] Sevanti Ninan, 'The Airwaves Belong to Us', *The Hindu*, 16 November 1997.

[42] Max Frankel, 'Money: Hard, Soft and Dirty', *The New York Times Magazine*, 26 October 1987.

[43] *The Hindu*, 19 October 1998.

[44] Sean MacBride, *Many Voices One World*, op. cit., part III, chapter 1.1.

The Indian Police: expectations of a democratic polity

R.K. RAGHAVAN

The Background

The last few years have generated an animated discussion in diverse forums on the quality of public administration in the country. A critical look at the Indian police therefore seems appropriate: we may ask, how well do the various public service agencies, especially the police, fit into the current democratic milieu? The basic problem, in my view, is that of the elected representatives of the people—the members of parliament (MPs) in Delhi and members of legislative assemblies (MLAs) in the states—wanting to exercise near total control over the civil service, at all levels. They believe that this is the only way they can discharge the trust reposed in them by the sovereign, namely, the people. Among the several state agencies, the police feel the impact of this influence the most, because of the coercive authority they enjoy vis-à-vis the rest of society.

The power wielded by the political executive controlling the government at any point of time is enormous, and is very often used to consolidate partisan gains. The resultant situation is marked by extra-legal, if not illegal, instructions to the police who constitute an important arm of the executive. Complaints of partisan action on the part of the police are very often made to the judiciary, and a near confrontation between the latter and the executive ensues. The judiciary's fulminations over the police's lack of objectivity disregard the fundamental flaw in the existing legal system, which makes the police subservient to the executive. Important recommendations of the National

Police Commission (NPC) of 1977 to free the police from such subordination have not yet been acted upon.

Unfortunately, there has been little informed debate on the role of the police in the present Indian polity. Very few observers of the public scene have ventured to analyse the state of policing in India at this historic moment.[1] Beyond the expression of general dissatisfaction at its performance and the demand for making it more autonomous, humane and civilized, there has been little by way of an assessment of its strengths and shortcomings or its successes and failures.[2] Recognizing that there have been two distinct periods in the history of the police in India helps us evaluate the current scene. Broadly speaking, these are identifiable as the period beginning with the promulgation of the Police Act (1861–1947) and concluding with the attainment of independence in 1947, and the post-Independence era, 1947–99.

During the first period, the focus of the police was on perpetuating alien rule; naturally, the service element received little attention. This was especially pronounced after the freedom movement, spearheaded by Mahatma Gandhi under the banner of the Indian National Congress, gained nationwide momentum and posed public order problems of great magnitude. In the second period, i.e., since Independence, which is germane to the present exercise, one is pained to see evidence of vestiges of the colonial mentality acquired by the police under British rule. An adversarial relationship with the community is still apparent in the day-to-day conduct of the police at the street level. The broader bases of recruitment to the police, better working and living conditions, and the accent on modernization—such as scientific aids to investigation, radio communication and computerization—have not brought about any visible change in police attitudes towards the common man. Unfortunately such attitudes have diluted significant police successes in tackling terrorism of the most militant variety. One difference between the two periods, however, is that the police are currently under greater public scrutiny than before and are subject to more accountability.[3]

The period since 1947 can be conveniently divided into four parts. In the first—a span of nearly three decades, 1947–75—attempts were made to impart direction to the economy as well as the administration and, incidentally, to set up strong democratic traditions. The process suffered a major reversal in 1975 when the controversial national Emergency was imposed, with its attendant impact on the civil services. The second phase, 1977–80, albeit brief, was significant for the administrative apparatus, including the police, for its bold yet unsuccessful efforts towards reforms aimed at transparency and a revival of the rule of law. The third phase saw a generally disturbed law and order situation. This—if one treats the insurgency in the North-east as a class apart—had its genesis in the Sikh militancy of the early 1980s, which led to the historic Operation Blue Star (June 3–6, 1984), the tragic sequel of Mrs Indira Gandhi's assassination (October 31, 1984) and countrywide anti-Sikh riots. The virulence of Sikh terrorism undeniably paved the way, perhaps indirectly, for militancy of different hues and for a general disrespect of authority. This added a new dimension to the polity as a whole, and to police work in particular. Finally, we have the current fourth phase, in which judicial activism is making the police task of tackling crime through strictly legal methods, somewhat easier.

Organization of the Police in Free India

According to the Constitution of India, 'police' and 'public order' fall within the law-making competence of the twenty-five states into which the Indian Union is divided. Policing is, therefore, essentially a state activity although, interestingly, since Independence one has seen the creation of several federal police forces directly under the central government in Delhi, to meet special needs. Among these are policing international borders as auxiliary to the defence forces; protection of central government installations in the states; and security of national railway stock (Table 1).

During the five decades since India attained freedom, there has been a manifold increase in the numerical strength of the police. From a mere 0.7 million in 1971, the strength of the civil police in

Table 1   Growth of Central Police/Forces

1986	1987	1988	1989	1990	1991	1992	1995	1996
458,170	420,017	463,304	485,439	520,485	554,433	567,851	560,896	579,520

Sources: Crime in India (1995) and IPS Central Association (1994).[4]

the country is now nearly 1.3 million. There are 39.5 policemen per 100 sq. kms. and 137 for a population of 100,000.[5] There is a police force, headed by a director-general of police (DGP), in each state. Additionally, there is a force for each of the seven union territories which come under the direct control of the central government. The higher echelons of the forces are manned by officers belonging to the Indian Police Service (IPS) who are appointed by the central government, but allotted to different state police forces to man supervisory positions. These officers are liable to be drawn in to serve in central police organizations, on deputation from the state governments, for specific periods.

Responsibilities: Maintaining Public Order

Since attaining independence, India has gone through several traumas on the law and order front. The first problem to confront the nation was one of political consolidation; this called for establishing control over some of the princely states whose rulers were anxious to retain their autonomy even after the British departed. Kashmir and Hyderabad were two such states where decisive action was called for. In Kashmir, it was the Indian army that tackled the problem by throwing out the raiders (a group comprising armed tribals and members of the Pakistan army) sent by Pakistan to pressurize the ruler into opting for Pakistan. In Hyderabad, it was the police who were employed. The Nizam of Hyderabad, with total disregard for all logic and geography, wanted to accede to Pakistan. Responding to popular sentiment which favoured India, the central government sent a police force into the state which swiftly brought about a surrender of the Nizam's forces. This remarkable operation—remembered even today as the Hyderabad Police Action—highlighted the professional skills and discipline of the Indian police.

The next test of police efficiency came from the same area in the south, in a cluster of districts called Telengana, during 1947–51. Uneven distribution of land and gross ill-treatment of farm workers by landlords generated a strong leftist movement here. The peasants, under the aegis of the Communist Party, indulged in large-scale violence against landholders. Since the police from Hyderabad was unequal to the task, large contingents were requisitioned from the neighbouring Madras State (now Tamil

Nadu). The movement was contained in the course of time, although the methods employed by the police were denounced by some as brutal and illegal. This area has again been the scene of violent activity by Left extremists under the banner of the People's War Group (PWG), whose tactics have taken the form of laying landmines on police routes and attacking police stations. There have been several encounters between them resulting in heavy police and civilian casualties.

The problems faced by the police on the law and order front since 1950 fall into the following broad categories:

   (i) violent agitations by linguistic groups to redraw the political map so as to earmark one state for each language;

 (ii) similar tactics by tribal groups, particularly those in the North-east;

(iii) demands for the redistribution of land ownership, voiced initially by the Communist Party, and subsequently by extremist groups, arising out of the Indian communist movement, leading to the liquidation of 'class enemies' and police informants;

 (iv) violent agitations engineered by political parties, ostensibly in support of some live economic or social issue, but mainly to bring down lawfully elected governments;

  (v) terrorism by groups in Punjab and Kashmir wanting to secede from the Indian Union;

 (vi) violent clashes arising out of the unconcealed fundamentalism espoused by the two most prominent religious groups, namely, Hindus and Muslims, with some of the latter being aided and abetted by Pakistan;

(vii) endemic caste clashes in the rural hinterland, often centering on antagonistic land claims and related problems between landlords and agricultural workers; and

(viii) the emergence of a sharp division between the forward and backward classes following the introduction of a quota system for distribution of places in educational institutions, and for government staff selections.

The Police Response

A few general observations are possible here. Large parts of the country suffer from attempts by various groups to tinker with public order. The violence varies only quantitatively. As a result, police forces have to be in a perpetual state of readiness. Almost every state, at some time or other, seeks the central government's help to provide police forces, such as the Central Reserve Police Force or Border Security Force, to bring what is usually euphemistically described as 'a disturbed situation' under control. Requisitioning the police of a neighboring state is also common. The resort to firearms by the police to quell riots is the order of the day. Very often, this is followed by a popular demand, backed by political parties in the Opposition, for a judicial inquiry to find out whether such use was justified by the circumstances of an incident. Except in a very few cases, such inquiries always end in favour of the police.

Two aspects of the current public order situation—terrorism and inter-religious conflict—deserve detailed consideration for a balanced evaluation of police performance in post-Independence India.

Counter-terrorism—While there has been much criticism of the Indian police, some of it justified, a serving officer can only say that, on the whole, the police response to terrorism in Punjab and in Jammu & Kashmir has been commendable. High qualities of leadership and courage have been displayed.

Two aspects of the scene, one positive and the other negative, compel attention. The militant tactics of terrorists have demanded a great degree of professionalism on the part of the state police. This has called for standards of recruitment and training on par with those of the army and central government police forces, such as the Border Security and Central Reserve Police Force. On the negative side, police retaliation against terrorist violence has occasionally been assailed as amounting to over-reaction. There have been numerous complaints of excesses which have generated a public debate on issues associated with human rights, and have exerted tremendous pressure on the police at the ground level.

Again, on the positive side, while the situation in J&K remains uncertain, the transformation in Punjab is remarkable. Elections to the state assembly in Punjab were held in February 1992, after a lapse of several years. A popularly elected government has been in place since 25 February 1992. The state has since gone through another round of democratic elections, an amazing turnaround. An internationally supported and heavily armed terrorist movement has been neutralized through a painstakingly devised multi-pronged strategy. This deserves a study by itself. The central government has played a constructive role in giving shape to the strategy and its follow-up. It has provided enormous logistical support, an example of what an effective and enlightened federal government can do. The Government of India can take pride in its reaction to an extraordinary public order situation in one of its states.[6]

Communal Riots—Again, on the negative side, we can say that one major criticism of the Indian police during the past three decades has been its apparent inability to handle inter-religious conflict professionally. There have been many clashes, commonly known as communal riots, between members of different religions, especially between Hindus and Muslims. Two specific complaints have been, a bias in favour of the Hindu rioter, and the delayed and excessive use of force. Several commissions of inquiry have looked into the causes of these riots. They have been particularly concerned with the part played by those in the civil administration charged with the task of preventing riots, or at least with quelling them in the early stages, so as to minimize damage to life and property.

The gravamen of the charge upheld by many commissions is that of an initial lack of police firmness against the rioters. The observation of the Jaganmohan Reddy Commission,[7] which studied the September 1969 riots in Ahmedabad and other Gujarat towns in which 524 people lost their lives, is relevant:

> The police lost the initiative and, once the situation got out of control at the very commencement of the riot, they were overwhelmed by the situation which confronted them.
>
> A lack of judgement of a developing situation is another shortcoming. The District authorities, police and the magistracy, very often ignored evidence in the form of isolated incidents that could ignite religious feelings. As a result, in a short time, they were faced with a situation that required action which was beyond their capacity.

Another commission also referred to interference from the higher echelons of government. In its view, this greatly cramped the

style and autonomy of field officers, thereby affecting their ability to contain riots.[8]

Perhaps the most serious complaint has been the alleged police failure to project a neutral image. The Justice Jitendra
Narayan Commission which looked into the 1979 Jamshedpur
riots, criticized the pro-Hindu action of the Bihar Military Police. In the Aligarh riots of 1979 and the Moradabad riots of
1980, a similar impression of police bias against the minority
community was dominant among the public.[9] Deeply concerned
with the effect of repeated clashes between religious groups on
the social fabric, the central government maintains an active
dialogue with state governments. One significant development
is the identification of trouble-prone, communally sensitive districts in every state. These require so much special attention
that a continuous monitoring of inter-religious relations is maintained

On the positive side, possibly the most effective of the moves
initiated so far to tackle communal riots has been the creation
of a Rapid Action Force (RAF) within the Central Reserve Police Force. The RAF is a crack force that is normally airlifted to
trouble spots so that quick action can be initiated to contain an
explosive situation. The RAF performance till now appears to
this author to have been satisfactory. However, until a serious
study of its effectiveness is available, there cannot be a meaningful public debate on its role.

Crime: Statistics and Fluctuations

Efforts to study crime in terms of numbers began with the Police Commission of 1860 prescribing a set of forms, refined by
the Police Commission of 1902. In 1953, the central government introduced *Crime in India*, an annual publication (somewhat similar to the *Uniform Crime Report* of the FBI in the U.S.)
with comprehensive statistics on all crime reported to the police in the twenty-five states and seven union territories, and to
a few enforcement agencies in the central government.

Crime in India is now the responsibility of the National Crime
Records Bureau (NCRB) of the central government. The NCRB
depends solely on the goodwill of police forces in the states and
union territories for prompt dissemination of information. The

process, till recently manual, has been substantially computerized. Crime is studied in terms of 'crime rate', i.e., offences per 100,000 of the population. This facilitates comparison across the board with other countries such as the U.S.: for example, the overall crime rate in India during 1995 was 654.3, as against the U.S.'s 5277.6.

During 1951–91, the first four decades of India as a sovereign nation, the population went up by 135.3 per cent. Crime rose by 158.2 per cent and the crime rate by 9.8 per cent. From a total of about 650,000 offences under the Indian Penal Code (IPC) and a crime rate of 179.9 in 1951, one saw both escalating to 1,696,000 and 185.1 respectively in 1995. From nearly 50,000 in 1953, *violent crime* went up to 245,000 in 1995, an almost 500 per cent rise. Homicides alone registered a 45 per cent increase during the decade 1985–95. Equally serious is the fact that rapes—13,754 in 1995—almost doubled during the same period.[10]

The Police Role in Government

The use of the police in free India has been frequent and extensive, amidst complaints that the force is utterly lacking in political neutrality. The impression of a bias in its day-to-day operations has unfortunately become stronger over the years, because the campaign to promote its non-partisan character has remained feeble. Basically, the Indian police has been weighed down by the scrutiny and criticism of the three segments of the polity, namely, the executive (both government and political), the legislature and the judiciary. The situation is compounded by the enormous pressure exerted on it by the citizen who expects the police to be law abiding, and at the same time, effective in the maintenance of peace and detection of crime.

Relations with the Executive—We noted earlier that independent India has passed through several distinct phases. The most devastating was the 20-month Emergency from June 1975 to March 1977, during which period the police operated without the usual political safeguards. Following the defeat of Indira Gandhi in the 1977 elections, a new Janata government—the first non-Congress government since Independence—took office. Responding to public outrage over the Emergency's excesses, it established a National Police Commission (NPC). Two things are noteworthy about this Commission. Firstly, it was the first, and only, body to be appointed at the national level since Independence, to propose police reforms; and secondly, its recommendations had still not been implemented when Mrs Gandhi and the Congress party returned to power in 1980.

The exhaustive analysis of the Indian police by the NPC is extremely relevant here. The six-member Commission, headed by a retired Governor of Karnataka, Dharma Vira, submitted eight reports between February 1979 and March 1981.[11] It is the path-breaking second report (August 1979) which is most germane to this paper. The Commission addressed itself in this report to the task of how to confer greater operational autonomy on policemen in the field, without however diluting their accountability. In this context, it quoted extensively from the Shah Commission of Inquiry. This had enquired into the excesses alleged to have been committed by the administrative machinery during the Emergency. One excerpt from the Shah Commission's Interim Report II (26 April, 1978) is vivid in its description of the scene:

> Police officers behaved as though they are not accountable at all to any public authority. The decisions to arrest and release certain persons were entirely [based] gon political considerations. . . . The Government must seriously consider the feasibility and desirability of insulating the police from the politics of the country and employing it scrupulously on duties for which alone it is by law intended.[12]

The NPC described the existing relationship between the executive and the police thus: 'The insistence on prompt obedience and execution of all orders lawfully issued by any competent authority underlines the total submission of police to executive authority'.[13]

The Commission thereafter proceeded to draft a new Police Act (to replace the 1861 Act) to articulate its definition of the role of the police. This draft is yet to find government acceptance. Two recommendations made in this connection—a fixed tenure of four years for the police chief, and the constitution of a state security commission headed by the state minister in charge of the police—also remain to be implemented.

In the opinion of many police officers, past and present, most of the odium that attaches to the Indian police over the years is due to the situation so graphically described by the NPC. There is a noticeable difference between the executive's political expectations, and the non-partisan responses of a law-abiding and conscientious policeman. The failure to insulate the police from politics is unfortunate, because it places the force under tremendous psychological pressure and militates against objective and professional policing. Governments hold a very different opinion to justify the subordinate status they accord to the police. In their estimation, the police tend to take a very narrow and legalistic view of events, and therefore ignore the compulsions of a democracy. Second, governments argue that the control exercised over the police ensures that they do not commit excesses that violate human rights, so sacrosanct in a democracy. Finally, it is the executive that is the policy-maker and the representative of the people, in whom sovereignty resides. Only governments are competent to dictate priorities so that policing remains focused on community needs.

Rival viewpoints have their merits. The NPC was quite alive to this reality and also to the need to harmonize the police role with democratic aspirations. Obviously, it was this perception that prompted them to suggest the creation of a state security commission. This was to be headed by the state minister in charge of the police and consist of six other members. The commission would include two members of the state legislature, one from the ruling party and the other from the Opposition. The commission would lay down policy guidelines for the police, besides evaluating its performance for the benefit of the legislature. It would also entertain representations by supervisory officers of the rank of superintendent of police and above against 'illegal or irregular orders' received by them while performing their duties.

The NPC recommendation on the state security commission has not yet been accepted. Views on whether such a commission would be effective are varied. There are those who believe that the commission is no panacea to all of the police's current ills; others feel that the proposal is hardly practical. In their estimation, the commission would only hinder the police force further in its day-to-day work. In my view, the creation of such a commission would be a step forward in rendering the police more transparent and accountable. While it will give the executive a feeling of greater control over the police, it would at the same time assure the latter that its performance will be evaluated more objectively.

Relations with the Legislature and Legislators—There are two facets to the relationship between the police and the legislature, one inside the precincts of the legislature, and the other outside. First, the inside relationship. The presiding officers of parliament in Delhi, and legislative assemblies/councils in the states, are the supreme authority within their respective houses. For the purpose of preserving order therein, they have their own watch and ward staff, independent of the government. It is only under extremely grave circumstances, rendering the latter incapable of dealing with a situation, that the police are called in, under the specific orders of the speaker/chairman, as the case may be. In free India, there have in fact been many such contingencies.

What we are here concerned with more intimately is the outside relationship, the day-to-day interaction between legislators and policemen in the field. The executive's instructions to the police regarding the treatment of MPs and MLAs could not be clearer than they are. They require the utmost courtesy in receiving legislators at police stations and other police premises, and a quick response to representations on behalf of citizens. While, generally speaking, senior officers take every care to be polite and sensitive, it is at the police station that there are often problems. Instances are legion of complaints of disrespect shown to MLAs/MPs by lower police functionaries. The police themselves charge that unreasonable, and sometimes extra-legal, demands are made on them by legislators, demands that lead to unseemly and avoidable verbal duels. The countrywide police agitation in 1979 was triggered by a trivial altercation between a Haryana traffic policeman and a legislator. The relationship between the police and MLAs/MPs is extremely delicate, calling for great restraint on both sides. In recent years, fortunately, an aggressive media and an active judiciary have improved this relationship.

Relations with the Judiciary—A general distrust of the police by the legal profession, and especially the judiciary, has characterized India since the days of the Raj. While many readers may endorse this distrust, it is important to understand that the police believe they are unreasonably constrained. For example, the National Police Commission shared the distress of the police that, even three decades after Independence, the force was so distrusted. It was particularly concerned about the stipulation of the Raj's second police commission, the Fraser Commission of 1902–3 that 'the Constable shall not be associated with any criminal investigation,' and its faithful carry-over to the Criminal Procedure Code (CrPC) of 1973.[14]

The police feel that the courts also lack faith in them. For instance, the Indian Evidence Act, which is an effective aid to the trial court, lays down (Sec. 25) that no confession made to a police officer shall be admissible in evidence. The exception (Sec. 27) is when such confession leads directly to the discovery of a material fact, such as the recovery of a murder weapon. Only then does that part of the confession become admissible. This is a major source of discontent for police officers at all levels.

The most important restraint on police investigators, however, is the constitutional mandate that no person arrested without a warrant shall be held in police custody for longer than twenty-four hours, before which time he has to be produced before a magistrate. This time limit has been found to be unreasonable and impractical by many experienced police professionals. The Supreme Court of India and several high courts have imposed many restrictions on the power of arrest vested in police officers, and have prescribed certain guidelines. In *Joginder Singh v. State of Uttar Pradesh* (1994), the Supreme Court stated that an arrest should not be made merely because it was lawful to do so. The officer concerned should actually be able to justify such action. In *Charan Das Chawla v. Commissioner of Police, Delhi* (1994), the Delhi high court dealt with the issue of information being demanded by a magistrate about a person alleged to be held in illegal custody. It decreed that the police officer concerned must file an affidavit within a day or two and also produce the arrestee before that magistrate. A refusal to file such an affidavit would amount to contempt of court. Also, while the CrPC permits examination of witnesses during investigation at the police station itself, no male below the age of fifteen, or a woman, can be summoned to a police station. Section 160 of the CrPC is emphatic that these persons shall be examined at their place of residence.

It must be admitted that the record of the police in respect of human rights leaves much to be desired. Fortunately, the judiciary in India has been acutely sensitive to complaints of human rights violations by the police. Superior courts have found it necessary to make stern observations whenever these come to their notice and have also initiated punitive action. Custodial deaths in particular have invited their ire, leading to criminal prosecution and the award of stiff sentences to erring personnel. Significant here is the formation in 1993 of a National Human Rights Commission headed by a former chief justice of India. The NHRC has been extremely proactive and has caused quite a lot of discomfiture to those in the police ranks with low regard for human rights. The creation of a similar body in some states has also placed policemen in the field under pressure.

Some judgements, it must be admitted, have helped free the police from unwarranted governmental interference. This section on the judiciary would not be complete without referring to a momentous January 1996 Supreme Court order. In this case, *Vineet Narain and Others v. The Union of India,* the Court was disposing of a petition which alleged that the Central Bureau of Investigation (CBI) and revenue authorities had failed to perform their duty to bring certain offenders to book, because the latter were highly placed in society and were influential. The Court examined cases in which an investigating agency filed a final report stating that there was no material to proceed further against an accused person, and the case had therefore to be closed. The Supreme Court stated that it had the right to satisfy itself that this conclusion had been arrived at on reasonable grounds.[15] This was a landmark pronouncement. It established the Court's role in monitoring an investigation and in ensuring that it was fair and fearless, without being influenced by those in authority who may have had a vested interest in shaping an investigation on lines desired by them.

It is true that this is a significant development that limits police discretion, but it ensures that such discretion is not used to favour offenders because of their high position in society. In a sense, the Supreme Court stand promotes a major objective of the National Police Commission recommendations, namely, the insulation of the police from manipulation by the political machinery.

Another landmark ruling of the Supreme Court came in December 1997. This aimed at substantially freeing the premier investigating agency of the country, the Central Bureau of Investigation, from the control of the executive. The Court stated that the CBI did not have to seek the prior permission of the government in launching investigations against senior civil servants. It thus reversed what was known as a 'single directive' of the government which required the CBI to obtain the government's prior concurrence in the matter. Further, the superintendence of the CBI's work would be vested in a central vigilance commission, to be given Statutory status. The Court also laid down a new procedure for the appointment of the director of the CBI. The Court's pronouncements on the CBI evoked mixed reactions, and a nationwide debate has ensued. (A central vigilance commissioner and a director of the CBI appointed through the procedure contemplated by the Supreme Court are now in position, and a central government law regularizing this may be adopted in parliament very soon.)

Relations with the Public—As long ago as 1969, after a detailed study of the Indian police that incorporated an extensive public opinion survey, David Bayley wrote:

> The survey results demonstrate forcefully what many close observers of police-public relations in India have long thought, namely, that the Indian public is deeply suspicious of the activities of the police. A considerable proportion expect the police to be rude, brutal, corrupt, sometimes in collusion with criminals, and very frequently dealing unevenly with their clients.[16]

Opinion surveys on behalf of the NPC, conducted nearly a decade later, did not show any great change in public perception. In its Fifth Report (November 1980), the Commission expressed its anguish over the poor state of police-public relations.[17] It believed that the Fraser Commission's observation in 1902 that people 'do all they can to avoid any connection with the police investigation' held true even after a lapse of nearly 80 years, and it went on to say: 'People now may not dread the police, but they certainly dread getting involved with it in any capacity.'[18] Media reports of the recent past do not show policing in a better light. The common man is visibly exercised over their obvious lack of courtesy towards citizens during day-to-day interactions.

Failure to register complaints, impolite responses to requests for help in dealing with bullies, and blatant favouritism towards the more affluent of two contending parties, even if that party happens to be the aggressor, are common complaints against the police.

Perhaps the most serious allegation, described briefly in the previous section, is the tendency of investigating officers to use physical force, or what is commonly referred to as the 'third degree', in dealing with crime suspects. The charge gains credence from the frequent deaths in police custody, an average of 70 to 80 being reported annually. Both the central and state governments are highly sensitive on this issue and have conveyed several instructions to curb police misconduct. The most striking aspect of public perception relates to the quality of crime investigation. The average citizen strongly believes that policemen indulge in corrupt practices at every stage, beginning with the registration of a complaint. The 1902 Fraser Commission said: 'The complainant has often to pay a fee for having his complaint recorded. More money is extorted as the investigation proceeds. When the officer goes down to the spot he is a burden often to the whole village.'[19] Lamenting this, the NPC (1977) observed in its Third Report, 'What the Police Commission said in 1903 would more or less fully apply even to the present situation. If anything, the position has worsened.'[20] The Commission identified several areas and stages of investigation—registration of a complaint; arrest/non-arrest and release/non-release of the accused on bail; and recording of witnesses' statements—as vitiated by corruption. It recommended 'a system of surprise checks and inspections and effective supervision by honest and well motivated officers at the different levels of command within the hierarchy itself'.[21]

Complaints voiced through the media, court pronouncements at all levels, and periodic reviews of vigilance agencies in state and central governments reinforce the impression that there has been no perceptible change in the integrity of police investigators. This is despite the fact that criminal investigation, notwithstanding the excessive attention to public order matters, gets high priority in the police training curriculum. The recruit, at all three levels, constable, sub-inspector and assistant/deputy superintendent, is substantially exposed to the fundamentals of crime work.

Once he or she is assigned to the field, the focus gets distorted, and it acquires an obsession with the maintenance of law and order, as distinct from crime prevention and detection.[22] This is because of the high political stakes involved for the government.

The movement in favour of community policing in many parts of the world, especially in the U.S., has not acquired any great momentum in India. Here and there one sees individual officers with some imagination and dynamism making some strides, and the NPC acknowledged that some efforts had been made to improve the situation in the form of crime prevention weeks, setting up of boys' clubs, etc. But these are sporadic. For instance, according to the Commission, no crime prevention week has been held since 1971. The Commission suggested that the police should not merely highlight the responsibilities of the public, but should go beyond, to focus attention on their own difficulties and how citizens can help to mitigate them. In this context, it referred to a majority response to one of the questions in its questionnaire, which favoured the more liberal appointment of special officers (permitted by Sec. 17 of the Police Act, 1861) from the community so as to aid the police in especially difficult law and order situations. It endorsed the suggestion that this arrangement be an ongoing process, rather than one invoked on special occasions.

Expectations of the Public

The Indian scene is marked by acute public dissatisfaction with the quality of police service. This is most evident in the urban centres where violent crime is on the rise and clearance rates have been dismal. As everywhere else in the world, the public expects safer streets and swifter response to distress calls. Greater police visibility is another demand in towns rocked by violent incidents. The popular complaint is that precious police manpower is diverted to take care of dignitary protection (popularly known as 'VIP security') at the cost of basic police services to the community.

Another common complaint is the hostile reception accorded to the public in police stations when they go to report a crime. The widespread feeling is that they are unwelcome and that a complaint will receive attention only after payment of a bribe.

The public demands a sea-change in the police station environment that will ensure greater friendliness and sensitivity. Less deliberate suppression of complaints of crime and decisive action against anti-social elements, even if it means the police breaching the law, characterize popular expectations of the force.

Expectations of the Police

The Indian police, especially those at the police-station level, articulate many grievances. These relate to a poor pay structure, long hours of work, an unhygienic work environment and unsatisfactory living conditions, in terms of low quality government housing and medical care. But what police constables are most bitter about is the lack of humane treatment by their supervisors. The situation has no doubt been changing for the better, thanks to a vigilant media that does not fail to pick up stories on this issue. But there remains a basic feeling of lack of consideration for the sensitivities of subordinate policemen.

Recent judicial activism has had an impact, both positive and negative, on police investigators. The willingness of courts to uphold police processes, such as the arrest of top politicians and civil servants, and searching and freezing the ill-gotten wealth of public servants, has been extremely welcome. Nevertheless, the close judicial scrutiny of investigation is of concern to the police. Directives impinging on police discretion with regard to arrests, and the dropping of further action at the end of investigation when no evidence is forthcoming, also cause a ripple in police circles. The standards of objectivity which the judiciary expects of the police, even in cases where members of a government may be adversely involved, embarrass the police greatly. Viewed in this light, the police feel that the judiciary does not appreciate the hard realities of the field situation.

Recent Developments

India's polity is at a crossroads. The strident demand for greater probity in public life, the proactive stance of the judiciary which has shown itself to be quite independent, and the investigative reporting of the media that has whetted public appetite, are all distinct features of the current Indian scene. These are going to place the whole polity, including service agencies such as the police, under public scrutiny and a consequent pressure to be transparent.

The specific demand on the police will, increasingly, be one of strict political neutrality and fearless investigation, even when big public figures are involved. The pressure is felt particularly by anti-corruption agencies at the Centre and in the states. A former prime minister, and a serving and few former state chief ministers have recently been arraigned by the CBI/state anti-corruption bureaus. This points to new courage among police investigators and sets the trend for the future. On a Public Interest Litigation (PIL) filed by a former director-general of police of Uttar Pradesh, the Supreme Court of India issued a directive in 1998 to the union home ministry in Delhi to report on action taken to reform the police structure on the basis of the recommendations of the 1977 National Police Commission. This was another significant development in the effort to make the police more professional and less partisan. As a sequel, the home ministry appointed a committee headed by former Punjab DGP, Julio Ribeiro, to go into the NPC recommendations and report on what needed to be done. The committee has since submitted its report, which the ministry has placed before the Supreme Court. Further directions of the Court are awaited. It is against this backdrop that the Indian police will have to contend with problems described in the succeeding paragraphs.

Coalition Governments—Trends at the federal government level and in some states point to coalition governments becoming more and more common. This has its own implications for the bureaucracy, especially the police, which had become accustomed to the unified rule of a single party. Apart from bickering between coalition partners as to who should control the police, there are bound to be conflicting directions to the police hierarchy on how to handle a particular situation. The Uttar Pradesh (U.P.) experiment (1996–7) of a change in the chief ministership once in six months between the two coalition partners, was at the time a uniquely interesting experiment, but this type of arrangement could be repeated. It could also raise new issues of administrative propriety, causing further confusion and demoralization within the police force. It may take several decades before coalition politics establishes salutary practices that permit the police to be clear about their role in such an environment. Until then, the forces will muddle along, hopefully without disastrous consequences for the community.

Criminalization of Politics—There is strong evidence available in many parts of the country of the growing nexus between some political parties and individuals with proven criminal records. This is no new phenomenon, but the relationship has come out into the open during the past few decades, with muscle power and money beginning to determine the outcome of elections, especially those fought in villages.[23] Two frequent crimes committed by thugs on the eve of elections, at the instigation of some political elements, are murder and kidnapping. It is widely known that on the day of polling, the coercion of citizens to vote for a particular party, or to stay away from the polling booth, is a tactic for which political parties use anti-social elements. It was against this background that in July 1993 the central government appointed a committee headed by N.N. Vohra, former home secretary, to explore the growing politician–criminal nexus. The Committee's 1993 report was placed before parliament on 1 August 1995. The report concluded:

> It is apparent that crime syndicates and mafia organizations have established themselves in various parts of the country [and] have developed significant muscle and money power and established linkages with governmental functionaries, political leaders and others to be able to operate with impunity.[24]

The report referred to the observation of the Intelligence Bureau (IB) director that 'warning signals of sinister linkages between the underworld, politicians and bureaucracy have been evident with disturbing regularity'.[25] The director was reported to have added that criminal gangs in certain states like Bihar, Haryana and U.P. enjoyed the patronage of local politicians and the protection of government functionaries. The dependence of politicians on crime syndicates for financial support to fight elections enhanced the latter's clout in dealing with the official machinery. As a sequel to the Vohra Report, a nodal agency was set up in the central government for exchange of information among central agencies for effective follow-up action.[26] It is not yet known how effective this agency has been.

Unless there is a strong political will here, the police will not be able to stem the rot. The reported decision of the Central Election Commission to bar persons with a record of conviction in a criminal case from contesting elections should help to keep out a few really bad elements. Beyond this, with the high degree of proof required by courts, one cannot be sanguine that the Election Commission's move will bring about any great transformation of the scene.

Judicial Activism—The question uppermost in the minds of many enlightened citizens, including police officers, is whether the judiciary will be able to sustain its present momentum for long. This misgiving is traceable to an apprehension that vested political interests, affected by many recent judicial decisions, will somehow align themselves to scuttle future processes. While the fear seems a little exaggerated, it undoubtedly succeeds in throwing up uncertainty before the police, in its capacity for professional action in sensitive investigations. This is an unhappy situation, not likely to be resolved unless judicial independence remains unhindered for at least a few years to come. The police desire for autonomy will stand or dissipate, depending on the future strength of the judiciary.

Broader Recruitment—The new scheme of quotas for admission into professional colleges and for entry into the civil service, following the implementation of the Mandal Commission recommendations, should see the induction of more rural youth from relatively underprivileged sections of society into the Indian Police Service. While this is true of the Indian Administrative Service and other higher civil services as well, it has particular import for the police. At least in theory, it should lead to greater police sensitivity to the problems of the lower strata. This is important in the context of galling tales of police apathy to the poor, vis-a-vis the privileged treatment of the moneyed class who can often 'buy' police attention. This author will not go so far as to agree with many of his cynical colleagues, who are positive that it is still the better-placed individual who will continue to be privileged in the police station context. I look upon this as a possible area for future research: will the new class composition of the IPS alter police attitudes towards the rural poor?

Centre–State Relations—Notwithstanding the strong sentiments heard frequently in favour of greater autonomy for states vis-à-vis the central government, it is likely that collaboration between state and central forces will expand rather than diminish. Even states that are traditionally reluctant to be a part of the national mainstream, acknowledge the indebtedness of their police to the home ministry of the central government in Delhi.

The Central Reserve Police Force will remain the mainstay for states to tackle major threats to peace. The continuous expansion of the CRPF is a direct recognition of the faith placed in it by the states. Recruitment to the CRPF may therefore have to be more broadbased, in response to various regional pulls, so as to bring about its greater acceptability. One issue that may be raised in the future is: how far is dependence on a central force expedient for a state government, especially when the latter is controlled by a political party that is opposed to the ruling party at the Centre? Another that requires attention is the impact of excessive reliance on the CRPF, on the quality of state armed police battalions, and especially on their state of training and preparedness.

Conclusions

The widespread impression, nationally, is that the Indian police force is excessively law and order oriented and that it has done precious little to reverse the rising trend of crime. This is buttressed by daily media reports on police activity in different parts of the country and the continual expansion of para-military forces. While this impression can be faulted for being sweeping—one that ignores the fact that a spurt in crime, especially of the violent variety, is not peculiar to India—what is inescapable is the feeling that police performance is invariably evaluated by the government mainly in terms of handling protest demonstrations in public, and quelling riots. This is a legacy carried over from pre-Independence days, marked by large-scale political agitations that aimed at disrupting administrative processes. Critics of the police believe that this continued obsession with law and order, even fifty years after Independence, is unfortunate because it is oblivious to the new functions imposed on the police by an evolving society. Vocal sections of the population such as Scheduled Castes and Tribes and women expect greater police sensitivity to their grievances and new innovations which will give them a feeling of security in what is considered a sharply fractured society.

In essence, the community expects the police to be more proactive than reactive as they have always been known to be. In real terms, the desire is for a more consumer-oriented police that assigns a higher priority to service functions than to maintenance of the status quo. In this connection, attention is drawn to the activism displayed by the judiciary in the recent past. This is attributed to the judiciary's perception of a changing society and the need to adapt itself to modern requirements. The innovation of PIL whereby any member of the public can seek swift judicial intervention in cases of gross injustice or administrative impropriety, and the judiciary's visible concern over matters of environmental protection are cited as the latter's willingness to assume a new role. The discerning critic asks why the police cannot similarly get rid of its colonial baggage and become service-oriented, especially when such activism does not require Constitutional amendments, a task that is circumscribed by elaborate procedure. Here, the accusation is that the police leadership, particularly the IPS variety, has been smug and conservative.

Notwithstanding this failure to be proactive, the police role in holding the nation together against the onslaught of centrifugal forces cannot be exaggerated. The resources placed at its disposal for discharging its duties are no doubt expanding; the positive interest evinced in this area by the central government to bolster state police forces is commendable. It is a moot point, however, whether police resources are adequate. There are additional constraints in the form of the executive's unconcealed anxiety to keep the police under its strict control, thereby denying the latter the degree of operational freedom that it requires to prove itself effective. The distrust of the judiciary for police procedures, especially in matters of crime investigation, weighs heavily on the police, and leads to morale problems. Police personnel management therefore, is going to be increasingly important in the days to come; in this, more than with the judiciary and the executive, it will be the police leadership, represented by IPS officers, that will be severely tested.

Notes

[1] R.K. Raghavan, 'Fifty Years of Policing', *The Hindu*, 27 August 1997.

[2] For studies of the Indian police in the post-Independence period, see David H. Bayley, *The Police and Political Development in India* (Princeton, NJ: Princeton University Press), 1969; S.K. Ghosh and K.F. Rustamji (eds), *Encyclopaedia of Police in India*, vol.1 (New Delhi: Ashis Publishing House), 1993; and R.K. Raghavan, *Indian Police: Problems, Planning and Perspectives* (New Delhi: Manohar), 1989 and *Policing a Democracy: The Case of India and the U.S.* (New Delhi: Manohar), 1999. For additional research focusing on women in Indian police, see Shamim Aleem, *Women in Indian Police* (New Delhi: Sterling), 1991; S.K. Ghosh, *Women in Policing* (New Delhi: Light and Life Publishers), 1981; and M. Natarajan, 'Women Police Units in India', *Police Studies*, vol. 19, no. 2 (1996).

[3] For reports on police in the pre-Independence period, see J.C. Curry, *The Indian Police* (London: Faber and Faber), 1932; K.S. Dhillon, *Defenders of the Establishment: Ruler-Supportive Police Forces of South Asia* (Shimla: Indian Institute of Advanced Study), 1998. S.M. Edwardes, *Crime in British India* (Reprint of 1924 edition) (New Delhi: ABC Publishing House), 1983; P.G. Griffiths, *To Guard My People: The History of the Indian Police* (London: Ernest Benn), 1971; A. Gupta, *Crime and Police in India, up to 1861* (Agra: Sahitya Bhawan), 1974 and *The Police in British India, 1861–1947* (New Delhi: Concept Publishing), 1979, c. 1978; and S.D. Trivedi 'The Origin and Development of Police Organization in Ancient India' in S.K. Ghosh and K.F. Rustamji (eds) *Encyclopaedia of Police in India*, vol.1, op. cit. For Studies examining the police during the transition from the British Raj to Independence, see Inspector General of Madras, *The History of Madras Police*, (1959); S.K. Jha, *Raj to Swaraj: Changing Contours of Police* (New Delhi: Lancer), 1995; and B.P. Saha, *Indian Policy: Legacy and Quest for Formative Role* (Delhi: Konark), 1990.

[4] Government of India, *Crime in India 1996* (New Delhi: National Crime Records Bureau, Government of India), 1998; and IPS Central Association, 'Memorandum to the Fifth Central Pay Commission' (New Delhi), 1994.

[5] Government of India, *Crime in India 1996*, op.cit.

[6] Additional research on the police and counter-terrorism can be found in Ved Marwah, *Uncivil Wars: Pathology of Terrorism in India* (New Delhi: HarperCollins), 1995; and Vijay Karan, *War by Stealth: Terrorism in India* (New Delhi: Viking), 1997.

[7] Government of Gujarat, *Commission of Inquiry on Communal Disturbances at Ahmedabad and at Various Places in the State of Gujarat on and after 18th September 1969*. Chairman: Jaganmohan Reddy. (Ahmedabad: Home Department, Government of Gujarat), 1971.

[8] P.R. Rajgopal, *Communal Violence in India* (New Delhi: Uppal), 1987a.

[9] See Jitendra Narayan, *Communal Riots in India: A Case Study of an Indian State* (New Delhi: Ashish Publishing), 1992 and P.R. Rajgopal, *Communal Violence in India*, op. cit.

[10] For additional information on crime statistics, see S. Venugopala Rao, *Dynamics of Crime: Spatial and Socio-economic Aspects of Crime in India* (New Delhi: Indian Institute of Public Administration), 1981 and G.P. Joshi and J.C. Arora, *Crime in India: A Trend Analysis, 1951–91* (New Delhi: Bureau of Police Research and Development), 1994.

[11] Government of India, *Reports of the National Police Commission*, vols. I to VIII, (Delhi: Controller of Publications), 1979–81.

[12] Shah Commission, *Interim Report, Shah Commission of Inquiry* (Delhi: Controller of Publications), 1978.

[13] Government of India, *Report of the National Police Commission* (Second) (Delhi: Controller of Publications), 1979, p. 11.

[14] Government of India, *Report of the Indian Police Commission, 1902*. The Andrew H.L. Fraser Report (New Delhi: Government of India).

[15] Known as the Jain diary, or the *Hawala* case, this document recorded alleged money laundering by a private businessman, and payment of bribes by him to public officials, both political leaders and civil servants. Several important personalities were indicted, and the Supreme Court has closely monitored the investigation of the case.

[16] David H. Bayley, *The Police and Political Development in India*, op. cit., p. 203.

[17] Government of India, *Report of the National Police Commission* (Fifth), op. cit., p. 48.

[18] Government of India, *Report of the Indian Police Commission 1902*, op. cit.

[19] Ibid., p. 16.

[20] Government of India, *Report of the National Police Commission* (Third), (Delhi: Controller of Publications), 1980, p. 25.

[21] Ibid., p. 26.

[22] The Indian Police, at the cutting-edge level, is principally divided into three wings: 'law and order', 'crime' and 'traffic'. 'Law and order' is analogous to the patrol bureau found in U.S. police departments. This wing handles all disorders in public places, including minor and major riots. While the crime wing no doubt investigates offences flowing from such disorders, its primary preoccupation is with offences against property such as theft, burglary, and robbery. In the Indian environment, these two aspects of police routine are viewed very much in isolation from each other, and there is not much of an appreciation of the fact that effective patrolling by the law and order wing could prevent crime, both against human body and property.

For additional information on police training, defence of law and order and relations with the public, see Indian Institute of Public Opinion, *Study on Police Image* (New Delhi: Ministry of Home Affairs, Government of India), 1979; K.M. Mathur, 'Policing for Internal Security', *Administrative Change,* vol. 19, nos. 1–2, June 1992; Kuldeep Mathur, 'The State and Use of Coercive Power in India', *Asian Survey*, vol. 32 no. 4, April 1992; S. Misra, *Police Brutality: An Analysis of Police Behaviour* (New Delhi: Vikas), 1986; Government of India, *Report of the Committee on Police Training* (New Delhi: Government of India), 1973; P.R. Rajgopal, *Social Change and Violence: The Indian Experience* (New Delhi: Uppal), 1987b; N.S. Saksena, *Law and Order in India* (New Delhi: Abhinav), 1987; and P.D. Sharma, *Police and Political Order in India* (Delhi: Research), 1984.

[23] R.K. Raghavan, *Policing a Democracy: The Case of India and the U.S.,* op. cit.

[24] Vohra Committe Report, Ministry of Home Affairs, Government of India, New Delhi, 1993.

[25] Ibid.

[26] *The Hindu,* 2 August 1995.

Judges and Indian Democracy: the lesser evil?

RAJEEV DHAVAN

I

Against impossible odds, and after fierce resistance, the judiciary has become India's most controversial institution of governance. Consisting, at any given point, of some 500-odd Supreme and high court judges, India's higher judiciary has claimed more than the general custodianship of the Constitution.[1] If, in the early years, it was content to do no more than contain the socialist excesses of planned development, after the Emergency (1975–7), the Supreme Court has become the god of many, if not all, things—large and small.

An Indian adaptation of an Anglo-American institution, the judiciary has constantly been viewed with subdued suspicion. It has been depicted as a potential 'Frankenstein monster' by a prominent member of the Constituent Assembly,[2] forgivingly chastised by an angry Nehru for having 'purloined' the Constitution,[3] attacked by Indira Gandhi for being anti-development and anti-poor,[4] vilified by virtually the whole nation during the Emergency for its pusillanimity and making 'the darkness of the darkest period of the history of Independent India . . . complete',[5] accused of taking over the governance of the nation under the guise of public interest litigation,[6] and constantly threatened with constitutional amendments seeking to circumscribe the vast range of its powers.[7]

The judiciary has borne most of these unfriendly humiliations with relatively statesmanlike rectitude. In the 1950s, the judges beat a retreat, claiming to have been misunderstood.[8] If the 1960s supported the compromise that judges would do their part to engineer transformative social change,[9] the Supreme Court was unhappy about being driven into a position of constitutional subservience.[10] By the early 1970s, it had struck down overtly political initiatives to nationalize banks,[11] to abolish the 'privy purses' of the erstwhile rulers of princely states,[12] and to control India's powerful newspaper media.[13] In 1973, in what is celebrated as one of the more significant and globally acknowledged Constitutional decisions of this century, the Court made it clear that every Constitution has a basic structure which is inviolate and immune from constitutional amendment.[14] An irate Mrs Gandhi retaliated by punishing some of the judges, refusing to appoint any of the allegedly more 'dangerous' ones as chief justice of India. Confronted with their record during the Emergency when judges refused to interfere even on mala fide detentions without trial, they simply apologized.[15] In the decade that followed, the Supreme Court crafted new socio-economic promises into the Constitution, inviting social activists to use the Court to obtain effective remedies through the new-found 'public interest litigation'. This seemed like a good judicial offer of 'love' at a time of 'political cholera', which simultaneously created a new constituency of support for the judges. No sooner was this offer made than it was seized upon by social activists, lawyers, and journalists to wedge open a backdoor entry into matters of governance from which they were otherwise excluded.

Accused of enlarging the scope of judicial intervention to areas where the judiciary normally fears to tread, the judges of the 1980s demurred, arguing that they were doing no more than interpreting the Constitution as they understood it—an explanation that wore thin as more and more issues got entangled in the judicial web.[16] By the mid-1990s, as the chorus of those mal-affected by judicial decision-making grew louder, the judges defended their intervention as a temporary antidote to the collapse of institutions of governance, and a weakening of the rule of law.[17] These judicial explanations are as ingenious as the complaints that give rise to them. Yet, somehow, the controversies have helped rather than hindered the judiciary in acquiring its own pivotal place in the institutions by which India is governed.

Constitutional arrangements that place the judiciary in institutional polarity to the political sovereign so as to permit 'judges' to strike down the 'actions' and 'laws' of the 'ruler' are alien to traditional notions of governance in India. The Dharmashastra, which in varying degrees permeated civil society, was a *jurist-based* system, directly targeted towards the people. Aware that such a system must adapt and be adapted to how people actually lived, considerable scope was built into the shastra for local and regional variation, even to the point of accepting that *sadachara* (custom) could override a thousand texts.[18] Judges may not have been important to the efficacious working of the system. Judicial procedure found its pride of place in various texts, including some (like the *Narada Smriti*) where it was profiled for more pointed attention.[19] The king's justice could have included judges, who may have displeased rulers from time to time by acting according to dharma, but most disputes were resolved at village level by the powerful 'wise men' of the village, who no doubt fudged the shastra to their advantage.[20] Founded on a concept of 'law' wholly different from the institutionalized 'political' concept prevalent today, the shastra avoided confrontations between the commands of the ruler and the dharma from which the king himself derived his authority. In the ultimate analysis, dharma would prevail over royal edict,[21] but the judiciary was not the institutional instrument through which kings were reminded of their duties to their people, or the eternal order of things of which they were a part.

This system was not too greatly disturbed by the Muslim rulers, who enforced their edicts if and when it became politically expedient and 'revenue-necessary' through their administrators and qazis. If the Emperor Jahangir's famous bell symbolized the king's justice as his own, the labours of dispensing justice were shared with qazis who, at least occasionally, were known to remind the king of the Islamic law which, like the shastra, was also an elaborate *jurist-based* system directed towards observance by civil society. Too much cannot, and should not, be made of the (albeit legendary) skirmishes that may have taken place between various Hindu and Muslim rulers and their 'judges'. The latter were by no means the seat of institutional opposition to their kings. To pretend that this was so is unnecessary, even if it is a good retaliatory 'nationalist' response to condescending imperial descriptions depicting indigenous systems of law as 'dotages of brahmanical superstition'.[22] Yet, even if judges were neither the custodians nor the carriers of the shastra or the shariat, the broad influence of these systems on indigenous native thinking about 'law' cannot be ignored. They represent an alternative concept of law, developed by jurists rather than the state, directed towards day to day life in civil society. Amidst innumerable adaptations, variations and negations, this alternative approach to law—which may be called a Value-Based Social Legal System (VBSLS) approach—drew its support directly from institutions in civil society which skilfully avoided confrontation with the king but constantly reminded him that he was answerable to the shastra or shariat, and not above it.

By the time the British arrived and consolidated their power in India, they were already committed to a singularly different Statute-Based Political Law System (SBPLS) whereby the 'commands' of the sovereign (whether king or parliament) were deemed to be the overriding 'law' of the land.[23] The declarations of the political sovereign expressed in the form of statutes and rules had supremacy over the open-textured common law. Bentham had triumphed over Blackstone;[24] and India became the laboratory for 'whiggish' nineteenth-century experiments on law reform.[25] The *Code Indica*, which continues to govern India and many former colonies to this day, was created.[26] Whatever was not codified by statute, such as personal, customary and other laws, did not escape institutionalized restatement. A strongly bureaucratized judiciary recast all the personal and customary laws so that the institutionalized restatement of the shastra, shariat and customary laws, rather than the social law itself, became the law of the land.[27] It is no doubt true that the British SBPLS displaced the Indian VBSLS, and that asking for the restoration of the aborted (VBSLS) indigenous system is more sentimental than realistic.[28] But, the VBSLS represents an approach to law which is radically different from the approaches of SBPLS. Even though Indian law is now statute-based and thoroughly 'western' in its approach, it should not surprise us if the basic instinct of Indian judges is to retain a dharmashastric approach to otherwise Anglo-phonic laws. This might explain their affinity to widely stated doctrines of judicial reviews including, perforce, the famous 'basic structure' doctrine,[29] which powerfully re-states the case for constitutionalism in ways that it has never before been stated.

Initially, the British were extremely wary about creating too powerful a judiciary, especially one that could be used as an instrument to challenge the Raj. Their initial experiences showed both how the English themselves abused the judicial process[30] as well as the 'utter want of connection between the (various) courts'.[31] By 1834, the idea of the judiciary being the seat of institutional opposition to the Raj was firmly rejected in, and by, a famous dispatch:

> A judiciary utterly uncontrollable by the government and, on the contrary, controlling the government, recognising the highest authorities of the State only as private individuals and the tribunals which administer justice in all its forms to the great body of the people only as foreign tribunals, is surely an anomaly in the strictest sense of the word.[32]

But this was, to say the least, problematic. If one imperative arising from the 'anomaly' lay in codifying the law so as to contain juristic creativity within the confines of 'law' declared by the state, it was no less necessary to profile the British Indian judiciary as an independent and creative institution in its own right. If it was to acquire credibility in Indian eyes, it had to be seen not as a 'foreign tribunal', but one to which all people brought even their personal and social disputes. The solution evolved by the Raj was to create a lower judiciary that would attract disputes and decide them according to British laid-down law. Above the lower courts was a high court system that consolidated the work of the lower courts, upheld the supremacy of British Indian law, and reformulated the 'traditional' indigenous law in British terms under the broad aegis of 'justice, equity and good conscience'.[33] At the apex was a Privy Council based in London to ensure that any juristic excess committed by judges remained under the control of London.

Special care was taken to ensure that the Imperial State was virtually immunized from civil actions in respect of most of its functions.[34] But, more importantly, the British made sure that Indian high courts had no powers of judicial review that would enable them to institutionally oppose and strike down the actions and statutes of the Raj as unconstitutional. The power to issue High Prerogative writs was given only to the high courts of the Presidency towns of Calcutta and Bombay; and the Privy Council made sure that Presidency high courts could exercise their powers only up to the administrative limits of these towns and no further.[35] Given the choice to use and abuse the British justice systems, Indians flocked to the courts and choked their work to a point that a special committee had to be appointed in 1925 to look at the mounting arrears in civil courts.[36] This did not stop Indians from complaining that the system was biased, insensitive to Indian sentiments and guilty of committing what Gandhi called 'egregious blunders'.[37] Be that as it may, British law had triumphed, native law was reformulated and restricted in its scope by the courts of the Raj and placed under the shadow of the British legal system, to which it was subordinated and with which it was to be intermingled.

Curiously, India's 'freedom' movement did not ask for too many radical changes in the legal system. A demand for a Bill of Rights was made as early as 1895.[38] The Nehru Report's demand for a Supreme Court in 1928 was more to do away with appeals to the Privy Council in London.[39] The White Paper, following the Round Table Conferences of 1930–2, readily acceded to the need for a 'federal court' to resolve disputes between the various states comprising of, and associated with, the federal system proposed for the future, but was less sanguine about the need for a Supreme Court to replace the Privy Council. Eventually, only the federal court was set up by the Government of India Act of 1935 to adjudicate inter-state disputes, to interpret the Act of 1935, to hear civil cases above a certain value, and generally to decide matters for which the court itself granted special leave to appeal.[40]

When the Special Committee appointed by the Constituent Assembly considered the design for a future Supreme Court of India, its Report of 21 May 1947 did not deviate too markedly from the 'federal court' model, other than approving the new title of 'supreme court' and generally making the Supreme Court both a general court of appeal (to replace the Privy Council) and a 'federal' court to deliberate on inter-state issues and the interpretation of the Constitution.[41] No more was done than to 'indigenize' the Imperial apex of the judiciaries of the Raj. Perhaps nothing more was necessary, since the more momentous decisions concerning the judicial enforcement of the proposed Bill of Rights had yet to be taken.[42] Nor was the British-Indian judiciary seriously attacked as being unsuited to independent

India. In the Memorandum of the Chief Justices to the Drafting Committee in 1948, it was openly stated:

> Thanks to the system of administration of justice established by the British in this country, the judiciary, until now, has, in the main, played an independent role in protecting the rights of the individual citizen against encroachment and invasion by the executive power.[43]

If anything—more so after the Constitutional Advisor visited the United States—the 'lawyer' and other members of the judiciary became wary about granting the judiciary too much power.[44] The great New Deal crisis of the United States—read along with the turn of the century record of the American Supreme Court's bias towards property and business—confirmed some of the worst fears of the most legally knowledgeable conservative members.[45] The events of Partition added precautionary fuel to conservative ardor.[46] Over the months that followed, the Bill of Rights was elaborated so that the original 'due process' clause was replaced by an 'any process' clause; and the incidence of judicial intervention was both curtailed and straitjacketed.[47] Judges could not examine what was the 'due' or appropriate process, but only whether some process had been laid down by law. It is not surprising that although the Assembly did consider various alternatives of collegiate, judicial, and political models for appointments to the higher judiciary,[48] there was very little said about the kind of judges who should be considered for such appointments. For Nehru, the criterion was simply that any judge appointed to the Supreme Court should have distinguished himself as a judge of the high court.[49]

What must not be lost sight of is the fact that a strong judiciary was really inconsistent with the SBPLS that the British had installed both at home and abroad. British politicians had fought hard to achieve the supremacy of Parliament; they were not about to hand their victory over the king to a bunch of judges who, even if they belonged to the same social class, could create political mischief under the guise of judicial decision-making. This traditional British antipathy towards the judiciary was even more deeply rooted among workers and the Labour party which was in power at the time India's Constitution was being drafted. The Left had suffered much at the hands of the judiciary. In an unbroken experience from the Wilkes controversies of the eighteenth century, through committals for contempt for calling judges 'bewigged puppets', and the Laski and Foot trials, there was much that the Labour movement had against judges.[50] E.P. Thompson's famous memoir in *Whigs and Hunters*,[51] that the rule of law was a mixed blessing for the poor, had yet to be written. To this day, the British constitutional system is unhappy about creating an enforceable Bill of Rights which would empower the judiciary to the exclusion of Parliament.[52] Nehru's planning commission model of governance sought to use 'law' as an instrument of social change.[53] As long as the judiciary behaved itself and did not stand in the way of Nehru's plans for India, nothing more needed to be said. The judiciary was an extra, to be respected for what it was; and, perforce, to be feared if it got out of hand.

II

There was never any great dissonance between Nehru's developmental plans for the Indian people and the positivist theory of law that the British had bequeathed to the courts of independent India. The fact that the Constituent Assembly had scripted a judicially enforceable Bill of Rights into the text of the Constitution did not disturb the positivist credentials of Indian law. The 'fundamental rights' guaranteed to the citizen had been perceived as essentially 'legal rights' granted by a super-statute. Each one of the rights had been hedged in by limitations and was interpreted like any other statute.[54]

Troubled by his experiences in Avadh and Europe, Nehru was convinced that India's freedom movement had to be given a socio-economic face. The first mature step towards this was the Karachi Resolution of 1931, which became as controversial as it was ambiguous.[55] Nehru's only significant contribution to the Constituent Assembly was his 'Objectives Resolution', which was based on the Karachi Resolution and became the Preamble to the Indian Constitution.[56] Despite the discontent in the Assembly over the form and timing of the Objectives Resolution, there was broad social and political consensus on the view that the only way India could dispense substantive *socio-economic* justice to its people was not just through planned development, but by an effective transformation of Indian society. It was not merely a question of allocating resources in order to build a technological infrastructure for a 'modern' society; rather, the goal was to change attitudes and behaviour so that 'untouchability' was abolished as a social practice, gender equality was assured, equal opportunities were created for the poor, the 'personal' laws of various communities were assimilated into a uniform civil code, poverty and exploitative practices were done away with, and ruler and ruled alike looked at things in a 'rationally' more progressive way. Much of this was placed within the Directive Principles of State Policy, which were not enforceable, but were somewhat guardedly declared to be fundamental to the governance of the nation.[57] The upshot of all this was the creation of a positivistic welfare state that demanded enormous legal empowerment to effect the social and economic transformation of India. If 'law' had any role to play, it had to be functionally geared towards achieving this politically ordained social change.

India was not alone in committing itself to a model of state-induced 'law and development'. America's New Deal was founded on creating a regulatory and welfare state, created by 'law' and administered through powerful bureaucratic agencies. Just after World War II, the Soviet Union stood out as an example, demonstrating how planned development could transform a society into a major industrial nation with a tolerably reliable agricultural base. If Keynesian economics canvassed the case for state expenditure, the Labour government which swept into power in Britain in 1945 presented India and various colonies with a model of how a welfare state could be created through 'law' and the parliamentary process. The very fact that the world was divided into 'developed' and 'developing' nations suggested that the latter had to do something about catching up with the former. The then contemporary answer lay in empowering the state with regulatory and transformative powers, creating huge, powerful bureaucracies and new norms of administration and administrative adjudication, enacting a vast number of social, welfare and regulatory laws, rules and regulations and underpinning the entire system with criminal sanctions, so that the directives of the state and all its allied agencies were obeyed even when they were not respected.

The planning commission 'law and development' model of social change was very much in vogue. All the international agencies, public and private, recommended it, and most political systems were addicted to it. Legal scholarship touted the law and development model for universal application throughout the world.[58] It had acquired the status of a theology, spanning many prescriptive disciplines. It was not until the 1970s that the halo around the law and development model began to lose its glow. American scholarship, which had exported this model to developing nations, found itself in 'self-estrangement' over its results.[59] No society could be commanded into change. But this wisdom was not vouchsafed to nation-builders like Nehru and others who had good cause to believe that the societies in which they lived would comply for the good of the cause.

In this Nehruvian concept of 'law and social change' the essential ingredients of law as an instrument of planned development in a liberal democratic society could perhaps be summarized as follows:

(i) Law is not a mystical creation.

(ii) It consists of rules that are created by a sovereign parliament and other legislative bodies.

(iii) Law acquires legitimacy if and when: (*a*) it serves the overall principles of justice; and (*b*) it is arrived at by a process of democratic discussion.

(iv) Once a law is made it cannot be undermined but has to be respected.

(v) If people want to change the law, they have to do so by constitutional methods; and, the Constitution imposes no substantive limits on the change.

(vi) Law can be an instrument to achieve social and political transformation; but such changes have to be crafted into a law and not just left to the good sense of the people.

(vii) In order to achieve social and economic change, powerful bureaucracies have to be created to enable the transformation of society.

(viii) Such bureaucracies, along with the assistance of courts, where necessary, are expected to plan, persuade, cajole, threaten and punish in order to effect compliance where there is a lack of congruence between a declared norm or goal and its compliance.

(ix) The courts are not centres of rebellion; they are needed to interpret the law and to keep the various bureaucracies from straying too greatly out of their jurisdiction and exceeding their powers.

(x) People have fundamental rights; but judges are expected to interpret these in a reasonable way.[60]

Faced with the tour de force of Nehru's— as indeed the rest of
the world's—intense concern with 'law' and 'development', how
was the judiciary and its performance to be judged? Where exactly did judges fit into all this? And if they did not, what would
happen? Would there be a fight between the legislature and the
courts? Would the legislature overturn the decisions of the
judges? And, would they go further and disempower the judiciary? Or, having done that, would judicial appointments be
made to recruit judges who understood the imperatives of
planned development? If judicial appointments were, like the
Constitution, 'made to measure', what would happen to the
judiciary?

Judges were not the only ones to be concerned. As the Independence movement came to an abrupt halt, lawyers, who had
been significant participants in that movement, were also concerned about what lay in store for them. Way back in 1947,
lawyers, troubled by a sense of nemesis, formally passed a resolution 'protest(ing) . . . the growing tendency in responsible ministerial circles to undermine the profession of law and lawyers',
and 'affirm(ing) that law is an honourable profession and that
for the good government of any government, lawyers are absolutely necessary'.[61] We have already seen the reaction of the conference of the chief justices during the process of constitution-
making declaring their crucial role in defending individual
rights.[62] The law journals were full of lawyers and judges tracing their learning back to Indian antiquity and pledging their
self-stated importance to the future of the nation.[63] But what
exactly would be their role? Apart from the rhetoric, no one
quite knew what it was. At the time the Constitution came into
being, there were no great expectations from judges; nor, for
that matter, were there any great fears that judges would place
any major impediment in the way to planned social change
through law. With its 'any process', as opposed to 'due process',
clause, the Constitution had given an edge to parliament over
the judiciary.[64] The judges had no other choice but to accept
the 'procedure' enacted by the legislature, even if they felt that
it fell short of what they would have wished. The judges themselves had been schooled in the 'black letter' law tradition. Deep
down, even within that tradition, the judges knew that their
job was a lot more creative than simply 'interpreting' the law.

However, given the juristic techniques they had inherited, they were expected to get involved in controversies; at the same time they were expected not to be controversial. It did not take long for these assumptions about the judicial role to be disproved.[65]

III

How exactly has the judiciary performed? There are as many opinions as there are complaints and evaluations. The truth is that there are very few rigorous accounts of both the pre- and post-Independence judiciary. What has attracted scholarship and comment has been the ongoing battle between the Congress government of the day and the courts, principally, the Supreme Court. If Nehru's pique against the judiciary was ideological, successor governments personalized this discontent. As long as this public, and necessarily political, controversy dominated the critique of the judiciary, a balanced view was not, and never has been, possible.

It might, therefore, be a useful starting point to examine how the Supreme Court has figured in the political controversies of the day. From that standpoint, it is possible to divide the political and public evaluation of the judiciary into various distinct, but overlapping, phases. In the first phase, the early 'tension' years of the 1950s, the government accused the judiciary of standing in the way of progress. In the second phase, from 1960 to around 1965 or so, came the 'compromise' years dominated by Justice Gajendragadkar, when the judiciary became interested in using the law for 'social engineering' and evolved compromises, seeking a quietus to the controversy. The third phase overlaps with the second, and is largely an assertion of judicial power, leaning in favour of 'libertarian' values. The fourth phase comprised the ill-fated years of the Emergency, when judicial power was curbed and the judiciary lost some of the ground that it had won for itself. The fifth phase was the post-Emergency phase, when the judges not only placed their power over all authorities, public or private, but claimed the status of an independent institution of governance that had its own separate public interest, people-oriented, constitutional goals. This put many vested interests on the defensive, protesting that public interest litigation was a dangerous hoax in excess of the judiciary's appointed constitutional role. The sixth phase was essentially a consolidation of the post-Emergency one, even though the judges of the late 1980s and early 1990s have sometimes been criticized for blunting the radical edge of the 'public interest litigation' that had been developed immediately after the Emergency. The seventh, contemporary, phase represents the Supreme Court's direct involvement in issues of governance, forcing other institutions of governance to do what they are supposed to do by using the new and powerful methods of investigation of public interest litigation. This has exposed government, politicians and public persons who, along with the media, have severely chastised the judiciary for having usurped the judicial future.[66]

This over-stylized history of the conflicts between the judiciary and politicians of various hues represents how the judiciary has been popularly, or sometimes unpopularly, depicted, and how it is largely responsible for producing the various criticisms directed against it. It overlooks the unparalleled range of civil and criminal cases that are dealt with by even the Supreme Court every day, and the diversity of judicial approaches on virtually each and every issue; a public image has been conjured up of an over-contentious, anti-government judiciary inimical to India's social justice needs.

From this distinct political point of view, the consequences of judicial decisions speak for themselves. In this 'consequentialist' evaluation of the judiciary, judges had stood by agrarian landlords at a time when the legislatures were trying to abolish feudalism; sided with business against labour; and generally supported a monopolistic press, undeserving princes, the corporate sector, and privileged property owners. And, having come thus far, the judiciary dealt the final blow to the sovereignty of parliament and the people by denying legislatures the power to amend the Constitution.[67] From such a consequentialist analysis flows the further charge that the judiciary is essentially class-biased— a charge to which the judiciary reacted with elegant but compromising vehemence by declaring politicians who gave voice to this charge, guilty of contempt of court![68] Masquerading both as academic analysis as well as political rhetoric, these indictments and accusations resulted in the government formulating a policy of appointing 'committed' judges who were 'ideologically suitable' and politically loyal to the higher judiciary, passing over the claims of certain 'not-so-suitable' judges to be chief justices of India.[69] However, the consequentialist argument that the judges were class-biased necessarily fizzled out because of the Emergency, when the government's commitment to planned development and poverty alleviation became preeminently suspect. It suffered a further setback during the early years of the public interest law movement, when judges wore their social consciences on their sleeves and reinterpreted the law in favour of poor tenants, workers of all fortunate or unfortunate description, and the unemployed.[70] It revived a little a decade later, when judges were less positive about the social justice concerns of the earlier phase of the post-Emergency public interest law movement. The consequentialist argument regarding class bias continues in a nebulous, less exaggerated form.[71]

Explanations of the judiciary that concentrate wholly on the class affiliation of judges are politically shrill, analytically crude, historically muddled and hopelessly confused about the nature of 'law' in the hands of judicial institutions. Nor would it be easy to describe the four thousand or so judges who have been part of the higher judiciary since 1950 as necessarily belonging to the same class. A prosopography would suggest deep divisions and many differences, more so in recent years.[72] They do, of course, share the characteristic of having been part and parcel of what has often been described as a 'middle class' intellectual profession which has always been, and sought to be, at the forefront of social and political activity. That is why one study of the Supreme Court has suggested that:

> In the end, we must regard the attitude of Supreme Court judges as typical of the decision-making habits of metropolitan Indians: technically unpredictable, not influenced by imitative cosmopolitan habits, conditioned by native instinct to a depth not yet predictable by the psychologist or documented even by the novelist, the dramatist or the fiction writer, and suffering from an over-sensitive opinion of their lonely and unparalleled position.[73]

The social backgrounds of the judges are not unimportant; nor, indeed, is the fact that aspects of 'class ideology' are imbricated in 'law' as a discipline. Judges elsewhere in the world have often been crudely 'instrumental' in trying to achieve certain ends.[74] But, in this day and age, the discourse of 'law', founded as it is on an architecture of universal principles from which it draws social legitimacy, does not easily admit an overly reductionist class analysis drawn from a crude consequentialist analysis of decision-making. In the Indian context, such an analysis is an expression of political pique expressing discontent with the finality of judicial decisions from which there is no further appeal.

IV

Populist and political versions and critiques of the judiciary tend to obscure empirical realities as well, while simultaneously paying insufficient attention to the overall purpose and function of a judiciary in any particular society.[75] The best-laid plans of legislators and Constitution-makers suffer transformation, as legislation and institutions get hijacked for purposes other than those for which the legislation or institution in question was designed.[76] Despite the best efforts of the Constitution-makers to give India's judiciary a low profile and to ensure that it would enhance, rather than obscure, the government's 'developmental image' as a matter of blind faith, the judiciary has grown in status and importance as an independent institution of governance. We need to examine the nature of the judiciary's transformation from an institution of state to an institution of governance in its own right.

For the moment, it might be safer not to confound our review of transformative changes in the higher Indian judiciary by considering whether it is now a 'populist' or 'political' institution.[77] This would be treading on all manner of contentious terrain and getting embroiled in all kinds of definitional controversies over contra-distinguishing 'political' or 'populist' institutions from others which are not so. Although India's post-Independence judiciary has cast off many of its imperial clothes, it may be a useful starting point, albeit for heuristic purposes, to examine the broad premises on which the pre-Independence judiciary worked. For the British, the judiciary of the Raj was preeminently an institution of state.[78]

There were three expectations from the imperial judiciary. To begin with, it was expected to contribute to the overall aims and objectives of the state and not to act in institutional polarity to the government. To this extent, the judiciary possessed virtually no powers to counteract the actions of government or to render them liable for their actions in any extravagant sense. Second, and notwithstanding the first expectation, the judiciary was also expected to profile its independence in such order that it might acquire social legitimacy. This meant that while retaining its fidelity to the overall purposes of the imperial state in matters of interpretative discretion and application of the law, it had to be seen to uphold the rule of law: *fiat justitia ruat caelum*. The seeming contradiction between the first and second expectations was resolved by the third, i.e., that the judiciary would act as both the conscience and problem solver for the government, which reacted to what the judiciary said or decided with dignified respect—even if the government overturned the decisions of various courts from time to time by legislation.

This construction of the judiciary as an institution of state paved the way for regarding it as different from other bureaucracies of the state that were directly subjected to operational, day to day line management control. They were also under a positive mandate to give effect to all or any directions from the political rulers. No doubt civil servants enjoyed a great deal of autonomy in their work, and were also expected to be independent in their dealings with the local populace. In one sense, it could be argued that the judiciary was also a bureaucracy of the state in light of the positivist conception of law by, and through, which the Raj was governed, and the fact that judges were appointed by the government, had greater security of tenure than civil servants, and were basically bound by instructions issued by the government in the form of legislation, rules and notifications. But, despite all these comparisons, if the judiciary was, and is, a state bureaucracy, it is unlike any other bureaucracy of state. If seen as a bureaucracy, it is unique and has no parallel. Even if it is a bureaucracy, it is necessarily a hybrid one whose agenda is not determined by the government but by social, economic, and political forces in society which invite the judges to determine and pronounce on causes of action placed before them. The judiciary has to be visualized as more than a unique bureaucracy and seen as an institution of state. However, the 'bureaucracy thesis'[79] serves as a reminder that many judiciaries never quite acquired the status of an institution; or, having acquired it, were often in danger of losing it at the hands of an intemperate executive or unsympathetic populace.

The judges of the Supreme Court in 1950 broadly accepted the 'institution of state' model of the Raj as a working attitude towards the new independent state.[80] Judges of the Supreme Court protested, both in their judicial and extra-judicial comments, that they had never intended to upset the status quo. There are suggestions (no less in my own writing as in the writings of others) that the judiciary, by and large, upheld the welfare and regulatory legislation of the government. However, there is enough evidence to suggest that, amidst dissension among themselves, the judges made conscious efforts to flex their judicial muscles in order to secure independent recognition for the judiciary as a self-standing constitutional institution in its own right.

Apart from the land reform cases which led to a major political conflict with the government, the Supreme Court cast doubts on the 'public order–police power' of the government, set aside a large number of local government schemes which interfered with the right of local businessmen, scrutinized and struck down aspects of state control of religious endowments, and generally made it clear that it would use its newfound powers to carefully scrutinize legislation and government actions.[81] Unlike the imperial judiciary, the Indian judiciary set itself up in a position of institutional polarity to the government while making, at least, a tongue-in-cheek declaration that the government had little to fear from its much misunderstood judiciary. To the extent that individual judges had different points of view, the judges of the early court were also divided in their approach, with some of them being more keen to declare their latent power to oppose the government if the need so arose. If the events of the executive–judicial conflict of the early Nehru era admit to ambiguity, it is because the judges, when faced with a sharp attack from government, sought refuge in ambiguity.[82] Meanwhile, they continued to establish their position of institutional polarity while making sure that they did not leave too much room for criticism. If the figure of Chief Justice Gajendragadkar looms large in the 1960s, it is precisely because he stabilized relations with the government, backed off from controversy even when pushed by his colleagues to enter into it, and generally toned down the posture of the judiciary.[83]

However, in the first long reign of Mrs Gandhi even this 'institutional polarity' model was not acceptable to the government, which wanted a judiciary which at best was an institution of state (in the British sense), and at worst, receptive to the demands of the regime in power.[84] Pushed into defending their pitch, it is well known that the Court made a series of decisions on newsprint, bank nationalization, pricey privy purses, and the inviolability of the basic structure of the Constitution that led to a fresh crisis of tension between the judges and the executive, retaliatory action by the latter, and an abandonment by the judges of the 'weak' institutional polarity model floated as a compromise in the 1960s. But, if in Nehru's era the judiciary was placed on the defensive, in the early 1970s there was a marked support for it that was partly political and partly the expression of discontent with the overtly majoritarian, arbitrary and increasingly personalized rule of Mrs Gandhi. She knew that she could not appoint pliant regime judges who simply did what she or her regime in power asked them to do. If anything, the 'institutional polarity' model had come to stay, and was further entrenched by some measure of social and political support. All these gains were squandered during the Emergency when the Supreme Court was accused of becoming not just an 'institution of state' but a 'regime' judiciary—a charge exacerbated by a distinguished Supreme Court judge dispatching an injudicious, vastly overwritten paean in the form of a letter to Mrs Gandhi on her return to power in 1980.[85]

The immediate post-Emergency phase of the judiciary turned out to be a dramatic social double promotion for the judiciary. Not only did it recover from its all-time low as a regime judiciary and restore its position in constitutional polarity to the government, it slowly worked its way into becoming an institution of governance. Such an institution is one that arrogates wide powers and responsibilities to itself to achieve the public good, has a direct rapport with the people, and acts with a self-assured sense of autonomy to achieve the purposes for which it claims to be ordained. There are several complex reasons for this further evolution in the Indian judiciary. Even during the Emergency, various high courts had in fact adopted a constitutional stance against the government on issues of censorship and detention; and at least one Supreme Court judge had dissented in the infamous detention case for which the Supreme Court is criticized. More significantly, even as the successor Janata government crumbled and the middle classes became aware that the judiciary was not just a backstop but a corrective institution of last resort, faith in the judiciary was consistent with the growing tendency on the part of privileged litigants to rush to the courts. This is self evident from the fact that the filing of anti-government cases had increased steadily since 1950.[86] The 'law and development' model of progress had brought nothing but grief to everybody. The middle classes groaned against excessive regulation and the poor were constantly aware that welfare schemes and resources designated for them had been hijacked by politicians. But it is to the credit of the astuteness of Justice Krishna Iyer—and Justices Bhagwati, Desai and Chinnappa Reddy with support from others including Chief Justice Chandrachud and, later on, Justice Venkataramiah—that in the short time available to him before his retirement in 1980 he masterminded a judicial policy that made two significant, enduring moves towards establishing the judiciary as an institution of governance.[87] The first of these was to invite ordinary people—which in effect meant social activists—to locate their causes before the Supreme Court, and to devise a new procedure to deal with such causes. The public interest law movement was directed to establish a direct link with India's discontented elements and give them a voice in governance of a kind they had never had before. The simultaneous second step was to make social justice the essential goal of the Constitution, making the judiciary the custodians of social justice with a positive obligation to ensure that it was achieved. Lawyers, activists and press persons took on this invitation with a zest paralleled only by their memories of arrogant exclusion from governance by virtually all political regimes in power. All of a sudden, a new institution of governance was born, replete with its own support and with a high-profile capacity to order the direction of governance.

But, as the public interest law advanced tendentiously into a position of autonomous strength and institutional self-sufficiency, the Court itself began to have doubts.[88] By training, judges were unaccustomed to deviating too sharply from a combination of the 'institution of state' and 'institutional polarity' models described above. Apart from America, the judiciaries of the rest of the Commonwealth had been forbearing, with the English judiciary in a state of perpetual caution that judges not stray into areas that they felt were 'judicially unmanageable'. This was another way of re-stating the political question doctrine which was a symbolic, but otherwise meaningless, statement by the judiciary that it would not enter the political domain except for limited constitutional reasons. In fact, the judiciary of the 1990s beat a hasty retreat; and, while accepting the broad tour de force of the new public interest law, returned to the practices of the 1960s whereby judges monitored official action for illegality, unreasonableness and procedural lapses, but saw themselves as self-restrained and cautious interlopers on issues of governance. In this incarnation, the judiciary was, more or less, an overseer of the rule of law, a problem-solver when issues became too hot politically, and a facilitator when the government defaulted from fulfilling its duties.

This retreat is self-evident in the new labour and landlord–tenant jurisprudence of the Supreme Court, and in the Supreme Court's problem-solving decisions in the *Affirmative Action, President's Rule*, and *Babri Masjid* cases.[89] However, this cosy retreat had to be cut off by insistent circumstances that the judges could not ignore. To begin with, it soon became clear that Indian governance was riddled with corruption and human rights atrocities on a disturbingly excessive scale. The second and parallel concern was that corruption and atrocities were not just eating into the foundations of the rule of law, but eroding India's infrastructure of natural, ecological, human and administrative resources to levels from which there could conceivably be no reprieve.[90] Governance had failed. The Supreme Court stepped in with a dramatic revival of public interest law in areas concerned with the environment, corruption, and the failure to take appropriate action regarding human rights atrocities. With notable exceptions, there was less concern about the social justice issues that had animated the Court's prominence after the Emergency. By the mid-1990s, an essentially conservative Supreme Court found itself at the centre of issues relating to governance. Instead of braving the storm the judges publicly went on the defensive. Prompted by their conservatism, they declared their reluctance to be directly involved in running the country. Faced with a situation in which systems of governance hovered on the edge of ruin, they rushed in to do their bit. The architect of a soft version of this policy was Chief Justice Venkatachaliah, with judges like Justice Kuldip Singh venturing forth into prominence with aggressive passion about the judicial role.[91] Chief Justice Ahmadi did not resolve these dilemmas; but Chief Justice Verma, who had generally been cautious about moving too fast on matters of judicial review, took on the mantle of supervising criminal investigations into corruption and entering into many areas where natural and other resources were being depleted. But he somewhat uncharitably chastised 'activists' rather than their transgressors for spoiling the public interest law movement. He devised new procedures that shut out many voices that had earlier graced and given strength to the cause of the judiciary as an institution of governance.[92] Given the present membership of the Supreme Court, this plausibly contradictory stance of juristic conservatism and high-profile intervention will continue as India drifts towards the end of millennium.

Having stormed into prominence on the strength of the public interest law movement, the Supreme Court and high courts seemed to overlook the fact that the important transitions made by the Indian judiciary (from being an institution of state, to being in institutional polarity to the other organs of state, and then an institution of governance in its own right) was rendered possible because of the large measure of support it had received from lawyers, the media and various interests in society. The judiciary would be making a fatal mistake if it took the view that it is already larger than the social forces that sustain its claims to prominence.

It is not necessary for the judiciary to evolve a populist juristic agenda in order to retain support from the constituencies that support it.[93] But the new juristic tradition of the later 1970s and early 1980s evolved a new jurisprudence based on more rigorous concepts of substantive equality and distributive justice. In the words of a distinguished judge: 'In the inevitable chemistry of social change judges [can] certainly [not afford to be seen as] . . . anti-catalysts.'[94] This vision seems to have been abandoned by the judiciary of the 1990s. Although it has been profiled as judicially activist because of its orders in various cases concerning important political personages, its juristic activism is actually in relative decline.[95] Adding to this decline is the markedly idiosyncratic behaviour of individual judges at the cost of cohesive institutional development. Charges of corruption compound these tendencies in a structure in which judges of the higher judiciary cannot be called to book except by the complex and unreliable process of impeachment.[96]

In sum, the judiciary has made important transitions from being an institution of state, to being an institution in constitutional polarity to the government, to an institution of governance in its own right. These transitions have been uneven, but significant. Judges have not always handled the media, the public or even the lawyering community, well. At times, they have played to the gallery; at others, directly to the tune of the party in power. Some have been the epitome of courtesy, others have been rude and acerbic. Faced with declining standards, the abrasive shortsightedness of the judiciary in dealing with lawyers, litigants and the public may put some of its unparalleled achievements in jeopardy.

V

In the course of the many controversies that have plagued the judiciary in India, one of the deeper and more reasoned charges against it has been that it is essentially an élitist and anti-democratic institution. It places too many important decisions in the hands of a few men and women in black robes who have been arbitrarily appointed and given security of tenure, and who are accountable to no one for their decisions. Such a charge is not peculiar to the Indian judiciary, and is invariably met with the counter-argument that judges are answerable to the 'law', and that day-to-day accountability to others for decision-making subverts the very nature of the judicial function.[97]

The claim that judges are accountable to the law ineluctably draws us into controversies about the meaning of law. In both simple and sophisticated versions of the positivistic conception, 'law' is derived by institutional processes external to the judges who accept socially and politically evolved criteria to distinguish between 'social' and 'legal' norms. Leaving aside the fact that judges are also party to determining what these criteria should be—a fact highlighted in the various 'revolution' cases from Rhodesia, Pakistan and elsewhere[98]—there are some grounds for judges to make the claim that the 'law' they consider and are obliged to follow is not created by them, but by social forces external to them. A similar argument is made in respect of 'value-based' statements that portray 'law' as a normative expression of justice. This, it is claimed, is 'Law's Empire'[99]—fashioned from principles that are external to the judges who, in turn, give weight and dimension to these principles and interpret and apply them to particular cases.

In earlier writing, I have tried to explicate the consequences that flow from these arguments by making a distinction between 'primary' and 'secondary' accountability.[100] The need for primary accountability inheres in a person or institution when the decision or decisions in respect of which accountability is sought can be directly or primarily attributed to that person or institution. Thus, it can be said that legislatures (whether elected or otherwise) are primarily responsible for the laws created by them. Using this positivistic conception of 'law', it can be argued with some conviction that in a democratic society legislatures are primarily accountable to the people for the creation of any law. To this extent, judges can—and, in the black-letter law tradition or even otherwise, do—claim to be only secondarily accountable because they claim to do no more than 'interpret' and 'apply' the law. To the extent possible, judges immunize themselves from moral stress by claiming to accept the validity of even immoral and unjust laws. In such a state of affairs, in the words of one of the most distinguished legal philosophers of this century, H.L.A. Hart: 'The society in which this was so might be deplorably sheep like; the sheep might end in the slaughter-house; but there [would be]. . . little reason for thinking that it could not exist or for denying it the title of a legal system.'[101]

Unfortunately, too broad a judicial claim of secondary accountability wears thin because judges are responsible for determining what the criteria for identifying 'law' should be. More significantly, even though 'modern law' places judges in a position of claiming secondary accountability by virtue of being mere interpreters within interstitial parameters, legal professionals know that in any mature system it is the statutory 'law' that yields to the body of judicial or juristic doctrine by which the law is sought to be interpreted, rather than the other way round. Even as interpreters of it, judges create law. Pretending not to do so is a useful political myth and legal fiction by which the balance of power between the executive and judiciary is maintained and justified.[102] Thus, although greatly constrained in modern times (and much more so in constitutional systems with bills of rights), judges are primarily accountable for their decision-making and cannot be permitted to hide behind claims of secondary accountability. This is especially true of judicial decision-making in post-Independence India. Judges have been malleable in their approach, attributing primary responsibility to the Constituent Assembly or the legislature, as the case may be, but invariably reworking the meaning of the Constitution and the laws to suit their judicial interpretation.

If judges are primarily accountable, how is this accountability to be discharged? Here, too, I rely on a distinction between 'structural' and 'value' accountability. Democracy reposes its faith in structural accountability by arguing that the burden of accountability is fully discharged when democratic structures ensure that decision-making is arrived at by a process which directly or systematically involves the explicit or tacit approval of, if not participation by, the people. The greater the participation and the more incisive the ability of a structure to counter complex conurbations of power in a society, the greater the democratic accountability of the system. Since democratic structures (as well as utilitarian appeals to the greatest good of the greatest number) are essentially majoritarian in nature, it is felt that decisions should not only be democratically accountable in structural terms, but also 'value' accountable, so that the ends of justice are fairly met.

These distinctions between 'structural' and 'value' accountability can perhaps be applied in critiquing and evaluating the judiciary. To the extent to which judges claim secondary accountability for law created by democratic legislatures, they can hide behind the apron of electoral democracy. But, as explained earlier, such a claim is necessarily limited in scope. The essential claim of the judges is that they are repositories of justice and social values. If they fail in discharging this responsibility, they become less an institution of governance and more an institution of state. But judges do not exactly forgo the claim of structural accountability simply because they are not, or may not be, elected. Even in structural terms, what judges can claim is that their procedures are designed so that anyone can approach them. All proceedings are usually in open court, and justification has to be provided if courts retire in camera. Judicial decision-making follows due process principles, so that decision-making is done without bias and after giving a hearing to those concerned. In some courts, non-parties are allowed to intervene. And in public interest cases, access to raise issues is given to a large number of persons who, individually and collectively, have the standing to mobilize the jurisdiction of the courts. Finally, decisions are not made arbitrarily but on the basis of detailed reasoning in justification for the decision. On this basis, it could be argued that within the broad parameters of primary and secondary accountability and structural and value accountability, the judiciary is a sufficiently accountable institution of governance.[103]

This is no less true of the Indian judiciary. Amidst a great deal of political patronage, the most crucial appointments to the higher judiciary have not been arbitrarily made by politicians, even if they have often played a significant role. Once appointed, those selected have ensured that judicial processes are fair, with public interest litigation opening the doors for a much larger number of persons to make the judiciary a forum through which accountability can be obtained from those in power. Many of these processes can be improved. Often arbitrary in approach and with more than occasional lapses, decisions of the higher judiciary in India are based on reasoned judicial decision-making. If we have given the judiciary the power to decide, we must tolerate the fact that this includes the possibility that judges may err—as long as they do not do so for perverse reasons. It is true that there is growing irresponsibility in the judiciary and allegations of corruption and intemperate behaviour by judges are on the increase. While state high courts are empowered to examine complaints against the lower judiciary, the only way—short of impeachment—of dealing with errant judges is the power of the President (in consultation with the Supreme Court) to transfer a high court judge from one state to another; or pressure by the Bar and Bench to get them to resign. Supreme Court judges cannot be transferred; like high court judges they can only be removed by impeachment. India badly needs to evolve new informal and formal mechanisms to ensure that judicial indiscipline is checked, and that there is effective examination and redress of complaints against the judiciary. The only impeachment that took place in respect of a Supreme Court judge resulted in the judicial committee, which examined the charges, finding the judge guilty; parliament acquitted him because the Congress members in parliament abstained from voting for or against the motion of impeachment.[104] Short of impeachment, high court judges have been transferred to other courts, and some have been forced to resign.[105] The entire judicial system is overloaded and there are fantastic delays. No doubt, the system needs to be overhauled; but it cannot entirely be faulted on the grounds that the judiciary as an institution is not accountable for its decision-making.

VI

This effort to essay certain intuitions about the judiciary does not admit to easy summary. Over the centuries, India's judicial system has changed along with the social and political systems. The pre-British native legal systems were jurist as opposed to judge-based, with judges playing a minor, if any, dispositive role to deal with disputes. The British system introduced in India brought in a legal system in which the judge figured strongly as the custodian of the 'law'. But, the 'law' so introduced by the British was the positive law of the state, which displaced the local legal systems with far greater vehemence than the common law system was displaced in England. Nehru's India—for that is the most apposite description of the first few years following independence—sought to use this positivist conception of law to advantage by placing a great premium on using law as an instrument for planned development. Judges were not expected to stand in the way of this 'great' social and political experiment. Analysis of the judiciary gets locked into political exchange and over-reductionist conclusions about the consequences of judicial decision-making, leading to allegations of class bias. In fact, a more exacting analysis of the judiciary is long overdue. For its part, the judiciary has made important transitions from being a mere institution of state to an institution of governance in its own right. These transitions have been complex and intricate. As a hybrid institution of state, the agenda of the judiciary is not determined by the government but by lawyers, litigants and other interested parties who approach the court; and, perforce, the judges. As Indian governance has dissolved into corruption and there is an increasing spiral of atrocities committed by the state and state officials, the judiciary has exercised greater power of review over them, adding support to its claim to be an institution of governance. Judged by simple norms of electoral democracy, the judiciary has been portrayed as élitist and anti-democratic. But if its work is evaluated against broader notions of accountability, both the judiciary in general and the Indian judiciary in particular can be seen as responsible institutions that are accountable for their work. As India meets the challenge of a billion mutinies that animate and plague its life every day, the judiciary is not just the lesser evil but a crucial ingredient of the democratic process by which India is governed.

Notes

[1] See *Vineet Narain v. Union of India*, (1998), 1 SCC 226 at pr. 51–2, when the Supreme Court claimed the power to 'fill the void in the absence of suitable legislation' and to 'provide a solution till such time as the legislature acts to perform its role by enacting proper legislation to cover the field'. For general accounts of the Supreme Court see Rajeev Dhavan, *The Supreme Court of India: A Socio-legal Critique of Its Juristic Techniques* (Bombay: N.M. Tripathi), 1977; R. Dhavan, *The Supreme Court of India and Parliamentary Sovereignty: A Critique of Its Approach to the Recent Constitutional Crisis* (New Delhi: Sterling Publishers), 1976; R. Dhavan, *Justice on Trial: The Supreme Court Today* (Allahabad: A.H. Wheeler), 1980; R. Dhavan, *The Supreme Court under Strain: The Challenge of Arrears* (Bombay: N.M. Tripathi), 1979. On the controversial post-Emergency transition, see Upendra Baxi, *The Indian Supreme Court and Politics* (Lucknow: Eastern Book Company), 1980; and U. Baxi, *Courage, Craft and Contention: The Indian Supreme Court in the Eighties* (Bombay: N.M. Tripathi), 1984. For an early account of the public interest law movement see U. Baxi, 'Taking Suffering Seriously—Social Action Litigation in the Supreme Court of India', in R. Dhavan et al. (eds) *Judges and the Judicial Power: Essays in Honour of Justice V.R. Krishna Iyer* (London: Sweet and Maxwell;

Bombay: N.M. Tripathi), 1985, pp. 289–315. For the 1980s, see R. Dhavan, 'Law as Struggle: Public Interest Law in India', *Journal of the Indian Law Institute,* 36 (1994), pp. 302–38. An estimate of the Supreme Court for the 1990s is yet to be written.

[2] A phrase used by T.T. Krishnamachari in the Constituent Assembly.

[3] Jawaharlal Nehru, Speech in Parliament: (1951) XII–XIII *Parl. Deb.* Col 8832 (16 May 1951). 'Somehow we have found that this magnificent Constitution that we have framed was later kidnapped and purloined by lawyers'.

[4] The best account of the stance of Mrs Gandhi's government is articulated through Mohan Kumaramangalam, *Judicial Appointments* (New Delhi: Oxford & IBH Publishing Co.), 1973; V.A. Seyid Mohammed, *Our Constitution for Haves or Have Nots?* (Delhi: Lipi Prakashan), 1975; cf. Nani Palkhivala, *Our Constitution Defaced and Defiled* (Delhi: Macmillan India), 1974.

[5] H.M. Seervai, *The Emergency, Future Safeguards and the Habeas Corpus Case: A Criticism* (Bombay: N.M. Tripathi), 1978, p. vii.

[6] This challenge was voiced by academics and lawyers. See D.C. Jain, 'The Phantom of Public Interest' (1986), 3 SCC (Jnl) 30–7; S.K. Agarwala, *Public Interest Litigation in India* (Bombay: N.M. Tripathi), 1985; T.R. Andhyarjuna, *Judicial Activism and Constitutional Democracy in India* (Bombay: N.M. Tripathi), 1992; and, more generally, provoking comments and proposals for legislation in Parliament. Judges themselves have been somewhat divided on the nature and scope of public interest litigation (see note 88).

[7] For a review of the various amendments, see S.P. Sathe, *Constitutional Amendments 1950–1988: Law and Politics* (Bombay, N.M. Tripathi), 1989); on the infamous Forty-second Amendment see R. Dhavan, *The Amendment: Conspiracy or Revolution?* (Allahabad: A.H. Wheeler), 1978.

[8] See, for example, Chief Justice Patanjali Shastri's speech to the Madras Bar, reported in *AIR 1955,* Journal 25.

[9] This is best exemplified by Justice P.B. Gajendragadkar (see note 83),

[10] This is shown by the progressive discomfort of the Supreme Court in accepting constitutional amendments that both reversed Court decisions and challenged constitutional limitations of judicial power. (See *Sajjan Singh v. State of Rajasthan,* AIR 1966 SC 845; *Golak Nath v. State of Punjab,* AIR 1967 SC 1643; *Kesavananda v. State of Kerala,* AIR 1973 SC 1461.) Out of these decisions evolved the 'basic structure' doctrine which limited the power to amend the Constitution to matters other than those that were part of its basic structure.

[11] *R.C. Cooper v. Union of India,* AIR 1970 SC 564.

[12] *Madhav Rao Scindia v. Union of India,* AIR 1971 SC 530.

[13] *Bennet Coleman v. Union of India,* AIR 1973 SC 106; see also *Express*

Newspapers Ltd., AIR 1958 SC 578; *Sakal Newspapers v. Union of India*, AIR 1962 SC 305; *Indian Express Newspapers (Bombay) P. Ltd. v. Union of India*, (1985) 1 SCC 641 and, more recently, *Printers (Mysore) Ltd. v. Ass.CTO*, (1994) 2 SCC 434. Further, see R. Dhavan, *Only the Good News: On the Law of the Press in India* (Delhi: Manohar Publications), 1987.

[14] *Kesavananda v. State of Kerala*, op. cit.

[15] Chief Justice Chandrachud apologized after his retirement for his decision in the Emergency detention case (*ADM Jabalpur v. S.B. Shukla*, AIR 1976 SC 1207) in May 1978.

[16] For example, Justice P.N. Bhagwati, 'Judicial Activism and Public Interest Litigation', *Columbia Journal of Transnational Law* (23) 1985, p. 561.

[17] For example, Chief Justice Ahmadi's Zakir Hussain Memorial Lecture (1996) 2 SCC (Jnl) 1–15 'Law Day Lecture' (1997) 2 SCC (Jnl) 3–6 and his Pune Speech on the judicial process reproduced at (1996) 4 SCC (Jnl) 1–10.

[18] For accounts of the Dharmashastra, see R. Lingat, *The Classical Law of India* (Berkeley: University of California Press), 1973; and P.V. Kane's monumental *History of the Dharmashastra* (Poona: Bhandarkar Oriental Research Institute), 1968 edn.

[19] 'Proof' and 'ordeals' intermix to constitute evidence. Narada's Dharmashastra deals with these aspects. See J. Jolly *Naradiya Dharmashastra: Judicial System in Ancient India* (Delhi: Takshila Handbounds), 1981 edn, as also Richard Lariviere's 'Introduction' to, and translation of, *The Divyatattva of Raghunandan Bhattacarya: Ordeals in Classical Hindu Law*, (Delhi: Manohar), 1981. More generally, see P.V. Kane, *History of the Dharmashastra* (1968 edn), vol. II, pp. 242–368.

[20] The operational and institutional location of the Dharmashastra is based on conjecture; as, indeed, the alleged schools of thought which British courts profiled for attention; see further, Ludo Rocher, 'Schools in Hindu Law', in J. Ensink and P. Gaeffke (eds.), *India Major: Congratulatory Volume Presented to J. Gonda* (Leiden: E.J. Brill), 1972.

[21] See J.D.M. Derrett : 'The Criteria for Distinguishing between Legal and Religious Commands', *AIR 1953* Journal 61.

[22] A remark made by H. Maine that incurred the wrath of Indian jurists. See especially S.S. Dhavan, 'Indian Jurisprudence and Theory of State in India' (mimeo) (Mussoorie: National Academy), 1962; see also G.W. Keeton; 'How Ancient is Indian Law', *Question* 78, (1971); cf J.D.M. Derrett, 'Sir Henry Maine in India', *Judicial Review* (1959), pp. 40–55.

[23] The formula used by the British was the Roman formula of 'justice, equity and good conscience' (JEGC) whereby judges had to obey statute, but had a discretion to apply such other customary or other laws

consistent with JEGC. On the Roman origins of this formula and its Indian application, see J.D.M. Derrett, 'Justice, Equity and Good Conscience in India' (1962) 64 Bom. LJ (Jnl) 129, 145 and J.D.M. Derrett, 'Justice, Equity and Good Conscience', in J.N.D. Anderson (ed.), *Changing Law in Developing Countries* (London: Allen and Unwin), 1963, pp. 114–53.

[24] This is not to get into academic controversies between Bentham and Blackstone, on which see J.U. Lewis 'Blackstone's Definition of Law', *Irish Jurist* 337 (1968); H.L.A. Hart, 'Blackstone's Use of the Law of Nature', *Butterworths South African Law Reporter* 169 (1955–7); K.L. Vick, 'Rebuttal of Bentham and Austin on Blackstone', (1966-7) 13 *Loyola LR* 71; J.M. Finnis, 'Blackstone's Theoretical Intentions', (1967) 12 *Nat. L.F.* 163. Had Bentham not triumphed over the Blackstonian view, Indian law would have progressed differently. See Macaulay's speech to the House of Commons, 10 July 1833 (*Hansard* 3rd edn) XIX, pp. 531–3.

[25] Benthamite influence on law reform in India is self-evident. See Eric Stokes, *The English Utilitarians and India* (Oxford: Clarendon Press), 1959.

[26] The Anglo-Indian codification of English law is regarded as a masterly restatement. See generally Whitely Stokes, *The Anglo Indian Codes: Vol. I: Substantive Law; Vol. II: Procedural Law* (Oxford: Clarendon), 1887; C. Ilbert: Indian Codification (1889) 5 LQR 347–69.

[27] The Anglo-Indian judiciary of the British Raj restated the dharmsastric law. See R. Dhavan, 'Dharmashastra and Modern Indian Society: A Preliminary Exploration', *Journal of the Indian Law Institute* 34 (1992):515–40. The same is true of Islamic and other laws.

[28] See M. Galanter, *Law and Society in Modern India* (Delhi, New York: Oxford University Press), 1989, Chapters II and III, reproducing his earlier essays, 'The Displacement of Traditional Law in Modern India' and 'The Aborted Restoration of Indigenous Law in India'.

[29] The 'basic structure' doctrine is to be found in *Kesavananda* (see note 10). This is not to advance the proposition that dharmashastric notions overrode the 'given' western law, but only to emphasize the intuition which may have animated the quest for a wider and more fundamental value-based approach to law that is not alien to western legal traditions. See R. Dhavan, 'Juristic Enthrology of Kesavananda's Case', *Journal of the Indian Law Institute* 19 (1977), pp. 489 and R. Dhavan, 'The Basic Structure Doctrine: A Footnote Comment', in R. Dhavan et al. (eds), *The Indian Constitution: Trends and Issues* (Bombay: N.M. Tripathi), 1978, pp. 160–78.

[30] English abuses of the processes of law are well known. Apart from Clive's statement to the House of Commons that he was 'astonished' at

his 'moderation' in pillaging the riches of the Empire, the impeachment of Warren Hasting was, inter alia, over manipulations in legal proceedings. See Anindita Mukhopadhyay, 'Rule of Law' in Shiv Vishwanathan and Harsh Sethi (eds), *Foul Play: Chronicles of Corruption* (New Delhi: Banyan Books) 1998, pp. 291–316. The most celebrated of these cases is the trial of Raja Nand Kumar. See J.F. Stephen, *The Story of Nuncoonar and the Impeachment of Sir Elijah Impey* (London), 1885; cf. J.D.M. Derrett, 'Nand Kumar's Forgery', *English Historical Review,* (1980), pp. 223–38, and M.P. Jain, *Outlines of Indian Legal History* (Bombay: N.M. Tripathi), 1972, pp. 105–65.

[31] C.E. Grey, *Appendix to the Report on the Affairs of the East Indies* (London: Parliamentary Papers), 1862. p. 75.

[32] Despatch No. 44, prs. 55–6. quoted in M.P. Jain (see note 30), p. 406:

[33] On British uses of the 'Justice, Equity and Good Conscience' formula, see note 23.

[34] For a review of the nature of state immunity, see *Kasturi Lal v. State of U.P.*, AIR 1965 SC 1039 and *Vidyawati v. State of Rajasthan*, AIR 1962 SC 933, and the long line of cases cited there tracing the origins of these decisions to nineteenth-century precedents.

[35] The Privy Council restricted the judicial review powers of the Presidency high Courts. See further, R. Dhavan, 'On the Future of Western Law in India: Reflection on the Post-Emergency Supreme Court', *Journal of the Bar Council of India* 8 (1981), pp. 61–86, on the absence of the tradition of judicial review.

[36] The Rankin Committee Report on *Civil Justice* (Government of India), 1925. The crisis of the work load caused by arrears in pending cases remains a continuing problem in courts; it has been examined by various commissions such as the (S.R. Das) Committee on Arrears in High Courts (1948); (J.C. Shah) *Report of the High Court Arrears Committee* (1972). The Law Commission has also written many reports on judicial administration, including Report No. 14: *Reforms on Judicial Administration* (1958); Report No. 44: *Appellate Jurisdiction of the Supreme Court in Civil Matters* (1971); Report No. 45: *Civil Appeals to the Supreme Court on a Certificate of Fitness* (1971); Report No. 58: *Structure and Jurisdiction of the Higher Judiciary* (1974); Report No. 77: *Delay and Arrears in Trial Courts* (1978); Report No. 79: *Delay and Arrears in Appellate Courts* (1979); Report No. 95: *Constitutional Division within the Supreme Court: A Proposal* (1984); Report No. 99: *Oral and Written Arguments in the Higher Courts* (1984); Report No. 100: *Litigation By and Against the Government: Some Recommendations for Reforms* (1984); Report No. 114: *Gram Nayayalaya* (1986); Report No. 115: *Tax Courts* (1986); Report No. 116: *Formation of an All India Judicial Service* (1986); Report No. 117: *Training of Judicial Officers* (1986); Report

No. 118: *Method of Appointment to Subordinate Courts/Subordinate Judiciary* (1986); Report No. 119: *Access to Exclusive Forum for Victims of Motor Accidents under Motor Vehicles Act, 1939* (1986); Report No. 120: *Manpower Planning in Judiciary: A Blueprint* (1986); Report No. 121: *A New Forum for Judicial Appointments* (1987); Report No. 122: *Forum for National Uniformity in Labour Adjudication* (1987); Report No. 123: *Decentralisation of Administration of Justice: Disputes Involving Centres of Higher Education* (1988); Report No. 124: *The High Court Arrears—A Fresh Look* (1988); Report No. 125: *The Supreme Court—A Fresh Look* (1988); Report No. 126: *Government and Public Sector Litigation—Policy and Strategies* (1988); Report No. 127: *Resource Allocation for Infrastructural Services in Judicial Administration (A Continuum of the Report on Manpower Planning in Judiciary: A Blueprint)* (1988); Report No. 129: *Urban Litigation—Mediation as Alternative to Adjudication* (1988); Report No. 130: *Benami Transactions—A Continuum* (1988); Report No. 131: *Role of the Legal Profession in Administration of Justice* (1988); Report No. 136: *Conflict in High Court Decision on Central Laws—How to Foreclose and How to Resolve* (1991); Report No. 137: *Need for Creating Office of Ombudsman and for Evolving Legislative and Administrative Measures, inter alia to Relieve Hardships Caused by Inordinate Delays in Settling Provident Fund Claims of Beneficiaries* (1990); Report No. 144: *Conflicting Judicial Decisions Pertaining to the Code of Civil Procedure* (1908); Report No. 151: *Admiralty Jurisdiction.*

[37] Gandhi's statement is reported in *The Hindustan Times*, 7 August 1926. I am grateful to George Gadbois Jr. for this reference; see his 'Evolution of the Federal Court in India' in *Journal of the Indian Law Institute* 5 (1963), pp. 19–26.

[38] See 'Constitution of India Bill 1895', in B. Shiva Rao (ed.), *The Framing of India's Constitution: Study* (Delhi: Indian Institute of Public Administration), vol. I (1966–8), pp. 5–14. Note also the 'Commonwealth of India Bill, 1925', in B. Shiva Rao (*supra*) I, pp. 43–50.

[39] See *The Nehru Report* (1928) in B. Shiva Rao, op. cit., vol. I, pp. 58–75.

[40] On the federal court, see George Gadbois, 'Evolution of the Federal Court of India', op. cit., 'The Federal Court of India: 1937–1950' *Journal of the Indian Law Institute*, 6 (1964), M.V. Pylee, *The Federal Court of India* (Bombay: Manaktalas), 1966.

[41] 'Report of the Ad Hoc Committee on the Supreme Court', in B. Shiva Rao, op. cit., vol. II, pp. 587–91, written by S. Varadachariar, A.K. Ayyar, B.L. Mittal, K.M. Munshi, B.N. Ramu.

[42] For the discussion on the Bill of Rights, see B. Shiva Rao, *Study Volume* (see note 38), pp. 170–318; Granville Austin: *The Indian Constitution: Cornerstone of a Nation* (Oxford: Clarendon), 1966, pp. 50–115. For a

full account of how the Assembly dealt with the Bill of Rights, see R. Dhavan: *Tidy Intuitions, Untidy Discourse: Conversations and Exchanges on Human Rights Discourse in the Constituent Assembly* (1983) PILSARC Working Paper No. 20—forthcoming as a separate publication.

[43] 'Memorandum Representing the View of the Federal Court and of the Chief Justices of all the Provincial High Courts of the Union of India', (March, 1948) in B. Shiva Rao, op. cit., vol. IV, pp. 193–204 at 194.

[44] See B.N. Rau, 'Notes on Fundamental Rights—2 Sept. 1946', in B. Shiva Rao op. cit., pp. 21–38. See generally B.N. Rau's *India's Constitution in the Making* (Calcutta: Orient Longman), 1960.

[45] See Arthur Selwyn Miller, *The Supreme Court and American Capitalism* (New York: Free Press), 1968. It cannot be overlooked that the 16th Amendment to the American Constitution became necessary because the Supreme Court declared income tax unconstitutional, in *Pollock v. Farmers Loan & Trust Co.* (1895) 157 U.S. 129; 158 U.S. 601.

[46] For example, A.K. Ayyar's letter to B.N. Rau, 4 April 1947 (B. Shiva Rao, op. cit., pp. 143–6), and the concern of the advisory committee (ibid., 264–7).

[47] Although a due process clause was introduced in an earlier Draft (see B. Shiva Rao, op. cit., vol. II, pp. 22–3, 122, 143–4, 240–4, 284–6; vol. III *Constituent Assembly Debates (CAD)* 468), it was abandoned after a short debate (see VII *CAD*, pp. 842–57, 6 December 1948); pp. 999–1001 (13 December 1948)).

[48] For the various discussions in the Constituent Assembly, see R. Dhavan's *Justice on Trial: The Supreme Court Today*, op. cit. pp. 27–50. The present position is summed up in the Judges' cases (see *Supreme Court Advocates-on-Record Association v. Union of India* (1993) 4 SCC 441 modifying the earlier pro-executive stance in *S.P. Gupta v. Union of India* (1981) Supp. SCC 87 so that after 1993 the judges—in fact, the Chief Justice of India—have the more decisive say. This view has now been reversed, to give a decisive say to a collegium of the five senior most judges of the court. (See special Reference No. 1 of 1998 5 *Scale* 629.

[49] Jawaharlal Nehru, Speech in Constituent Assembly (1948) VIII *CAD* 247.

[50] See R. Dhavan, *Contempt of Court and the Press* (Bombay: N.M. Tripathi), 1980, pp. 28–36.

[51] E.P. Thompson, *Whigs and Hunters: The Origin of the Black Act* (New York: Pantheon). Cf. R. Johnson, 'Thompson, Genovese and Socialist Human History', *History Workshop*, 6 (1978) p. 79; see also T. Campbell, *The Left and Rights: A Conceptual Analysis of the Idea of Socialist Rights* (London, Boston: Routledge and Kegan Paul), 1983.

[52] See generally M. Zander, *A Bill of Rights* (London: Sweet and Max-

well), 1985 3rd edn.; S.H. Bailey et al., *Civil Liberties: Cases and Materials* (London: Lexis Law Publishing), 1995, pp. 1–26 and the extensive materials cited there.

[53] The term 'planning commission' model of law and development is taken from R. Dhavan (note 60); and R. Dhavan 'Introduction' to Marc Galanter's *Law and Society in Modern India* (Delhi, New York: Oxford University Press), 1989, pp. xii–xxxii.

[54] For the earlier strict interpretation, see R. Dhavan, *The Supreme Court of India,* op. cit., 1977, pp. 69–95.

[55] See J.K. Mittal, 'Nehru and the Objectives Resolution', in R. Dhavan (ed.), *Nehru and the Constitution* (Bombay: N.M. Tripathi), 1992, pp. 22–44.

[56] The Karachi Resolution (1931) finally found voice in the Objectives Resolution (which Nehru piloted with some difficulty in the Constituent Assembly) which eventually became the Preamble to the Constitution. On this development, see R. Dhavan, 'Introduction', in R. Dhavan (ed.), *Nehru and the Constitution,* op. cit., pp. xix–xxv.

[57] Although the jurisprudence of the courts has given a much more accommodating status to the Directive Principles after *Kesavananda's* case (see note 10), the importance of socio-economic rights has not been firmly established (see further, R. Dhavan, 'Ambedkar's Prophecy: Poverty of Human Rights in India', *Journal of the Indian Law Institute*), 36(1994), pp. 8–36 even though the public interest law movement has absorbed their significance in its agenda (see R. Dhavan: 'Law as Struggle: Public Interest Law in India', op. cit.)

[58] For a review of literature, see R. Dhavan: 'Law as Concern: Reflecting on Law and Development', in Yash Vyas, et al. (eds), *Law and Development in the Third World* (Nairobi: University of Nairobi), 1994, pp. 25–50; E.M. Burg, 'Law and Development: A Review of the Literature and a Critique of 'Scholars in Self-estrangement',' (1977) 25 *A.J.C.L.* 492; F. Snyder, 'Law and Development in the Light of Dependency Theory' (1980) 14 *Law and Society Review* 723. In the Indian context, see also R. Dhavan, 'Borrowed Ideas: On the Impact of American Scholarship on Indian Law', (1985) 33 *A.J.C.L.* 505.

[59] The famous 'self-estrangement amongst American scholars' controversy can be found in D. Trubek and M. Galanter, 'Scholars in Self-estrangement: Some Reflection on the Crisis in Law and Development Studies in the United States', (1974) Wis. L.R. 1062; R. Seidman, 'The Lessons of Self-estrangement: On the Methodology of Law and Development' (1978) *Research in Law and Sociology* 1; Trubek and Galanter's reply, 'Scholars in the Fun House: A Reply to Professor Seidman', (1978) 1 *Research in Law and Sociology* 31.

[60] This catalogue is an improved version of an earlier statement in a lecture to the Faculty of Law at Jammu University entitled, 'If I Contra-

dict Myself, Well then I Contradict Myself. . .: Nehru, Law and Social Change', reproduced in R. Dhavan (ed.), *Nehru and the Constitution*, op. cit., pp. 45–62.

[61] Third Uttar Pradesh Lawyers' Conference 1947, Kanpur, High Court Administration File III Resolution 4. I am indebted to Dr Gillian Buckee for this reference.

[62] See note 43.

[63] See R. Dhavan, *The Supreme Court of India*, op. cit., pp. 1–13, for examples of these protests.

[64] The 'any process' approach was affirmed by the Supreme Court in 1950 (see *Gopalan v. State of Madras*, AIR 1950 SC 27—note the dissent of Fazl Ali J); but abandoned for wider approval in R.C. Cooper (see note 11) and Maneka Gandhi's case (AIR 1978 SC 597). For discussions in the Constituent Assembly, see note 47.

[65] The judicial assertion of constitutionalism was subdued but implicit in the first Nehru phase—see M.C. Setalvad's masterly review of this period, *The Indian Constitution 1950–65* (Bombay: University of Bombay), 1966, after which it acquired more confidence to create the basic structure doctrine to curtail Parliament's power to amend the Constitution. (On the 'basic structure' cases, see note 10). For the judicial struggle of Indian judges to find their Indianness, see generally R. Dhavan, *Supreme Court of India*, op. cit.

[66] This upsurge of using the judiciary to make governance accountable under court supervision, is new. A good example of this trend is *Vineet Narain's* case (see note 1).

[67] See note 10.

[68] See *E.M.S. Namboodiripad v. T.N. Nambiar*, AIR 1970 SC 2015; and more generally R. Dhavan, *Contempt of Court and the Press*, op. cit.

[69] For the discussions in parliament, see Lok Sabha Debates *Vth Series* Part XXVII No. 46 Col. 311–402 (2 May 1973); ibid. No. 45 col.136–157 (26 April 1973); ibid. No. 48 Col. 228–32. Note: M. Kumaramanglam (ed.), *Judicial Appointments* (New Delhi: Oxford & IBH Publishing Co.), 1973 or N. Palkhivala (ed.), *A Judiciary Made to Measure: A Collection of the Nationwide Protests against the Supercession of Justices Shelat, Hegde and Grover for the Office of the Chief Justice of India* (Bombay: M.R. Pai), 1973; Kuldip Nayar (ed.), *Supercession of Judges* (New Delhi: Indian Book Co.), 1973.

[70] For an account of this early period, see Upendra Baxi, 'Taking Suffering Seriously. . . .' (see note 1); R. Dhavan, 'Law as Struggle' op. cit.

[71] The class bias of the judiciary was the subject of litigation in 1970 (*supra* note 68). Many of the pro-poor and pro-worker gains of the public interest law movement of the 1980s were lost in the 1990s.

[72] For earlier portraits of the Supreme Court, see G. Gadbois, 'Indian

Supreme Court Judges: A Portrait', (1968) 3 *Law and Society Review* pp. 317–66; R. Dhavan. *The Supreme Court of India,* op. cit., pp. 19–31; R. Dhavan, *Justice on Trial,* op. cit., pp. 27–81.

[73] R. Dhavan, *The Supreme Court of India,* op. cit., p. 961; see also generally Gobind Das, *The Supreme Court in Quest of Identity* (Lucknow: Eatern Book Company), 1987.

[74] For such an instrumental analysis, see J.A.G. Griffiths, *The Politics of the Judiciary* (Manchester: Manchester University Press and Atlantic Highlands, NJ: Humanities Press), 1977; Morton Horwitz, *The Transformation of American Law, 1780–1860* (Cambridge: Harvard University Press), 1977. For a critical review of such reductionist approaches, see D. Sugarman's, review of Horwitz's book in *British Journal of Law and Society* (1980).

[75] This is a weakness in U. Baxi's post-Emergency tour de force (see his *The Indian Supreme Court and Politics,* op. cit.

[76] There is a vast literature on 'symbolic' and 'instrumental' aspects of legislation (see Gusfied, 'Moral Passage: The Symbolic Process in Public Designations of Deviance', *Social Problems,* 15 (1967), p. 175 and W.S. Carson, 'Symbolic and Instrumental Dimensions of Early Factory Legislation', in Roger Hood (ed.), *Crime, Criminology and Public Policy: Essays in Honour of Sir Leon Radzinowicz* (New York: Free Press), 1975. Such legislation is extant in India, especially in areas of socio-economic reform.

[77] Cf. U. Baxi, *The Indian Supreme Court and Politics,* op. cit., G. Gadbois, 'The Supreme Court of India as a Political Institution', in R. Dhavan et al. (eds), *Judges and the Judicial Power,* op. cit., pp. 251–67.

[78] As 'colonial' British governance became more 'imperial', the use and understanding of 'law' and 'legal' institutions also became more sophisticated. See D.A. Washbrook, 'Law, State and Agrarian Society in Colonial India', *Modern Asian Studies,* 15 (1981), pp. 649–72. For an assessment of juristic developments, see J.D.M. Derrett, 'Legal Science in India during the Last Century', in M. Rotondi (ed.), *Inchieste di Dirrito Comparato* (Padua), 1976 edn, pp. 413–35.

[79] See R. Dhavan, 'Judicial Decision-Making' (mimeo., lectures to the Faculty of Law, University of Delhi). 1979.

[80] This can be seen in the acceptance of 'any process' as approved to a due process clause (see notes 47 and 64); as also in the initial subordination of Directive Principles (see note 54).

[81] For example, on the limited interpretation of security of state, see *Romesh Thapar v. State of Madras,* AIR 1950 SC 124; *Brij Bhushan v. State of Delhi,* AIR 1950 SC 129. On the various local business cases, note *Rashid Ahmed v. Municipal Board, Kairama,* AIR 1950 SC 163; *Chintamani Rao v. State of MP,* AIR 1951 SC 118; *Mohd. Yasin v. Town Area Committee,* AIR 1952 SC 115; *Dwarka Das v. State of U.P.,* AIR 1954 SC 224.

[82] Note Chief Justice (Punjab), Sastri's speech (see note 8).

[83] On Justice Gajendragadkar, see his autobiography *To the Best of My Memory* (Bombay: Bharatiya Vidya Bhavan), 1983; Vidya Dhar Mahajan, *Chief Justice Gajendragadkar: His Life, Ideas, Papers and Addresses* (Delhi: S. Chand), 1966; S.N. Dhayani: 'Justice Gajendragadkar and Labour Law' *Jaipur Law Journal*, 7 (1969), pp. 69; P.K. Tripathi, 'Mr. Justice Gajendragadkar and Constitutional Interpretation', *Journal of the Indian Law Institute*, 8 (1966), pp. 419.

[84] Note N.A. Palkhivala's *Our Constitution Defaced and Defiled*, op. cit., and *A Judiciary Made to Measure*, op. cit.

[85] Justice P.N. Bhagwati, a sitting judge, wrote a letter congratulating Mrs Gandhi on her election to office; see further R. Dhavan, 'On the Future of Western Law in India: Justice Bhagwati's Letter to the Prime Minister', (mimeo.) 1980.

[86] See R. Dhavan, *The Supreme Court under Strain,* op. cit., which gives statistical data that was updated in R. Dhavan, *Litigation Explosion in India* (Bombay: N.M. Tripathi), 1986.

[87] Apart from his own voluminous writing, a lot has been written on Justice Krishna Iyer; see especially Hari Swarup, *For Whom the Law is Made* (Delhi: Veenu Publishers); K.M. Sharma, 'The Judicial Universe of Mr. Justice Krishna Iyer', in R. Dhavan, et al. (eds), *Judges and the Judicial Power: Essays in Honour of Justice V.R. Krishna Iyer,* op. cit., pp. 316–36. On Justice Bhagwati, see Mool Chand Sharma, *Justice P.N. Bhagwati: Court, Constitution and Human Rights* (Delhi: Universal Book Traders), 1995; and Sheeraz Latif A. Khan, *Justice Bhagwati on Fundamental Rights and Directive Principles* (Delhi: Deep & Deep Publications), 1996. On Justice O. Chinnappa Reddy, see R. Venkataramani *Judgments of O. Chinnappa Reddy—A Humanist Judge* (Delhi: International Institute of Human Rights), 1989. On Justice Y.V. Chandrachud, see V.S. Deshpande, *A Chandrachud Reader* (New Delhi: Documentation Centre for Corporate & Business Policy Research), 1985. Comprehensive accounts of the contributions of various judges and, with notable exceptions, even of the Supreme Court of India are conspicuous by their absence.

[88] For example, see Pathak J. in *Bandhua Mukti Morcha v. Union of India*, AIR 1984 SC 802; Khalid J. in *Sachidanand Pandey v. State of West Bengal*, (1987) 2 SCC 295; Venkatachaliah J. in *Sheela Barse v. Union of India*, (1988) 4 SCC 226; Mukerjea J. in *Chettria Pradushan Mukti Sangarsh v. State of U.P.*, AIR 1990 SC 2060; K.N. Singh J. in *Subhash Kumar v. State of Bihar*, AIR 1991 SC 420.

[89] *Indra Sawhney v. Union of India*, (1992) *Supp.* 3 SCC 217 (on affirmative action); *S.R. Bommai v. Union of India*, (1994) 3 SCC 1 (on President's Rule); *M. Ishmail Faruqui v. Union of India*, (1994) 6 SCC

300 (on Babri masjid). More generally on this problem-solving approach, see R. Dhavan, 'The Supreme Court as Problem Solver', in V.A. Pai Panandikar, *The Politics of Backwardness* (Delhi: Konark Publishers), 1997, pp. 262–332.

[90] Apart from investigating into corruption cases (e.g., *Vineet Narain* see note 1), the environment cases are significant (in particular *Vellore Citizen's Welfare Forum* (1996) 5 *SCC* 647 (on the precautionary principle); *Indian Council for Enviro-Legal Action v. Union of India* (1996) 5 SCC 281 (on the non-toleration of infringement); *M.C. Mehta v. Kamal Nath*, (1997) 1 SCC 388 (on the concept of public trust); and many others including cases on pollution in Delhi (*M.C. Mehta v. Union of India*, (1996) 4 SCC 351 and (1996) 4 SCC 750); and on the Taj Trapezium (*M.C. Mehta v. Union of India*, (1997) 1 Scale 61) among others.

[91] Justice Kuldip Singh is associated with 'environment' cases (see note 90) and for imposing exemplary damages on allegedly corrupt ministers (*Common Cause v. Union of India*, (1996) 6 SCC 530, Rs 50 lakh damages); (*Shiv Sagar Tewari v. Union of India*, (1996) 6 SCC 558; also (1997) 1 SCC 444, Rs 60 lakh damages).

[92] Justice Verma devised a procedure whereby all public-interest parties had to speak through the court appointed *amicus curiae*, who were not always sensitive to consultation.

[93] Cf. U. Baxi, *The Indian Supreme Court and Politics,* op. cit.

[94] A phrase taken from Justice Krishna Iyer in *Kunhu Mohammed v. T.K. Ummayithi* (1969) LR 629; see also Dhavan J. in *Basai v. Hasan Raza Khan*, AIR 1963 All 340.

[95] Much has come to depend on the personality of the judge. A writ petition on the scope of public interest litigation awaits determination by the Court (see *Sudipt Majumdar v. State of MP*, (1983) 2 SCC 258) 96.

[96] Judicial corruption is on the increase. In one case concerning a Supreme Court judge, the Tribunal affirmed charges against Justice V. Ramaswami, but impeachment was averted by parliament. Corrupt high court judges have been transferred. A controversy resulting virtually in a newspaper trial was started against the appointment of Justice Punchhi as Chief Justice of India (see R. Dhavan, 'Enough is Enough', *The Hindu* 3 October 1997; and 'Trial by Newspaper', *The Hindu*, 19 December 1997; and J.R. Jai (ed.), *Assault on Judiciary* (Delhi: Associated Legal Advisers, 1997). There is a need for proper mechanisms to investigate the judiciary (see R. Dhavan, 'Removing Judges: The Quest for Fair Solutions', *Indian Bar Review*, vol. 17 (1991), pp. 42–57.

[97] On various forms of accountability, see R. Dhavan, 'Judges and Accountability', in R. Dhavan et al. (eds), *Judges and the Judicial Power,* op. cit., pp. 165–82.

[98] The famous 'grundnorm' cases are from Pakistan (*State v. Dosso* PLD, 1958 SC 533; *Asma Jilani v. Government of Punjab*, PLD 1972 SC 139); Rhodesia (*Madzimbamuto v. Lardner Burke*, (1969) AC 645); Ghana (*Sallah v. Att. Gen.* (1970) ref. in 20 ICLQ 315); and Nigeria (*Laknami v. Western State*, (1970), noted in 20 ICLQ 177). For an interesting analysis see J.W. Harris, 'When and Why Does the Grundnorm Change', *Cambridge Law Journal* 103 (1971); and for an incisive analysis of the Pakistan cases, see Paula R. Newburg, *Judging the State: Courts and Constitutional Politics in Pakistan,* (Cambridge and New York: Cambridge University Press), 1995.

[99] A phrase taken from the title of a book by R. Dworkin, *Law's Empire* (Cambridge: Belknap Press of Harvard University Press), 1986.

[100] This analysis is taken from R. Dhavan (see note 27).

[101] H.L.A. Hart, *The Concept of Law* (Oxford: Clarendon), 1961, p. 114.

[102] For Indian and English antics on this subject, see G.P. Singh, *Principles of Statutory Interpretation* (Nagpur: Wadhwa), 1996, 6th edn, pp. 8–20, 47–49.

[103] See R. Dhavan (note 97).

[104] This is the case of Justice V. Ramaswami. For the report of the impeachment Committee, see *Report of the Inquiry Committee in Regard to the Investigation and Proof of the Misbehaviour Alleged against Justice V. Ramaswami, Judge, Supreme Court* (New Delhi: Government of India), 1992, two volumes. For the debate in Parliament on 10–11 May 1993, see Vol. 22 *Lok Sabha Debates* (LSD) *Xth Series*. For an informative and one-sided view, see S. Sahay (ed.), *Gone at Last? The Story of V. Ramaswami's Impeachment,* (New Delhi: Har-Anand), 1993.

[105] This was a policy used by Justice Venkatachaliah when he was chief justice. Even if appropriate in the circumstances, such a policy cannot but be an unsatisfactory way of dealing with the problem.

Hindu Nationalism and Democracy

CHRISTOPHE JAFFRELOT

No wing of the Hindu nationalist movement, whether the militant youth of the Bajrang Dal or political parties like the Jana Sangh or its successor, the Bharatiya Janata Party, has ever been really attracted by the fascist, putschist strategy. The Rashtriya Swayamsewak Sangh and its offshoots probably never promoted a coup d'état because they did not regard state power as the most important object of conquest—they preferred to work at the grassroots level with a long-term perspective.[1] They could have stayed out of the institutional framework or even the political domain, as many RSS leaders argued they should in the late 1940s to early 1950s. However, the Jana Sangh and the BJP, and before them the Hindu Mahasabha, have always played the game of electoral politics. The Jana Sangh distanced itself somewhat from the elections in the 1970s, when A. B. Vajpayee considered that it was 'becoming increasingly difficult to dislodge the Congress by the ballot-box since elections proved to be an unequal battle, since the Congress has money power'.[2] But this stand was not uncommon then—as the JP (Jayaprakash Narayan) movement was to testify—and, in any case, the Jana Sangh continued to contest elections.

Does this rejection of putschist strategies mean that Hindu nationalism fully adheres to democracy? My paper proposes to give some answers to this question by analysing how the Sangh Parivar and the Hindu Mahasabha have approached this political system even before Independence, by studying the kind of democracy they tended to favour and by highlighting the limits of their democratic credentials.

The Hindu Nationalist Ideology of Democracy

India, a Democracy from Time Immemorial

Even before Hindu nationalism crystallized in the inter-war period, Hindu revivalists were not averse to the notion of democracy. On the contrary, they argued that democracy was not alien to India. Aurobindo even claimed that democracy was born in India; it was merely returning via the British after a long journey. All that was needed was to free it from the foreign elements which were now affecting it.[3] This discourse naturally reflected a nationalist strategy: the British prided themselves on being democrats, and members of the Indian intelligentsia (and among them, Hindu revivalists) did not want to see their country lagging behind. The Hindu nationalists inherited this conception from the revivalists in the 1920s and 1930s.

As did many others,[4] the first Hindu nationalist ideologues emphasized the existence of a democratic precedent in India. This they generally situated in Buddhist institutions, the village, and the ancient 'republics'. Radha Kumud Mookerji, a professor of history at Lucknow University in the inter-war period, was one of the intellectuals of the Hindu Mahasabha who advocated such ideas.[5] In *Hindu Civilization*, the first edition of which came out in 1936, he explains that the monarchy of Vedic times was far from absolute: 'Within the framework of autocracy, there were operative certain democratic elements, the significance of which should not be missed.'[6] For instance, Mookerji found that 'the *Atharvaveda* has several passages indicative of the people choosing their king'.[7] But the republics were naturally seen by the author as the main embodiments of democracy in ancient India:

> The growth of republics as a feature of Indian political evolution implied that of the necessary democratic procedure by which their working was regulated and governed. It is a remarkable testimony to the popular republican instincts and traditions of the times that democratic procedure was applied in every sphere of life, political, economic and even religious. The Pali texts furnish interesting information on the working of the Buddhist Samghas in strict and minute conformity with genuine democratic principles. The essence of democracy is government by decision based on discussion in public meetings or assemblies. The Pali texts describe the meetings of religious assemblies or Samghas in all their stages.[8]

Mookerji emphasizes the role of voting in the making of decisions within the Buddhist Samgha.[9] So-called democratic procedures typical of a *religious* body, the Buddhist community, were used to substantiate the claim that ancient India knew *political* democracy.

This kind of discourse was not confined to the Hindu Mahasabha. Hindu traditionalist Congressmen made assiduous use of it, as the 1946–1950 Constituent Assembly debates testify. When the question of regime type arose in the Assembly, many of them declared that India could choose only democracy, because that is what she had always known (before she was conquered by 'foreigners'). To substantiate this claim, soon after the opening session of the Constituent Assembly, Purushottam Das Tandon, well known for his Hindu traditionalist leanings,[10] established a parallel between this Assembly and an illustrious Buddhist precedent:

> After centuries, such a meeting has once more been convened in our country. It recalls to our mind our glorious past when we were free and when assemblies were held at which the Pundits met to discuss important affairs of the country. It reminds us of the Assemblies of the age of Asoka [the third Emperor of the Maurya dynasty who lived and ruled till 232 BC].[11]

The assemblies presented here as the precursors of the Constituent Assembly were in no way political: the pundits evoked by Tandon were Brahmans versed in Sanskrit scriptures who could have debated questions of theology or ritual, but even for these purposes, they were not representatives of society. As far as the assemblies convened by Asoka are concerned, they also undoubtedly had a religious vocation: the Emperor, it seems, had indeed convened the third Buddhist Council and thus contributed to the building of the canon of the religion to which he had been converted.

Like many Congressmen, and especially Hindu traditionalists such as Tandon, Hindu nationalist ideologues were not hostile to democracy insofar as it appeared to be rooted in Indian soil and culture. To that extent, it was a prestigious feature adding to the country's glory.

An Anti-individualistic Conception of Democracy

Even though Hindu nationalists have generally praised democracy and appreciated its advent in India, they have tended to distinguish their conception of democracy from the Westminster model borrowed from Britain in the 1950 Constitution. This argument was made clear during the 1975 Emergency. At that time, the RSS and its affiliates projected themselves as being at the forefront of the fight against Indira Gandhi, but this claim needs to be qualified. First, the RSS fought less for democracy than for regaining a right to legal existence. (The then RSS chief, Balasaheb Deoras, proposed to Indira Gandhi that she accept its collaboration. The RSS launched its anti-Emergency agitation *after* she refused.[12]) Second, Hindu nationalists suggested that the democracy for which they fought was not necessarily that of the parliamentary system. For instance, D. Thengadi, who was one of the main RSS leaders underground, declared:

> The Constituent Assembly imposed British-type institutions on the people. India too has had a democratic tradition, a tradition of thousands of years, and the temperament of the Indian people can be easily moulded accordingly. But the Indian democratic system has been different. Its nature is different from that of the British democratic system.[13]

Thengadi does not explain here what the differences are, but he is more explicit in other writings, borrowing heavily from the organicist worldview of his mentor, Golwalkar.

In Defence of Social Organicism

Golwalkar's favourite political arrangement combined territorial representation (election by constituencies) with functional representation, where each corporate body nominates delegates at the request of both its local branches and the central organization. This mechanism was described as merely giving concrete shape to what was already practised in ancient India, where each of the varnas chose its representative for its village council (gram panchayat) and thence to the royal council.[14] Golwalkar did not hesitate to demand, if necessary, a revision of the Constitution to put this plan into action.

This programme looks like an Indian variant of the corporatist state, since the group, not the individual, is regarded as the relevant unit; this group can be the family, the village, the varna, but also the 'industry'. Indeed, Thengadi, who was the founder of the Bharatiya Mazdoor Sangh in 1955, proposed a parallel system from the trade unionist point of view:

Bharatiya culture believes that the 'Nation', and not the 'class', is the basic unit of human society. Horizontal division of the world is a fiction. Vertical arrangement of it is a fact . . . . [In ancient India] like a family, the community had its life based upon mutual love and confidence, and consequently, its horizontal division could not even be dreamt of. It was further realized that the various communities are but different limbs of the same organism, i.e., the Bharatiya Nation. The Bharatiya social order thus implied the industry-wise arrangement and not class-wise arrangement.[15]

Thengadi not only dealt with 'economic democracy', he also criticized the foreign inspiration of parliamentary democracy, in comparison with the Indian version of democracy, because 'Unlike the western form of democracy, which is more intellectual, the Indian alternative—the dharmic system—is based on human values.'[16] Thengadi even suggested constitutional reform because 'checks and balances provided by the Constitution and our legal systems can be effective only if they are supplemented by checks and balances in human, social mind as a result of appropriate *samskaras17 of* dharma'.[18] Thengadi's discourse bears testimony to the latent hostility of Hindu nationalists towards a secular form of democracy, a political system separated from religious notions such as the most all-embracing one, dharma, which also underlies social organicism.

Thus, Hindu nationalist leaders disapprove of parliamentary democracy because it is alien to religious (dharmic) notions and does not fit into their non-individualistic view of society. Today, these conceptions are propagated not only by old-timers or more or less sidelined leaders such as Thengadi, but also by mainstream ideologues. In the BJP, K.N. Govindacharya for instance, has adopted the same perspective in a recent assessment of India after fifty years of independence:

The Constitution is not the product of our soil; a minimum addition is required to make it more responsive. Consensus, instead of majority-minority concept, suits the country better. Occupational representation (participation of various social groups based on their occupation) in the system will deliver the goods. Such a system will be in conformity with our traditions and ethos. . . .

It is clear the system has to be rooted in our soil. Public and political education are essential ingredients for our evolution. M.K. Gandhi, Aurobindo Ghosh and M.N. Roy had reservations about the system right since its inception. There was skepticism about the

efficacy of adopting the parliamentary system of democracy. Dr. B.R.
Ambedkar emphasized the need of having an Indian Union—a true
reflection of our ethos—instead of federation. Jay Prakash Narayan
favoured party-less democracy. RSS founder M.S. Golwalkar considered 'unanimity' as the mode of elections, with an added component
of functional representation as the best model of governance.

I feel Golwalkar's view is best suited for our society. In the pro-
cess of evolution, the system is bound to tend towards this goal.
As of now, I am not pessimistic about the survival of our system.
We need improvement, not change in the system.[19]

Like his predecessors, Golwalkar and Thengadi, Govindacharya
does not reject democracy, but shows a strong inclination for a
reformed version of parliamentary democracy. Interestingly, he
does not draw his inspiration from Golwalkar alone but also
from Gandhian views. Indeed, this variant of the Hindu nationalist conception of democracy overlaps with ideas propagated
by Gandhi and his disciples.

Does Hindu Nationalism Echo Gandhian Views?

It is well known that Gandhi's first and only book, *Hind Swaraj*
(1908), is not only an indictment of western, modern material-
istic civilization, but also of parliamentary democracy:

The condition of England at present is pitiable. I pray to God that
India may never be in that plight. That which you consider to be
the Mother of Parliaments is like a sterile woman and prostitute.
Both these are harsh terms, but exactly fit the case. That Parliament has not yet of its own accord done a single good thing, hence
I have compared it to a sterile woman. The natural condition of
that Parliament is such that, without outside pressure, it can do
nothing. It is like a prostitute because it is under the control of
ministers who change from time to time.[20]

Gandhi agrees with one of the main ideas of the opponents of
parliamentary democracy, namely that deputies are too corrupt
to represent the voters, that they waste their time in useless
debates and that they stick to their parties' programme without
thinking for themselves. The Mahatma, then, preferred the reign
of 'a few good men'.[21] This stand reflected a strong distrust of
the people who allegedly are not able to make up their minds;
they live under the influence of the press and populist leaders.

In a book professing to be a reflection on 'democratic values', Vinoba Bhave opposed *raj-niti* (power politics) to *lok-niti*

(democratic ethics). This view implied the dissolution of parties and the relinquishing of any electoral system aimed at reaching a consensus. Bhave's anti-individualism encompassed a germ of authoritarianism. He wrote that social harmony would reign if everyone fulfilled his or her duty in the social order: 'if every limb were to function smoothly, the whole body would function properly'.[22]

The main work of Jayaprakash Narayan (JP) (another Gandhian leader mentioned by Govindacharya), *A Plea for Reconstruction of Indian Polity,* is also an indictment of parliamentary democracy which, as he saw it, implied excessive centralization of power and systematically betrayed the wishes of the people. In parliamentary democracy, the electors are 'manipulated by powerful, centrally controlled parties, with the aid of high finance and diabolically clever methods and super media'.[23] In setting forth his political ideal, JP also claimed he drew upon models from ancient India, and particularly from the interpretation of these models provided by Aurobindo who, like Gandhi, was one of his sources of inspiration. Going back to the thesis of this author about a century later, JP maintained that the political order of ancient India was based 'on the system of the self-governing village community', which only British colonization was able to destroy.[24] Ancient India, therefore, held the key to 'an organically self-determining communal life', and for JP, the challenge at hand was just 'a question of an ancient country finding its lost soul again'.[25]

Obviously, JP opposed parliamentary democracy because he wanted a democracy expressed through a truly decentralized system of governance. Gandhi's political ideal was already a network of independent villages, drawing its inspiration from the orientalist stereotype of the 'village republics:'

My idea of Village Swaraj is that it is a complete republic, independent of its neighbours for its vital wants, and yet interdependent for many others in which dependence is a necessity. . . . The government of the village will be conducted by the Pancayat of five persons, annually elected by the adult villagers, male and female, possessing minimum prescribed qualifications. These will have all the authority and jurisdiction required. Since there will be no system of punishments in the accepted sense, this Pancayat will be the legislature, judiciary and executive combined to operate for its year of office.[26]

The RSS and its offshoots were also in favour of a decentralized state. As early as the 1950s, the Jana Sangh proposed in its election manifestoes to divide the Indian territory into about one hundred large districts, or *janapadas*. These would be much smaller than the states and would, it was argued, promote village autonomy. In its 1954 election manifesto, the party committed itself to make the village councils, or panchayats, 'the foundation of administration', granting them an increase in financial resources and (re)establishing the so-called traditional rule that their members would be elected unanimously.[27] However, the Hindu nationalists' emphasis on the unity of Indian society led them to advocate a unitary rather than a federal state, a move which reflected their basic difference with the Gandhians, that is, their rejection of diversity. While the latter have always stressed pluralism, Hindu nationalists cannot accommodate the notion of a plural society.

The Limits of the Hindu Nationalists' Commitment to Democracy

Democracy, the Most Convenient Regime for a Majority
Hindu nationalists favoured democracy before Independence not only because of the prestige they could draw from the claim that India has been a democracy since its antiquity; they also espoused it as early as the 1930s because this regime relied on the notion of majority rule. Hindu nationalists were increasingly obsessed by demographic figures from the late nineteenth century onwards, when the first censuses showed a limited but steady erosion in the proportion of Hindus in the population of India. This sensitivity led them to over-emphasize the fact that Hindus formed a majority in India, and that it was their nation for this reason. In addition, they could claim to be its first inhabitants. Democracy has suited them more than any other regime because it relies on the principle of 'one man, one vote'.

This first became clear in the speeches of Veer Savarkar after he took over as chief of the Hindu Mahasabha. In the presidential address he delivered at the 1937 session of the party he declared, 'Though we form an overwhelming majority in the land we do not want any privileges for our Hindudom'.[28] In fact, Savarkar did not want any privileges for any community *because* the Hindus were in a majority. From this perspective, he added:

> Let all citizens of Indian States be treated according to their indi-
> vidual worth, irrespective of their religious or racial percentage in
> the general population. Let their language and script be the na-
> tional language and script of the Indian State which is understood
> by an overwhelming majority of the people, as happens in every
> other State in the world. Let no religious bias be allowed to tamper
> with that language and script. Let 'one man, one vote' be the gen-
> eral rule irrespective of caste, creed, race or religion.[29]

Savarkar was favourably inclined towards democratic principles, because they guarantee the domination of the 'overwhelming majority', that is, the Hindus—a logic which would
enable Hindi to become the national language. The universalistic
discourse of democracy was evidently hijacked in order to promote communal interests.[30] The Hindu Mahasabha leaders seem
to have been deeply convinced that they could make their point
through the use of universalistic values, so much so that the
party's working committee decided to refer the Hindu-Muslim
question to the League of Nations in 1940.[31]

This discourse heralded the present-day propaganda of the
RSS and its offshoots in favour of the disbanding of the Minorities Commission. Even though this Commission was established
by the Janata Party, of which the former Jana Sangh was a component, the Hindu nationalist movement quickly criticized it
as an institution responsible for the 'division of the nation'. The
BJP, the Jana Sangh's successor, proposed to replace it with a
Human Rights Commission,[32] which would have enabled it once
again to use the language of universalism for particularistic ends.
The aim was to remove some of the protections granted to the
minorities because of their vulnerability and, in effect, to assert
the strength of the Hindu majority.

The BJP shaped the notion of 'minorityism' in the same perspective. The term was first used by L.K. Advani after he took
over as BJP president in 1986. In January 1987, in an address to
the BJP's National Council, he referred to the 'dangers of
minorityism' in an obvious allusion to the Congress government's
concern to protect certain interests of the Muslims, as exemplified in the Shah Bano controversy.[33] Advani had specifically con-
demned the Muslim Women's (Protection of Rights in Divorce)
Bill on behalf of modern, universalistic values. Addressing the

plenary session of the BJP as the party's incoming president, he stated in 1986 that in the Shah Bano affair some Muslim leaders had acted as 'obscurantists' and 'fanatics' because they disregarded the rights of their community's wives.[34]

Hindu nationalism has thus become adept at promoting the interests of the majority community in the guise of universalistic values that are pillars of liberal democracy. In reality, Hindu nationalists appreciate the majority rule of democracy because it means that Hindus can never lose power, provided they vote *en bloc*, which is indeed their chief objective. As Sudipta Kaviraj has suggested, the main enemies of democracy in India are those who would like to merge democracy and 'majoritarianism', as if both things would mean the same. They do not oppose democracy openly; on the contrary, 'they are in fact the greatest supporters of majority rule. But they do not want democratic government to be a complex arrangement in which majority rule is counterbalanced by a system of secure enjoyment of minority rights.'[35]

This analysis can be applied to different categories, including the Other Backward Classes (OBCs) and the Hindi-speaking population, but, of course, it is especially relevant in the case of Hindu nationalism. Savarkar's reaction to the abolition of separate electorates by the Constituent Assembly is very significant in this respect. In May 1949, soon after Sardar Patel made this decision known, Savarkar sent him the following telegram:

> I heartily congratulate you and the Constituent Assembly on leading and adopting the resolutions doing away with separate electorates, reservations and weightages based on invidious racial or religious distinctions and on having thus vindicated the genuinely national character of our Bharateeya state.[36]

Savarkar did not reject a religion-based state to promote an individualistic civil space; he opposed separate electorates and reservations because they hindered his efforts to equate democracy and majoritarianism, that is the pursuance of 'a permanent unbeatable majority which would place [large groups] in power for ever'.[37] But in a true democracy, 'Large majorities are bearable only if there is a random element in them, if individuals and groups are sometimes in the winning and sometimes in the losing group.'[38]

Thus, while the Hindu nationalists look at democracy as something that is not alien to India, and furthermore, as an element of its historical prestige, they have promoted a non-individualistic version of it, and they have been especially interested in this political system because it is a convenient way to establish the domination of the majority community.

The Sangh Parivar and Democratic Procedure

Since Independence, the RSS has not been able to claim to represent the people because it did not contest elections, but its democratic credentials have been affected by its desire to influence those in power. In his attempts to transform the RSS into a kind of advisor to the government, Golwalkar drew his inspiration from the classic connection between temporal power and spiritual authority:

> The political rulers were never the standard-bearers of our society. They were never taken as the props of our national life. Saints and sages who had risen above the mundane temptations of self and power and had dedicated themselves wholly for establishing a happy, virtuous and integrated state of society, were its constant torch-bearers. They represented the *dharmasatta* [religious authority]. The king was only an ardent follower of that higher moral authority.[39]

Golwalkar was invoking the Hindu tradition of the king's guru (*raj guru*) and, because of the RSS's emulation of the values of renunciation—the *pracharaks* are known for their ascetic lifestyle—he proposed for his organization the traditional function of 'dharmic' counselor to state power:

> We aspire to become the radiating centre of all the age-old cherished ideals of our society—just as the indescribable power which radiates through the sun. Then the political power which draws its life from that source of society, will have no other [goal but] to reflect the same radiance.[40]

Golwalkar's successor, Deoras, tried to play the role of the *raj guru* during the Janata phase when he met Morarji Desai, Charan Singh, and Jayaprakash Narayan in order to influence power from outside. This activity, as noticed by D. R. Goyal, tended to turn the RSS into a 'supra party' and 'extra-constitutional authority'[41] that was incompatible with the logic of democracy, simply because this centre of power was not subject to the verdict of the polls.

The problem became even more acute after the BJP came to power in 1998. Even though the new prime minister, Atal Behari

Vajpayee, was known for not being as close to the RSS as, for instance, Lal Krishna Advani, the then BJP president, he had been trained in this organization and still regarded it as his 'family'.[42] He praised the 'RSS ethos' in general and the way it 'change[d] . . . the collective mind'. While in power, the BJP enabled the RSS to exert a stronger influence over Indian politics. Sangh leaders regularly met the prime minister and key ministers such as Advani. In July 1998, two meetings were convened by the RSS chief, Rajendra Singh, for interacting with the 180-odd BJP MPs. Vajpayee and Advani attended parts of this event. Such meetings had been organized previously, but this time the BJP MPs were the pillars of the ruling coalition.[43] More importantly, in Uttar Pradesh, Rajendra Singh was allowed to address a group of about fifty-five top bureaucrats, including the chief secretary and the director general of police, on 'how they could emerge as ideals before the public'.[44] The meeting took place in the presence of ministers of Kalyan Singh's government; bureaucrats could hardly miss Rajendra Singh's message since their political bosses were obviously supporting what he said.

The RSS and its offshoots have traditionally been apprehensive about elections, which they never really regarded as the legitimate procedure for filling posts of responsibility. The Jana Sangh and then the BJP have professed that they were more democratic than other parties. For one thing, they limited the number of terms of the party chief (as in the BJP today, where the term of the president can only be renewed once); for another, they held party elections often. Through these elections local committees designate state units, which then nominate delegates to an all-India council, which in turn elects the party president. The Jana Sangh and the BJP have certainly held party elections more often than other parties, but in contrast with what has happened in the latter, there have been very few *contested* elections. Most of the time, there has been one candidate per post, because the very notion of contested elections is rejected as divisive.[45]

Inner democracy is not very evident in any other Indian political party or organization. During the 1920s, the Congress had been given a more representative AICC by Gandhi; even so, it suffered from the Mahatma's interference—as testified by the 'dismissal' of Subhas Chandra Bose in 1939. After Independence, Nehru forced P. Tandon to resign and, more importantly, there were no party elections for the twenty years between 1972 and 1992. However, this was largely due to factionalism which was a form of pluralism that is rejected by the BJP today. When the BJP itself was affected by groupism and factionalism as a result of its coming to power in several states in the early 1990s, it preferred not to conduct party elections in several regional party branches, such as Madhya Pradesh.

The limited role of elections in the functioning of the Jana Sangh and the BJP is well in tune with what happens in their mother organization, the RSS. The latter was obliged to draft a constitution after its ban in the wake of Gandhi's assassination. This document required local branches of the RSS to elect provincial assemblies whose members would nominate the delegates to the Akhil Bharatiya Pratinidhi Sabha (ABPS—All India Delegate Assembly). This body was empowered to elect the general secretary, who in turn appointed the executive committee. In practice, there have never been more candidates than posts to be filled, and the general secretary has more or less been free to nominate, transfer, or even suspend the pracharaks. Similarly, the Sarsanghchalak, the RSS chief who embodies supreme authority, cannot be voted out. He remains at the helm until his death or until he resigns. He is not elected, but designated by his predecessor, as in 1940 and 1973, when Hedgewar and Golwalkar, respectively, designated their successors.

The taste for personalizing power that is evident in the structure of the RSS and its offshoots partly explains the interest of the Hindu nationalists in the presidential system. Whereas members of a parliamentary cabinet are responsible to parliament, in the presidential system, members of the executive are any persons chosen by the president, and are responsible to the president alone.

Parliamentary Democracy or Presidential System?
The BJP reaffirmed its faith in a presidential form of government in 1991, as a means to guarantee a stronger Centre.[46] Several of its top leaders elaborated on this point while assessing the achievement of India after fifty years of independence. A.B. Vajpayee went into this question more deeply than any other BJP leader. In the 13th Desraj Chowdhary Annual Memorial

Lecture which he delivered on 11 November 1996, he declared that 'the *present* system of parliamentary democracy has failed to deliver the goods and that the time has come to introduce deep-going changes in our structure of governance'.[47] Among the 'ills of the present system of parliamentary democracy. . . fashioned after the British model nearly five decades ago',[48] Vajpayee highlighted the incapacity of parliament to satisfactorily exert its legislative function and to launch serious debates. As a remedy, he envisaged, first, the presidential system; or second, proportional representation (PR); or third, the strengthening of democracy within the political parties. While everybody will agree with the third proposal, the first two are debatable; they seem to be contradictory, since the presidential system is intended to concentrate the authority of the state, while the main asset of the electoral system known as PR lies in its capacity to represent different opinions.

However, the strengthening of the president's role is obviously favoured by Vajpayee, and a subsequent interview suggests that this process would have authoritarian implications:

It's 50 years since Independence and time we reviewed the functioning of our institutions. I have made a few suggestions. For example, I feel that where political parties are unable to form a government at the Centre, the President should carry on the administration with the help of advisers.[49]

Such a schema, which amounts to extending a kind of president's rule to the Centre, has clear anti-democratic consequences. First, the president would acquire significant prerogatives even though he would not be elected by the people, but by members of Parliament and of the legislative assemblies. Second, it would be very difficult to assess 'where political parties are unable to form a government'—the president could interpret the situation according to his personal inclinations. Third, the president would be free to choose his advisors, and not necessarily from among elected politicians whose legitimacy derives from universal suffrage. Vajpayee's formula reflects a certain fascination for strong, personalized power, which is well in tune with the middle-class craving for the replacement of politicians by bureaucrats and technicians.

After the 1998 elections, the BJP and its coalition partners evolved a National Agenda for Governance, in which one of the items read: 'We will appoint a Commission to review the Constitution of India in light of the experience of the past 50 years and to make suitable recommendations.'[50] In April 1998, L.K. Advani, the home minister, virtually spelt out the terms of reference of such a commission: whether the political system needed to be decentralized, whether to continue with the parliamentary system, and whether the electoral system needed to be reformed.[51] A few days later, during the BJP National Council session, he explained that the proposed commission would go into the 'merits and demerits' of the parliamentary system and the presidential system to make recommendations, but he pointed out that parliamentary democracy was not among the basic features of the Constitution which could not be changed.[52]

The presidential system is not necessarily opposed to democracy, even though it reflects an inclination towards concentration (even personalization) of power. In fact, the growing attention that is paid to this system is not limited to the Hindu nationalist milieu. Several Congressmen, for instance, have been toying with this idea for some time,[53] and it is even referred to by many politicians who are concerned with the need to reform the state. Yet, the form that presidentialization of the regime would take under the auspices of the BJP appears to be more threatening than it would under other parties, because of the BJP's ideological background and the way in which the RSS and its offshoots function.

The Sangh Parivar: Stronghold of Social Status Quo?

The BJP: Still the Party of an Elite
One of the major changes on the Indian political scene since the late 1980s has been the rise of the Other Backward Classes (OBCs) and the Dalits. The share of the former among the MPs of the Hindi belt—where the BJP won most of its seats and where social change was much slower than in the South—has increased from less than five per cent in the 1950s to about 25 per cent in the 1990s. For the first time, the Lok Sabha harbours a large proportion of agriculturists (many of them from the lower castes), whereas it used to be a stronghold for lawyers and other professionals. In many respects, this trend represents a democratization of Indian democracy. However, the BJP, until recently, did not participate in this process.

Classifying Lok Sabha members according to their profession is difficult because of the large number of those who declare agriculture as their profession, even though they may have some land but do not cultivate it themselves. In the table below, which analyses Uttar Pradesh, Bihar, Madhya Pradesh, Rajasthan, Haryana, Himachal Pradesh, Chandigarh, and Delhi, the MPs who, in *Who's Who in Lok Sabha*, have given agriculture as their profession but hold an LLB have been classified as lawyers. Nonetheless, the 'agriculturalists' category remains very heterogeneous, since it encompasses landlords as well as tenants. In spite of these caveats, it is noteworthy that the share of the agriculturalists among the BJP MPs has tended to increase, while that of the lawyers has been on the decline. However, the group composed of traders and industrialists represents about one-fourth the total member of BJP MPs in the 1990s—compared to less than four per cent for the Janata Dal and six per cent for Congress—a clear indication that in parliament the BJP still represents the business community to a greater extent than do other parties.

The proportional over-representation of upper caste MPs among the BJP members elected from the Hindi belt and Gujarat, where the party won most of its seats, was evident from 1989. Their percentage declined in the 1996 election, but remains prominent and much more important than in the Congress and the Janata Dal. Interestingly, in 1996 the erosion of the upper castes' share benefits the MPs from the Scheduled Castes, who are largely elected by non-SC voters, as much as those from the OBCs. In fact, very few Dalits vote for the BJP, as testified by the exit poll made by the Centre for the Study of Developing Societies in 1996. This poll also shows that the upper castes are still over-represented among the BJP electorate, while the Scheduled Tribes are significantly under-represented. The OBCs are also under-represented, but to a lesser extent.

The forward castes' votes polarize in favour of the BJP in Maharashtra, Uttar Pradesh, and Bihar, where respectively 50, 64, and 67 per cent of the upper castes preferred this party. The BJP also remains a predominantly urban party. Thirty-two per cent of the urban dwellers voted for it, as against 19 per cent of the people living in rural constituencies. As for the upper-caste graduates living in towns and cities, 52 per cent of this category opted for the BJP in 1996.

The Upper-caste Middle Class and the BJP

The upper-caste middle class has always been overrepresented within the Hindu nationalist movement, to such an extent that the Jana Sangh was known as a 'Brahmin-baniya' party. The Sangh Parivar held some attraction for these milieus for two main reasons. One was its sanskritized style and defence of social hierarchy; the other was its economic liberalism and defence of the 'middle world', a world, according to Bruce Graham, composed of 'the provincial professions, small industry, and country trading and banking'.[54] The affinity between Hindu nationalism and these categories was particularly noticeable in the towns of the Hindi belt. Since the late 1980s, however, the BJP has benefited from the growth of a new middle class that has emerged largely as a result of economic liberalization. The system of values of this rising social category is based, in theory at least, on merit gained through hard work. Its members thus show little concern for the poor[55] and disapprove of reservation systems in principle. These views overlap with those of the BJP. The party advocates a more vigorous liberalization of the domestic economy. It also expresses apprehensions about caste-based reservations, though publicly it has to moderate its stand so as not to alienate the OBC voters. In fact, the Mandal affair was probably as important as the Ayodhya movement in rallying upper caste middle-class support around the BJP in the early 1990s.

This middle class not only shares the BJP's concern about the rise of new groups (the OBCs and the Dalits)—that is, its apprehension regarding the social dimension of democracy— they also have in common with it a growing questioning of parliamentary government. In 1993, an opinion poll conducted in Bombay, Delhi, Calcutta, Madras, and Bangalore revealed that 58 per cent of interviewees agreed with the following proposition: 'If the country is to progress, it needs a dictator.'[56] The anti-parliament attitude underlying this stand reflects the opprobrium affecting politicians. The survey conducted by the Centre for the Study of Developing Societies during the 1996 elections showed that only 22 per cent of the interviewees thought that their MP cared for the people (as against 27 per cent in 1971).[57] The authoritarian option, however, seems to be considered by the urban middle class alone. Among the

Table 1: Occupational distribution of Hindi-belt MPs of the three main parties

Occupation	1989 BJP	1989 Cong	1989 JD	1991 BJP	1991 Cong	1991 JD	1996 BJP	1996 Cong	1996 JD
Agriculturalist	14 / 21.8%	13 / 37.1%	34 / 32.3%	16 / 18.6%	23 / 38%	19 / 35.8%	35 / 28.8%	10 / 29%	10 / 40%
Lawyer	15 / 23.4%	5 / 14.2%	20 / 19%	9 / 10.4%	12 / 20%	8 / 15%	18 / 14.8%	6 / 17.6%	1 / 4%
Trader	5 / 7.8%	2 / 5.7%	3 / 2.8%	12 / 13.9%	3 / 5%	1 / 1.8%	19 / 15.7%	2 / 5.8%	1 / 4%
Industrialist	2 / 3.1%	0	0	6 / 6.9%	0	1 / 1.8%	5 / 4.1%	0	0
Ex-Civil Servant	2 / 3.1%	0	0	2 / 2.3%	0	0	4 / 3.3%	0	0
Ex-Army	1 / 1.5%	0	1 / 0.9%	5 / 5.8%	2 / 3.3%	1 / 1.8%	4 / 3.3%	1 / 2.9%	1 / 4%
Policeman/Pilot	1 / 1.5%	1 / 2.8%	0	0	1 / 1.6%	0	0	1 / 2.9%	0
Journalist	2 / 3.1%	0	6 / 5.7%	1 / 1.1%	1 / 1.6%	2 / 3.7%	1 / 0.8%	1 / 2.9%	0
Writer & Artist	0	0	2 / 1.9%	1 / 1.1%	0	0	2 / 1.6%	2 / 5.8%	3 / 12%
Teacher	5 / 7.8%	3 / 8.6%	9 / 8.6%	5 / 5.8%	5 / 8.3%	6 / 11.3%	9 / 7.4%	2 / 5.8%	3 / 12%

Doctor	4 6.25%	0	2 1.9%	6 6.9%	0	0	7 5.7%	1 2.9%	0
Engineer	0	0	2 1.9%	1 1.1%	0	3 5.6%	0	2 5.8%	3 12%
Trade Unionist	0	2 5.7%	1 0.9%	0	0	2 3.7%	0	0	1 4%
Social Worker	4 6.25%	2 5.7%	3 2.8%	6 6.9%	0	3 5.6%	10 8.2%	2 5.8%	2 8%
Political Worker	5 7.8%	5 14.2%	19 18%	3 3.4%	10 11.6%	5 9.4%	1 0.8%	1 8%	0
Former Ruler	2 3.1%	1 2.8%	0	2 2.3%	1 1.2%	0	2 1.6%	2 5.8%	0
Religious Figure	2 3.1%	0	2 1.9%	8 9.3%	0	1 1.8%	3 2.4%	0	0
Sportsman	0	0	0	2 2.3%	2 3.3%	1 1.8%	0	0	0
Other, Not Known		1 2.8%	1 0.9%	1 1.1%	0	0	1 0.8%	1 2.9%	0
Total	64 100%	35 100%	105 100%	86 100%	60 100%	53 100%	121 100%	34 100%	25 100%

Table 2: Caste and community background of the Hindi belt and Gujarat MPs (party-wise, in %)

Castes & Communities	BJP 89	Cong 89	JD 89	BJP 91	Cong 91	JD 91	BJP 96	Cong 96	JD 96	BJP 98	Cong 98	JD +SP +RJD 98
Upper castes	**46.67**	**34.21**	**28.45**	**51.40**	**27.69**	**16.99**	**42.75**	**27.27**	**14.28**	**43.26**	**22.22**	**15.22**
Brahmin	17.33	15.79	6.90	24.30	10.77	1.89	19.57	15.91	4.76	18.44	6.67	-
Rajput	16.0	7.89	14.66	17.76	6.15	13.21	13.77	4.55	7.14	12.77	2.22	15.22
Bhumihar	-	2.63	1.72	-	3.08	1.89	1.45	-	-	1.42	2.22	-
Baniya/Jain	6.67	5.26	1.72	3.74	3.08	-	5.07	4.55	-	4.96	6.67	-
Kayasth	2.67	-	2.59	1.87	3.08	-	2.17	-	2.38	2.13	2.22	-
Other*	4.0	7.89	15.52	9.35	13.85	1.89	7.97	20.45	-	8.51	2.22	-
Intermediate	**8.0**	**7.89**	**15.52**	**9.35**	**13.85**	**1.89**	**7.97**	**20.45**	-	**8.51**	**22.22**	-
Castes												
Jat	-	2.63	11.21	2.80	10.77	1.89	4.35	13.64	-	4.26	11.11	-
Maratha	1.33	2.63	-	0.93	1.54	-	0.72	2.27	-	0.71	2.22	-
Patidar	6.67	-	4.31	5.61	1.54	-	2.90	4.55	-	3.55	4.44	-
Bishnoi	-	2.63	-	-	-	-	-	-	-	-	4.44	-
OBC	**16.0**	**5.26**	**26.72**	**14.02**	**13.85**	**39.62**	**18.1**	**11.36**	**54.76**	**17.02**	**8.89**	**50.0**
Yadav	1.33	-	14.66	-	1.54	22.64	1.45	-	33.33	1.42	2.22	21.74
Kurmi	5.33	5.26	4.31	7.48	4.62	9.43	5.80	-	4.76	7.09	-	10.87
Lodhi	2.67	-	0.86	2.80	-	-	2.90	-	-	2.13	-	-
Other	6.67	-	6.90	3.74	7.69	7.55	7.97	11.36	16.67	4.26	6.67	17.39

SC	16.0	18.42	16.82	15.38	24.53	21.01	11.36	14.29	15.60	11.11	17.39
ST	9.33	23.68	4.67	21.54	-	7.97	22.73	-	6.38	26.67	-
Muslim	1.33	5.26	-	4.62	13.2	-	4.55	14.29	0.71	4.44	13.04
Sikh	1.33	-	0.93	-	-	0.72	-	-	0.71	-	-
Christian	-	2.63	-	-	1.89	-	-	2.38	-	-	2.17
Sadhu	-	-	1.87	-	-	-	-	-	-	-	-
Unidentified	1.33	2.63	0.93	3.08	1.89	1.45	2.27	-	7.80	4.44	2.17
Total	100.0	100	100	100	100	100	100	100	100	100	100
	N=75	N=38	N=107	N=65	N=53	N=138	N=44	N=42	N=141	N=45	N=46

*Khattri, Amil, Tyagi

Table 3: Caste background of the parties' electorates

	Cong(I)	BJP	NF/LF	BSP	State Parties	Others
Forward	29	33	17	1	10	10
OBC	25	23	25	2	18	7
SC	31	11	21	16	14	7
ST	47	17	15	2	7	12

Source: India Today, 31 May 1996, p. 27.

interviewees of the 1993 survey, 68 per cent declared that they belonged to the 'middle class' (as against eight per cent to the 'lower-middle class', nine per cent to the 'upper-middle class', and 10 per cent to the 'working class'). Indeed, the masses continue to regard the act of voting as useful, as testified by the fact that ordinary people vote more than the élite groups.[58]

The urban middle class obviously aspires to a more orderly day-to-day life and a kind of discipline that is regarded as a precondition for economic progress. This is one of the reasons for the attraction the BJP holds for this group, since it is known for its RSS background. The urban middle class also approves of the BJP's crusade against corruption, a theme that it has cashed in on despite allegations that some of its leaders had been involved in corruption. The common assumption is that parliamentary democracy not only needs to be disciplined; it also needs to be purified.

Conclusion

Historically, the Hindu nationalists have supported democracy largely because, in contrast to today's advocates of 'Asian values' in South East and East Asia, for whom democracy is an import from the West, they have regarded it as a *national* regime. According to them, India was always a democracy—before foreign invasions—and to say so was a good means for regaining one's self-esteem in front of the British. This 'traditional' democracy, however, does not meet the criteria of parliamentary or liberal democracy, since Hindu nationalists have tended to be favourably inclined towards an organicist arrangement. This approach is not fundamentally different from the Gandhian view of democracy.

The democratic credentials of Hindu nationalists can be questioned for other reasons. First, they supported democracy as the most convenient regime for establishing a permanent Hindu domination, since Hindus were a majority. Second, the RSS has been keen to exert some influence on the political domain even though it has not contested elections itself. Third, even though the BJP holds internal elections more often than most other organizations and parties, the RSS and its offshoots are not ruled by democratic procedures, since there is often only one candidate for one post and the personalization of power, as well as the repression of any dissent, are commonplace. Today, these authoritarian leanings find expression in a more or less openly declared interest in a presidential system of governance.

The fourth factor affecting the credibility of the Hindu nationalist commitment to democracy lies in its sociological composition: the movement is still identified with the upper castes, since a large number of its leaders, militants, and voters belong to this milieu. Though the BJP is gradually promoting low-caste cadres within the party apparatus, it still does not contribute to the present day (social) democratization of Indian (political) democracy.

Notes

[1] I have developed this point in the first chapter of my book, *The Hindu Nationalist Movement and Indian Politics, 1925–1990s* (New Delhi: Viking), 1996.

[2] *The Hindu*, 16 September 1974.

[3] Sri Aurobindo, *Collected Works* (Pondichery: Sri Aurobindo Ashram Trust), 1970, vol. 1, 'Bande Mataram', pp. 767-9 (article dated 20 March 1908).

[4] See, for instance, K.P. Jaiswal, *Hindu Polity: A Constitutional History of India in Hindu Times* (Calcutta: Butterworth), 1924; and even Beni Prasad, *The State in Ancient India* (Allahabad: The Indian Press), 1928, p. 170.

[5] R.K. Mookerji belonged to the Bengal Hindu Sabha and was one of the opponents of the Communal Award in 1932. See J. Chatterji, *Bengal Divided: Hindu Communalism and Partition, 1932-1947* (Cambridge: Cambridge University Press), 1994, pp. 26–7.

[6] R.K. Mookerji, *Hindu Civilization: From the Earliest Time up to the Establishment of the Maurya Empire* (Bombay: Bharatiya Vidya Bhavan),

1950, p. 99.

[7] Ibid.

[8] Ibid., p. 209.

[9] Ibid., p. 214.

[10] In the late 1940s, he was closely associated with Hindu nationalist leaders (such as Shyama Prasad Mookherjee), for his fight on behalf of Hindi and the refugees from East Bengal.

[11] *Constituent Assembly Debates* (New Delhi: Lok Sabha Secretariat), 1989, vol. 1, p. 65.

[12] For more details, see C. Jaffrelot, *The Hindu Nationalist Movement*, op. cit., p. 273.

[13] D.P. Thengadi, 'Lamp at the Threshold', preface to P.G. Sahasrabuddhe and M.C. Vajpayee, *The People versus Emergency: A Saga of Struggle* (New Delhi: Suruchi Prakashan), 1991, p. 45.

[14] M.S. Golwalkar, *Bunch of Thoughts* (Bangalore: Jagrana Prakashan), 1966, pp. 37–8.

[15] *Organiser*, 24 October 1955, p. 6 and p. 12.

[16] 'Adhivakta Parishad wants checks and balances through Dharma in Constitution', *Organiser*, 5 January 1995.

[17] Here, the notion of *samskaras* does not refer to 'rites of passage' but, as often in the RSS's discourse, to all the good influences which can be exerted on the formation of character (for more details, see C. Jaffrelot, *The Hindu Nationalist Movement*, op. cit., p. 48).

[18] Ibid.

[19] 'Agenda', *The Pioneer*, 6 April 1997.

[20] M.K. Gandhi, *Indian Home Rule* (Madras: Ganesh and Co.), 1922, 5th edn, p. 26.

[21] Ibid., p. 27.

[22] Cited in D. Dalton, 'The Concept of Politics and Power in India's Ideological Tradition', in A. Jeyaratnam Wilson and Dennis Dalton (eds), *The States of South Asia: Problems of National Integration* (London: Hurst), 1982, p. 186.

[23] Jayaprakash Narayan, *A Plea for Reconstruction of Indian Polity* (Kashi: Akhil Bharat Sarva Seva Sangh), 1959, p. 66.

[24] Ibid., p. 22.

[25] Ibid., p. 26.

[26] M.K. Gandhi, 'The Kingdom of Rama', in K. Satchidananda Murty (ed.), *Readings in India History, Politics and Philosophy* (London: George Allen and Unwin), 1967, p. 186.

[27] 'Manifesto-1954', in Bharatiya Jana Sangh, *Party Documents*, vol. 1 (New Delhi: BJS), 1973, p. 62.

[28] *Indian Annual Register*, 1938, vol. 1, p. 420.

[29] Ibid.

[30] Savarkar reiterated this stand in even more explicit terms in his 1938 presidential address: 'The Hindu Sannathanist Party aims to base the future Constitution of Hindusthan on the broad principle that all citizens should have equal rights and obligations irrespective of caste or creed, race or religion, provided they avow and owe an exclusive and devoted allegiance to the Hindusthani State.'. . . No attitude can be more National, even in the territorial sense than this and it is an attitude in general which is expressed by the curt formula "one man, one vote".' *The Indian Annual Register*, vol. 2, 1939, p. 325.

[31] *The Indian Annual Register*, 1940, vol. 1, p. 10.

[32] See, for instance, the Party's election manifesto in 1996. Bharatiya Janata Party, *For a Strong and Prosperous India: Election Manifesto 1996* (New Delhi), 1996.

[33] L.K. Advani. Presidential Address, 9th National Council Session, 2–4 January 1987, pp. 8–9.

[34] L.K. Advani, Presidential Address, BJP Plenary Session, 9 May 1986, p. 465.

[35] S. Kaviraj, 'Democracy and Development in India', in A.K. Bagchi (ed.), *Democracy and Development* (London: Macmillan), 1994, p. 123.

[36] S.S. Savarkar and G.M. Joshi (eds), *Historic Statements: V.D. Savarkar* (Bombay: Popular Prakashan), 1967, p. 224.

[37] S. Kaviraj, 'Democracy and Development in India', op. cit., p. 124.

[38] Ibid., p. 124.

[39] M.S. Golwalkar, *Bunch of Thoughts*, op. cit., pp. 92–3.

[40] Ibid., p. 103.

[41] D.R. Goyal, *Rashtriya Swayamsevak Sangh* (New Delhi: Radha Krishna Prakashan), 1978, p. 196.

[42] Interview with A.B Vajpayee, 'Sangh is My Soul', *Organiser*, May 1995, reprinted in *Communalism Combat*, February 1998, pp. 28-9.

[43] *The Hindustan Times*, 21 July 1998.

[44] Ibid., 27 July 1998.

[45] For more details, see C. Jaffrelot, *The Hindu Nationalist Movement*, op. cit., p. 149 ff.

[46] *The Statesman* (Delhi) 16 January and 2 February 1991,

[47] A.B. Vajpayee, 'Challenges to Democracy in India', *Organiser*, 24 November 1996, p. 4.

[48] Vajpayee reiterated his attacks on the foreign origin of parliamentary democracy on several occasions. Delivering the M.S. Golwalkar Memorial Lecture organized by the Deendayal Research Institute on 22 February 1997, he considered that the low level of the socio-economic development in India resulted from 'the present system of parliamentary democracy, which we borrowed blindly from the British'. (Vajpayee Advocates a Change in Our System of Governance', *Organiser*, 9 March

[49] *India Today*, 15 May 1997.

[50] Digvijay Singh, the chief minister of Madhya Pradesh, for instance, recently advocated a presidential form of government (*National Mail*, 21 October 1996).

[51] 'National Agenda for Governance', *Organiser—Varsha Pratipada Special*, 29 March 1998, p. 29.

[52] *The Hindu*, 27 April 1998.

[53] Ibid., 5 May 1998.

[54] B. Graham, *Hindu Nationalism and Indian Politics* (Cambridge: Cambridge University Press) 1990, p. 158.

[55] See R. Kothari, 'Class and Communalism in India', *Economic and Political Weekly*, 3 December 1988.

[56] *The Times of India*, 28 December 1993, pp. 1 and 11.

[57] *India Today*, 31 August 1996, p. 31.

[58] Among those who voted more, one finds the 'very poor' people (+2.9 points above the average turnout), the Scheduled Castes (+ 1.9 point), and the villagers (+1.1 point). Among those whose turnout is below the average, one finds the upper castes (-1.6 point), urban dwellers (-3 points) and graduates and post-graduates (-4.5 points) (Ibid., pp. 30–9).

The Transformation of Hindu Nationalism? Towards a reappraisal*

AMRITA BASU

To inquire into the implications of Hindu nationalism for Indian democracy is to enter a quagmire, for it was only in the
period leading to the 1989 parliamentary elections that the
Bharatiya Janata Party (BJP) began its spectacular growth. The
historical record is thin, our capacities to predict are limited,
and the commitment of the BJP to democratic norms is highly
questionable. Nonetheless, speculating on the fate of Indian
democracy without asking whether it is undermined, enhanced
or untouched by the growth of Hindu nationalism would be a
futile exercise; Hindu nationalism undoubtedly represents one
of the major challenges Indian democracy has faced in its fifty
years of existence, and the BJP is its principal proponent. However incomplete our knowledge or speculative our interpretation,
we will have to confront the thorny issue of the relationship
between Hindu nationalism and Indian democracy.

The analytic question that this paper poses is: under what
conditions can a party that abides by the *formal* rules of democracy be considered anti-democratic? Many theorists subscribe
to a minimalist view of democracy which holds that political
parties which support free and fair elections, inclusive suffrage,
freedom of expression, and associational autonomy can be considered democratic.[1] Such minimalist views were expounded
amidst the demise of authoritarian regimes and transitions to

* I received helpful comments on this paper from participants in the conference on 'Democracy and Transformation: India After Fifty Years of Independence,' held in New Delhi in November 1997. Mary Katzenstein, Mark
Kesselman and Ritu Menon made excellent suggestions on an earlier draft.

democracy in Latin America. Subsequently, however, they have reviewed their earlier optimism and devised more demanding standards for evaluating democratic parties and regimes.[2]

I will examine the pertinence of these different standards in the Indian context. India might be seen as experiencing a transition to either a more or less democratic system. Overall, the Congress party has declined, regional parties have become prominent national actors, and short-lived coalition governments have supplanted a stable, one-party-dominant system. My particular focus is on the BJP, which in 1996, paradoxically, won the largest number of seats in the parliamentary elections in India, yet was unable to form a durable national government.

Let us, for a moment, consider some of its distinguishing features: The BJP functions as a party, a movement and, often, as a government at the state level; it operates differently when in power than in opposition; and it has deep and enduring ties to a range of allied organizations. Chief among these are the Rashtriya Swayamsevak Sangh (RSS), a cultural organization, and the Vishva Hindu Parishad (VHP), an affiliated religious organization. Thus, to study the growth of Hindu nationalism necessitates an inquiry into the BJP's multiple identities in each of these contexts.

The first part of this essay explores how the BJP positions itself on questions of secularism, democracy and minority rights. Far from challenging the founding principles of the 1950 Constitution, it seeks to demonstrate that it now champions the very principles that its erstwhile opponent, the Congress party once embraced. Its acceptance of them suggests that the BJP wishes to gain support by presenting itself as a centrist party that endorses the common values of Indian politics. The second part examines the extent to which the BJP has been influenced by the centripetal pressures of electoral democracy. While it has moderated its sometimes aggressive public stance in response to social and political pressure, it also periodically succumbs to competing demands to sustain its commitment to militant Hindu nationalism. This becomes evident if we shift our focus away from the BJP's formal pronouncements to its routine actions; and away from its electoral stance to the interplay between elections and riots. This is the case even when the party occupies office at the state level, and since 1993, after which its overall stance has become more moderate.

Hindu Nationalism as the Common Sense of Indian Politics

The BJP has so far escaped the stigma often attached to religious 'fundamentalist' parties. Terms like 'fanaticism' or 'extremism' have been used to describe individuals and particular acts of violence, rather than the BJP as a whole. One reason for this reluctance to condemn the BJP outright may be the nature of Hindu nationalist discourse itself. As Christophe Jaffrelot rightly argues (in this volume) this can sometimes be anti-democratic, but the BJP's deployment of democratic and secular discourses is deliberate and significant: it has earned Hindu nationalists the support of the educated middle classes in India and abroad, and has distinguished them from religious fundamentalists.

Unlike most fundamentalist movements which reject the separation between religion and politics, Hindu nationalists accept it, in principle. It is true that on the issue of the Babri masjid the BJP brought India to the brink of disaster, but it has not yet clearly articulated a position on the creation of a Hindu state. Partha Chatterjee argues:

> The persuasive power, and even the emotional charge the Hindutva campaign appears to have gained in recent years does not depend on its demanding legislative enforcement of ritual or scriptural injunctions, a role for religious institutions in legislative or judicial processes, compulsory religious instruction, state support for religious bodies, censorship of science, literature and art in order to safeguard religious dogma, or any other similar demand undermining the secular character of the existing Indian state.[3]

Even during its most militant phase (1989–92), the BJP did not challenge secular and democratic principles. Rather, it decried the 'pseudo-secular' Congress party presenting itself as truly secular. It was the most strident critic of Rajiv Gandhi's actions during the Shah Bano controversy, his overturning of a Supreme Court ruling that provided maintenance to an elderly Muslim woman, and his enacting of a law that debarred Muslim women from availing of the provisions of civil law. It also emerged as the major advocate of a Uniform Civil Code governing all legal matters pertaining to the family. The BJP seized on the issue as another opportunity to expose the Congress party's failure to provide equality to men and women before the law. At the same

time, it was responsible for creating a political climate in which
the passage of such a code would no longer signify an extension of women's rights, with the result that today the women's
movement has withdrawn its long-standing demand for a UCC
for fear that this might be construed as an attack on the Muslim
community.

The very grounds on which the BJP supports secularism in
fact undermine it. The BJP holds that the Indian conception of
secularism is inspired by the notion of *sarva dharma sambhava*,
or equal respect for all religions, rather than the western conception of secularism, which entails separation of and often,
opposition between, religion and the state. Significantly, the BJP
criticizes the state for its *unequal* treatment of Hindus and Muslims; the examples it cites demonstrate the state's 'appeasement'
of Muslims and its 'discrimination' against Hindus. Atal Behari
Vajpayee, generally considered the party moderate, argues that
the state has failed to properly implement family planning
programmes and to draft a UCC for fear of 'hurting' Muslim
religious sensibilities. Further, it has unfairly denied majorities
the right it accords to minorities to establish and manage educational institutions of their choice. The state discriminates
against Hindus, the argument continues, by deeming their cultural practices 'religious' and thereby restricting them to the
private domain. Atal Behari Vajpayee argues,

> Practices like lighting a lamp at the inauguration of state functions or
> breaking a coconut at the time of launching a new ship are not con-
> nected with the rituals of any religion but are part of Indian culture
> and tradition. . . . Social festivals like Diwali, Dussehra and Holi should
> not be associated with any specific form of worship. These festivals
> have manifested our cultural wealth and its diversity right from the
> days of the Puranas.[4]

The implication is that whereas Hindu religious practices are
part of the fabric of Indian cultural life, Muslim observance is
not. The major impediments to secularism in India are, thus,
the state and the Muslim community. The VHP is more explicit.
A pamphlet authored by Rajmohan argues that Hinduism is secular by nature. 'It assimilates all creeds and sects in the same
way the ocean takes into it various rivers.' By contrast, 'If one
traverses through the preachings required by Muslims, leaving
not even the minute details, one will be shocked to see the cruel

treatment meted out to those who belonged to religions other than Islam. . .'.[5] After documenting the barbarism that Islam mandates in great detail, Rajmohan concludes that it is fundamentally incompatible with secularism.

Hindu nationalists argue that the state should favour the interests of Hindus over those of Muslims because they constitute a majority of the population, and because Hinduism is more tolerant than Islam. Their argument that the state treats Hindus and Muslims unequally in effect, proposes the denial of minority rights and religious liberty for Muslims. This in turn explains the BJP's opposition to the National Minorities Commission and its desire to abrogate Article 370 of the Constitution, which accords a special status to Kashmir. By opposing the state's attempt to protect minority interests, the BJP seeks to redefine democracy as majority rule, and minority rights as a matter of special bargaining. In the process it has transformed the universe of political discourse. Rajeev Bhargava best captures this when he argues, 'Words integral to the established vocabulary of democratic and liberal discourse were gradually detached from it, evacuated of their original meanings and recast, indeed hijacked, for a new brand of extremist politics'.[6] He goes on to note that Hindu nationalists conflate democracy with power ensconced in a permanent majority:

> Democracy means neither the rule of the majority nor of a minority, but primarily the acceptance of a common framework that prevents the concentration of power in either. Since democracy is a central value of our Constitution and majority rule is inimical to proper democratic functioning, equating democracy with majority rule is neither fully democratic nor properly constitutional.[7]

The Taming of the BJP

Most students of Indian politics would concur that if the surge of militant Hindu nationalism in the early 1990s challenged Indian democracy, the challenge was shortlived. Lloyd and Susanne Rudolph have argued persuasively that one of the most striking features of Indian politics is its persistent centrism.[8] All political parties that seek or exercise power are subject to centripetal pressures. Atul Kohli observes that between March and June 1996, Congress, the BJP, and the United Front—each of which briefly took up the reins of government—all felt the need to move towards an invisible centre by adopting similar policies on the same set of issues.[9] Neither the Rudolphs nor Kohli comment specifically on the BJP's trajectory, but others who do, like Ashutosh Varshney, find that it too has increasingly become a centrist party.[10] Although it rose to prominence by associating itself with a disruptive, violent movement in Ayodhya, the closer it has come to the exercise of national power, the more moderate has been its actual functioning.

Recall that on December 6, 1992, Hindu nationalists organized a massive campaign that culminated in the destruction of the Babri masjid in Ayodhya. The riots that followed, which were often one-sided attacks on the Muslim community by the police and Hindu organizations, resulted in well over two thousand casualties. The BJP hoped to reap enormous political capital from its actions, so much so that its 1993 election manifesto devoted eleven paragraphs to the campaign, which it described as 'the biggest mass movement in the history of independent India'. It went on to hail the movement as 'both a symbol and a source of our national solidarity, economic power and social cohesion'. Barely a year later it was chastened by humiliating electoral setbacks. Public opinion polls conducted after the demolition of the mosque showed that 52 per cent of the population disapproved, 39 per cent approved, and eight per cent had no opinion. Fifty-two per cent of those who were surveyed believed that the BJP had broken the law.[11]

The November 1993 legislative assembly election results are widely regarded as a public referendum on the events of the previous December. Significantly, the BJP's losses were greatest in Madhya Pradesh, followed by Uttar Pradesh, states in which its posture was most militant and riots were numerous. By contrast, it retained power in Rajasthan, where it benefited from the moderate, relatively secular leadership of Chief Minister Bhairon Singh Shekhawat. The election returns suggest that a strategy that sought to polarize the electorate along religious lines by fomenting violence, had ceased to pay. The BJP took heed. At its national council meeting in Bangalore in June 1993, it projected itself as a responsible alternative to the Congress party and highlighted its commitment to opening up the economy and ending corruption. It reaffirmed its faith in a secular state and downplayed the possibility of building a temple in Ayodhya. Two years later, at the Goa conclave, the BJP was trying hard to tone down its anti-Muslim posture. The then party president, L.K. Advani, asked party members to try to rid Muslims of their 'misapprehensions of the BJP'.

In state elections held in 1995, following the pattern established two years earlier, the electorate delivered an anti-establishment vote: the BJP came to power in only two states, neither of which it had ruled before, as a result of popular discontent with incumbent governments. Anti-establishment sentiment generally worked to the advantage of anti-establishment parties: the Telugu Desam in Andhra Pradesh, the Janata Dal in Karnataka, and Congress in Orissa, as well as the BJP in Maharashtra and Gujarat. In these two states, the BJP benefited from the vote of dissatisfaction that had previously gone to the Janata Dal. The BJP–Shiv Sena alliance came to power in Maharashtra with a slim majority, just one per cent over Congress, while the BJP came to power with a comfortable two-thirds majority in Gujarat.

The more successful the BJP has been in occupying office at the state level and in attaining power at the Centre, the more it has been forced to participate in coalition governments. Regional parties are heavily represented among coalition partners, and their interests lie in effecting a devolution of power from the Centre to the states. In working out an alliance with the Akali Dal and the Haryana Vikas Party (HVP) in July 1997, the BJP threatened an agitation if, by the end of the year, the Centre failed to implement the Sarkaria Commission recommendations to restructure Centre–state relations. It also demanded that the Centre consult with state governments in the appointment of governors. That a party committed to a centralized state should demand the devolution of power is a mark of the extent to which electoral compulsions can influence the BJP's agenda. There are several additional explanations for the BJP's retreat from its militant stand of the early 1990s. As social movement theorists point out, single-issue campaigns are highly effective but short-lived: it was much easier to mobilize people to destroy the Babri masjid than to undertake the mundane work of building a Hindu temple. The violence associated with the campaign may have worked in the short run, but it backfired ultimately. Even if

Muslims were the worst victims, Hindus also suffered from political instability, material losses and threats to their physical safety.

The BJP's centrism may also be the inadvertent result of the party's diminished organizational coherence. The BJP has experienced what has been called 'Congressization', as it evolved from a narrowly-based, disciplined-cadre party into a mass party. Expansion has brought about a more disparate, corrupt, unprincipled membership, rendering the party less equipped to either play a transformative role or to maintain a stable government. Indeed, dissension and rivalry within the party was a major reason for the fall of the BJP government in Gujarat in 1996. One of the most important impediments to the BJP's continued militancy has to do with its regional confinement to north-western India. The BJP won more seats than any other political party in the 1996 parliamentary elections, but 74 per cent of these seats were from the Hindi heartland (including Bihar but excluding the Punjab). The addition of Gujarat and Maharashtra in the west accounted for 96 per cent of seats won, but only four per cent of these were from south, east and north-eastern India. Although it recorded a significant growth in Andhra Pradesh and West Bengal in 1991, it had declined in these states by 1996. It is essential for the BJP to make inroads into south and east India in order to form a national government, but to do so, it has had to divest itself of certain north Indian trappings; for example, it has abandoned its insistence on Hindi as the national language. To attain power at the Centre, the BJP must also achieve significant gains among the lower castes. Exit polls for the 1996 parliamentary elections showed that although it succeeded in fracturing the Other Backward Classes (OBC) vote, only 11 per cent of the Scheduled Castes supported the BJP, compared to 31 per cent for the Congress, 21 per cent for the National Front, and 16 per cent who supported their own new party, the Bahujan Samaj Party (BSP).[12] Indeed, notwithstanding the shortlived alliance between the BSP in the state and the BJP in Uttar Pradesh, lower-caste parties remain the major antidote to the BJP and the strongest supporters of secularism.

There are serious, enduring strains between the upper and lowest castes. Although the BJP's upper-caste leadership has been quite successful in attracting OBC votes and candidates, it has been relatively unsuccessful among the lowest castes. At a deeper level, the strongest defence of secularism has always come from those parties and leaders who are most committed to economic redistribution, cultural pluralism and democratic renewal. Today, amidst the demise of Congress and its socialist commitments, lower-caste parties are the major proponents of a social democratic agenda.

Overall, Muslims' response to the events surrounding the Ayodhya campaign has been an important impediment to xenophobic Hindu nationalism. The BJP can only polarize religious communities if it provokes a militant Muslim response. However, most Muslims have distanced themselves from the opportunistic Muslim leadership, and have affirmed secular values. One indication of this is the emergence of several Muslim organizations committed to reforming religious laws and becoming active in community work. Another indication is the community's disinterest in participating in activities that Muslim leaders have organized around Ayodhya since 1993. Syed Shahabuddin sponsored a meeting on 3 July 1993 to discuss the reconstruction of the mosque, but what had been billed as a day-long meeting ended within two hours because it met with so little enthusiasm.

The Muslim community's electoral response to the BJP has changed as well. In the immediate aftermath of the demolition of the Babri masjid, Muslim leaders urged community members to vote for whichever party would defeat BJP candidates. However, this strategy ultimately worked in the BJP's favour by encouraging the upper castes to rally round the BJP. Today, no single Muslim position prevails on whether to vote for or against them. A discussion with a group of Muslim men from Nizamuddin in November 1997 demonstrated how Muslim views on the BJP had evolved.[13] The group did not believe that the BJP's ideology had changed fundamentally since 1992; an elderly maulvi commented, 'The BJP has simply washed its old clothes. But some stains are so bad that no amount of laundering can remove them.' What had changed, however, was their view of how the Muslim community should respond to it. Muslims had fallen into the BJP's trap, they said, by exaggerating the significance of the temple issue. If the BJP built the temple, as it repeatedly claimed it would, they would not resist. Their priority was to attend to the real needs of the Muslim community, particularly better and more extensive educational facilities. Meanwhile, they would lend support to lower castes, both within and outside the party, who would pose the major challenge to the BJP. Their respect for Mulayam Singh Yadav matched their disdain for Syed Shahabuddin.

The Endurance of Hindutva

If, as we have seen, the BJP has moderated its stand on some of the controversial issues it had raised earlier, it is not in its interests to simply abdicate its commitment to Hindutva when this is what distinguishes it from other political parties. The BJP is keenly aware of the cost of assimilating into the political mainstream and has, for years, sought to avoid doing this without at the same time, becoming a pariah party. Before and after 1993, the period of relative moderation, the BJP periodically revived Hindu-Muslim conflicts to keep alive public memory of Hindutva. .

The BJP may give less importance today than it did earlier to the temple in Ayodhya, but it has nonetheless sought to keep memories of it alive. Although some BJP leaders apologized for the destruction of the mosque just after it had occurred, others later defended it. Uma Bharati suggested that December 6, the day the Babri masjid was demolished, be commemorated as a national holiday.[14] Lest her views be regarded as aberrant, Atal Behari Vajpayee, whom the party regards as its most moderate leader, defended the destruction of the mosque by arguing that it had occurred in reaction to Muslim vote-bank politics. In an essay entitled 'The Sangh is My Soul', he lauded the regeneration of Hindu India that the demolition signalled and argued that 'this was the prime test of the RSS. Earlier Hindus used to bend before an invasion. Not now, this change in Hindu society is worthy of welcome.' Far from repudiating Vajpayee's essay, the BJP posted it on the website that it established for its 1998 election campaign,[15] and its 1996 and 1998 election manifestoes reiterated the party's commitment to building a temple at Ayodhya.

It is hard to reconcile the BJP's apparent turn to moderation after 1993 with its decision to ally with the Shiv Sena, a political party that in popular perception is synonymous with xenophobic violence. Shiv Sena chief Bal Raj Thackeray had gloated over the demolition of the Babri masjid and over having 'taught Muslims a lesson' during the December 1992–January 1993 Mumbai riots.[16] There is no question about the Shiv Sena's complicity in the Mumbai riots which claimed a thousand lives. But after the BJP formed a government in Maharashtra in 1995, it did not repudiate the Shiv Sena's violent past. Instead, it withdrew all charges against Thackeray, disbanded the State Minorities' Commission, and terminated the Srikrishna Commission, which was charged with investigating the Mumbai riots.[17] It has generated insecurity among the Muslim population by passing bills against cow slaughter and in favour of a Uniform Civil Code in the state assembly. It has also prohibited entry of Bangladeshi immigrants, whom it terms 'infiltrators', into the state. This policy stokes subliminal fears among Hindus that a growing Muslim population may be turning the former into a minority in their own land.

Political parties cannot adopt and shed identities at will—they are subject to pressures by leaders and constituencies to abide by past commitments, which makes it extremely difficult for them to reinvent themselves. Changes in strategy are more likely to be cyclical than permanent. As a result, to a greater extent than with other political parties, the BJP engages in doublespeak. It seeks to simultaneously demonstrate its moderation and its militancy. A good example is its revival of a campaign against cow slaughter, this time seeking the support of Muslims. 'If the cow is sacred to Hindus because of religious reasons,' Uma Bharati argued at a convention of Muslim youth in Delhi in December 1997, 'it is also sacred to Muslims because they drink cow milk.'[18] The BJP's 1998 election manifesto provides an especially striking instance of its double-edged approach. The party remains committed to the core demands that are associated with the militant stance it adopted in 1989. These include building a temple at Ayodhya; the abrogation of Article 370 of the Constitution; introduction of a Uniform Civil Code; the abolition of the Minorities Commission; and a total ban on cow slaughter and beef exports. Its election manifesto states, 'The BJP is convinced that Hindutva has enormous potential to regenerate this nation and is committed to facilitating the construction of a magnificent temple at the Ram Janmasthan in

Ayodhya.' However, it quickly moderates this impassioned statement by promising 'consensual, legal, constitutional means to facilitate the construction of the Ram Mandir'. It also stated that it might drop some of the demands in its election manifesto once elected.

The BJP knows that polarizing the electorate along Hindu–Muslim lines can sometimes pay rich electoral dividends. This was surely one of the chief lessons it learnt from the 1991 parliamentary elections, in which it was the beneficiary of the violence it had instigated in connection with Advani's *rath yatra* in October 1990. It is true that other political parties, most notably the Congress, have employed communal appeals and violence to gain the support of the majority community. However, the BJP is unique in the extent to which it has precipitated violence with the explicit intention and effect of influencing electoral outcomes. The BJP provoked riots just before the 1991 elections in several Uttar Pradesh towns and cities, including Agra, Varanasi and Aligarh; it went on to win a majority of votes in each of these towns and in the state as a whole.[19] The BJP's share of the vote in Uttar Pradesh went up to 20.08 per cent from 11.36 per cent in the previous elections. It also came to power in Gujarat and Maharashtra in 1995, following serious incidents of communal violence two years earlier.

A commonly heard assertion is that the BJP is more communal in opposition than in office. While there is some truth to this statement, it must be qualified; after all, it was when a BJP government was in office in Uttar Pradesh that the Babri masjid was demolished by Hindu nationalists. Rajasthan, which has a reputation for having been peaceful, historically, experienced two riots, in 1989 and 1990, the latter when the BJP was in office. The first riot occurred in 1989, just before the parliamentary elections. Since the BJP's election campaign had been extremely communal, members of Jaipur's civil liberties organization, the People's Union of Civil Liberties (PUCL), met with the chief minister and asked him to take measures to prevent a riot.[20] However the BJP's candidate, Girdharilal Bhargava, took a procession through a sensitive Muslim neighbourhood where it shouted provocative, anti-Muslim slogans. A riot broke out. Hemlata Prabhu, the PUCL president, asked Shekhawat to issue a statement condemning the violence, but he refused.[21] In

October–November 1990, Jaipur, Udaipur, and Kotah experienced riots when the central government arrested L.K. Advani in connection with his procession to Ayodhya, and local BJP units organized protest movements in response.

Furthermore, even when the BJP has not been implicated in riots, it has often pursued policies which have targeted Muslim communities and undermined communal amity. The BJP government in Madhya Pradesh engaged in a massive slum eradication campaign in the early 1990s. What distinguished this particular campaign from others organized by Congress governments in the past was the extent to which it targetted poor Muslim slum-dwellers. The worst abuses in the BJP's anti-encroachment drive occurred while relocating 628 families. Two hundred and twenty-eight were sent to Badwai and 400 to Gandhinagar, about 13 kilometres from Bhopal. The BJP government's actions were particularly callous because a large proportion of the slum dwellers were victims of the Bhopal gas disaster in 1984. Many residents suffered health problems for which they needed to make hospital visits three times per week. Rajiv Lochan Sharma, a doctor who worked closely with the victims of the gas disaster, said that many of the people who had been evicted to Gandhinagar had suffered lung damage that required more elaborate treatment than they were receiving.[22] He feared that in many cases the move to Gandhinagar would be fatal.

One obstacle that prevents the BJP from pursuing a centrist path is its membership in a broad network of Hindu organizations. The most important of these are the RSS and the VHP. Both uphold an organic understanding of nationalism, which is intolerant of divergent interests. This is best illustrated by their refusal to enter into negotiations with the government or with Muslim groups on the temple issue. Although differences in the philosophies of the BJP and RSS have grown in recent years, particularly in Rajasthan, Madhya Pradesh, Maharashtra, Uttar Pradesh and Gujarat, the two organizations are unlikely to sever their ties. In the BJP the RSS has found a vehicle for influencing political life without incurring the risk of direct participation.

In its relations with the RSS, the BJP faces a more difficult proposition. While loosening its ties with this vehicle of Hindutva would make it more acceptable to other parties and thus increase its prospects of electoral success, the BJP is unlikely to do so for several reasons. First, the RSS and affiliated organizations have been vital to the BJP's phenomenal growth since the late 1980s. They spearheaded the campaign around Ayodhya, and their activities have enabled the BJP to claim that it is a social movement, one that is able to mobilize people on a larger scale than any other political party in India today. The BJP's ties to the RSS have also gained it the support of many state functionaries, who themselves have long-standing ties with the RSS. The extent of this support became evident during the move to demolish the mosque and the accompanying riots. Many public officials, including the police, dropped the pretence of impartiality and openly sided with the BJP.

Second, it is hard to visualize a split between the RSS and the BJP when the BJP's leadership is dominated with men of RSS backgrounds. Approximately 70 per cent of BJP officials at the national level, and 60 per cent at the state level are RSS members. In the BJP's central office, 28 out of 41 BJP officials are of RSS background.[23]

Third, the BJP has become dependent on the RSS to mend rifts that have formed in the party, particularly in the states in which it has occupied office. In November 1996, the RSS directly confronted the problem of growing caste, personality and organizational divisions within it and decided to monitor the BJP more directly. The RSS's identity centres on its profound and enduring commitment to militant Hindu nationalism—as long as the BJP remains affiliated with the RSS, it will have to remain similarly committed.

The BJP's relationship with the VHP is more complicated. In return for its crucial role in the Ayodhya campaign, the VHP extracted from the BJP a share in selecting candidates to contest the 1991 elections. However, during the 1993 elections, tensions between the two organizations emerged. As a result of the VHP's key role in demolishing the mosque, the BJP resisted its escalating demands, and with the approach of the 1995 assembly elections, the BJP made it clear that the VHP's commitment to building temples at Kashi and Mathura were not part of its agenda.

Although its relationship with the VHP has become increasingly strained and the latter has become less visible in BJP campaigns, the party still supports much of the VHP's agenda. In preparation for the 1996 parliamentary elections, the BJP released a forty-point agenda. Among its demands were the following: the passage of new laws to hand over the Ayodhya site to one of its committees, the Ram Janmabhoomi Nyas; discarding the Place of Worship Act; abrogating Article 370 of the Constitution; and imposing a ban on cow slaughter. It was only after the BJP incorporated most of the VHP's agenda into its own platform, that the VHP, in turn, promised it support.

Links between the BJP and VHP have endured partly because they have been sustained by such prominent leaders as Uma Bharati and Vijaya Raje Scindia, who have strong ties with both organizations. Uma Bharati has publicly chided the BJP for putting the temple issue on the back burner, and not taking up the VHP's demands on Kashi and Mathura.[24] More importantly, given the pressures the BJP faces to temper its stance, it can rely on the VHP to keep alive a broad commitment to Hindutva, allowing the BJP to represent a moderate position. This dual-faceted strategy was clearly evident in the 1995 legislative assembly elections in Gujarat. Sadhvi Rithambara, a VHP rabble-rouser, travelled through the state delivering incendiary speeches. At the same time, the BJP embarked on a populist campaign which promised something to everybody: wheat at two rupees per kilo within three months of coming to power, for people below the poverty line; two pairs of school uniforms for primary school students; bicycles for tribal female students; land for the homeless; subsidies to women for self-employment; and loans to initiate businesses and sustain the self-employed. Thus the VHP serves as both a useful ally and a convenient scapegoat for the BJP.

Cycles of Moderation and Militancy

If, as I have argued earlier, the BJP's shifts from a militant to a moderate strategy are cyclical rather than linear, what are the points at which these shifts occur? A few general patterns are striking. First, there is a strong correlation between the emergence of Hindu nationalist militancy and the character of the state; specifically, Hindu nationalism has been most militant when state power is in flux and political leaders have accommodated its demands. Conversely, when the state exercises a high degree of authority and refuses to accede to their demands, Hindu nationalists have moderated their stance.

There have been three periods since Independence when Hindu nationalism has taken a militant turn. The first concerns the RSS in the late 1940s; the second, the Bharatiya Jana Sangh (predecessor to the BJP) in the mid-1960s; and the third, the BJP in the late 1980s. The immediate catalyst for RSS militancy was the Partition of India, for which the RSS blamed both Congress and the Muslim leadership. The conditions that permitted such militancy were the collapse of state power amidst decolonization and a temporary leadership vacuum at the Centre. Increasing militant Hindu nationalism culminated in the assassination of Mahatma Gandhi by Nathuram Godse, a former RSS member. In response to Gandhi's assassination, Jawaharlal Nehru took several steps that defined India as a secular state and curtailed the influence of religion in politics. He also banned the RSS. As a result, the RSS and Jana Sangh adopted a low profile and eschewed explicitly communalist appeals.

Militancy recurred in the mid-1960s. The RSS attempted to resume its militant posture only after Jawaharlal Nehru's death in 1964. Assuming that Indira Gandhi would be more accommodating than her father, Hindu organizations formed a committee for the protection of the cow, and demanded that the government ban cow slaughter immediately. When a massive demonstration organized by the RSS in November 1966 turned violent, Prime Minister Indira Gandhi issued 1400 arrest warrants, fired officials she suspected were implicated in the movement, and imposed stricter controls on the RSS. Her government also reconstituted the National Integration Council and introduced a Criminal Law (Amendment) Bill that established new ways of combating communalist and paramilitary organizations. The Jana Sangh responded by shunning Hindu militancy. The moderate A.B. Vajpayee became party president (1969–72) and sought to integrate the Jana Sangh into the political mainstream.

The third and most significant period of Hindu nationalism dates back to the late 1980s. This period was marked by the BJP's unprecedented growth and militancy. Equally unparalleled was the leadership vacuum that was created by the erosion of Congress dominance and the accommodation of Hindu nationalism, first by the Congress and later by the National Front. The BJP experienced a remarkable growth between 1989 and 1991.

The story of the Congress party's complicity in the growth of Hindu nationalism is well known. By the early 1980s, the Congress' commitment to secularism and the authority of political institutions were both in decline. Indira Gandhi responded to the crisis in the Punjab and to the waning of her traditional support among minorities and Scheduled Castes by appealing to the Hindu majority. A few years later, her son, Rajiv, succumbed to pressure from the conservative Muslim leadership in the infamous Shah Bano case. In an apparent attempt to balance its concessions to Hindu nationalists with the concessions it had made to Muslim 'fundamentalists', the Congress paved the way for the Ram Janmabhumi campaign. In 1986, the district sessions judge in Faizabad ordered the Uttar Pradesh government to unlock the gates of the Babri masjid and allow devotees to pray there. The government did nothing to stop this. Shortly thereafter, Hindu nationalists demanded that the government permit them to build a temple at the site. The BJP's appeals became more militant.

The National Front, led by V.P. Singh, contributed to the BJP's growth by relying on its support to form a government at the Centre. Furthermore, in negotiations with the BJP prior to the 1989 elections, the National Front failed to condemn it for refusing to compromise its position on the Ram Janmabhumi campaign. In its anxiety to supplant the Congress, it tacitly encouraged the BJP to pursue the militant approach it was fostering. Even after L.K. Advani embarked on his *rath yatra* to Ayodhya in October 1990, V.P. Singh was slow to check the BJP for fear of precipitating the government's downfall.

Several patterns can be discerned in this trajectory. First, the growth of the Jana Sangh, and subsequently the BJP, *followed* periods of militancy. In the 1967 parliamentary elections, the Jana Sangh received nine per cent of the vote, an increase from six per cent in 1962 and four per cent in 1957. It paid for its subsequent moderate phase under Vajpayee's leadership, for it received only seven per cent of the vote in the 1971 elections. In 1989, at the start of the Ram Janmabhumi campaign, the BJP received 11 per cent of the vote, and by the 1991 elections, when the campaign was in full flower, it had 20 per cent of the national vote. The BJP

could only have concluded that militancy pays much richer electoral dividends than moderation; and even if it failed to pay off at
certain points, as in the 1993 elections, it was likely to bear fruit
again following a period of moderation.

Second, in 1967 and again in 1989, the BJP combined militant
Hindu appeals with participation in coalitions; at the state level in
1967 and at the national level in 1989. The BJP's double-edged
approach, which simultaneously embraced militant and populist
appeals, has been a critical reason for its success. If its alliance
with the RSS enabled it to demonstrate its militancy, its alliance
with non-Congress coalitions allowed it to display its moderation.

Third, Hindu nationalism has become stronger and more
militant when political parties have adopted an inclusive stance
towards it, both by lending support to its demands and by including it in coalition arrangements. The Congress party has
done the former, the United Front the latter. In the Punjab, Kashmir and Assam, the Congress' appeals to the majority community escalated ethnic mobilization, which in turn provoked a
backlash from Hindu nationalists. During the most recent phase
of militant Hindu nationalism, the BJP's opposition to movements to self-determination in Kashmir formed a key feature of
Hindutva ideology.

Varieties of Identity Politics

In general, regionally based ethnic movements, from linguistic
mobilization for the reorganization of state boundaries in the
1950s, to the territorial demands of Punjabi Sikhs and Kashmiri
Muslims in the 1980s, have responded in a manner very different
from that of the Hindu nationalists. As Atul Kohli has argued,
when the authority of the central state is institutionalized and
the ruling party is accommodating, self-determination movements are likely to trace the shape of an inverse U curve;[25] they
will inevitably decline in intensity once the state makes some
genuine concessions. This pattern does not hold in the case of
religious nationalism.

There have been two periods of ethnic mobilization in India.
The first, over linguistic demands, occurred in the aftermath of
Independence when a broad coalition of ethnic and linguistic
groups protested the domination of Hindi-speaking states and

demanded a bilingual national language formula. The Centre conceded their demand and the movement ended. In its place, various states organized a movement for the reorganization of state boundaries along linguistic lines. Following mass movements that eroded the strength of the Congress party, the government agreed to the creation of Andhra Pradesh in 1953, followed by Maharashtra and Gujarat in 1960 and Punjab and Haryana in 1966.

There was a resurgence of ethnic mobilization in the 1980s in Kashmir, Assam and the Punjab. All these cases, unlike the movements of the 1950s, entailed extensive violence. The state's refusal to concede the legitimate demands of a moderate leadership was a major cause for this. In the Punjab, Indira Gandhi precipitated the growth of extremist politics by undermining the moderate Akali Dal leadership and refusing to accommodate its demands. In Kashmir, she similarly undermined the National Conference government of Farooq Abdullah and paved the way for political extremism. In Assam, the Congress party bore major responsibility for the Nellie massacre which claimed the lives of 1400 people in February 1983. Hoping to capitalize on minority resentments, Congress ignored the demand of the indigenous Assamese linguistic community to defer elections until the government had revised the electoral rolls. Conversely, the Assam Accord, which Rajiv Gandhi negotiated in August 1984, showed that the central government could settle the conflict by conceding some of the movement's demands.

In the abstract, it would seem that an accommodating state can placate, both, ethnic self-determination movements and Hindu nationalism; as we have seen, however, the dynamics of the two movements are exactly the opposite. In practice, an accommodating state has moderated the demands of ethnic movements but radicalized the demands of religious nationalists. Hindu nationalists are likely to gain a sympathetic hearing from the state because their core supporters, upper-caste Hindus, are so heavily represented within it. By contrast, ethnic minorities are less represented in the state apparatus and have less possibility of gaining a sympathetic hearing from state officials.

Furthermore, the BJP is a national political party that has its sights fixed on attaining power in New Delhi. Electoral considerations dictate that it discredit the ruling party rather than accept its concessions, and that it sustain agitation movements rather than bring them to closure. By contrast, ethnic self-determination movements have traditionally had their sights fixed on attaining power at the state level. As a result, their demands tend to be finite and negotiable. Once satisfied, it makes sense for them to cultivate good relations with the Centre and turn their attention to regional issues.

In several cases, such as Punjab and Kashmir, religion has provided ethnic minority movements with the language of militancy. Although in both instances the initial demands of these movements were economic, political and territorial in nature, they expressed their identities and aspirations in religious terms as they became increasingly frustrated, defensive and intransigent. The state contributed to this development by depicting these movements as secessionist and failing to respond constructively to their negotiable demands. Their expression of religious militancy provoked the state to resort to greater repression, thereby leading to spiralling cycles of violence. Thus, today, several movements that have taken on a religious colouring started out as ethnic movements.

The central question that emerges from this comparison of ethnic and religious movements concerns their implications for democracy. Although the process of democratic change may give rise to varied forms of identity politics, the consequences of each form of identity politics for democracy, are quite different. In general, ethnic movements that are accommodated by the state have strengthened democratic processes. Once regional parties have assumed power, they have not only ushered in stable governments but often, also more democratic ones, which in some measure have redistributed power from the upper to the middle and lower castes.[26] Furthermore, both the state's adoption of a multilingual policy and its linguistic reorganization of states has strengthened cultural pluralism. It has done so by encouraging people to uphold regional and national identities simultaneously. By contrast, whenever the BJP has assumed power at the state level, its leadership has been primarily upper caste. Nor has it fostered strong regional identities; on the contrary, it has consistently asserted the overriding significance of Hindu identity for a sense of Indian nationalism. The common Hindu nationalist claim that Muslims are anti-national stems precisely from the belief that they cannot simultaneously maintain a strong religious and national identity although, ironically, Hindus can and should do so.

Similarly, Hindu nationalists fear that a heightened salience of caste will confound religious identities. Despite its formal pronouncements in support of the Mandal recommendations, the BJP actually opposed reservations for OBCs. Advani admitted that the government's decision to implement the Mandal Commission recommendations provoked the BJP into withdrawing support from the National Front government in 1990, although he was evasive about why the BJP opposed such reservation.[27] Its opposition was expressed more pointedly at the state level. Presumably, one of its major fears was that heightened caste consciousness would undermine a common sense of Hindu identity.

Compared to Hindu nationalists, ethnic minorities and lower caste groups do not tend to think of their identities in a similarly exclusive fashion. One reason is that caste identities and alignments vary greatly from one region of the country to the next, making it difficult for any single caste or ethnic group to organize on a national scale. This in turn means that politicians seeking to advance the interests of particular communities are best served by building broad alliances with members of other communities. By contrast, while Hindu nationalists can hope to claim the loyalties of only a single community, it is a community that constitutes an overwhelming majority of the population.

Conclusion

Many observers have concluded that the BJP has become increasingly centrist. As evidence they note that, by the late 1990s, it had formed electoral alliances with ideologically diverse partners including regionally based parties which opposed Hindu nationalism. Just prior to taking office in March 1998, the BJP sought to accommodate its coalition partners by publishing a national agenda which omitted the controversial issues of the temple, the Uniform Civil Code, and Kashmir's special constitutional status. After coming to power, the BJP was forced to expend so much energy maintaining its fragile coalition and assuaging temperamental coalition partners like Jayalalitha Jayaram, that it was unable to pursue Hindu nationalist goals.

This characterization of the BJP is not wholly wrong, but it is overly simple. First, while the BJP's dominant appeals have become increasingly inclusive, it has never repudiated its anti-Muslim position. L.K. Advani commented in an interview that one of the BJP's lasting achievements was to have set the agenda of Indian politics.[28] Indeed, the BJP has had a significant impact on the question of minority rights. Congress and the National Front have not devoted adequate attention to the question of increasing educational and employment opportunities for minorities; neither of them would dare raise the question of reservations for Muslims, although they both support reservations for women—it would be suicidal to do so in the political climate that the BJP has fostered. Most importantly, many Muslims would fear for their safety in the event of the recurrence of communal violence, particularly with a BJP government in office. One noted that when Mulayam Singh Yadav was chief minister of Uttar Pradesh, he ordered preventive arrests of large numbers of Hindus in order to avert a communal riot. He could not imagine a BJP government taking such a step.[29]

The BJP's cultivation of the apparently moderate Atal Behari Vajpayee and the militant L.K. Advani are symptomatic of its tendency to engage in doublespeak. Vajpayee as prime minister and Advani as minister for home affairs personify the BJP's attempt to sustain these two different identities, as well as the relative priority it assigns to each of them. Just after the BJP government was formed, L.K. Advani argued that the 50th anniversary of Indian independence offered a good opportunity to review the functioning of the Constitution and to propose some reforms. A few days later, Vajpayee assured the Opposition that the BJP had no intention of changing the Constitution.[30]

The 1998 parliamentary elections confirmed the strength of BJP–RSS ties. Even while taking pains to assert the moderate, secular character of the BJP government, Atal Behari Vajpayee praised the RSS for its dedication to the well-being of the country. Not surprisingly, opposition parties claimed that the BJP was being run by 'remote control'.[31] The composition of the BJP government's cabinet also reveals the extent of RSS influence. Some of its key appointments include L.K. Advani, minister of home affairs; Murli Manohar Joshi, minister of human resource development and Uma Bharati, his counterpart, as minister of state; M.L. Khurana, minister of parliamentary affairs; and Sushma Swaraj, erstwhile minister of information and broad- casting, and subsequently, chief minister of Delhi.

Furthermore, the BJP has sought to utilize new channels for propagating its Hindu nationalist agenda. Since achieving power in New Delhi, it has been able to permeate a variety of institu- tions. One important example is the Indian Council for His- torical Research (ICHR). In June 1998 Murli Manohar Joshi appointed new members to the ICHR who subscribe to the BJP's views on the mosque–temple dispute at Ayodhya. The World Archaeological Congress has already censured two prominent members of the reconstituted ICHR. The BJP has also broad- ened its Hindu nationalist agenda. The best illustration of this was its decision to explode nuclear bombs soon after it came to power. The nuclear explosion enabled the BJP to buy time for their crisis-ridden coalition. In the days preceding, it seemed beleaguered by its domestic woes: 'fatigued', 'indecisive', and 'tired' were how a government minister described the prime minister. An editorial writer for *India Today* wrote that if the prime minister did not engage in nuclear testing, he might just as well 'roll out the red carpet for Sonia Gandhi'.[32] With the explosion of the bomb, Prime Minister Vajpayee simultaneously asserted his strength and silenced Mamata Bannerjee and Jayalalitha Jayaram.

The nuclear issue provided the BJP with an ideal way to rein- carnate Hindu nationalism as Indian nationalism. Its commit- ment to Hindu nationalism had been vital to the party's growth, and it was unwilling to relinquish it. But as a party in power it could not afford to be as blatantly anti-Muslim as it had once been. The BJP's revamped Hindu nationalism had to be capa- cious enough to include Indian Muslims while directing its anti- Muslim hostilities towards Pakistan. The scientist who played a leading role in developing the bomb, A.P.J. Abdul Kalam, is Muslim—a secular Muslim, the BJP will point out, as if most other Muslims are fundamentalist. While including a few In- dian Muslims, the BJP has expressed extreme aggression towards predominantly Muslim Pakistan.

There is a religious dimension to the BJP's revamped Hindu nationalism, and it recalls its campaign in Ayodhya. The makers of the bomb christened it 'Shakti', the principle of female energy or strength. The VHP announced that it would construct a temple called Shakti Peeth 50 kilometres from the site of the explosion. The VHP general secretary, Govindacharya, stated that Pokhran was 'an ideal place for the Shakti Peeth'; this is where a Hindu social reformer is worshipped 'for the reforms he brought about in society, especially for waging a movement for the protection of women'. Govindacharya's comment that the temple would honour the protection of women might read more broadly as Hindu nationalists' attempt to protect an India that is both traditional and yet modern.

What, then, is the challenge that Hindu nationalism presents to Indian democracy? It is certainly less dramatic than the challenge other postcolonial states have faced, for it entails neither territorial disintegration, as in Nigeria, nor the creation of a religious state, as in Iran. What is at stake, however, is no less important. From diverse quarters, intellectuals, policymakers and political functionaries are questioning India's traditions of cultural pluralism and minority rights. The answers that the BJP provides to these questions could entail a more contested and truncated understanding of Indian democracy in the years to come.

Notes

[1] This understanding is inspired by Robert Dahl's concept of polyarchy. See Robert Dahl, *Democracy and Its Critics* (New Haven: Yale University Press), 1989.

[2] One of the most important voices in the early debates and in subsequent reconceptualizations of democracy is Guillermo O'Donnell. See, for example, his 'Illusions about Consolidation', *Journal of Democracy,* vol. 7, no. 2, (1996), pp. 34–51.

[3] Partha Chatterjee, 'Secularism and Toleration', *Economic and Political Weekly*, vol. XXIX, (9 July 1994), p. 1768.

[4] Atal Behari Vajpayee, 'Secularism: The Indian Concept', (New Delhi: Bharatiya Janata Party Publication), 1992, pp. 22–6.

[5] S. Rajmohan, 'Can Muslims Become Secular?' A Pamphlet Published by the Vishva Hindu Parishad (Sankat Mochan Ashram, Hanuman Mandir, New Delhi), nd, pp. 3–4.

[6] Rajeev Bhargava, 'Secularism, Democracy and Rights', in Mendi Arslan and Janaki Rajan (eds), *Communalism in India: Challenge and Response* (Delhi: Manohar), 1994, p. 62.

[7] Ibid., p. 69.

[8] Lloyd I. Rudolph and Susanne Hoeber Rudolph, *In Pursuit of Lakshmi: The Political Economy of the Indian State* (Chicago: University of Chicago Press), 1987.

[9] Atul Kohli, 'Can the Periphery Control the Centre? Indian Politics at the Crossroads', *The Washington Quarterly*, vol. 19, (Autumn 1996).

[10] Ashutosh Varshney, 'The Self Correcting Mechanisms of Indian Democracy', *Seminar* (January 1995).

[11] 'A Nation Divided', *India Today*, 15 January 1993, p. 18.

[12] The remaining 14 per cent supported state parties and 7 per cent supported other parties. 'How India Voted', *India Today*, 11 May 1996, p. 50.

[13] I conducted these interviews in Nizamuddin, New Delhi on 18 and 20 November 1997.

[14] Asghar Ali Engineer, 'Communalism and Communal Violence, 1996', *Economic and Political Weekly*, 5 February 1997, p. 325.

[15] 'The Sangh Is My Soul' was first published in *The Organiser*, in 1995. The BJP subsequently posted it on the website it established in connection with the 1998 elections.

[16] *India Today*, 28 February 1995.

[17] Under pressure from the national leadership, the BJP–Shiv Sena government reinstated the Srikrishna Commission in May 1996.

[18] 'BJP: Dilli Dur Ast?' *Outlook*, 15 December 1997, p. 21.

[19] Paul R. Brass, 'The Rise of the BJP and the Future of Party Politics in Uttar Pradesh', in Harold A. Gould and Sumit Ganguly (eds), *India Votes: Alliance Politics and Minority Governments in the Ninth and Tenth General Elections* (Boulder: Westview Press), 1993, p. 275.

[20] Interviews with Mahesh Daga, *The Times of India* reporter, Jaipur, 25 June 1991.

[21] Interviews with Hemlata Prabhu, President, People's Union of Civil Liberties, Jaipur, 25 June 1991.

[22] Interview with Rajiv Lochan Sharma, 28 December 1990 in Bhopal.

[23] N.K. Singh, 'Hindu Divided Family', *India Today*, 15 December 1996, p. 69.

[24] *The Hindustan Times*, 17 May 1996.

[25] Atul Kohli, 'Can Democracies Accommodate Ethnic Nationalism? Rise and Decline of Self-Determination Movements in India', *Journal of Asian Studies*, vol. 56, no. 2 (May 1997).

[26] This point is well developed by Jyotindra Das Gupta in 'Ethnicity, Democracy and Development in India: Assam in a General Perspective', in Atul Kohli (ed.), *India's Democracy: An Analysis of Changing State–Society Relations* (Princeton, N.J.: Princeton University Press, 1998).

[27] See 'Why BJP Withdrew Support from Shri V.P. Singh Government?'

Speech delivered by L.K. Advani (MP) in parliament on 7 November 1990, (published by the Bharatiya Janata Party, New Delhi, 1990). In this speech, Advani criticizes V.P. Singh for the timing of his announcement that his government would be implementing the Mandal Commission recommendations, but does not come out against the principle of reservations.

[28] Interview with L.K. Advani, New Delhi, 27 January 1995.

[29] Interview with Syed Hashmi (pseudonym), New Delhi, 18 November 1997.

[30] Reuters newswire service, 31 March 1998.

[31] John Chalmers, Reuters, 29 March 1998.

[32] Swapan Dasgupta, 'Why Pussy Cats Can't Exercise the Nuclear Option', *India Today*, 18 May 1998.

India in Search... of a New Regime?

DOUGLAS V. VERNEY

What is a Regime?

There have long been proposals in India for a new 'regime'.[1] It is tempting, whenever yet another parliamentary coalition falls, to demand that India follow France's example under de Gaulle in 1958, and replace the present parliamentary regime with a form of presidential government.

But first we need to know what a new regime would involve. It is a term used by the French with some precision. For them, it signifies a new constitutional order, such as occurred in 1958 when the Fourth Republic was replaced by the Fifth. In the French sense, a change of regimes involves a new constitution. India has not had such a new *constitutional regime* since 1950. (An abortive attempt to establish a new constitutional regime was made by Mrs Indira Gandhi in 1975. She used her rump parliament to amend fifty-nine clauses of the Constitution by what was called, somewhat euphemistically, the Forty-second Amendment. Among its provisions were clauses denying judicial review over amendments affecting the basic structure of the Constitution. The Directive Principles of State Policy [Part IV of the Constitution] were given primacy over Fundamental Rights [Part III]. In the election of 1977, the people of India rejected Mrs Gandhi and her Congress (I), and the victorious Janata government restored much of the 1950 Constitution. Mrs Gandhi proved to be no Charles de Gaulle, a leader able to take advantage of a time of crisis to ensure a permanent constitutional regime change.) Elsewhere the term is used for changes much less formal than a new constitutional order. People speak of 'Mrs Gandhi's regime' or 'Mrs Thatcher's regime'. In the United States, the term has been used to describe the liberal era from Franklin D. Roosevelt's New Deal of the 1930s to the Great Society of the 1960s.[2] This is more accurately characterized as a *party regime* where the Democrats controlled Congress for much of the time.

In India it now appears that the era of one-party dominance is over and that the succession of minority governments, starting in 1989, reflects in part a social revolution that has brought new castes and classes into the political arena. Whether this will lead to a permanent multiparty system, it is too early to say. Even so, there has been a change in the party regime. Another change that may merit the term 'regime change' is the economic liberalization process that accelerated after 1991. We may perhaps call this a new *policy regime*. Changes in party alignments and in economic policy are important, but changes of party and policy regime do not involve the change in constitutional regime that France experienced in 1958. For India to replace its present parliamentary system by a presidential form of government would involve such a change.

Presidential government takes many forms, from the authoritarian governments experienced over the years in much of Latin America, to centralized authority in France, or to the American presidency with its separation of powers in Washington and its distribution of power among the fifty states.

Some critics have concluded that India's succession of minority governments shows that the parliamentary system has, in effect, broken down. They argue that a strong president able to offer firm government from Delhi must replace it. Other observers have decided that the Indian government is too centralized. They argue that the emergence of so many state parties is an indication that a more federal system of government is required. In a more federal India, even with a presidential government, the president would have limited power. The difference between a centralized presidency and a federal presidency can define alternative constitutional regimes.

This chapter explores some of the problems associated with any transformation into what is, often, all too loosely called a 'presidential regime', and examines India from a comparative perspective.

Many people in India are concerned about the gridlock in government that results from unstable coalition government. But only a minority appears willing to consider a constitutional regime change that would involve a transfer to a presidential form of government. There are good reasons for this skepticism. Mrs. Gandhi was advised to consider a presidential form of government in the 1970s. Her Emergency of 1975, which established a form of government more patrimonial than presidential, left bitter memories. More recent proposals have had the support of the Bharatiya Janata Party (BJP), a party that its opponents claim would use such a regime to establish authoritarian government. The chapter ends with the suggestion that proponents of change need to give more thought to making Indian government more responsive to its increasingly federalized polity and society. Such institutions as the Rajya Sabha, the Interstate Council, and the Legislative Councils (the upper houses of state legislatures) need to reflect this diversity. Finally, it should be noted that the present parliamentary regime has not been all that bad. In their increasingly diverse membership, successive parliaments and state legislative assemblies have reflected many of the changes in society. Various governments have responded to the demand for liberalization of the economy by changing their economic policies.[3] Indeed, it is by no means certain that a constitutional regime change involving a more powerful presidency would improve matters in India. The American presidential system, or to be more precise, its 'presidential–congressional federalism', did not prevent two government shutdowns in 1995. And while this may have been only a ploy by both sides, it could one day prove to have set a precedent. The French system of 'presidential quasi-parliamentarism' has also not been an unqualified success, and has on occasion resulted in an awkward relationship between the president and the prime minister. By contrast, the United Kingdom, with a parliamentary form of government on which India's own system is based, has been able to renew itself. It has done so not by adopting presidential government but by remodelling the political parties. The two major parties, the Conservatives under Margaret Thatcher and the Labour Party under Tony Blair, have learnt to adapt to the changing world.

The Search for a More Stable Regime

India could add to its parliamentary tradition a presidential system on the French model, providing a seven-year tenure for an elected president, alongside a Lok Sabha elected for four years. If the president's party were defeated in the quadrennial parliamentary elections, the president would still complete his or her seven-year term. This has happened several times in France. After the electorate rejected President Mitterand's Socialist Party in 1986, the president appointed the conservative leader, Jacques Chirac as prime minister. Mitterand's role became more like that of a head of state in a parliamentary regime. In 1997, the conservative Chirac in turn had to appoint a socialist premier, Lionel Jospin. The 1986–8 'cohabitation' demonstrated the capacity of the French presidential/quasi-parliamentary regime to alternate between a de Gaulle-style presidential system and one that was largely parliamentary. Both regimes have worked, and the French have been gratified to see their system adopted in other countries. However, under a strong president the executive is no longer responsible to parliament. The legislature in effect becomes a 'quasi-parliament'.

To replicate the French model in India is easier said than done. France is not only a unitary nation-state, it is even more centralized than most other nation-states, including the United Kingdom. India, by contrast, is a federation that has an increasing number of states, now twenty-eight, including Delhi. Specific powers are allocated to the states under the 1950 Constitution. In addition, there are a number of autonomous regions and a system of local government that has been constitutionalized since 1993. India now has a complex multi-tiered federalism to handle the problems of its billion people. Some conservative Indians are intrigued by the notion of a presidential executive directly elected by the people, especially were India to be seen as having definitely entered an era when unstable multiparty coalition governments became the rule. The assumption is that with a president elected for a definite term (say five years), India would be able to enjoy stable government, however often the government of the prime minister in the Lok Sabha had to be replaced.

India already has constitutional provisions for dealing with national emergencies, provisions invoked on several occasions. When unstable government gets out of hand in the Indian states, President's Rule can be instituted. Although India is in many ways a federation, it still has the centrally appointed Indian Administrative and Police Services, the IAS and IPS, and the judiciary. In times of crisis, state governors exercise discretionary powers even more extensive than those of the prefects in the French departments. Moreover, India is not France. The French presidential/quasi-parliamentary political system operates in a society that, until the post-war immigration, shared a comparatively homogeneous culture. The French form of presidential government has been less successful in diverse societies, for example, in Sri Lanka, where the Sinhalese majority has to deal with a Tamil minority that would prefer some form of federation. Then, in India, there are many important minorities, for example, the Muslims. It would be difficult to ensure that a Hindu president had the support of Muslims, and also the backing of a majority in the major regions of the country (a requirement of the Nigerian Constitution). Unlike the French president, a powerful president of India might well find it difficult to stay above the fray.

Presidential–Congressional Federalism as in the United States?

In size and diversity, India is more like the United States than France. The U.S. is a large country with a population not far short of India's at Independence, and its political system is also a federation. Its election campaigns take many months, enabling the candidates to become widely known. But even the United States is hardly comparable to India in its heterogeneity. In addition, America's 'presidential–congressional federalism' is very different from the federation that has traditionally been attached to parliamentary government in India. Federalism is the main principle on which the American Constitution is based. For proof we need look no farther than the composition and role of the American Senate. It is a powerful and independent body, a small upper house of 100 members (and originally of only twenty-six), in which each state is represented equally by two senators. A visitor to the offices of individual senators is given the impression that senators are also ambassadors, with a status superior to that of legislators in upper houses elsewhere. Members of the House of Representatives also have offices and staffs, an indication that they are not at all comparable to the 'backbench' MPs of the United Kingdom, India or Canada. In the U.S., the two houses share the legislative power, and disputes between them are resolved through conference committees. Because of the powers given to the Senate, the United States has in many (but not all) ways rejected the principle of majority rule. The eight smallest states, with a combined population of about five million people, each return the same number of senators as California, with its 31 million inhabitants. There are, therefore, sixteen senators representing five million people, compared to two senators who represent California's 31 million. It is this stress on the federal character of the polity that makes the American system of government unique. By contrast, the activity of legislatures in parliamentary federations like Canada and India is still based on the British tradition of majority rule. Unlike the American Senate, the upper house plays a subordinate role. Most decisions are taken by the lower house, and by a simple majority. Both countries would have to make fundamental changes to their systems of government to become anything like as federal as the United States. Now they are simply federations, that is to say they have a distribution of powers between the national and state governments.[4] The national government in Canada and India, like the government of the United Kingdom, is responsible to the lower house alone. No Canadian prime minister (and probably no Indian prime minister) has ever suggested a modification of this basic British assumption: majority rule. The closest that Canadians have come to considering an upper house comparable to the American Senate, is the support in the Canadian west for a so-called Triple-E Senate (that is, one that would be equal, effective and elected). The Triple-E Canadian Senate proposed by Alberta would represent all the provinces equally, would be as effective as the House of Commons in government, and would be elected by the voters of each province. Such a federation would be much more federal than today's Canadian regime.

Nevertheless, one feature of the U.S. that has not been copied elsewhere is its state-based party system. Instead of national parties there are the Republican and Democratic National Committees. These have minimal influence on the policies of the various state parties, and the platforms they produce every four years for the presidential nominating conventions rarely determine national policy. Over the years, minor parties have come and gone: the two major parties, with roots in every state, remain. The two-party system is the cement that binds the American federation together. In each state, there is a Republican and a Democratic party organization. The policies of the parties vary considerably from state to state. This means that after congressional elections the party caucuses in the House and the Senate rarely unite on a recognizable 'party policy' of the sort that characterizes parties in Europe. The 1994 Republican 'Contract with America' was a striking exception. State autonomy allows a kind of diversity unknown elsewhere.

Party discipline in the American Congress is weaker than in most parliamentary systems. The dependence of senators on the support of the voters in their states, and of congressmen and women on support in their districts, helps to explain one of the most disconcerting features of American politics. This is the necessity for the president to cobble together a majority (and a different majority) of members of Congress to get each piece of legislation approved. The various states also play a unique role. In each state there is a governor who is popularly elected, like the president. There is a bicameral legislature (except in unicameral Nebraska). Each state is responsible for the conduct of elections; the national election commission has limited powers.

Knowledgeable Indians favouring a new regime are not inclined to recommend the American presidential pattern, based as it is on the principle of federalism. The political system of the United States is a different regime. It is a country without a parliamentary tradition, and without nationally organized parties. It has two equal houses of Congress operating independently of the president. The American political system is too different from India's to be a model. There needs to be one caveat to this. Should India's system of national parties ever be wholly replaced by a congeries of state-based parties, it might be fruitful for Indian political scientists to study the American party system. The United States has somehow managed to combine state-based party organizations with a national and state two-party system. It is hard to visualize a national Indian nominating party convention with American-style hoopla, but few would have predicted a hundred years ago that there would be just such conventions in Canada by the 1920s. There may be more to the American party conventions than most of us are prepared to admit.

Are there any models other than the United States and France for a constitutional regime change? The lessons from the various communist regimes are mixed. In the 1970s and 1980s, communist legislatures were unable to adapt to the changes in society by broadening their membership to include non-communists. Some communist governments, notably in the Soviet Union and Cuba, found it difficult to liberalize the economy. It is true that the Chinese communists appear in many—but by no means all—areas to have done much more than their Russian counterparts to improve the economic condition of the people by liberalizing the economy. However, the economic achievements have not yet been accompanied by political freedom and may yet come unstuck. In India itself, the present Chinese model of governance is not generally thought of as an alternative to parliamentary federation.

India's New Party Regime

Many of those who oppose a new constitutional regime for India live in the hope that a stable new party system will emerge as an alternative. For while the Constitution has not been replaced, there has been considerable, if gradual, change in the Indian party system. Since 1977 there have been a number of coalition governments, providing an alternative to the one-party dominant political system that India so long enjoyed. In the process, the party system has been transformed, so much so that while there has been no new constitutional regime, we might perhaps be justified in describing the changes in terms of a new 'party regime'.

The last thirty years have seen a number of what were once called 'Opposition' governments. These have varied considerably. Although the first, the Janata government of 1977, was a hurriedly formed coalition of parties to fight a suddenly called election, it managed to obtain control of a majority of seats in the Lok Sabha. By contrast, the second coalition, the National Front of 1989, remained a minority government dependent on the outside support of the BJP and the Left Front. It is more difficult to classify the third 'Opposition' government, formed by Chandrashekhar in 1991 out of a rump of fifty-eight members of his breakaway Samajwadi Janata Party. During this rump period, the Indian National Congress performed the extraordinary feat of being the main supporter of the minority government, and at the same time, the official Opposition. The fourth substitute for the Congress party, the United Front government formed in 1996, was different again. This government, like that of 1989, was a minority coalition, but dependent on Congress, not on the BJP. India's search for an alternative party system, in other words a new 'party regime', appears to be continuing. The BJP government formed in March 1998 was also a minority government, though the BJP was by far its largest component.

An alternative party system could take several forms. It might turn out to be a system consisting of a right-wing BJP, a coalition of left-wing parties, and a centrist Indian National Congress. Alternatively, India could conceivably develop a system composed of the BJP and a United Front coalition, with the INC reduced to the status of a 'third party'. Both Britain (with the Liberal party) and Canada (with its New Democratic Party) are familiar with what Canadians call a '2 1/2 party' regime. There are of course many other permutations, including those involving a coalition dependent on the support of a number of regional parties. It was because of fears of what the 1996 regime might lead to that, in June 1997, the former president of India proposed that the United Front and Congress formalize their relationship to ensure some stability of governance.

In sum, the political parties in India have had to face the possibility of coalition government in many of the elections since 1977. Since 1989, they have increasingly had to come to terms with the probability that such a coalition might be unable to form a majority government. In 2001, following a period of transitional minority coalitions, the earlier 'one-party dominant' regime appeared to have been succeeded by a third form of party regime, one in which governments came to rely on relatively stable majority coalitions. So far, the parties have shown ingenuity in producing a parliamentary system dependent on complex coalitions. India has managed to have governments that reflect the will—some might say whims—of the voters.

But if the effort to form a stable government fails, and if the parliamentary system appears in danger of breaking down, then the parties could conceivably consider a change not simply of the party regime but of the parliamentary regime itself. It is to this topic that we now return.

Choosing a Constitutional Regime

India has, of course, from the beginning modified the
Westminster parliamentary regime. For one thing, it has combined parliamentary government with a federation, something
the English are only now beginning to contemplate in their dealings with Britain's Scottish, Irish and Welsh minorities. For another, it has never reproduced the British two-party form of
parliamentary government, moving instead from one-party
dominance to a multiparty system.

Although from time to time there have been suggestions, particularly from the BJP, that India replace its Westminster system
with one that would be more presidential, there is little indication at present that India will be tempted to do something so
drastic as to adopt a new constitutional regime. Even so, the
political situation has become sufficiently volatile for us to ask
whether there could be a better political system. Some consideration therefore needs to be given to possible alternative constitutional regimes, and to the implications of adopting such a
new regime.

The most likely constitutional modification, given the present
debate, would involve adding to the existing parliamentary federation some form of presidential government. The present parliamentary regime was not adopted without much thought. At
the time of the first search for a form of government, during the
constitutional debates, a choice had to be made between an
American-style presidency and the British form of parliamentary
rule. The decision was made to reject presidential government in
favour of the Westminster parliamentary system. This was not surprising. Some of India's leaders had served as chief ministers of
provinces in pre-war British India and had watched (with varying
degrees of astonishment) the British attempt to transform the role
of the imperial governor into one where he acted as a parliamentary head of state. These Indian leaders were therefore familiar
with British parliamentary government. Presidential government
had not succeeded in Latin America; indeed, at that time only the
Americans appeared to have been successful with such a form.

The federal distribution of powers outlined in the Indian Constitution was also based on precedent. Although the British system, unlike the American, was not devised for a federal state, it

had been adapted to federal government in Canada and Australia. In 1867, the Canadians had chosen to retain the parliamentary system they had already adopted in the various provinces, and in forming a Confederation they simply added on to this the federal distribution of powers. The Australians did the same thing in 1900. The Indians simply followed suit in 1950, establishing a form of regime known as 'parliamentary federation'. The proposal to replace this with some form of presidency has been made by a number of critics who have found the parliamentary federation wanting.

Since Mrs Gandhi's time in the 1970s, there has been talk of introducing some form of presidential government, in the belief that only under a president could there be a strong national government able to deal with the various states. Today it is not an American-style presidential regime that is proposed, but one that retains the prime minister and parliament. What seems to be favoured is something comparable to the French form of presidential/quasi-parliamentary government. The French managed to introduce presidential government without abandoning their familiar parliamentary institutions: prime minister, cabinet government, and National Assembly.

A number of Commonwealth countries, among them South Africa and Sri Lanka, have also opted for a form of presidential/quasi-parliamentary government. The recurrence of unstable minority governments in India has revived the debate on presidential government. There is some concern that with the rise of regional parties holding the balance of power in the national parliament, government in India could become as unstable as it has been in Italy and in France during the Third (1875–1940) and Fourth (1946–58) Republics. There is also the fear that India could become ungovernable. The more pessimistic observers even fear that the country will disintegrate unless a new and better political system is adopted. Liberal defenders of the existing system argue that a single presidential executive would only exacerbate India's problems. They are alarmed that the promoters of a new regime are associated with conservative elements in Indian society that may be willing to adopt an authoritarian form of government.

The complexities of the form that a new 'presidential' regime would have to take in a country as diverse, and as conservative, as India have not been subjected to close political scrutiny.

Certainly, none of the proposals made so far appears to have been examined in their relationship to a federal polity and remarkably heterogeneous society. This is not surprising. Although through-out the English-speaking world there is now a considerable lit-erature comparing presidential and parliamentary democracy, neither form of government appears to have been examined from the point of view of its relationship with federalism.[5]

It used to be assumed that in the analysis of political systems, there were three basic approaches to democratic government:

(i)   parliamentary government with its fusion of the government and the assembly in a parliament (as in Britain);

(ii) presidential government, in which the assembly remained an assembly, separate from the executive (as in the United States); and

(iii) government by the assembly itself, as in the Convention which briefly held sway in France in 1792–3.[6]

Since 1958, there has been a fourth type, the so-called presi-dential–parliamentary form of government of the French Fifth Republic. The French system is more accurately described as presidential/quasi-parliamentary, because the president is not responsible to the National Assembly. None of these four forms of government can be adopted in a federation without consid-erable modification, and India, unlike France, is of course a fed-eration. Any new Indian regime would therefore be even more complex than the French. It would have to be not only presi-dential/quasi-parliamentary, but a presidential/quasi-parliamen-tary federation.

Would such a complex form of government be feasible? The only example of a presidential/quasi-parliamentary federation so far appears to be the form of government outlined in the new Russian Constitution. After much resistance in the Duma, many of whose members wanted a parliamentary system, President Yeltsin was able to prevail by submitting his proposed Consti-tution to the public in December 1993. In a French-style refer-endum, the people of Russia approved a Constitution that gave the president considerable powers. In denying the Duma the power to make the executive responsible to the legislature, the Constitution in effect established a new presidential/quasi-parliamentary federation. It remains to be seen just how the new Russian Constitution will work out in practice. There are many critics of the way Russia was governed by Yeltsin. Russian governance, like governance in India, is not a very tidy affair, and the Russian federation too is replete with asymmetrical arrangements. On the other hand, there are few indications that the Russians are dissatisfied with the Constitution itself, and no indication that the Russian public expects it to be replaced.[7]

If the Russian Constitution is successful in combining presidential/quasi-parliamentary government with federalism, it may well have imitators. Such a system would no doubt have something in common with other complex regimes, but it would still be different from both the presidential/quasi-parliamentary regime of the French Fifth Republic and the presidential-congressional federalism of the United States.

What Should India's Model Be?

Were India to decide to adopt some form of presidential government, keeping its parliamentary tradition and federal distribution of power, neither the French nor the American models would be of much use. The American presidential system is federal but has none of the parliamentary features with which Indians are familiar; the French presidential system has parliamentary features but is in no way federal.

If neither the presidential/quasi-parliamentary government invented by de Gaulle, nor the presidential–congressional federalism invented by the framers of the American Constitution, is suitable, what then? Clearly, a different political system would have to be considered. We should be under no illusions regarding the difficulty of modifying, let alone replacing, any existing system of government, particularly one as entrenched as India's parliamentary regime. The French succeeded because

(*a*) there was a serious constitutional crisis;

(*b*) General de Gaulle was able and willing to serve as president;

(*c*) de Gaulle had his aides prepare a new constitution, one that he was able to persuade the people of France to accept in a referendum; and

(*d*) de Gaulle proved himself to be a (reasonably) constitutional president.

Such a coincidence as this would appear to make France's experience unique. However, let us consider what happened in Russia in the early 1990s:

(*a*)   there was a serious constitutional crisis;

(*b*)   President Boris Yeltsin was able and willing to serve as president;

(*c*)   Yeltsin had a new constitution prepared, which he was able to persuade the people of Russia to accept in a referendum; and

(*d*)   Yeltsin proved himself to be a (reasonably) constitutional president.[8]

Might India also one day undertake a similarly dramatic and unusual course of action? If so, would it be able to select as leader someone as innovative as de Gaulle or Yeltsin? And would whoever was chosen as president understand the need to establish a presidential/quasi-parliamentary system that was also a federation?

Unless there is an urgent need for a change of regimes, Indians keen on such a change would be well advised to wait and see how Russia manages. Barring a grave, unforeseen crisis, the most likely course of action for India is to continue its slow adaptation of the present system to changing conditions of unstable coalition government.

Some Indians appear to assume that with this preferred form of incremental change India could gradually shift to a presidential/quasi-parliamentary regime. It remains to be seen whether this is feasible. Certainly neither France nor Russia changed regimes incrementally. Nor did seventeenth-century England or eighteenth-century America. It is true that constitutionally all that would be necessary to transfer power to the president would be a deletion of the addition to Article 74 (1) made by the Forty-second Amendment. The original article could be restored, reading, 'There shall be a Council of Ministers with the Prime Minister at the head to aid and advise the President.' If parliament could limit the powers of the president in 1976, then it could presumably remove these limitations if it so choses.[9] However, giving more powers to the president is one thing: transforming India into a presidential/quasi-parliamentary federation would be much more difficult.

A Presidential/Quasi-Parliamentary Federation?

Parliamentary government has proved itself to be adaptable to societies as different as Germany, Japan, Canada and India. Some states, including India, have added federations to their parliamentary tradition, creating a hybrid form of government. The institutions of parliamentary federations such as today's India and Canada are nothing like as federal as those of the United States. The positions of the Indian president and Canadian governor general are still treated as analogous to that of the queen; each is constitutionally head of a parliamentary, not a federal, state. The formal head of state is subordinate to the prime minister and cabinet.[10] The cabinet is still responsible to the lower house of parliament alone, where majority votes prevail. The Indian Rajya Sabha and Canadian Senate, upper houses nominally representing the states and provinces, are much the weaker of the two chambers.

No doubt many of those who have proposed a presidential system for India have thought of it in terms of another 'add-on'. That is to say, just as the federal distribution of powers was added on to parliamentary government, so a presidency would be added on to the parliamentary regime. This may be wishful thinking. A 'presidential/quasi-parliamentary federation' would in practice probably turn out to be very different from any of the regimes so far envisaged. For one thing, it would mean the transfer of certain powers to the president, with a quasi-parliament (as in France or Russia) acting more as a regulatory body than as the director of policy. For another, it would mean recognition of the federal principle, with the transformation of the legislature into a body in which the upper chamber really did represent the interests of the states. For the Indian system to become federal on the American model, the Rajya Sabha would have to be as effective as the Lok Sabha, and be its equal. It would have to be equal in two senses: as representing all the states equally, and as the equal of the lower chamber in its powers. Such a development is unlikely.

Let us, then, assume that the transformed Indian parliament would not become federal like the U.S. Congress, a reasonable assumption. Would it have to be subordinate to the executive as in Russia? Unlike the situation in the existing parliamentary federations of Canada or India (or what would have been the case in Russia if the Russian parliamentarians had had their way), the emphasis in presidential/quasi-parliamentary federalism would no longer be on the parliamentary tradition. The president would play a greater role. This, as we have seen, is a major problem. Whereas in France the president has lost power when a hostile National Assembly has been elected, the absence of a majority party in Russia enabled President Yeltsin (up to August 1998) to pursue his own policies. If in India, no party won a majority of seats in Parliament, the situation could be more like contemporary Russia than France. In the upper house of the Russian parliament, called the Federation Council, each of the components of the federation is represented by two members. But a novel feature of the council is that one member is drawn from the legislative branch and one from the executive.[11] This increases the power of the executive at both levels of government, something that Indians might oppose.

A weakness of the Russian system is said to be that while it transfers power to the regional components of the federation, it does not adequately integrate them in national policy. The Russian Constitution appeared to increase the powers of the president at the expense of parliament, but to weaken Moscow's influence over the federation. There is the danger that with a president weaker than Vladimir Putin, the various republics and autonomous districts would be even less under national control. (It is not stated in the Russian Constitution who elects or appoints the executive of the various components of the federation.) The heterogeneity of Russia is different from India's. Because the other union-republics of the Soviet Union have separated from the Russian Federation, the Russians are an even more dominant ethnic group in the new country. By contrast, Hindi speakers may still be a minority in India. Moreover, not only are many of the states in India very large, but several of them have long histories as independent entities. With the greater emphasis on state identities in recent years, provision may have to be made for a greater recognition of the states in national institutions than is at present provided by the Rajya Sabha.

Three Possible Reforms

It is possible to institute certain reforms without adopting a new regime. One reform involves the recognition that, in a crisis situation between the Centre and the states, the president may have to take more responsibility than at present, by chairing the interstate Council that Article 263 authorizes him to establish. Another reform, at the state level, is to ensure that there are legislative councils, and that these are designed to represent, and even over-represent, the small regions of the states.

1. Normal and Crisis Administration: A New Division of Powers

India could make such provision by instituting something new for handling crises involving the states. In addition to the traditional separation and distribution of powers, there could be a new *division of powers* for crisis situations. This would be different from the traditional separation of powers between the three organs of governance (legislative, executive and judicial) and different also from the distribution of powers between two levels of governance. The division of powers would be between what we may call 'normal' administration and 'crisis' administration. 'Normal' administration would be handled by the prime minister and cabinet. 'Crisis' administration would involve the president and the federation. The president and the interstate council chaired by him would handle crises. Power would therefore not be concentrated in the president as in Russia. Instead it would be divided between four institutions: the president; the prime minister and cabinet; a legislature representing not only the population through the lower house but the states as well; and the states themselves, through an interstate council chaired by the president.

How this model would operate cannot be described in any detail here.[12] It is of course an ideal type. No doubt if India moved in the direction of presidential/quasi-parliamentary federalism it would depart from the suggested model. After all, India (like Canada) modified both its parliamentary tradition and its federalism to suit its own requirements. The proposed model reflects the influence of France, Russia, the United States and Canada, as well as India's own experience as a parliamentary federation. Like the Constitutions of France and Russia, the model offers a combination of a more powerful president (elected for, say, five years, compared to seven in France and four in Russia), with a legislature to which only the prime minister and government are answerable. The presidency of India would no longer be compared to the British monarchy.[13] Nor would the prime minister and the government be dependent only on the Lok Sabha: any model which includes a more powerful president and a federation will be incompatible with majority rule by the lower house. The proposal replaces the present weak upper house with one that is the equal of the lower house, and that represents the states equally.[14] In the model, governors, like the president, are elected, and also have a special federal responsibility through the interstate council.

Some of the changes envisaged for this new presidential/quasi-parliamentary federalism already have their counterpart in Canada. While the Canadians have not yet developed the sort of interstate council envisaged here for India, there have long been meetings of first ministers and the development of what has been called 'executive federalism'. As for a more powerful upper chamber, we have noted that Alberta has proposed a new Triple-E Senate for Canada, one in which the senators would all be elected, would represent the ten provinces equally, and would be as effective as MPs.[15]

If there is one thing that distinguishes India, it is the diversity of its rapidly changing society. We are assuming that, even if India does not adopt a form of presidential government, the institutions of governance need to recognize India's increasingly federative character more than they do at present. One means of achieving response to change would be to have direct triennial elections to the Rajya Sabha and the legislative councils of the states. (Half the upper houses could be elected every three years.) Two other institutions would reflect India's diversity.

2. The Interstate Council (ISC)

The present interstate council does not adequately reflect the federal character of India. The proposed reformed council would be composed of thirty-one people, divided into three categories. First, there would be the president and vice-president, representing the federation. Second, there would be the prime minister, and the ministers for finance, home affairs and defence, representing the Government of India. The third category would consist of the twenty-five state governors representing the states. The governors would be elected, not appointed by the Centre, and so they would be able quite properly to represent their states' concerns. All these thirty-one people would be drawn from the executive branch of government, and could be presumed to act responsibly. They would meet annually to review crisis policy.

The executive committee would handle crises in the states that, up to now, have been dealt with by invoking President's Rule through Article 356. The committee would consist of eight persons drawn from the three categories noted above: the president and vice-president; the prime minister and home minister; and four governors. The president would convene the committee before a state of emergency was declared.[16] If successful, the new interstate council might lead to a more federal finance commission and planning commission, both of which are at present under the Centre. It might also lead to a reappraisal of such Constitutional provisions as Articles 370 and 371, and the rationalization of the asymmetrical federalism that has gradually developed.[17]

3. State Legislative Councils

It is not enough to reorganize the Rajya Sabha simply to represent the various states. Within the large states, there are diverse regions demanding autonomy. Even in the smaller states, such as Kashmir, there are significant differences between Jammu, the Vale and Ladakh. Some regions would be best dealt with by treating the state as a mini-federation. Instead of regional autonomy there could be an upper house of the state legislature, the legislative council, designed to represent the smaller regions, ideally giving all the regions within a state equal representation.

In sum, the model of presidential/quasi-parliamentary federalism proposed here would call for a more federal political system. For the most part, it would simply require that the law of the Constitution become the practice. Take, for example, the position of the president of India. Already, like the president of France, the president is not allowed to be a member of parliament, and is legally responsible to the Constitution. As in France, the decisions of the president have to be countersigned by the prime minister on behalf of the cabinet. The main differences lie in the fact that India is a federation. A more federal India would give the president more powers, but nothing like the power of the president of France.

Conclusion: A Word of Caution

This essay has assumed that many people in India have searched, and that some of them are still searching, for a new regime.

In general they want their government (or regime) to reflect
the many changes that are taking place in Indian society; to
respond to the pressures for economic liberalization and globalization; and above all to deliver what it promised. Our analysis indicates that it is by no means certain that a presidential
regime, as often envisaged, could in itself produce all of these.
For one thing, Indians will want to keep their parliament; for
another, they may come to terms with the fact that India is more
of a federation than it used to be. If this is so, modifications
need to be made to the centralized character of India's administration, rather than choosing a new presidential regime. Hence
the discussion of a new role for the interstate council and state
legislative councils.

In any case, it is unlikely that there will be a new constitutional regime unless India finds itself in a serious crisis. But
then it will be too late to begin thinking of the alternatives, or
to undertake an examination of the problems that will have to
be resolved. There can be little doubt that the most likely alternative, some form of what we have called a ' presidential/quasi-
parliamentary federation', would be difficult to establish in
India. Indeed, initially it might seem too complex. Even so, as
liberalization and decentralization continue, as the standard of
living rises, and as the demand from the states for participation
increases, it will be necessary to explore the possibility of additional federal institutions. Among these is a much-improved
interstate council, together with state legislative councils representing the regions within states.

Any new arrangements have their risks. As the Russian Constitution suggests, two major dangers loom. One is the possibility of the concentration of power in the office of an authoritarian
president; the other is the fragmentation (and disintegration)
of the Indian polity. Indeed, the first type of change may accelerate the propensity towards the second.

As we said near the beginning of the paper, the regime established in 1950 has much to commend it. In fact, India has a
right to be proud of the constitutional labours of the framers,
work that has lasted so well. There is always the possibility that
once the voters tire of minority government, they will, in the
next election, vote for a new party alignment, with a new party
regime that gives reasonable stability, in which case India's search

would be over. If minority governments persist, then crises may be alleviated by the reforms suggested here. These include crisis management by the ISC under presidential leadership, and reform of the Rajya Sabha and legislative councils to reflect India's diversity.

Notes

[1] See, for example, A.G. Noorani, *The Presidential System: The Indian Debate* (New Delhi: Sage), 1989.

[2] David Plotke, 'Was the Democratic Order the Last American Regime? National Politics After the 1960s', (mimeo.) (Washington DC: APSA), 1997.

[3] Rob Jenkins, 'The Political Management of Economic Reform in a Federal Democracy: The Case of India', (mimeo.) (Washington DC: APSA), 1997.

[4] See Douglas V. Verney, 'Federalism, Federations and Federative Systems: The United States, Canada and India', *Publius: The Journal of Federalism*, vol. 25, no. 2 (1995), pp. 81–97; and 'Are all Federations Federal? The United States, Canada and India', in Balveer Arora and Douglas V. Verney (eds), *Multiple Identities in a Single State: Indian Federalism in Comparative Perspective* (Delhi: Konark), 1995, pp. 391.

[5] Juan Linz and Arturo Valenzuela studied presidential regimes in the 1980s. In 1989 they organized a symposium entitled 'Presidential or Parliamentary Democracy: Does It Make a Difference?' The debate resulted in a number of publications in the 1990s. Among them have been: Arend Lijphart (ed.), *Presidential versus Parliamentary Government* (Oxford: Oxford University Press), 1992; Matthew Shugart and John M. Carey, *Presidents and Assemblies* (Cambridge: Cambridge University Press), 1992; Alfred Stepan and Cindy Skach, 'Constitutional Frameworks and Democratic Consolidation: Parliamentarism and Presidentialism', *World Politics,* vol. 46 (1993), pp. 1–22; Juan J. Linz and Arturo Valenzuela (eds), *The Failure of Presidential Democracy* (Baltimore and London: Johns Hopkins), 1994; and Kurt von Mettenheim (ed.), *Presidential Institutions and Democratic Politics: Comparing Regional and National Contexts* (Baltimore and London: Johns Hopkins), 1997.

[6] I myself did not consider the federal dimension when I wrote *The Analysis of Political Systems* (London: Routledge), 1959. Since then I have lived in Canada, which invented parliamentary federalism, and spent much time in India and the United States.

[7] It is difficult to obtain up-to-date and reliable information on the actual working of the 1993 Constitution. S.E. Finer, Vernon Bogdanor

and Bernard Rudden have much to say about the Constitutions they reproduce in their *Comparing Constitutions* (Oxford: Clarendon Press), 1995, except for the Russian.

The American scholars I have questioned have tended to dismiss the Russian Constitution as little more than a piece of paper. But visiting Russian political scientists I have consulted have suggested that it is in the process of being implemented, that it will continue to develop, and that in all probability it will ultimately become an important document.

[8] Many observers have doubted whether President Yeltsin is really a constitutional president who fully believes in liberal democracy. But this was also said of de Gaulle whose regime has been called 'a liberal dictatorship'. Yeltsin, like de Gaulle, may be succeeded in 2000 by a less powerful president and, by then, the system may have been firmly established.

[9] Article 74 is the first article of a section on the Council of Ministers. It was (and is) entitled 'Council of Ministers to aid and advise President'.

It is Article 53 that states the powers of the president. These powers remain unchanged by the Forty-second Amendment: The article reads:

(1) The executive power of the Union shall be vested in the President and shall be exercised by him either directly or through officers subordinate to him in accordance with this Constitution.

(2) Without prejudice to the generality of the foregoing provision, the supreme command of the Defence Forces of the Union shall be vested in the President and the exercise thereof shall be regulated by law.

The Forty-second Amendment made an addition to Article 74 after the words '. . . aid and advise the President'. The insertion was the phrase 'who shall, in the exercise of his functions, act in accordance with such advice'. Even so, if a prime minister dies or a government resigns, the president still has considerable discretion.

[10] There is an exception to this subordination. Where no party has a majority in the lower house, and when it becomes necessary to form a new government, the head of state may have to exercise considerable discretion, subject to the conventions of the Constitution.

[11] The 'components' of the Russian federation include twenty-one republics, six areas, forty-six provinces, the two cities of Moscow and St. Petersburg, the Jewish autonomous province, and ten autonomous districts.

[12] Appendices outlining the operation of a new constitution were made available at the Delhi conference, and will be incorporated in an

appropriate chapter of a later publication tentatively entitled, *Choosing a Regime.*

[13] '. . . He is more akin to the English King than the American President insofar as he has no "functions" to discharge, on his own authority'. D.D. Basu, *Introduction to the Constitution of India* (New Delhi: Prentice-Hall), 15th edn, 1993, p. 183.

[14] In recent years, a number of very small states have been created, especially in the north-east. For electoral purposes these might have to be grouped together.

[15] It should be noted that the Triple-E Senate is unlikely to obtain the support of the two large provinces, Ontario and Quebec.

[16] How far this body will be able to represent the states' interests it is hard to say. Much depends on who sets the agenda for the meetings. Complaints have been made in Canada and Australia, where a form of 'executive federalism' exists, that the federal government not only sets the agenda but also often gives little advance warning of what is to be discussed.

[17] While the Government of India might retain the power of appointing senior national officials, there are a number of offices that are also *federal* in nature. Provision could be made for some form of federal confirmation of such appointments as Governor of the Reserve Bank of India, the Chief Election Commissioner, and the head of Doordarshan.

Index